E BUSINESS

Beynon-Davies

palgrave
macmillan

First published 2004 by
PALGRAVE MACMILLAN
Houndmills, Basingstoke, Hampshire RG21 6XS and
175 Fifth Avenue, New York, N. Y. 10010
Companies and representatives throughout the world

PALGRAVE MACMILLAN is the global academic imprint of the Palgrave
Macmillan division of St. Martin's Press LLC and of Palgrave Macmillan Ltd.
Macmillan® is a registered trademark in the United States, United Kingdom
and other countries. Palgrave is a registered trademark in the European
Union and other countries.

ISBN 1–4039–1348–X

This book is printed on paper suitable for recycling and
made from fully managed and sustained forest sources.

A catalogue record for this book is available
from the British Library.

Library of Congress Cataloging-in-Publication Data
Beynon-Davies, Paul.
  e-Business / Paul Beynon-Davies.
  p. cm.
  Includes bibliographical references and index.
  ISBN 1-4039-1348-X (paper)
  1. Electronic commerce. 2. Business enterprises--Computer networks--Management. 3.
Information storage and retrieval systems. 4. Expert systems (Computer science) 5.
Database design. 6. Database management. I. Title.

HF5548.32.B485 2004
658'.05--dc22

                                                                        2003055880

10   9   8   7   6   5   4   3   2   1
13   12   11   10   09   08   07   06   05   04

Printed and bound in China

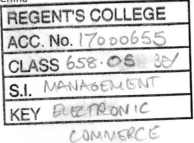

CONTENTS

PREFACE

Entities must not be multiplied beyond necessity

William of Occam

AIM

The term *electronic business* (e-business) is very topical and has overtaken the usage of the term *e-commerce*. Many courses and modules run at universities worldwide are starting to follow suit in the use of this terminology. The material now being taught in the e-business area is also beginning to stabilise in content.

There are a plethora of texts on e-business or e-commerce. However, part of the reason for writing this book was the belief that there are a number of deficiencies with current offerings in this area. Such deficiencies include:

- The vast majority of texts on e-business are US in origin and naturally take a perspective from the point of view of the North American continent.

- Many tend to focus solely on the business issues to the detriment of technical issues.

- A large proportion of such texts tend also to be directed towards consultancy rather than providing academic balance. As such they have been more interested in selling the phenomenon than in providing a systematic survey of the field in the sense of identifying clear patterns and synergy with established practice.

- The available academic literature in the form of academic textbooks tends to be structured in terms of an accumulation of topics rather than a theory-driven form of presentation. Many seem to multiply the number of concepts needed to understand and manage the phenomenon of e-business.

- There is a primary focus on the private sector within the existing literature. However, the dynamics of e-business are not exclusive to the commercial enterprise. The application and exploitation of ICT for organisational change is also equally relevant to the public sector organisation.

This text is clearly positioned in terms of these perceived limitations:

- It offers a worldwide perspective on e-business. For example, many of the examples cited are taken from the UK and European experiences of this phenomenon as well as from the US and Australasian experiences.

- It provides a balanced and integrated account of business and technical issues.

- The approach taken in this book has been field-tested in a number of advisory and consultancy projects undertaken by the author and is constructed as a holistic account of the phenomenon.

- It provides a rounded focus on the application of e-business principles in both the private and the public sectors. We have indicated wherever possible the relevance of e-business to the modernisation of public sector services. Hence electronic government is a key focus of the text.

- We have attempted to use the principle of Occam's razor in this text. In other words, we have attempted to use only sufficient concepts for the tasks of understanding and explaining the phenomenon of e-business. One particular concept we take to be foundational – that of system. Systems thinking drives the discussion of theory and practice in the text.

- It provides a systematic, theory-driven account of the field founded in organisational informatics. The book is clearly structured around a model of the e-business domain presented in the opening chapter and elaborated upon in the various parts of the work. Clear linkage is also made to three other texts published by the author in the Palgrave series – *Information Systems*, *Information Systems Development* and *Database Systems*.

AUDIENCE

The material in this book aims to impart a balanced, holistic overview of the phenomenon of e-business. As such, it covers the key business and technical issues associated with electronic business and electronic commerce. The material is intended to act as a foundation for further investigation in e-business, information systems or information and communication technology. As a core text the likely audience will be undergraduates in business-related subjects, information systems (IS) or computing. As a reference text its audience is likely to be MSc or MA students taking an IS course or a substantial amount of IS modules on an MBA or related programme. We believe that the material will also be of interest to practitioners in business generally and e-business particularly. It will also prove useful to the general reader wishing to learn about this important facet of the information society. For both groups of people, we hope it will provide some structured understanding of the apparent chaos that is modern e-business.

STRUCTURE OF THE BOOK

The book starts with an orienting chapter that provides an overview of the material presented in five major parts:

- *Business and systems*. We take e-business to be fundamentally concerned with the way in which various social and technical systems interact within an organisation. This part considers the key components of electronic business. We consider the foundation of the phenomenon in the concept of a system and its importance for understanding the complex socio-technical entities that are modern organisations. We also provide key distinctions between e-business, e-commerce and i-commerce. This leads us to examine the role of information systems in supporting business processes and some of the dynamics of the key front-end and back-end information systems infrastructure of modern business.

- *Technical infrastructure*. This part considers the technical infrastructure needed for successful e-business. We distinguish between remote access devices and channels and consider the use of such for the electronic delivery of goods and services. The technologies underlying the Internet and the Web are now critical aspects of the technical infrastructure. We also describe some of the important issues surrounding the front-end and back-end ICT infrastructure for e-business and conclude with an examination of the importance of data security to ICT systems and to data transmission.

- *E-business environment*. This part considers the economic, social and political environment for e-business. It examines the context that helps explain the rise of this phenomenon, but also some of the problems and difficulties of e-business. Topics include a consideration of electronic markets and hierarchies, the necessary preconditions for electronic service delivery and the use of ICT in government organisations and processes.

- *E-commerce*. This part considers the features and types of electronic commerce. We begin with an examination of various patterns of commerce and distinguish between business-to-consumer (B2C), business-to-business (B2B) and consumer-to-consumer (C2C) e-commerce. We locate these forms in terms of the supply, customer and community chains of organisations. A key aspect of customer chain activities is e-marketing while e-procurement is now significantly important to many supply chain activities.

- *Social infrastructure*. E-business demands a supporting social infrastructure – the specific organisational processes necessary for supporting e-business: planning, management, evaluation and development. We particularly concern ourselves with the continuous cycle of formulating e-business strategy and evaluating e-business performance.

◎ STRUCTURE OF THE CHAPTERS

Each part of the book is made up of a number of constituent chapters which are designed as independent learning units. Each chapter aims to impart a number of key concepts in the area of e-business and these are expressed as learning outcomes at the start of each chapter. The chapter is made up of a number of sections and each section contains a description of a pertinent concept and an example or examples to illustrate its application in the domain. Most sections also contain a reflective question that can be used as the basis for discussion in the context of some organised learning activity such as a tutorial.

Each part of the book and chapter includes a spider diagram. Spider diagrams were originally developed by Tony Buzan (1982) as an effective method of note-taking within study which exploits the natural ability of humans to associate. The idea of a spider diagram is simply to relate concepts together using free-form lines. The centre of the diagram is used to locate the orienting concept. Associated concepts are drawn radiating outwards, typically in a clockwise direction. Any concept on a spider diagram may act as an orienting concept on its own spider diagram. In this way, most of the structure of the book can be observed in the set of spider diagrams.

Spider diagrams are primarily used as a method within this work of summarising the organisation of information. However, we hope that the student of the area will also find them useful as a revision aid and the lecturer or instructor will find them useful as a way of summarising key elements of the domain.

At the end of each chapter we include a summary of key points and a set of activities. Activities are designed for the reader to pause and attempt to apply some concept to aspects of her own experience or understanding. Readers may wish to enter the results of such activity into some form of scrapbook, thereby keeping a record of progress.

Within each chapter a case is also provided. The cases provide real-world examples of e-business issues from both the private and the public sectors. Each case has been written based on published sources to integrate tightly with the concepts discussed in the chapter.

GLOSSARY AND BIBLIOGRAPHY

Two sources of material are provided as supplements to the main body of material provided. A complete bibliography highlights some key texts that you may use to pursue further study of key areas. A glossary/index is provided to define key terminology and enables quick access to individual topics in the main text.

ACKNOWLEDGEMENTS

My thanks to Ursula Gavin at Palgrave for encouragement and support in producing this book. My thanks also to a number of anonymous reviewers for their helpful suggestions.

WEB SITE AND FEEDBACK

A Web site, including a teaching pack for lecturers and instructors, has been produced to accompany the book and can be accessed at:

www.palgrave.com/resources

The author is keen to receive feedback on the current text. After all:

The idea is like grass.
It craves light,
Likes crowds,
Thrives on cross-breeding,
Grows better for being stepped on.

Ursula Le Guin, *The Dispossessed*

Any comments or suggestions should be addressed to the author (p.beynon-davies@swansea.ac.uk).

REFERENCE

Buzan, A. (1982). *Use Your Head*. BBC Books, London.

CHAPTER 1

THE E-BUSINESS DOMAIN

The power of technology as a competitive variable lies in its ability to alter competition through changing industry structure.

Michael Porter

Practical men who believe themselves exempt from any intellectual influence, are usually the slaves of some academic scribbler of a few years back.

John Maynard Keynes

LEARNING OUTCOMES

After reading this chapter, you will be able to:

- Distinguish between e-business and e-commerce
- Discuss the major elements in the environment of e-business
- Describe the major forms of e-commerce
- Relate the major features of the technical infrastructure for e-business
- Outline the major features of the social infrastructure for e-business

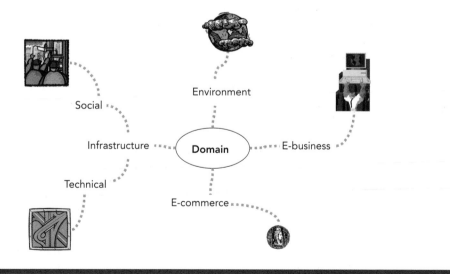

Social

Environment

Infrastructure · · · · · Domain · · · · · E-business

Technical

E-commerce

1.1 🌀 INTRODUCTION

Over a number of decades economic markets globally have been subject to two inter-dependent trends – the increasing centrality of information to effective activity and the increasing reliance on electronic communication networks for effective information transfer. Not surprisingly, many contemporary markets are electronic markets or e-markets – markets in which economic exchanges are conducted in whole or part using information and communications technology (ICT). The activity within electronic markets is generally referred to as electronic business (e-business) or electronic commerce (e-commerce). In this chapter we shall distinguish between these terms and use a model to discuss the key elements of e-business as a domain.

The eminent British scientist Michael Faraday once gave a tour of his laboratory to the then Prime Minister. He was asked what use the discovery of electricity could possibly have. 'I cannot say', Faraday replied, 'but one day Her Majesty's government will tax it'.

Prediction of the impact of technology is a tricky business. A key question frequently asked in relation to this area is how much will e-business revolutionise business? The opening sentence of this chapter should make it clear that this question somewhat misses the point. E-business has been happening for the last twenty to thirty years in terms of the use of ICT to change internal business practices. A much more valid question is how much e-commerce will revolutionise trade. Although e-commerce has impacted upon business-to-business trading, the case is still out as to its impact on customer-to-business and customer-to-customer relationships. The key aim of this book is to provide the reader with sufficient understanding to make an informed judgement about this fundamental question.

A note of caution: this chapter summarises the fundamental theory needed to understand the phenomenon of e-business. We would agree with Kurt Lewin that *there is nothing more practical than a good theory*. Therefore the current chapter serves as an orienting map for the book, since it provides a high-level view of the e-business terrain and provides the structure for the major parts of the text that follow. The reader is not expected to assimilate all the concepts discussed here in one pass, but should feel free to follow links to further chapters at any time. The chapter can be used at some later point as a way of reviewing the material covered.

Example

A major study (Dutta and Bison, 2001) of the effect of the Internet on large global corporations (listed in the *Fortune* Global 500 list) since 1997 concludes that:

- All large corporations have progressed in terms of establishing a presence on the Internet from a baseline of 50% of companies in 1997.

- The proportion of companies using the Internet for e-commerce has increased significantly. Initially most companies used the Internet as an advertising medium. Companies are now gradually enlarging their activities to handle commercial transactions.

- Most corporations have moved their existing business operations onto the Internet with little change to their fundamental business models.

- US corporations have been leading the business world in the use of the Internet. European corporations have gained the most ground in general advancement. Asian corporations continue to lag behind in e-business.

1.2 ⊚ ELEMENTS OF THE E-BUSINESS DOMAIN

The model in Figure 1.1 depicts the major elements of the e-business domain and also forms the basic structure for the book. Each of the component elements contained in the model is covered in more detail as a part of the book:

- *E-business environment (Part 3)*. A number of transformations in the economic, social and political spheres form the backdrop for organisational change stimulated by ICT in both the public and private sectors.
- *E-business (Part 1)*. We shall argue that e-business is both an old and a new phenomenon. It is an old phenomenon in that ICT has been used to innovate internal changes in business for a number of decades. It is a new phenomenon in that ICT is being used to innovate new forms of trading behaviour.

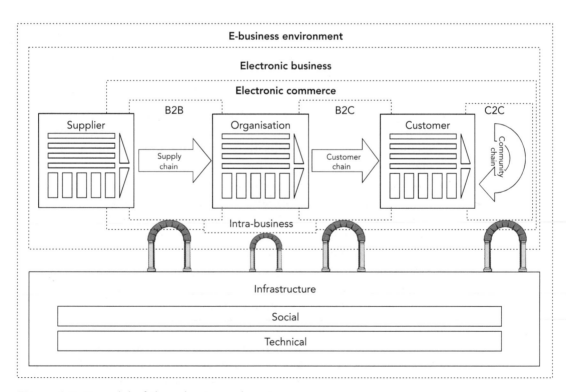

Figure 1.1 A model of the e-business domain.

- *E-commerce (Part 4).* The model distinguishes between three forms of e-commerce. Business to business e-commerce is one of the older and more established forms of ICT innovation in the area of trade. Business to consumer e-commerce has been critically affected by the rise of the Internet and the Web. Consumer to consumer e-commerce is probably the most radical and recent form of ICT innovation in the area of commerce.

- *E-business infrastructure.* The arches on the model presented in Figure 1.1 are meant to represent the important role that infrastructure plays in supporting e-commerce and e-business. We distinguish between social infrastructure and technical infrastructure. Social infrastructure refers to the necessary processes of planning, management, development and evaluation that must occur within organisations if they are to be successful in e-business (Part 5). Technical infrastructure refers to the necessary arrangements of information and communication technologies that make e-business possible (Part 2).

At the start of each part of the book this diagram is revisited with the appropriate component element highlighted for consideration. Within this chapter we consider each of these elements in turn, then summarise the interrelationships between the components.

1.3 E-BUSINESS (PART 1)

There has been some debate about the distinction between the terms *e-business* and *e-commerce*. We take e-business to be a superset of e-commerce. In turn, e-commerce can be considered a superset of Internet commerce or i-commerce:

- *E-business.* Business can be considered either as an entity or as the set of activities associated with a commercial organisation. Electronic business or e-business might be defined as the utilisation of information and communication technologies to support all the activities of business.

- *E-commerce.* Commerce constitutes the exchange of products and services between businesses, groups and individuals. Commerce or trade can hence be seen as one of the essential activities of any business. E-commerce focuses on the use of ICT to enable the external activities and relationships of the business with individuals, groups and other businesses.

- *I-Commerce.* Internet commerce is the use of Internet and Web technologies to enable e-commerce. Such technologies are becoming the key standards for intra- and inter-organisational communication.

These distinctions allow us to delineate the use of ICT to enable communication and coordination between the internal stakeholders of the business (intra-business e-business) such as employees and managers from the use of ICT to enable communication and coordination with external actors (e-commerce) such as suppliers, partners and customers.

1.3.1 SYSTEM

We use one fundamental and multi-faceted concept to explain e-business issues – that of a system. A systemic analysis of e-business corresponds to a holistic account of this phenomenon. We take e-business to be fundamentally concerned with the way in which various social and technical systems interact within the business. The systems concept is important because it allows us to relate together a number of critical concerns for e-business: the structure and dynamics of organisation – the issues of control and performance, management and decision-making, data and information, and activity and technology.

E-business is founded in systems (Chapter 2): systems of human activity, systems of information, and systems of information and communication technology. A system might be defined as a coherent set of interdependent components that exists for some purpose, has some stability, and can be usefully viewed as a whole. Systems are generally portrayed in terms of an input–process–output model existing within a given environment (Figure 1.2). The environment of a system might be defined as anything outside the system that has an effect on the way the system operates. The environment of a system can be defined in terms of the agents or agencies with which the system interacts. The inputs to the system are the resources it gains from agencies in its environment. The outputs from the system are those things that it supplies back to agencies in its environment. Inputs and outputs may be composed of either data or physical items. The process of the system is that set of activities that transform system inputs into system outputs. Systems can also be viewed hierarchically as a collection of subsystems and sub-subsystems....

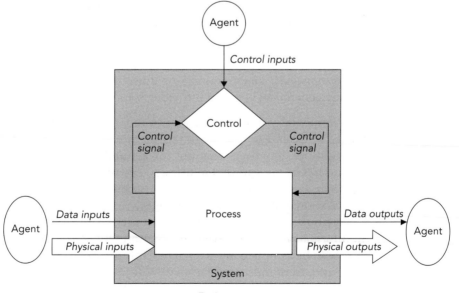

Figure 1.2 System components.

The systems concept has been applied to technology (ICT system), to information (information system) and to human activity (human activity system).

1.3.2 HUMAN ACTIVITY SYSTEM

Organisations, particularly business organisations, are human activity systems (Chapter 3) or more realistically complex chains of human activity systems. A human activity system (HAS) is a social system – sometimes referred to as a 'soft' system – and comprises a logical collection of activities performed by some group of people. A human activity system will have a distinct goal or goals that it fulfils. Another term now used as a synonym for a HAS is *organisational or business process*.

Organisations can be conceived of as chains of human activity systems associated with the production and dissemination of value. For commercial organisations such value will typically constitute products. For public sector organisations value will typically be embodied in the services that such organisations provide. Within the community value will constitute social capital – networks of information, trust and reciprocity.

1.3.3 VALUE CHAINS AND E-BUSINESS

Organisations can be seen as consisting of a series of interdependent chains made up of interdependent human activity systems that deliver value (Chapter 3). Four chains are significant for most businesses:

- *The internal value chain* consists of a series of HAS by which the organisation produces value.
- The *supply chain* consists of those HAS by which an organisation obtains goods and services from other organisations.
- The *customer chain* consists of those HAS by which an organisation delivers value to its customers.
- The *community chain* consists of those HAS in the 'community' that support value generation between individuals and groups.

Fundamentally e-business and e-commerce focus around organisational value chains. The trend to use ICT to re structure aspects of the internal value chain of organisations has been ongoing for a number of decades. Recently increasing interest has been expressed in using ICT to re-engineer aspects of the organisation customer and supply chains. ICT is also being used to build bridges between an organisation and the larger community.

Every human activity system within internal and external value chains will rely on information for effective collaboration and coordination of activity. Information will be supplied by associated information systems. ICT systems are an inherent part of most contemporary information systems.

1.3.4 INFORMATION AND INFORMATION SYSTEMS

Information is data interpreted in some meaningful context. A datum, a unit of data, is one or more symbols that are used to represent something. Information is interpreted data. Information is data placed within a meaningful context. The use of the term information therefore implies a group of people doing interpretation. An information system is a system of communication between people. Information systems are systems involved in the gathering, processing, distribution and use of information. Information systems support human activity systems in the sense that information is important for the coordination of human activity to meet established goals.

1.3.5 CONTROL AND PERFORMANCE

Control is the mechanism that implements regulation and adaptation in most systems. Systems generally exhibit some form of control to maintain the systems in some form of equilibrium and to enable the system to adapt to changes in its environment. Control can be viewed in terms of a monitoring subsystem that regulates the behaviour of other subsystems (Figure 1.2). This monitoring or control subsystem ensures defined levels of performance for the system through imposing a number of control inputs upon the system.

A monitoring subsystem may only work effectively if there are defined levels of performance (Chapter 2) for the system. Such performance levels will be defined by higher-level systems – a super-system for some given system. There are three main types of performance measure: efficacy, efficiency and effectiveness measures (Checkland, 1987):

- *Efficacy*. Efficacy is a measure of the extent to which a system achieves its intended transformation.
- *Efficiency*. Efficiency is a measure of the extent to which the system achieves its intended transformation with the minimum use of resources.
- *Effectiveness*. Effectiveness is a measure of the extent to which the system contributes to the purposes of a higher-level system of which it may be a subsystem.

Performance management of all three types is required for e-business. Information is critical to the measurement of performance in all three areas. The control signals on Figure 1.2 are fundamentally flows of information between the monitoring subsystem and its monitored process. Such signals feed back to the monitoring subsystem and trigger actions to maintain the state of some system within given bounds. In such terms, information systems and ICT are therefore critical for the effective management of modern organisations.

1.3.6 INFORMATION AND COMMUNICATION TECHNOLOGY

Information and communication technology (ICT) is any technology used to support information gathering, processing, distribution and use. ICT provides a means of constructing aspects of information systems, but is distinct from information systems. Modern ICT consists of hardware, software, data and communications technology.

- *Computer hardware.* This comprises the physical (hard) aspects of ICT, consisting of processors, input devices and output devices.
- *Computer software.* This comprises the non-physical (soft) aspects of ICT. Software is essentially programs – sets of instructions for controlling computer hardware.
- *Data.* This constitutes a series of structures for storing data on peripheral devices such as hard disks. Such data is manipulated by programs and transmitted via communication technology.
- *Communication technology.* This forms the interconnective tissue of ICT. Communication networks between computing devices are essential elements of the modern ICT infrastructure of organisations.

It is important to recognise that information systems have existed in organisations prior to the invention of ICT, and hence ICT is not a necessary condition for an IS. However, in the modern, complex organisational world most IS rely on hardware, software, data and communication technology to a greater or lesser degree because of the efficacy, efficiency and effectiveness gains possible with the use of such technology.

1.3.7 ICT SYSTEM

An ICT system is a technical system. Such systems are frequently referred to as examples of 'hard' systems in the sense that they have a physical existence. An ICT system is an organised collection of hardware, software, data and communication technology designed to support aspects of some information system. An ICT system has data as input, manipulates such data as a process and outputs manipulated data for interpretation within some human activity system. Hence most ICT systems are concerned with data manipulation or processing.

It is useful to consider an ICT system as being made up of a number of subsystems or horizontal layers:

- *Interface subsystem.* This subsystem is responsible for managing interaction with the user. This subsystem is generally referred to as the user interface, sometimes the human–computer interface.
- *Rules subsystem.* This subsystem manages the logic of the ICT system in terms of a defined model of business rules.
- *Transaction subsystem.* This subsystem acts as the link between the data subsystem and the rules and interface subsystems. Querying, insertion and update activity is triggered at the interface, validated by the rules subsystem and packaged as units (transactions) that will initiate actions (responses or changes) in the data subsystem.
- *Data subsystem.* This subsystem is responsible for managing the underlying data needed by the ICT system.

In the contemporary ICT infrastructure each of these parts of an application may be distributed on different machines, perhaps at different sites. This means that each part usually needs to be connected together in terms of some communications backbone.

1.3.8 INFRASTRUCTURE

Organised activity of whatever form requires infrastructure (Chapter 5). Infrastructure consists of systems of social organisation and technology that support human activity (Ciborra *et al.*, 2000). The arches on Figure 1.1 are meant to indicate that the technical and social infrastructures support activity in key areas of e-business. It thus becomes possible to speak of four vertical layers of infrastructure crucial to e-business:

- *HAS Infrastructure.* This constitutes the organisation of activity supporting the creation and distribution of value.
- *Information infrastructure.* This comprises the information necessary to support the HAS infrastructure.
- *Information systems infrastructure.* This consists of the information systems needed to support organisational activity in the areas of information collection, storage, dissemination and use.
- *ICT infrastructure.* This consists of the hardware, software, communication facilities and ICT knowledge and skills available to the organisation.

Such layers are organised hierarchically. The information infrastructure supports the HAS infrastructure. In turn, the information infrastructure is supported by the IS infrastructure. Finally, it is likely that the IS infrastructure of an organisation will be supported by an ICT infrastructure. We use the term *informatics* to encompass issues of information, information systems and ICT. Hence we may simplify and state that the human activity systems infrastructure of an organisation is reliant on its informatics infrastructure.

It is also possible to think of infrastructure in terms of a horizontal division between those processes and technologies concerned with external activities and those processes and technologies associated with internal activities. The former is frequently referred to as the front end or front office of the organisation. The latter is often referred to as the back end or back office of the organisation.

1.3.9 MANAGEMENT AS CONTROL

Information supports human activity in the sense that it enables decisions to be made about appropriate actions in particular circumstances. Decisions and decision-making therefore mediate between information and action and are a critical aspect of any human activity system.

Management can be seen as a control process within organisations. Management is a human activity system that controls other human activity systems. The primary activity of management is making decisions concerning organisational action. Effective management decision-making is reliant on good information, the effective definition of performance and the construction of effective performance management systems for managerial activity. Transactional data is critical to performance management.

1.3.10 TYPES OF INFORMATION SYSTEM

In terms of the control processes of organisations it is possible to distinguish between three major types of information system: transaction processing systems (TPS), management information systems (MIS) and decision support systems (DSS)/executive information systems (EIS).

Transaction processing systems form the major back-end information systems of the business and include sales order processing, purchase order processing, stock control, payroll and accounting. Such systems handle most of the essential operational information needed for running the business.

On this foundation a large number of other information systems are normally built. Such systems are front-end systems in the sense that they directly interface to the major stakeholder types of business: managers, employees, suppliers and customers (Chapter 4).

Various information systems may feed off the data provided by core information systems in the back-end infrastructure and summarise such data for effective management and planning. In effect this is a vertical extension to the back-end information systems infrastructure. These are the management-facing information systems of the business.

Extensions may also be made horizontally out from the core information systems of the business. Connections may be made from the core IS infrastructure to other information systems that interface to a company's customers, suppliers or employees. Such are the customer-facing, supplier-facing and employee-facing information systems of the business (Chapter 5).

1.4 TECHNICAL INFRASTRUCTURE (PART 2)

Figure 1.3 illustrates the key components of the ICT or technical infrastructure for e-business. The key message being promoted is that ICT is an enabler for organisational change focused around the redesign of the delivery of services and products to key stakeholders – customers, suppliers, partners and employees. Hence ICT is seen to offer the potential for more efficacious, efficient and effective delivery of value along supply, customer, internal and (potentially) community value chains.

ICT is being promoted within both the public and private sectors as a means of improving the efficacy, efficiency and effectiveness of the delivery of services and products to internal and external stakeholders.

A key distinction is essential between products, services and transactions. Products and/or services (represented as broad arrows on Figure 1.3) are typically the

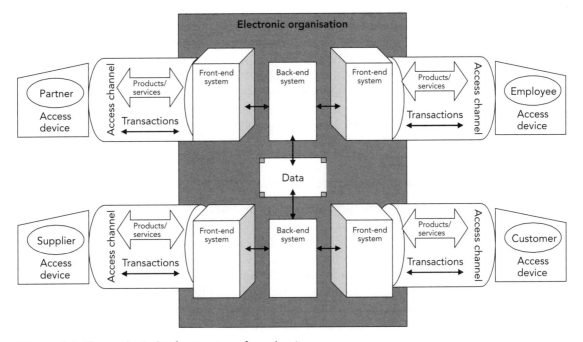

Figure 1.3 The technical infrastructure for e-business.

value delivered to the stakeholder. Hence products and/or services are typically the end points of processes or human activity systems undertaken by organisations (Checkland, 1987).

Information is needed to support most human activity systems, particularly in terms of transactional data. Transactions (indicated as narrow arrows on Figure 1.2) are ways of recording the delivery of products and services and hence are the essential raw data for modelling and evaluating organisational performance. Performance management systems cannot work effectively within organisations without such transactional data. Reducing the costs associated with the administration of transactions is also seen as the typical way of introducing cost savings with ICT.

The objective of redesigning organisational processes or human activity systems with ICT to support electronic delivery of products and services typically involves the changes described in Subsections 1.4.1–1.4.6.

1.4.1 INVESTIGATING AND IMPLEMENTING VARIOUS ACCESS MECHANISMS FOR DIFFERENT STAKEHOLDERS (CHAPTER 7)

In terms of interaction with the customer, face-to-face contact and telephone conversations are two of the most commonly used mechanisms for accessing an organisation's services and/or products. However, with an eye on the longer term, organisations in both the public and private sectors are either implementing or investigating access mechanisms that allow customers to interact with the organisation remotely using ICT. An access mechanism is typically composed of some access device and access channel. Typical remote access devices being supported are the Internet-enabled personal computer (PC) and interactive digital television (iDTV). There are a number of advantages to both the organisation and its external stakeholders in promoting the use of such access mechanisms. For instance, an organisation may be able to provide access to its services and products 24 hours a day, 365 days a year at relatively low cost.

1.4.2 PROVIDING EFFECTIVE DELIVERY OF INTANGIBLE GOODS AND SERVICES (CHAPTER 8)

Certain goods are primarily information-based or intangible in nature. Key examples here are software and music. As such, they are prime candidates for electronic delivery. This enables certain organisations to replace traditional physical distribution channels with electronic distribution. In this scenario the access channel on Figure 1.3 also becomes a distribution channel.

Many services are also intangible in nature. Key examples here are insurance, legal advice, news reports and monetary transfers. One would expect that such business areas would be prime candidates for electronic service delivery.

1.4.3 CONSTRUCTING FRONT-END ICT SYSTEMS TO MANAGE STAKEHOLDER INTERACTION (CHAPTERS 9, 10, 12)

The technological infrastructure for modern front-end ICT systems relies on two critical technologies: the Internet and the Web.

The Internet (Chapter 9) is a set of interconnected computer networks distributed around the globe and can be considered on a number of levels. The base infrastructure of the Internet is composed of packet-switched networks and a series of communication protocols. On this layer runs a series of applications such as electronic mail (e-mail) and more recently the World Wide Web – the Web for short. The Web (Chapter 10) is effectively a set of standards for the representation and distribution of hypermedia documents over the Internet. A hypermedia document consists of a number of chunks of content such as text, graphics and images connected together with associative links called hyperlinks. The Web has become a key technology for constructing the front-end ICT systems of organisations.

One of the most critical of such front-end ICT systems is the organisation's Web site (Chapter 12). The term *Web site* is generally used to refer to a logical collection of Web documents normally stored on a Web server. Such sites now constitute major ways of providing electronic delivery to customers.

Because of the increasing use of technologies such as the Internet and the Web by stakeholders such as customers, major investment is currently being undertaken by companies to increase levels of interactivity on their Web sites. The aim for many companies is to provide fully transactional Web sites in which customers can undertake a substantial proportion of their interaction with an organisation online.

1.4.4 RE-ENGINEERING OR CONSTRUCTING BACK-END ICT SYSTEMS (CHAPTER 11)

Effective back-end ICT infrastructure is critical to organisational success. The back-end ICT infrastructure of the organisation will particularly manage the operational data of the organisation. Hence, database systems are critical to back-end infrastructure.

A key focus within the e-business agenda is on re-engineering service delivery around the customer. This requires the effective integration and interoperability of back-end ICT systems. Hence, for example, when a customer enters personal details such as their name and address into one system this information should ideally be available to all other systems that need such data.

1.4.5 ENSURING FRONT-END/BACK-END ICT SYSTEMS INTEGRATION (CHAPTER 12)

To enable fully transactional Web sites, the information presented to the user needs to be updated dynamically from back-end databases. Also, the information entered by customers needs to update company information systems effectively. This demands integration and interoperability of front-end and back-end systems within the ICT infrastructure.

1.4.6 ENSURING SECURE TRANSACTIONS ALONG COMMUNICATION CHANNELS (CHAPTER 13)

For effective e-commerce people must trust electronic delivery. A major part of such trust is reliant on ensuring the privacy of electronic data held in ICT systems and the transactions flowing between ICT systems, particularly payments. A number of technologies now exist to ensure such security, including data encryption and digital certificates.

1.5 ◎ ENVIRONMENT (PART 3)

We have argued above that an organisation can be considered as a human activity system or more accurately as a series of interdependent human activity systems. An organisation is an open system. It receives inputs from its environment and feeds outputs into its environment. The environment also constrains what an organisation is able to do in terms of its human activity.

Therefore, by *environment* we mean anything outside of the organisation. The environment of most organisations can be considered in terms of the interaction between three major environmental systems: an economic system, a political system and a social system (Figure 1.4). The environment of an organisation constitutes a complex network of relationships and activities between the organisation and other agencies in the social, political and economic spheres.

An open systems model of the organisation emphasises that the relationship between environments and organisations is a dialectical one. Organisations are both affected by and affect environments. The shape of and trends within each area

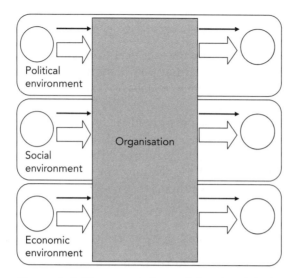

Figure 1.4 The economic, social and political environments.

of the environment will exert an impact on the e-business activities of an organisation. Likewise, the e-business activities of organisations are likely to impact on the social, economic and political spheres.

1.5.1   THE ECONOMIC ENVIRONMENT

For commercial organisations the economic environment (Chapter 14) of the organisation is probably the most important. An organisation exists within some economic system. At the level of the nation state we speak of such an economic system as being an economy. An economic system is the way in which a group of humans arrange their material provisioning. It essentially involves the coordination of activities concerned with such provisioning.

Two major sets of such activities are relevant to economic systems: production and distribution. Production is that set of activities concerned with the creation of goods and services for human existence. Distribution is the associated process of collecting, storing and moving goods into the hands of consumers and providing services for consumers.

Production and distribution are activities that deliver value. Hence economies can be seen as consisting of a multitude of chains of value both within and between organisations.

Economies have two basic mechanisms for coordinating the flow of goods and services in such chains of value: markets and hierarchies (Malone *et al.*, 1987).

● *Markets*. Markets form the competitive environment of the organisation. Markets are systems of competition and comprise media for exchanges between many potential buyers and many potential sellers. Markets coordinate the flow of goods and services through forces of supply and demand and record exchanges in terms of external transactions between individuals and firms.

- *Hierarchies*. Hierarchies form the cooperative environment of organisations. A hierarchy is a medium for exchanges between a limited number of buyers and sellers. The buyers and sellers exchange goods and services within established patterns of trade. Hierarchies coordinate the flow of goods and services by controlling and directing it at a higher level in management hierarchies.

Many contemporary markets are electronic markets (e-markets). By an e-market we mean one in which economic exchanges are conducted using ICT. In an e-market, electronic transactions between employees, buyers and sellers enable the efficient and effective flow of goods and services through internal, supply, customer and community chains.

In the modern electronic economy, electronic hierarchies will tend towards forms of inter-organisational information system (IOS). An IOS is an information system developed and maintained by a consortium of partner organisations for mutual benefit. Generally such systems provide an infrastructure for the sharing of information and services.

1.5.2 THE SOCIAL ENVIRONMENT

The social environment (Chapter 15) of an organisation concerns the cultural life of some grouping, such as a nation state. In recent times it has been popular to collect notions of society with the increasing impact of ICT under the umbrella term *Information Society*. There are a number of indicators of changes in Western societies that provide evidence for the Information Society, including changes to work structures, the growing use of transactional data and the rise of e-business and e-commerce itself.

In terms of e-business the social system concerns ways in which people relate to organisational activity. Although organisations are producing strategies to encourage their external stakeholders such as customers to use remote modes of access to their services and products, a number of preconditions exist to the successful uptake of such access mechanisms. These preconditions (Figure 1.5) represent the interaction of a range of factors in the social environment that are likely to affect take-up of electronic service delivery and include:

- *Awareness*. Stakeholders must be aware of the benefits of using various remote access mechanisms.
- *Interest*. Stakeholders must be interested in using various remote access mechanisms for their purposes.
- *Access*. Stakeholders must have access to remote access devices from some convenient location.
- *Skills*. Stakeholders must have the skills necessary to use access mechanisms such as the Internet-enabled PC effectively. This is frequently referred to as e-literacy.

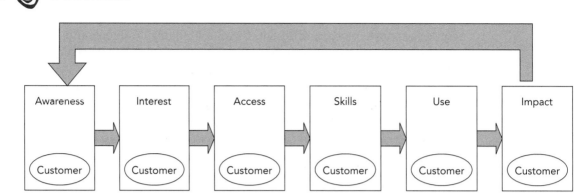

Figure 1.5 Preconditions for electronic service delivery.

- *Use*. Stakeholders must actively use remote access mechanisms on a regular basis in core areas of life such as work and leisure.
- *Impact*. Use of various access mechanisms must approach a threshold that encourages the provision of more content and services delivered electronically.

Social attitudes to issues such as data protection and privacy, as well as trust in e-commerce systems, affects such preconditions in a number of ways. For example, low levels of trust may keep the levels of interest in using transactional services at low levels.

A major concern is that the increasing use of ICT for private and public sector transactions is seen as potentially creating a 'digital divide' between those with access to technology and those who do not. The digital divide fundamentally refers to the phenomenon of differential rates of awareness, interest, access, skills and use among different groups in society. There is substantial evidence to suggest that the lower socio-economic groups in society are the least aware, are the least interested, have the least access to ICT, have the lowest levels of e-literacy and use electronic services the least.

1.5.3 THE POLITICAL ENVIRONMENT

The political environment (Chapter 16) or system concerns issues of power. Political systems are made up of sets of activities and relationships concerned with power and its exercise. The political environment is particularly concerned with government and legal frameworks within nation states and is a major constraining force on organisational behaviour. The practice of government continues to determine policy in the e-business and e-commerce areas.

The rate of development of the Internet as a tool for conducting business has brought challenges to legal systems at a greater rate than previously experienced with the advent of other innovative forms of remote communication. For instance, conventionally law involves a centralised sovereign actor such as a nation state exerting power within its territorial boundaries. This traditional concept of law is challenged by Internet commerce, since it lacks geographical boundaries and there is no centralised authority controlling the Internet. Some of the key areas of concern for e-business in terms of legislation include the use and enforcement of contracts and intellectual property rights.

The political environment of Western countries has been much subject to the influence of ICT in the areas of electronic government (e-government) and electronic democracy (e-democracy) in recent times. ICT and information systems are being used to re-engineer aspects of governmental processes and the relationship between government and the citizen. The interface between government and citizens in terms of services such as tax collection and benefit payment and the associated use of ICT systems to deliver these services via government agencies is sometimes referred to as *e-government*. The term *e-democracy* may be restricted to the use of ICT in the service of democratic representation between government and citizen and the associated use of ICT within democratic processes in government.

1.6 ⊚ E-COMMERCE (PART 4)

Commerce constitutes the exchange of products and services between businesses, groups and individuals. Commerce or trade can hence be seen as one of the essential activities of any business. Commerce of whatever nature can be considered as a process of exchange between economic actors with the following generic phases or states:

- *Pre-sale*. This involves activities occurring before a sale occurs.
- *Sale execution*. This comprises the activities of the actual sale of a product or service between economic actors.
- *Sale settlement*. This involves those activities which complete the sale of a product or service.
- *After sale*. This involves those activities which take place after the buyer has received the product or service from the seller.

It is possible to distinguish between three major patterns of commerce (Chapter 17) in terms of their frequency of occurrence (Whiteley, 2000). Repeat commerce is the pattern in which regular, repeat transactions occur between trading partners. Credit commerce is where irregular transactions occur between trading partners and the processes of settlement and execution are separated. Cash commerce occurs when irregular transactions of a one-off nature are conducted between economic actors. In cash commerce the processes of execution and settlement are typically combined (Figure 1.6).

E-commerce focuses on the use of ICT to enable all such trading activities and relationships of the business with individuals, groups and other businesses. Generally we may distinguish between three distinct forms of e-commerce.

1.6.1 B2C E-COMMERCE (CHAPTER 18)

Business to consumer e-commerce is sometimes called sell-side e-commerce and concerns the enablement of the customer chain with ICT. Customers or consumers

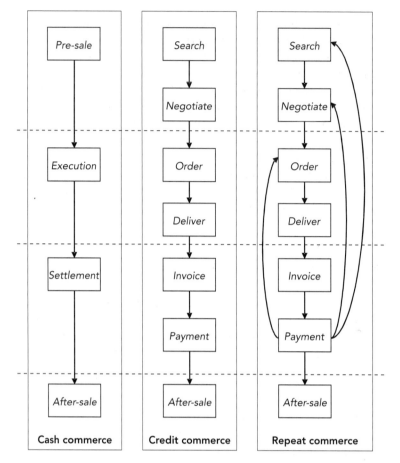

Figure 1.6 Forms of commerce.

will typically be individuals, or sometimes other organisations. B2C commerce typically follows a cash commerce model. Cash commerce for low and standard-priced goods typically follows the four stages of the generic commerce model quite closely. It typically involves a see/buy/get sequence.

For medium- to high-priced items some form of credit commerce will operate. In other words, organisations will search for a product, negotiate a price, order a product, receive delivery of the product, be invoiced for the product, pay for the product and receive some form of after-sales service. Typically, B2C e-commerce will utilise a market model of economic exchange.

1.6.2   B2B E-COMMERCE (CHAPTER 19)

Business to business e-commerce is sometimes called buy-side e-commerce and involves supporting the supply chain with ICT. B2B commerce is clearly between organisational actors – public and/or private sector organisations. This form of e-commerce invariably concerns the use of ICT to enable forms of credit commerce between a company and its suppliers or other partners. For high-priced and customised goods traded between organisations some form of repeat commerce model operates. In other words, the same processes occur as for credit commerce, but the processes cycle around indefinitely in a trusted relationship between producer and consumer. Hence typically some form of managerial hierarchy is employed to control the operation of the commercial relationship.

1.6.3   C2C E-COMMERCE (CHAPTER 20)

Consumer to consumer e-commerce concerns the enablement of the community chain with ICT. C2C e-commerce occurs primarily between individuals and typically involves forms of cash commerce generally for low-cost services or goods. Consequently, it tends to follow a market model for economic exchange. Other forms of value may be generated in the communities or social networks engaged in C2C e-commerce. Of particular interest is the degree of social capital that may be located in such social networks. Social capital is the productive value of people engaged in a dense network of social relations. Social capital consists of those features of social organisation – networks of secondary associations, high levels of interpersonal trust, reciprocity – which act as resources for individuals and facilitate collective action.

1.6.4   E-MARKETING AND E-PROCUREMENT

Two key sub-processes of B2C and B2B e-commerce are important because of their contemporary significance as key process strategies for improving organisational performance.

- *E-marketing.* In the case of B2C e-commerce electronic marketing (E-marketing) (Chapter 21) is an important way of impacting upon the efficiency and effectiveness of the customer chain. E-marketing is the use of electronic channels for the delivery of promotional material.
- *E-procurement.* In the case of B2B e-commerce engaging in electronic procurement (e-Procurement) is an important way to improve the efficiency and effectiveness of an organisation's supply chain (Chapter 22). The pre-sale activity of search, negotiate and order in the supply chain is frequently referred to under the umbrella term of *procurement*. Sometimes the term procurement is used to refer to all the activities involved in the supply chain.

1.7 ◎ THE SOCIAL INFRASTRUCTURE FOR E-BUSINESS (PART 5)

The social infrastructure for e-business consists of those human activity systems central to supporting the conduct of e-business. As well as the conventional competencies in areas of human activity such as finance, sales and production, the

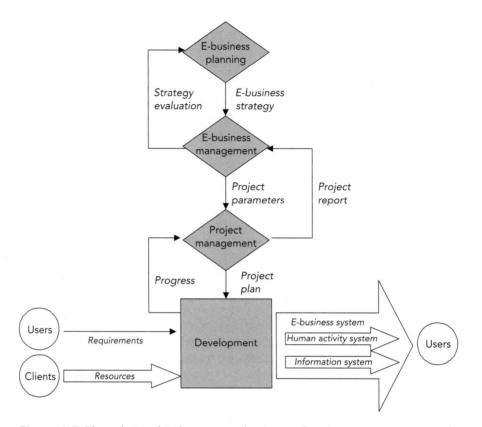

Figure 1.7 The relationship between e-business planning, management and development.

e-business must develop informatics competencies (Beynon-Davies, 2002) if it is to survive in the marketplace. These include competencies in e-business planning, management, development and evaluation. Figure 1.7 illustrates the relationships between these three of these critical processes. In systems terms, these processes can be can be envisaged in terms of a hierarchy of control. Planning controls management, which in turn controls development.

The major point to be made is that effective e-business planning, management, development and evaluation are critical for the effective alignment of human activity systems, information systems and ICT in business.

1.7.1   E-BUSINESS PLANNING

E-business planning (Chapter 23) is the process of deciding upon the optimal e-business infrastructure for an organisation. It is also the process of planning the transformation from one e-business infrastructure into another. E-business infrastructure includes both human activity systems infrastructure and informatics infrastructure. The key output from e-business planning is e-business strategy. The planning process also should include performance monitoring – information fed back from the management process – which is critical to the ongoing evaluation of strategy.

1.7.2 E-BUSINESS STRATEGY

E-business concerns itself with the juncture of ICT and the organisation. Therefore e-business must concern itself with the development of both organisational strategy and informatics strategy. In a sense, e-business strategy (Chapter 24) is both organisational and informatics strategy.

We would argue that there are at least three different viewpoints as to what e-business strategy constitutes. The appropriate viewpoint is defined by organisational context.

- *E-business strategy is organisation/corporate strategy.* In this viewpoint there is little or no distinction between organisation strategy and e-business strategy. This definition is appropriate if the e-business is effectively the entire corporation, as is the case in so-called 'clicks-only' companies – companies that run their entire business through electronic channels.

- *E-business strategy is business unit strategy.* In many companies the e-business strategy may only be applicable to a particular business unit. For example, some companies run their e-businesses as separate but parallel operations.

- *E-business strategy is a process strategy.* A key organisational process or human activity system, or perhaps an integrated set of such processes, may be chosen for radical redesign with ICT innovation. For example, a company may decide that it wishes to concentrate on redesigning its supply chain or customer chain processes with ICT innovation. We would argue that this is the most ubiquitous form of e-business strategy. It defines the most popular form of the so-called 'clicks and mortar' company – traditional businesses which have established an online presence.

1.7.3 E-BUSINESS MANAGEMENT

Two forms of management are delineated on Figure 1.7 – general e-business management and project management. E-business management (Chapter 25) is the process of putting e-business plans into action and monitoring performance against plans. E-business management will implement a portfolio of projects by defining and resourcing projects. However, individual projects need to be managed as autonomous fields of activity and progress reported to general management processes.

1.7.4 E-BUSINESS DEVELOPMENT

E-business development (Chapter 26) is the process of implementing the plans documented in strategy and resourced from management. E-business systems are

socio-technical systems consisting of information systems and the human activity systems they support. Such systems will be constructed by a development organisation and nowadays frequently employ Web-based standards and technologies. Detailed requirements are likely to be supplied by potential users of such systems to the development organisation. Clients such as managerial groups will typically supply key resources to the development organisation to enable such acts of 'engineering'.

1.7.5 E-BUSINESS EVALUATION

E-business strategy, project parameters and project plans are all control inputs in this hierarchy of control. Development progress, project reports and strategy evaluations are all forms of feedback. Figure 1.7 is meant to emphasise that planning, general management, project management and development are continuous processes. As in any human activity system it is important that the feedback loops work effectively for the social infrastructure of e-business to be a viable system. Information systems are equally critical to such processes as conventional business processes such as sales and manufacturing.

One critical subprocess within management is that of evaluation. Evaluation (Chapter 27) is the process of assessing the worth of something. At the highest level, evaluation is critical to the continuous assessment of strategy. At the lowest level, evaluation is critical to the assessment of ICT systems within their context of use and application, namely human activity systems.

1.8 ⊚ SUMMARY

- E-business is the utilisation of information and communication technologies to support all the activities of business. E-commerce focuses on the use of ICT to enable the external activities and relationships of the business with individuals, groups and other businesses. I-commerce focuses on the use of Internet and Web technologies for e-commerce.

- E-business is a superset of e-commerce. E-commerce is a superset of i-commerce.

- The key message being promoted by e-business is that ICT is an enabler for organisational change focused on the redesign of the delivery of services and products to key stakeholders – customers, suppliers, partners and employees.

- The objective of redesigning organisational processes or human activity systems with ICT to support electronic delivery of products and services typically involves remote access mechanisms, delivery of intangible goods and services, constructing front-end ICT systems to manage customer interaction, ensuring effective back-end systems integration and front-end/back-end systems integration, and ensuring the security of data and transactions.

- An organisation can be considered as a human activity system or more accurately as a series of human activity systems. An organisation is an open system. It receives inputs from its environment and produces outputs into its environment. The environment also constrains what an organisation is able to do in terms of its human activity. The environment of most organisations can be considered in terms of the interaction between three major environmental systems: an economic system, a political system and a social system.

- Economies are systems for coordinating the production and distribution of goods and services. Economic activity is organised in terms of markets or hierarchies. Markets are systems of competition. They are media of exchange between buyers and sellers. Hierarchies are systems of cooperation. Exchange is conducted on the basis of established trading arrangements.

- E-business and e-commerce are features of e-markets and e-hierarchies. E-markets and e-hierarchies are environments in which economic exchanges are conducted using ICT. E-markets are electronic environments for competition. E-hierarchies are electronic environments for collaboration.

- The political environment is particularly concerned with government and legal frameworks within nation states. The practice of government determines policy in the e-business and e-commerce areas. However, e-business is also a significant force in government. The political environment of Western countries has been much subject to the influence of ICT in the areas of electronic government and electronic democracy in recent times.

- The social system concerns ways in which people relate to organisational activity. Social attitudes to issues such as data protection and privacy as well as trust in e-commerce systems affects the practicality of e-business.

- A number of preconditions exist for the successful take-up of electronic service delivery, including awareness, interest, access, skills, use and impact.

- The increasing use of ICT for private and public sector transactions is seen as potentially creating a 'digital divide' between those that successfully engage with the preconditions and those who do not.

- Commerce of whatever nature can be considered as a process with the following phases: pre-sale, sale execution, sale settlement, after-sale. The precise form of the process of commerce will vary in terms of the nature of the economic actors involved, the frequency of commerce and the nature of the goods or services being exchanged.

- Electronic commerce (e-commerce) is the use of ICT to enable the external activities and relationships of the business with individuals, groups and other businesses. Generally we may distinguish between three major forms of e-commerce: B2C e-commerce, B2B e-commerce and C2C e-commerce.

- Two key sub-processes of B2C and B2B e-commerce are important because of their contemporary significance as key process strategies for improving organisational performance. E-marketing is the use of electronic channels for the delivery of promotional material. E-procurement is an important way to improve the efficiency and effectiveness of an organisation's supply chain.

● The social infrastructure for e-business consists of those human activity systems central to supporting the conduct of e-business. As well as the conventional competencies in areas of human activity, such as finance, management and production, the e-business must develop informatics competencies if it is to survive in the marketplace. These include competencies in e-business planning, management, development and evaluation.

1.9 🌀 ACTIVITIES

(i) Attempt to model at a high-level an organisation known to you in systems terms.

(ii) Find one example of an e-market and describe its key stakeholders and features.

(iii) Find one example of an e-hierarchy and describe its key stakeholders and features.

(iv) Choose an industrial or commercial sector. Investigate the degree with which B2B and B2C e-commerce has penetrated the sector.

(v) Find one example of an inter-organisational information system and analyse some of the reasons for its creation.

(vi) Investigate the take-up of e-business, e-commerce and i-commerce amongst companies in your local area.

(vii) Determine the costs and benefits associated with e-business.

(viii) In terms of a particular market sector determine whether customers in the sector meet the preconditions for electronic service delivery.

(ix) In terms of some organisation known to you determine the degree to which it engages in one or more of the aspects of the social infrastructure for e-business.

1.10 🌀 REFERENCES

Beynon-Davies, P. (2002). *Information Systems: an Introduction to Informatics in Organisations.* Basingstoke, Palgrave.

Checkland, P. (1987). *Systems Thinking, Systems Practice.* Chichester, John Wiley.

Ciborra, C. U., Braa, C., Cordella, A., Dahlbom, B., Falla, A., Hanseth, O., Hepso, V., Ljunberg, J., Monteiro, E. and Simon, K. A. (2000). *From Control to Drift: the Dynamics of Corporate Information Infrastructures.* Oxford, Oxford University Press.

Dutta, S. and Bison, B. (2001). Business transformation on the Internet: results from the 2000 study. *European Management Journal,* **19**(5), 449–462.

Malone, T. W., Yates, J. and Benjamin, R. I. C. (1987). Electronic markets and electronic hierarchies. *Communications of the ACM,* **30**(6), 484–497.

Whiteley, D. (2000). *E-commerce: Strategy, Technologies and Applications.* Maidenhead, McGraw-Hill.

PART 1

BUSINESS AND SYSTEMS

Pleasure is a thief to business

Daniel Defoe

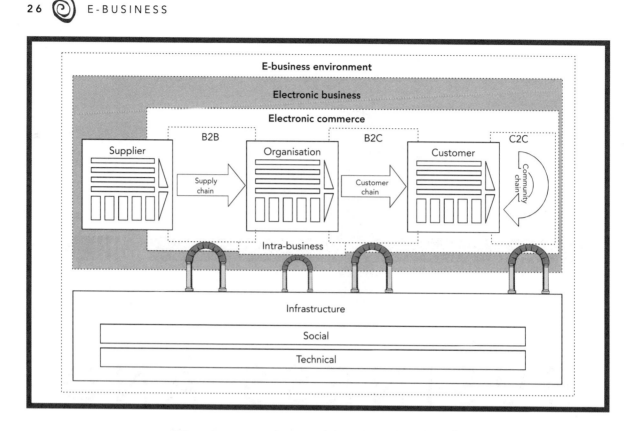

This part uses one fundamental concept to explain e-business issues – that of a system. A systemic analysis of e-business corresponds to a holistic account of this phenomenon. We take e-business to be fundamentally concerned with the way in which various social and technical systems interact within the business. The systems concept is important because it allows us to relate together a number of critical concerns for e-business: the structure and dynamics of organisation, the issues of control and performance, management and decision-making, data and information, and activity and technology.

E-business is founded in systems: systems of human activity, systems of information and systems of information and communication technology. In Chapter 2 we describe the fundamental components of all systems. The system components described in this chapter are used throughout further parts of the book to explain key aspects of the e-business phenomenon. In Chapter 3 we consider organisations, particularly business organisations, as human activity systems or chains associated with the production and dissemination of value. Every human activity system will have an associated information system. Chapter 4 describes the critical elements of an information system and distinguishes such systems from ICT systems. In Chapters 5 and 6 we consider the distinction between front-end and back-end information systems for business and describe some of the common infrastructure for information systems within modern companies.

A number of distinctions are important to understanding the division between the material of part 1 and further parts of the work. The organisational activity within electronic markets or hierarchies is generally referred to as electronic business (e-business) or electronic commerce (e-commerce). As represented on the e-business domain model above, e-business can be seen as a superset of e-commerce. In turn, e-commerce can be considered a superset of Internet commerce (i-commerce):

- *E-business*. Business can either be considered as an entity or as the set of activities undertaken by a commercial organisation. E-business might be defined as the utilisation of information and communication technologies to support all the activities of business.

- *E-commerce*. Commerce constitutes the exchange of products and services between businesses, groups and individuals. Commerce or trade can hence be seen as one of the essential activities of any business. E-commerce focuses on the use of ICT to enable the external activities and relationships of the business with individuals, groups and other businesses.

- *I-commerce*. Internet commerce is the use of Internet and Web technologies to enable e-commerce. Such technologies are becoming the key standards for intra- and inter-organisational communication.

These distinctions allow us to delineate the use of ICT to enable communication and coordination between the internal stakeholders of the business such as employees (intra-business e-business)

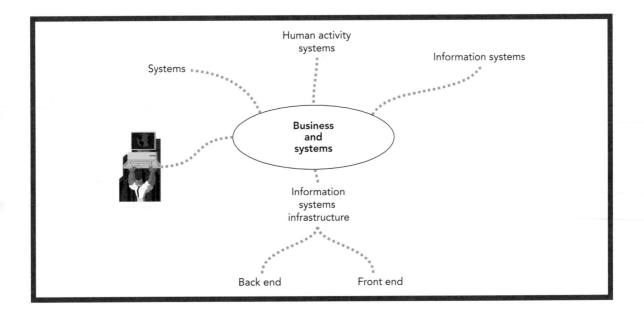

from the use of ICT to enable communication and coordination with external actors such as suppliers and customers (e-commerce).

In Part 1 we primarily consider intra-business issues. The use of ICT to automate, support and innovate internal processes has been ongoing for decades. In Part 4 we consider inter-business issues. The use of ICT to enable the processes of supply and consumption is in many senses a comparatively recent phenomenon in the organisational world.

CHAPTER 2

SYSTEMS

The whole is more than the sum of its parts

Aristotle

LEARNING OUTCOMES

After reading this chapter, you will be able to:

- Define the system concepts of inputs, outputs, process and control
- Describe how performance is measured in systems
- Detail various types of control mechanism experienced within systems
- Understand the key components of a system diagram
- Detail some of the relevance of systems thinking to business concerns

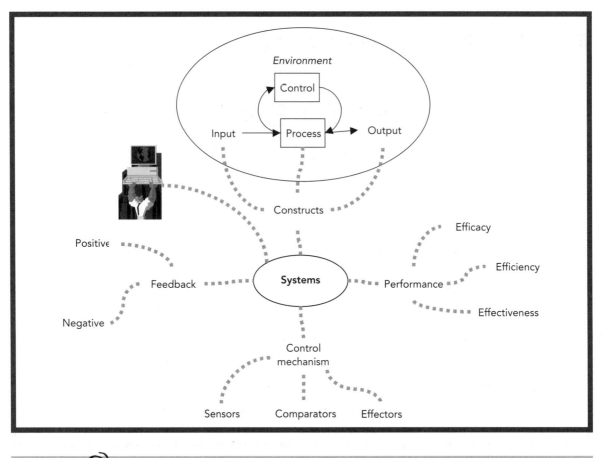

The concept of a system is central to modern thinking in numerous fields. In medicine it is seen as important to consider our bodies as being made up of various systems such as a digestive system and a central nervous system. In terms of astronomy we live on a planet that is part of the solar system. In the social sciences we engage with people in groups that form social, political and economic systems. In mathematics we are educated in the use of number systems. Modern organisations can be conceived of as systems of activity that would collapse without effective information systems.

We shall maintain that e-business is founded in the concept of a system. It is a key 'tool of thought' (Waddington, 1977) for understanding and explaining the impact of ICT on private and public sector organisations. E-business involves the interaction between three types of system – human activity systems, information systems and ICT systems. In this chapter we describe the general elements of systems that we shall use in subsequent chapters to build our description of systems of human activity, information and technology. We also introduce a simple technique for graphically representing systems that we shall use in further chapters.

2.2 SYSTEM

Systems thinking maintains Aristotle's dictum that *the whole is more than the sum of its parts*. Systems thinking proposes that it is important to investigate and understand complex phenomena holistically. The early ideas in systems thinking can be seen as a reaction against the reductionism inherent in the scientific method, i.e. the conventional approach to scientific investigation which involves dissecting a problem into its smallest parts.

A system can be defined as an organised set of interdependent components that exists for some purpose, has some stability, and can be usefully viewed as a whole.

- *Identity*. A system can be clearly distinguished as persisting over time. A boundary for a system can be clearly identified.
- *Organisation*. Systems are organised. Systems are different from aggregates or collections of things.
- *Purpose*. To say a system displays organisation implies that a system is organised to do something – systems are organised to achieve some goals.
- *Emergent properties*. Systems have emergent properties. A system is a complex entity that has properties that do not belong to any of its constituent parts, but emerge from the relationships or interaction of its constituent parts. The whole is more than the sum of its parts.

Example

A road network can be viewed as a system. It is made up of component parts such as roads, road intersections and vehicles. The purpose of a road network is likely to be to convey people and goods between points within some geographical space. In a road network a bottleneck experienced at some road intersection is the result of the interactions of a large body of components (cars) coming together in particular ways. A bottleneck is not a property of any one component (car); it is only a property of the system as a whole.

Systems thinking has been applied to both 'hard' and 'soft' systems (Checkland, 1978). Hard systems are not 'hard' in the sense of being any more complex than soft systems. They are 'hard' in the sense that they use system concepts as a means of investigating complex situations and taking rational action with the objective of achieving what are seen to be defined, unquestioned and frequently unproblematic goals.

Example

Large integrated manufacturing plants such as petrochemical plants can be treated as hard systems in the sense that the design of such plants to achieve production goals is unproblematic.

In contrast human systems are soft systems. They are collections of people undertaking activities to achieve some purpose. Human systems are soft because the boundaries or scope of the human system may be fluid and the purpose of the system may be problematic and certainly open to interpretation from many different viewpoints.

Questions

Consider the purposes of a private sector and public sector organisation as a system. What are the purposes of such organisations? How do such purposes differ?

2.3 SYSTEM CONSTRUCTS

Systems are generally portrayed in terms of an input–process–output model existing within a given environment.

- *Environment.* The environment of a system might be defined as anything outside the system that has an effect on the way the system operates. The environment of a system is typically defined in terms of a number of agents or agencies that interact with the system.
- *Inputs.* The inputs to the system are the resources it gains from agents in its environment, some of which may be other systems.
- *Outputs.* The outputs from the system are those things that it supplies back to agents in its environment, some of which may be other systems.
- *Processes.* The process of the system is that set of activities that transform system inputs into system outputs.

Examples

A manufacturing firm can be considered as a system that transforms raw materials (inputs) from its suppliers (agent) into finished products (outputs) for its customers (agent).

A flower can be conceived of as a system that transforms water, carbon dioxide and light (inputs) from the physical environment into carbohydrates and oxygen (outputs).

The inputs and outputs from a system may consist of two types of flow:

- *Physical flows.* The flow of physical or material things to and from the environment such as plant, machinery and foodstuffs. Since all matter can be described in terms of some energy equivalent, general systems thinkers tend to refer to such physical flows as energy flows.

- *Non-physical flows*. Accompanying the flow of physical material there will be a flow of data. Data is used to describe what is currently happening in a system, what has happened in the past or what is likely to happen in the future.

Questions

In what way is it appropriate to identify the inputs, processes and outputs of the educational system? What physical and non-physical flows are relevant to the educational system?

2.4 ◎ OTHER SYSTEM CONSTRUCTS

Systems are normally seen as comprising a number of other constructs. These include:

- System state and variety
- Subsystems
- Open and closed systems
- Control
- Feedback
- Comparators, sensors and effectors

2.5 ◎ SYSTEM STATE AND VARIETY

The behaviour of a system can be defined in terms of the notion of *state*. The state of a system is defined by the values appropriate to the system's attributes or state variables. At any point in time a value can be assigned to each of a system's state variables. The set of all values assumed by the state variables of a system defines a system's state.

Variety is a measure of the complexity of a system (Beer, 1972). It may be defined as the number of possible states of a system. For many systems, particularly those involving human activity, the variety of the system may be quite large in the sense that the number of possible states may not be precisely countable.

Examples

In a stock control system key state variables may record the level of raw materials stored and the current level of finished products. In a university admissions system key state variables may record the number of applications received, the number of offers made and the number of offers accepted.

In terms of variety we may adapt an example provided in Beer (1966). Assume we have a set of six different things labelled A–F. As a set of dissimilar things they constitute a collection but not a system. Now suppose we represent each thing as a node in a network and indicate relations between these things with directed lines, as in Figure 2.1. In this figure arrows are drawn in both directions between any two nodes to indicate that relation A → B is different from B → A. Suppose also that each relation is effectively a switch that may be turned on or off, perhaps indicating the effect of one node in the network on another. Here we have a simple system since the collection of things now interacts; it operates.

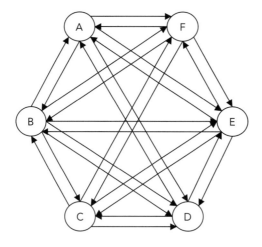

Figure 2.1 A dynamic system.

One state of the system is when the line A → B is open and all the other lines are closed. Another state is when A → B is closed and so on. Since there are two possible relations between each of the six nodes in the network it can be shown that there are $n(n - 1)$ possible relations between nodes, which is 30. If each line on the figure can take two possible states then there are over 236 possible states for the entire system. This is a measure of the variety inherent in this system.

Question   *What contributes to the high variety of most human systems such as businesses?*

2.6 🌀 SUBSYSTEMS

Systems can generally be seen as being composed of subsystems. Hierarchy seems to be an inherent property of most systems. In viewing systems we frequently use a recursive lens. In other words, we can view a system on various levels, each level of

which can be conceptualised in terms of a system. Hence the environment of a system may be viewed as a system in its own right and a process which is part of one system may be treated as a system in turn, and so on.

Examples

An automobile can be viewed as being composed of subsystems such as the electrical subsystem and transmission subsystem.

The human body consists of a number of subsystems such as the nervous system, the circulatory system and the digestive system.

2.7 OPEN AND CLOSED SYSTEMS

There are a number of ways in which we may define types of system. One of the most important distinctions is between open and closed systems. A closed system is one in which there is no interaction between the system and its environment. An open system is one in which there are interactions between the system and its environment. Open systems are generally more interesting than closed systems because they normally adapt to changes in their external environments.

Example

The discipline of ecology utilises the concept of open systems to explain the adaptations that animals and plants make to changes in the physical environment – their habitat. Darwinian natural selection defines the process by which such adaptations occur.

2.8 CONTROL

Control is the process by which a system ensures continuity. It is also the means by which system identity is sustained. Control can be conceived as both a process of regulation and a process of adaptation:

- *Regulation*. Regulation is the conservative side of control. It focuses on internal operation and involves maintaining the system's state within defined parameters. Regulation also ensures that a system recovers some stability after a period of disturbance caused by environmental changes.
- *Adaptation*. Adaptation is the evolutionary side of control. It focuses on the relationship between the system and its environment. Systems generally exhibit some form of control that enables the system to adapt to changes in its environment.

Control can be viewed in terms of a monitoring subsystem that regulates the behaviour of other subsystems. This control mechanism, subsystem or process ensures defined levels of performance for the system through imposing a number of control inputs upon the system.

For reasonably simple 'hard' systems such control inputs will normally be in the form of decision rules or a decision strategy. The rules are initially supplied to the control subsystem from outside of the system and are used to steer a system in a desired direction by supplying control signals to the process of the system.

The discipline of cybernetics (hence 'cyber-space') is founded on the study of such control systems (Wiener, 1948). The ancient Greek word *Kybernetes* means steersman. Wiener (1948) defined the discipline of cybernetics as the 'entire field of control and communication theory, whether in the machine or in the animal'. For complex systems of which human activity systems (Chapter 3) are examples, it may not be possible to specify precisely a decision strategy as a set of decision rules. Instead, the control inputs are likely to comprise an organisation's mission and strategy.

Hence a control mechanism is designed to steer a system in a certain direction. Generally such a direction is defined by the idea of *homeostasis* or steady state. The control system attempts to maintain the system it is monitoring within parameters defined by its control inputs. Such a form of regulatory control system is generally referred to as a *homeostat*. A homeostat is a control mechanism for holding some variable or variables within defined limits. The limits will be set by control inputs. Homeostasis is the process of achieving control in this manner. Homeostasis is the essential principle underlying the self-regulation of systems.

Example

In a heating system a set of thermostats will normally act as control subsystems. A thermostat is normally set at a desired temperature (control input). The device will then monitor the temperature of its environment. If the temperature reaches the set temperature then the heating components such as radiators will be switched off. Once the ambient temperature in the environment drops back below a defined range the thermostat will switch the heating components back on.

Questions

What constitutes control in a human system such as a business? In what way is a business strategy a set of control inputs?

2.9 (C) REPRESENTING SYSTEMS AS DIAGRAMS

To understand systems we must build a model that represents their key components and how they interact. Systems can be described in terms of natural languages such as English, as we have done in the examples presented above.

However, it is usually more convenient to represent systems in visual terms as a diagram. It is particularly easier to represent the interaction of system components on a diagram. To produce a diagrammatic representation of a system we require a graphical notation for the following constructs:

- *Inputs/outputs.* Generally speaking two main forms of input and output need to be represented on a system diagram for our purposes – physical and data inputs/outputs. Physical inputs and outputs are represented as broad labelled arrows. Data inputs and outputs are represented as narrow labelled arrows. The direction of both forms of arrow indicate the direction of physical or non-physical flow.

- *Process.* A process is represented on a system diagram as a labelled box of some kind. The label describes the key transformation of the process – what it does to inputs to produce outputs.

- *Agents.* The environment of a system is defined in terms of a number of agents or agencies that interact with the system. These are represented as rounded shapes on the system diagram and are generally used to indicate the boundary of a system with its environment.

- *Control.* A control process can be represented as a diamond shape on the diagram. Control inputs and control signals are a special case of data inputs to the control process and are represented as such on the system diagram
These elements are illustrated in Figure 2.2.

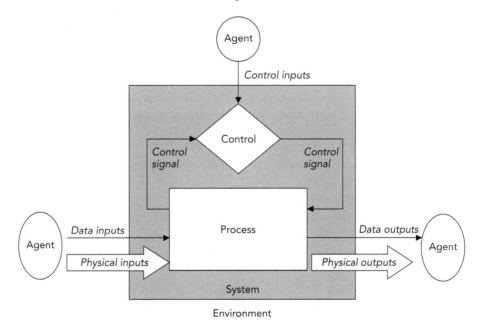

Figure 2.2 Components of a system diagram.

2.10 PERFORMANCE

Control is normally exercised in terms of some defined measures of performance. A monitoring subsystem may only work effectively if there are defined levels of performance for the system. Such performance levels will be defined by higher-level systems.

Examples

In terms of a physical system such as a thermostat a performance measure will be defined in terms of a temperature level.

In terms of a manufacturing plant a defined level of performance might be productivity level per manufacturing unit.

There are three main types of performance measure based on the transformation principle of a system: efficacy, efficiency and effectiveness (Checkland, 1999):

- *Efficacy*. Efficacy is a measure of the extent to which a system achieves its intended transformation. Fundamentally it is a check on the output produced by some system.
- *Efficiency*. Efficiency is a measure of the extent to which the system achieves its intended transformation with the minimum use of resources. Fundamentally it involves a check on the resources (inputs) used to achieve some output.
- *Effectiveness*. Effectiveness is a measure of the extent to which the system contributes to the purposes of a higher-level system of which it may be a subsystem. Fundamentally it amounts to a check on the contribution being made by the system to the purpose of some super-system of which it is a part.

Example

Consider a business unit such as sales. The efficacy of the sales unit may be measured in ways such as examining the number of sales of particular products over some chosen time span. The efficiency of the sales unit can be compared in terms of productivity measures, such as the number of sales per salesperson. The effectiveness of the sales unit can be determined in relation to its contribution to overall company profitability. The key role of the management of the sales unit will be to define and operate measures such as these to enable it to control the work of the unit successfully.

This example illustrates that specialist performance management systems in organisations are effectively control systems.

Question   *What sort of difficulties might be experienced in specifying efficacy, efficiency and effectiveness measures of performance for the business?*

2.11 COMPARATORS, SENSORS AND EFFECTORS

We can refine the idea of a control mechanism in a system by introducing three further system constructs (Figure 2.3):

- *Sensors.* These are mechanisms that monitor changes in the state of a monitored system and send signals to the control system representing such changes.
- *Comparators.* Comparators compare signals from sensors against control inputs and on the basis of established standards of performance send signals to effectors.
- *Effectors.* These components cause changes to a system's state. In other words, they introduce changes to system variables. Effectors are sometimes referred to as actuators because they cause action.

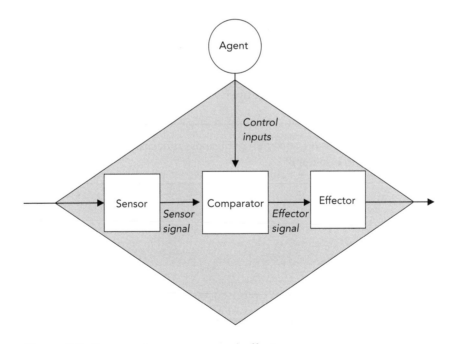

Figure 2.3 Comparators, sensors and effectors.

Example

In a security system sensors are likely to be placed at points of entry into a building, such as windows and doors. If a window is opened when the system is activated then a sensor sends a signal to the control unit. This unit is likely to identify the point of entry and send signals to effectors such as alarms.

In organisational terms any control process is therefore likely to be composed of four major stages (Anthony, 1988):

- A standard of desired performance is specified – the control inputs.
- There is some means of sensing what is happening in the organisation and communicating this information to a control subsystem – sensors.
- The control subsystem compares the information with the standard of performance – comparator.
- If what is happening does not correspond to the standard then corrective action is taken. This corrective action is conveyed back to the monitored system as information – effector. This is the process of feedback.

At a high level of abstraction it is possible to consider planning and management within organisations as control systems. Planning (Chapter 23) is a key organisational process whose output is strategy (Chapter 24). Strategy can be conceived of as a key set of control inputs for management (Chapter 25). Management is a key organisational process concerned with establishing key performance management systems (sensors) that provide data about operational performance and compares (comparators) such performance against objectives established in strategy. Divergence between operational performance and strategy leads to directives (effectors) which attempt to bring operations back within defined parameters.

Question

In a business organisation or business process, what constitute likely sensors, comparators and effectors?

2.12 ◎ FEEDBACK

Control is normally exercised within a system through some form of feedback. Outputs from the process of a system are fed back to the control mechanism. The control mechanism then adjusts the control signals to the process on the basis of the data it receives. Feedback has two major forms: positive and negative feedback.

2.12.1 NEGATIVE FEEDBACK

Control is normally exercised through a negative feedback loop. The monitoring subsystem monitors the outputs from the system through its sensors. The comparators in the monitoring system detect variations from defined levels of performance provided by control inputs. If the outputs vary from established levels then the monitoring subsystem commands some effectors to reduce the variation.

Examples

In a thermostat, if the temperature falls below some specified level then the thermostat initiates an action such as opening a hot water valve.

A company maintaining cash flow can be conceived of as a system with negative feedback in which the cash balance continually influences company decisions on expenditure and borrowing.

2.12.2 POSITIVE FEEDBACK

Positive feedback is a deviant version of control evident in many systems. Commonly known as a 'vicious circle' it involves the monitoring subsystem increasing the discrepancy between the desired and actual levels of performance.

Examples

The 'arms race' that occurred during the Cold War period is a classic example of a system characterised by a positive feedback loop. At the time, the USA increased its level of armament to improve its security. This prompted the USSR to increase its level of armament because of a perceived greater threat to its security. The USA responded by increasing its levels of armament, and so on.

In large information systems development projects there is a tendency to escalate decision-making such that more resources are thrown at an ailing project in the hope of preventing failure. What tends to happen is that costs escalate, demanding even more resources to be thrown at the project.

Question

What sorts of feedback are experienced in economic systems such as markets?

2.13 HUMAN ACTIVITY SYSTEMS, INFORMATION SYSTEMS AND ICT SYSTEMS

The idea of a system has had a profound influence on the domain of e-business. For instance:

- The term *system* is inherently embedded within the label 'information system' that we shall argue is the primary focus for bridging between human activity and information and communication technology. Hence the concept of a system has been applied both to technology such as hardware and software ('hard' systems) and to human activity ('soft' systems). In the modern organisational world information systems are key examples of hybrid systems – socio-technical systems (Emery and Trist, 1960).

- The concept of a system contributed to the development of modern information and communication technology in the sense that it heavily influenced the design of devices such as the modern computer. Systems thinking also influenced the creation of the communications revolution that underpins the modern 'information highway'.

- We shall argue that the treatment of organisations as systems underlies much of contemporary e-business thinking. As a consequence, much of e-business activity is based in the assumption that organisations can be designed by modelling them in system terms and implementing new processes within organisations to improve performance. ICT is seen as a key agent for organisational change.

These are the topics of subsequent chapters.

2.14 CASE STUDY: THE ELECTORAL SYSTEM IN THE UK

In this section we consider an area of human activity – the activity of electing governments in the UK – that is not normally associated with the concept of a system generally or with the appropriateness of systems of ICT. We include it here and in subsequent chapters to demonstrate the applicability of systems thinking generally and of e-business thinking in particular to governmental as well as commercial areas of life.

The UK is a parliamentary democracy and hence is reliant on an effective electoral system. General elections are held after Parliament has been dissolved either by Royal Proclamation or because the maximum term of office of five years for a government has been reached. The decision as to when a general election is to be held is taken by the Prime Minister.

For parliamentary elections the UK is divided into 659 constituencies – 18 in Northern Ireland, 40 in Wales, 72 in Scotland and 529 in England. For so-called general elections to Parliament the UK currently employs a 'first past the post' system, sometimes described as a single member plurality system. In this system

each voter uses a single poll card to cast a single ballot for one constituency candidate and each constituency elects a single MP on the basis of the majority of the votes cast. Each candidate in the general election generally represents a single political party and the party with the most seats in Parliament (not necessarily the most votes) will usually become the next government of the nation.

Figure 2.4 comprises a system diagram of this electoral system. The key inputs into the electoral system are ballot poll cards and ballot papers provided by the key agents, voters. The key outputs are a set of election results provided for each constituency. The key control process is one of electoral monitoring which establishes guidance on expected electoral practice and monitors the actual election to determine any deviation from such practice. The environment of the electoral system is the political system of the UK.

One can argue that a number of emergent properties result from the UK employing this form of electoral system. Some of such properties may be viewed as advantages to the democratic system of the UK; some might be conceived of as disadvantages.

- The electoral system is relatively simple to implement, use and understand.
- The system generally provides a clear choice between two main political parties.
- The system tends to promote strong single-party governments with a coherent government opposition.
- Political parties tend to be broad churches of political opinion in order to satisfy the demands of various shades of the electorate.
- The system tends to exclude extremist parties.

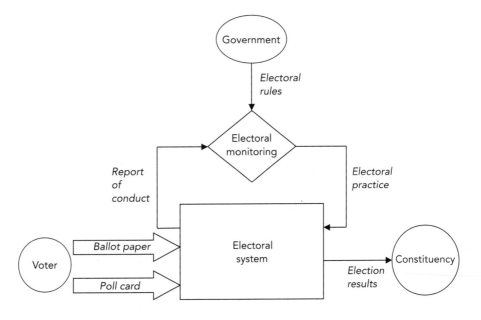

Figure 2.4 The electoral system.

- The system tends to exclude minorities from fair representation.
- Party government can maintain in control in the face of a substantial drop in popular support.
- The electoral system is susceptible to manipulation of electoral boundaries (constituency).

2.15 SUMMARY

- E-business is founded in systems thinking.
- A system is an organised collection of things with emergent properties and with some definable purpose.
- Critical features or components of all systems are subsystems, input–process–output, an environment and control.
- Systems may be classified in various ways, including open and closed systems.
- Control is the mechanism that implements regulation and adaptation in systems. Systems generally exhibit some form of control that enables the system to maintain state within defined parameters and to adapt to changes in its environment.
- Control mechanisms are built of sensors, comparators and effectors working in feedback loops.
- Control is normally exercised in terms of defined measures of performance – efficacy, efficiency and effectiveness measures.
- There are two main types of feedback: positive feedback and negative feedback.
- The concept of a system can be used to model human activity, information and technology.

2.16 ACTIVITIES

(i) Identify the system components of a computer – inputs, process, outputs and environment.

(ii) A computer would be described as a discrete or digital system. Investigate what this means in terms of the concept of system state.

(iii) Consider an educational organisation such as a school or university as a system. Try to identify some possible subsystems.

(iv) There are various other ways of classifying systems besides open–closed. Try to identify a number of other system types and examples of each type.

(v) Try to represent in high-level terms a university or school as a system diagram.

(vi) Identify appropriate measures for the efficiency and effectiveness of university teaching as a system.

(vii) Identify the functionality of sensors, comparators and effectors in terms of a thermostat.

(viii) Negative feedback is frequently used to maintain the homeostasis of some system. Investigate the term *homeostasis* in greater detail.

2.17 REFERENCES

Anthony, R. A. (1988). *The Management Control Function*. Boston, MA, Harvard Business School Press.

Beer, S. (1966). *Decision and Control: the Meaning of Operational Research and Management Cybernetics*. Chichester, John Wiley.

Beer, S. (1972). *Brain of the Firm: the Managerial Cybernetics of Organisation*. London, Allen Lane.

Checkland, P. (1999). *Soft Systems Methodology: a Thirty Year Retrospective*. Chichester, John Wiley.

Checkland, P. B. (1978). The origins and nature of 'hard' systems thinking. *Journal of Applied Systems Analysis*, **5**(2), 99-110.

Emery, F. E. and Trist, E. L. (1960). *Socio-Technical Systems. Management Science, Models and Techniques* (ed. C. W. Churchman and M. Verhulst). New York, Pergamon.

Waddington, C. H. (1977). *Tools for Thought*. St Albans, Jonathan Cape.

Wiener, N. (1948). *Cybernetics*. New York, Wiley.

3

HUMAN ACTIVITY SYSTEMS

If you can dream and not make dreams your master

If you can think and not make thoughts your aim...

Rudyard Kipling, *If*

Who can control his fate?

William Shakespeare, *Othello, Act V, Scene ii*

LEARNING OUTCOMES

After reading this chapter, you will be able to:

- Define the term *human activity system*
- Understand the concept of the value chain and describe the key elements of the value chain
- Distinguish between the supply, internal and customer chains of business
- Consider management as a control process
- Define the concept of a business model and its use in designing human activity systems

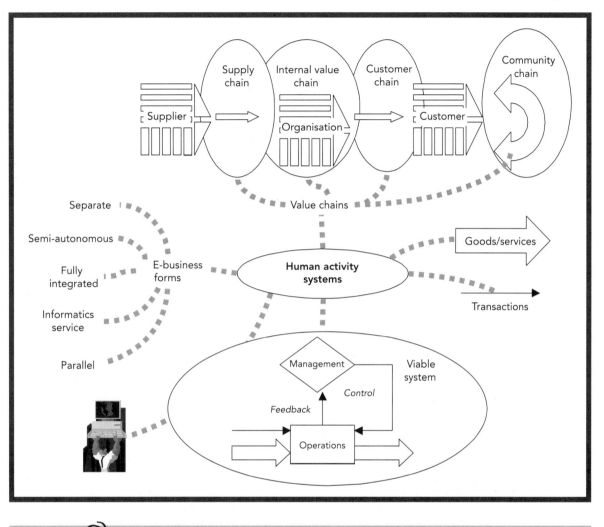

Most of the e-business literature takes a process or systems view of the organisation. Organisations are viewed in terms of a number of key human activity systems (Checkland, 1987) or business processes (Hammer, 1996). Information, information systems and information and communication technology support human activity in such systems.

In this chapter we describe some of the key characteristics of a human activity system. Such systems produce value that travels within and between organisations. Hence human activity systems provide the supportive mechanisms for the customer, supply and internal value chains of organisations. We outline key elements of such value chains and describe them primarily as conduits for the flow of goods, services and transactions both within and between organisations.

Such flows have to be controlled, and this we describe as the primary task of management. Management is described as the key control process for organisations, and as such feedback is a critical concern. The chapter concludes with a discussion of the issue of designing organisations in terms of the concept of a business model and considers the radical business model of the virtual organisation that is made possible with ICT.

3.2 CHARACTERISTICS OF A HUMAN ACTIVITY SYSTEM

An organisation can be seen as being made up of a limited number of human activity systems or business processes. A human activity system is a 'soft system'. It is a set of logically related activities by which organisations accomplish goals.

There are a number of key characteristics of any human activity system:

- *Human activity systems are systems*. As such we should be able to define the key processes of the system, inputs to each process, outputs from each process and the transformation undertaken by each process.

- *Human activity systems support core organisational competencies*. A general assumption is that most organisations consist of a limited number of human activity systems which contribute to fulfilling the key mission or purposes of some organisation.

- *Human activity systems frequently cut across structural and functional organisational boundaries*. A systems view of the organisation emphasises organisational dynamics rather than organisational structures. Human activity systems frequently cross the organisation cutting through traditional organisational structures such as divisions and departments.

- *Human activity systems can be designed*. Much of the e-business literature takes a rational stance on the organisation in assuming that work systems can be designed to optimise performance (Daft, 2001).

- *Human activity systems have definable measures of performance*. One consequence of the assumption that human activity systems can be designed is that objectives/goals/targets must be set for a human activity system and clear criteria established for measuring its performance in terms of efficacy, efficiency and effectiveness (Chapter 2).

- *Information and communication technology can be used to enable aspects of the design of a human activity system*. ICT is an effective tool which supports the design of new human activity systems or the redesign of existing human activity systems.

Example

A sawmill may be considered as various types of system. An industrial engineer may view it as a production system, a management scientist as a profit-maximising system.

The industrial engineer will be interested in the performance of the system in transforming logs into finished products using particular resources such as plant and machinery. The purpose of studying a sawmill in this way would be to determine effective procedures for controlling the production process. This might concern the physical placement of machinery, the way in which products are handled, and so on.

The management scientist would probably not be interested in the physical activities of the sawmill. He or she would be interested in the financial consequences of such activities. The sawmill may be conceived of as a series of subsystems, such as a log handling and storage subsystem, a finished goods and warehousing subsystem, a marketing subsystem and a financial control subsystem. The main interest of the management scientist is in the way in which each subsystem communicates its needs to other subsystems and how the flow of goods and information affects the financial performance of the firm. The system's environment in this case consists of the market for logs, the market for finished wood products and other elements such as the financial, labour and legal environment of the firm.

Question	How true is it to say that different persons will have different ideas about what constitutes a human activity system and what it is made up of?

3.3 PORTER'S VALUE CHAIN

Porter (1985) offers a template for considering an organisation's key human activity systems. This is a generic model of an organisation known as the value chain. In this view organisations are seen as social institutions that deliver value to customers through defined activities (Sawhney and Parikh, 2001).

Examples	In a manufacturing organisation key aspects of value will be associated with the qualities of the products manufactured. In the public sector an organisation's value will typically be associated with the qualities of the services it delivers. Hence a university may be judged in terms of the quality of the education it provides.

An organisation's value chain is a series of interdependent activities that deliver a product or service to a customer. Such activities are of two types: primary and secondary activities. Primary activities constitute the core competencies of the organisation. Secondary activities are important to the successful operation of primary activities. This is illustrated in Figure 3.1.

The processes in Porter's value chain are modelled on the ideal manufacturing organisation. However, these key human activity systems can be adapted to service-oriented organisations.

Primary activities in the value chain consist of the following:

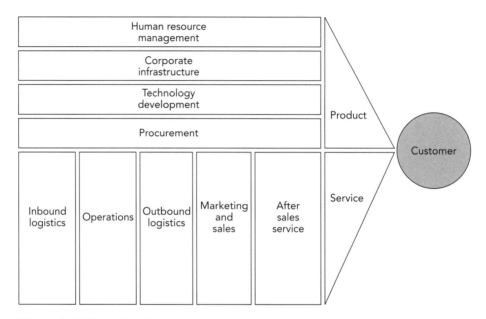

Figure 3.1 The value chain.

- *Inbound logistics*. This process involves the receiving and storage of raw material needed by the company to produce its products. It also involves the associated activity of distributing relevant raw material to manufacturing premises.
- *Operations*. This would traditionally be called manufacturing. It involves transforming inputs (raw materials) into finished products.
- *Outbound logistics*. This involves the storage of finished products in warehouses and the distribution of finished products to the customer.
- *Marketing and sales*. Marketing is the process of planning and executing the conception, pricing, promotion and distribution of ideas, goods and services to create exchanges that satisfy individual and organisational goals (Chapter 21). Sales is the associated activity involved in the management of purchasing activities of the customer.
- *After sales service*. These are services that maintain or enhance product value by attempting to promote a continuing relationship with the customer of the company. It may involve such activities as the installation, testing, maintenance and repair of products.

Secondary activities consist of the following:

- *Infrastructure activities*. These are support activities for the entire value chain such as general management, planning, finance, accounting, legal services and quality management.
- *Human resource management*. This involves the recruiting, hiring, training and development of the employees of a company.

- *Technology development.* This involves the activities of designing and improving the product and its associated manufacturing process. Traditionally it would be called the research and development function.
- *Procurement.* Procurement is the process of purchasing goods and services from suppliers at an acceptable quality and price and with reliable delivery (Chapter 22).

Example

Consider a supermarket chain. We may map some of the key processes from the internal value chain onto this type of business:

- *Inbound logistics* involves the management of the purchasing of foodstuffs and the distribution of foodstuffs to warehouses.

- *Operations* involves the unpacking of bulk deliveries and the presentation of foodstuffs on supermarket shelves.

- *Outbound logistics* involves the distribution of bulk foodstuffs from warehouses to supermarket stores.

- *Marketing and sales* involves the advertisement of product lines and the purchasing of foodstuffs from stores.

- *After-sales service* involves the handling of customer enquiries and complaints.

Question

How relevant is the idea of a value chain for understanding the dynamics of public or voluntary sector organisations?

3.4 SUPPLY CHAIN, CUSTOMER CHAIN AND COMMUNITY CHAIN

An organisation exists within a competitive environment. Porter's notion of the value chain focuses on the internal processes of an organisation. Two other chains of value critical to the competitive environment assume significance for most organisations: the supply chain and the customer chain. They are both chains in the sense that both customers and suppliers will typically be other organisations. Hence an economic system (Chapter 14) will be composed of a complex network of such chains.

The supply chain is illustrated in Figure 3.2. The broad arrows on the diagram indicate the flow of goods and services between organisations. On the diagram we distinguish between direct suppliers one step removed in the supply chain and indirect suppliers more than two steps removed in the supply chain. Indirect suppliers are sometimes referred to as channel organisations or intermediaries.

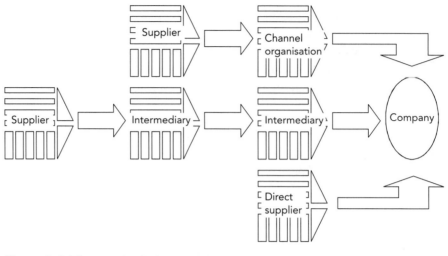

Figure 3.2 The supply chain.

Example   Typical intermediaries include warehousing companies, independent wholesalers, retailers and distributors.

The customer chain is the demand chain of the business. Figure 3.3 illustrates the customer chain of a particular organisation. We may distinguish between local customers in the immediate marketplace of some organisation and export customers in some form of global marketplace. For both forms of customers, but particularly in the global marketplace, forms of channel organisation or intermediary (such as distributors and retailers) may mediate between an organisation and its customers.

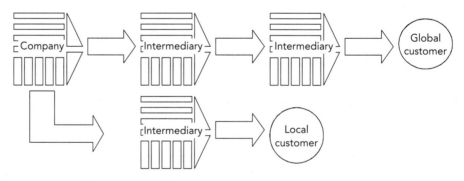

Figure 3.3 The customer chain.

Example

Clearly the value chain, including the supply and customer chains, will vary depending upon the type of business an organisation is in. In Figure 3.4 we illustrate three value chains:

- In automobile manufacturing, components are produced both by subsidiaries of the major car manufacturers and by external component suppliers. Such components are used to assemble cars which are passed on to the dealer network which sells cars to consumers.

- In food retail foodstuffs are supplied to supermarkets from warehouses and food-stuff suppliers and are sold on to the consumer.

- In insurance there is little in the way of a supply chain. Insurance products are sold on to consumers via agents and brokers.

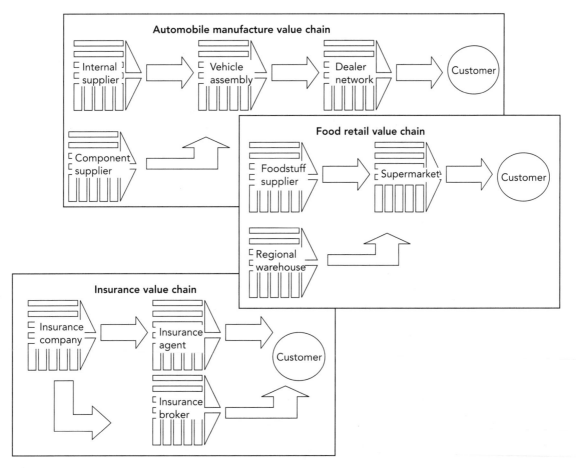

Figure 3.4 Three value chains.

The supply chain and customer chain define the immediate external environ-ment for organisations. One might argue that such chains overlap with another frequently ignored chain of value of increasing significance to most organisations. We refer to this as the community chain. The community chain is founded on social networks of individuals. The value of the community chain lies in its ability to generate social capital – one indicator of which is a high level of inter-personal trust – an essential prerequisite for many forms of business and commerce.

Question

What would constitute the supply and demand chains of a higher education institution such as a university?

3.5 ⊚ GOODS, SERVICES AND TRANSACTIONS

The internal, supply, customer and (to a certain extent) community chains of busi-ness are pipelines for the delivery of value. Such value is typically the delivery of goods and services. Associated with such delivery is a corresponding flow of data transactions.

- *Goods*. These constitute either physical (tangible) goods such as raw materials and finished products or non-physical (intangible) goods such as music, graphics or video.
- *Services*. These constitute the delivery of a service to a customer, either tangible or intangible.
- *Transactions*. Information is needed to support most human activity systems, particularly in terms of transactional information. Transactions are ways of recording organisational activity such as service delivery and are critical to the measurement of organisational performance.

Goods and services are the end points of business processes or human activity systems. Transactions are the necessary record of such delivery. The flow of phys-ical goods and services is supported by the flow of data.

Some services will be primarily information or transaction-based. Others will not be information-based services, but will nonetheless require certain transactions to record details of delivery (Chapter 8).

Example

Take the case of a local government authority in the UK. It is estimated that a typical unitary authority will have 70 different types of service that it provides to its customers. Some of these services will be primarily information-based. Major examples here are maintaining a land and electoral register and collecting revenues such as the council tax. Other services, such as waste disposal, although not information-based, will nevertheless rely on effective and efficient transmission of information to stakeholders. Hence, for example, effective waste disposal is reliant on the provision of accurate collection times to the customers of an authority.

Questions | When you buy an item of foodstuff from a supermarket, what constitutes a typical transaction? When you receive some medical treatment what constitutes the transaction involved?

3.6 MANAGEMENT AS A HUMAN ACTIVITY SYSTEM

Information supports human activity in the sense that it enables decisions to be made about appropriate actions in particular circumstances. Decisions and decision-making therefore mediate between information and action and are a critical aspect of any human activity system.

Management can be seen as a control process within organisations (Figure 3.5) (Beer, 1985). Management is a human activity system that regulates other human activity systems. The primary activity of management is making decisions concerning organisational action. Effective management decision-making is reliant on good information.

Decision-making is a key activity of management, but decision-making is performed at a number of levels within organisations. In terms of management decision-making we may identify three levels of management: strategic management, tactical management and operational management (Figure 3.5). Each of these three levels can be seen to be arranged in a hierarchy of control with higher levels of management controlling the behaviour of lower-level management.

Example | In a supermarket chain operational management is likely to involve management of particular supermarket stores. Tactical management will involve the overall management of distribution of goods to stores around the country. Strategic management will be involved with the overall direction of the company such as deciding on the quantity and siting of new stores.

At each of these levels effective management decision-making is reliant on the effective definition of performance and the construction of effective performance management systems for managerial activity. Transactional data is critical to performance management.

Certain levels of decision-making and hence of management, particularly at the operational level, can be automated in systems within an organisation. Hence,

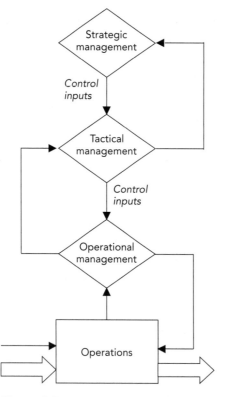

Figure 3.5 Management as a control process.

certain levels of modern management have become embedded in the information systems of the organisation.

Example

Consider the case of stock control as a human activity system. Traditionally organisations would construct a layer of operational management concerned with controlling the operations of warehouse staff. The performance of such a system would likely be defined in terms of maintaining optimal levels of inventory of raw materials for production. In a manual system decisions as to reordering stock would be taken on the basis of established reorder levels and continually monitoring stock levels within warehouses. In modern inventory control systems a degree of management decision-making will be embedded in the information system. Effective regulation of the activity system of stock control is therefore performed in large part by the technology.

Question

What sort of decision-making is conducted by an academic school, faculty or department in a university? How much of such decision-making is amenable to automation?

3.7 ◎ SINGLE AND DOUBLE-LOOP FEEDBACK

Feedback is the mechanism for exercising control. Single-loop feedback is the type of feedback discussed above and in Chapter 2, in which a single control process monitors variations in the state of a process, compares this state against some planned levels of performance and takes corrective action to bring performance in line with the plan. Single-loop feedback is that form of feedback relevant to the regulation of a system. In single-loop feedback the plans for performance (the control inputs) remain unchanged. This form of feedback is characteristic of control processed at the operational and tactical levels of management in business. Such systems are relatively closed in that they do not interact with the environment of the organisation and since their performance plans do not change are relatively easy to automate with ICT.

Example   Stock control, production control, budgetary control and standard costing are all examples of human activity systems in organisations that tend to be constructed in terms of single-loop feedback systems.

Double-loop feedback is a higher-form of control experienced in organisations. Ashby (1956) insists that double-loop feedback is essential to ensure that an organisation adapts effectively to changes in its environment. Double-loop feedback is that form in which the monitoring of lower-level single-feedback control systems in organisations as well as monitoring of the environment triggers examination and perhaps revision of the principles on which the control system is established. Colloquially, it is sometimes referred to as 'thinking outside the box'. At the simplest level, double-loop feedback may cause revisions to the control inputs of lower-level systems. At its most complex it will involve redesigning the processes and structures on which the lower-level systems are established.

Double-loop feedback is equally reliant on information as single-loop feedback. The information flows between operational, tactical and strategic layers of management on Figure 3.5 can be seen to be critical to this higher-order form of control as well as sensors for environmental changes.

Example   Consider a situation in which an organisation fails to establish double-loop feedback systems for its stock management. As a result, the organisation continues to use reorder levels and quantities which are inappropriate for current market demands. This either causes storage of excessive levels of stock or stocks run out with a consequent inability to fulfil customer demand quickly.

Question	What is the relationship between double-loop feedback and strategic management?

3.8 VIABLE SYSTEMS AND REQUISITE VARIETY

The work of Stafford Beer can be seen as an attempt to apply cybernetic thinking – the science of control – to management – the profession of control. Beer attempted to develop a model of the business enterprise founded in a biological analogy. In terms of this model, the key aim of any human activity system is survival in a volatile environment – what Beer refers to as a viable system. The key to effective survival is seen to rely on the effective use of information systems. Information systems are important in informing the organisation of changes in its environment and in the state of its internal processes.

Example	There appear to be similarities between the idea of corporate governance and that of control (Dunlop, 1998). Corporate governance may be defined as the system by which companies are directed and controlled. Boards of directors are responsible for the governance of their companies. The shareholders' role in governance is to appoint the directors and auditors and to satisfy themselves that an appropriate structure for governance is in place. The responsibilities of the board include setting the company's strategic aims, providing the leadership to put these aims into effect, supervising the management of the business and reporting to the shareholders on their stewardship.
	The overriding principle of corporate governance is one of stewardship. This bears a close relationship to the idea of the steersman familiar from the idea of control. The directors of a company have delegated authority from the company – its shareholders – and are required to be accountable to it.

However, there is an inherent limit to the degree to which control systems and the information systems on which they rely can work without human intervention. This is expressed as what Ashby (1956) calls the 'law of requisite variety', which states that only variety can absorb variety. Variety is a measure of the number of states a system can take. Hence for full control of the system it is monitoring a control subsystem should contain variety – number of states – (Chapter 2) at least equal to the system under control.

The consequence of this is that relatively simple control systems cannot be expected to control the multitude of activities characteristic of complex human activity systems.

Example	A budgetary control system will only be able to control a narrow range of an organisation's activities concerned with financial management.

Closed feedback systems are only suitable for simple, structured systems where there are enough predetermined control actions to match all possible control conditions. In organisations much disturbance and variation is caused by the influence of external variables. Many such variables are not controllable and hence are unlikely to be included in any control system. In systems where external variables interact with internal variables it is likely that an open loop feedback is required where managerial intervention is required to generate enough control variety.

Operational control systems are likely to be closed-feedback systems. Management control systems are likely to be open-feedback systems. The consequence of this law is that there are limits to the degree of automation possible in managerial systems. Any complex organisation will need certain degrees of management intervention to ensure successful adaptation.

Question	*What is the relationship between the concept of a viable system and that of sustainable business performance?*

3.9 ⊚ BUSINESS MODELS

We argued in Section 3.2 that human activity systems can be designed. This prompts the question as to how they should be designed. One useful concept that can help in this task is that of a business model (Timmers, 1998). A business model specifies the structure and dynamics of a particular enterprise, particularly the relationship between different stakeholders, benefits and costs to each, and key revenue flows. The presupposition of design implies that a given business has a number of different options in terms of the particular business model it may choose to adopt. With the rise of e-business and e-commerce such options multiply. Business strategies (Chapter 22) specify how a particular business model can be applied to a particular market sector to improve competitive position.

In a sense a particular business model specifies the structure of human activity systems appropriate for a particular business in terms of its market. A key part of the argument used for adaptive systems is that the model of the business must fit market circumstances. The so-called model for the business must be founded in its key value chains and be viable in this environment. In other words its activities must be sustainable over the long term.

Example

Take the example of a supermarket chain. Such a food retailer has relationships with its customers and suppliers. Revenue flows into its value chain from its customers and on to its suppliers. Customers are mainly attracted to supermarkets by a combination of low prices and a large variety of goods on offer. Supermarket chains typically sell large volumes of their products and hence their business strategy is typically one of low-cost/high-volume operations with typically low margins on each product. Costs are minimised in a number of ways, such as buying in bulk from suppliers and letting customers bear the costs of selecting products from shelves, packing products and transporting such goods to their homes. The critical success factor for a supermarket chain is therefore attracting sufficient customers to its store. This means that location of stores is critical. Stores need to be placed within easy reach of a sufficient catchment area of willing customers.

The provision of an e-commerce site changes the business model of a supermarket chain. Relationships with customers and suppliers change, as do costs and revenue. For example, if a supermarket fulfils online orders by having a member of staff walk around the store and picking and packing goods followed by transportation to customers' homes using delivery vans then the costs of the operation can substantially increase. Hence many supermarkets pass on this cost directly to the customer through a charge for delivery.

An alternative business model is to do away with the stores entirely. Goods may then be stored in and delivered from low-cost warehouses. Hence additional order fulfilment costs (picking, packing and transporting) can be balanced by lower operational costs (larger range, reduced inventory, larger volume, lower margins).

Question

What business model is appropriate to automobile retail in the modern electronic economy?

3.10 RELATIONSHIPS BETWEEN E-BUSINESSES AND TRADITIONAL BUSINESSES

For many companies a critical decision to make in establishing an online business model is the relationship of online activity to traditional business activity.

Rather ephemerally, traditional businesses have been referred to as 'bricks and mortar' businesses in the sense that they have a physical presence usually in terms of some buildings where they can be located. Traditional businesses that have moved into the world of e-business are frequently referred to as 'clicks and mortar' businesses. They still maintain a physical presence, but also offer services and products accessible by clicking online. Businesses that have emerged entirely in the online environment are known as 'clicks-only' businesses.

Moore and Ruddle (2000) propose a more sophisticated typology of e-businesses:

- *Separate organisation.* This is where a firm packages its e-business activities as a separate organisation isolated from the parent firm. The separate organisation is expected to innovate with new products and services.
- *Semi-autonomous organisation.* A halfway house between a separate organisation and a fully integrated organisation.
- *Fully integrated organisation.* Here e-business is integrated into the conventional firm under the control of specific business units.
- *Fully integrated within informatics service.* In this form e-business is run under the control of the informatics service of an organisation. The informatics service is that business unit tasked with developing and maintaining the informatics infrastructure of some organisation.
- *Parallel organisation.* A sister organisation is created, offering the same products or services as the parent company but through e-business channels.

We discuss some business models relevant for certain forms of e-business in Chapters 18 and 20.

Examples

The food retailer Tesco runs its e-tail operation as a fully integrated setup within the larger organisation.

The cosmetics company Avon originally designed its online sales arm as a separate organisation. More recently, after experiencing poor take-up of services, they have fully integrated it back into the mainstream activity, particularly designed as a vehicle for supporting their sales representatives.

Question

Michael Porter (2001) has recently argued that clicks and mortar firms are more likely than clicks-only firms to be viable in economic markets long-term. Why should this be the case?

3.11 VIRTUAL ORGANISATIONS

We have stressed in this chapter that ICT is an effective tool which supports the design of new human activity systems or the redesign of existing human activity systems. One of the most radical forms of such redesign is the virtual or network organisation (Hale and Whitham, 1997).

A virtual organisation has one or more of the following characteristics:

- Physical structures such as offices are reduced in number; perhaps they do not exist for the organisation.

- Workers are provided with electronic workspaces rather than physical workspaces.
- Where office space is required workers are encouraged to 'hot desk' – to share office facilities on a booking basis.
- Physical documentation is discouraged; electronic documentation is promoted.
- Work is organised in terms of loose projects which workers join and leave in a flexible way.
- The members of the organisation communicate and collaborate using ICT. The network becomes the organisation.

Virtual organisations have been particularly proposed as viable business models for knowledge-intensive industries and corresponding sets of knowledge workers. Sawhney (Sawhney and Parikh, 2001) has argued that entire industries will soon be organised around the supporting infrastructure of communication networks.

Example

First Direct is a telephone banking service created by the then Midland bank in 1989. At the time Midland was experiencing difficulties with its high street branch network and suffered heavy losses in 1988. The aim was to provide 24-hour banking services to customers. First Direct was deliberately started under a separate brand name. By 1994 the company had returned profits and by 1997 the company had become the largest 'virtual' bank in the world. Effective communications infrastructure and use of customer information systems enabled it to provide banking services far more cost-effectively than the branch network. It also managed to achieve high customer satisfaction ratings leading to a high retention rate for customers.

Question

In what respect may large-scale product design projects be organised in terms of virtual or networked organisations?

3.12 CASE STUDY: LOCAL GOVERNMENT IN THE UK

In this section we discuss the example of a local authority as a human activity system primarily tasked with the provision of public services to the community. The management of such provision is heavily reliant on effective information systems.

In the UK local government is organised as a three-tier system: unitary authorities, county authorities and district authorities. Unitary authorities were introduced during the mid-1990s and take on the role of both county and district councils in delivering services to their local community.

Unitary authorities are responsible for a wide range of services, including education, environmental health, planning, housing, personal social services, waste management and disposal, highways, libraries, recreation, cemeteries and crematoria. Authorities also assume some overseeing function in relation to the fire and police services.

Local authorities have both a democratically elected set of council members and a permanent administration of officers. The councils exercise decision-making powers only. Local authorities have been encouraged to operate a cabinet-style of governance structure under a programme to increase the accountability of decision-making. In association with this, members of council cabinets are beginning to manage crosscutting portfolios. This replaces the older-style system of members and officers with direct departmental responsibility and reporting directly to central government.

In terms of officer structure, a head of permanent administration (frequently termed the chief executive) is responsible for day-to-day implementation of policy decisions made by council. In line with changes in the democratic arrangements, a flatter organisation structure is now being introduced into many authorities, with crosscutting responsibilities for officers emulating the crosscutting nature of cabinet local government.

It is estimated that a typical unitary authority will have 70 different types of service. Some of these services will be primarily information-based. Major examples here are maintaining a land and electoral register and collecting revenues such as the council tax. For a number of such information-based services national standards and systems are being developed and promoted among authorities within the UK. These include:

- *Local Authorities Secure Electoral Register (LASER)*. The LASER project aims to provide electoral registers that are joined up, maintained and managed locally, and can then be accessible on a national level to authorized users. LASER aims to draw together all of the locally held registers of electors and make them available nationally to support e-voting

- *National Land Information Service (NLIS)*. NLIS is an online, one-stop shop that delivers land and property-related information from source data providers to conveyancers and homebuyers. At present, NLIS provides access to information held and maintained by local authorities, the Land Registry and the Coal Authority. Negotiations are now under way towards including searches relating to the water service companies and the Environment Agency

- *National Land and Property Gazetteer (NLPG)*. NLPG is a single, comprehensive, up-to-date list of addresses. Local authorities are essential participants because they start the process by naming streets and numbering buildings. The NLPG requires local authorities to convert their existing lists of addresses into a fully consistent national information system, held electronically, constructed to common standards, and based on unique property reference numbers for each property or piece of land. The NLPG is reliant on authorities producing and maintaining Local Land and Property Gazetteers (LLPGs) to a common standard

Other services, such as waste disposal, although not information-based, will nevertheless rely on effective and efficient transmission of information to stakeholders. Hence, for example, effective waste disposal is reliant on the provision of accurate collection times to authority customers.

3.13 SUMMARY

- Human activity systems are systems, support core competencies, frequently cut across functional boundaries, can be designed, have definable levels of performance and use ICT for support.
- The internal value chain can be used as a template for key organisational processes and consists of a set of primary and secondary activities.
- Two other chains of value critical to the competitive environment assume significance for most organisations: the supply chain and the customer chain.
- Internal, supply and customer value chains are pipelines for the delivery of goods and services. Associated with good and service flow is a flow of transactions.
- Management is the key control process for organisations.
- Two types of feedback are critical for ensuring effective control: single-loop and double-loop feedback.
- Single-loop feedback works within a closed system and plans for performance remain unchanged over time.
- Double-loop feedback works within an open system and involves continually adjusting plans to meet environmental circumstances.
- There is an inherent limit to the degree to which control systems can work without human intervention – the law of requisite variety which states that for full control the control subsystem should contain variety at least equal to the system under control.
- A business model specifies the structure and dynamics of a particular enterprise, particularly the relationship between different stakeholders, benefits and costs to each and key revenue flows.

3.14 ACTIVITIES

(i) Identify one human activity system known to you and identify its key components.

(ii) Try to model a public sector organisation such as a university in terms of the internal value chain.

(iii) Identify the elements of the supply chain of an organisation known to you.

(iv) Identify the elements of the customer chain of an organisation known to you.

(v) Service industries have been the largest growing sectors of Western economies. Identify some such industries and the services they supply.

(vi) When you purchase some product through mail order attempt to identify the flow of data transactions that accompanies the purchase.

(vii) Attempt to identify the various layers of management in an organisation known to you.

(viii) What we have referred to as tactical management in this chapter is also called middle management. This layer of management has disappeared from many economic sectors with the increasing use of ICT. Determine some of the reasons for this.

(ix) Describe the control systems one would expect in an organisation such as a university.

(x) Find examples of clicks and mortar and clicks only companies.

3.15 ◎ REFERENCES

Ashby, W. R. (1956). *An Introduction to Cybernetics*. London, Chapman & Hall.

Beer, S. (1985). *Diagnosing the System for Organisations*. Oxford, Oxford University Press.

Checkland, P. (1987). *Systems Thinking, Systems Practice*. Chichester, John Wiley.

Daft, R. L. (2001). *Organization Theory and Design*. Cincinnati, OH, South-Western College Publishing.

Dunlop, A. (1998). *Governance and Control*. London, Chartered Institute of Management Accountants.

Hale, R. and Whitham, P. (1997). *Towards the Virtual Organisation*. London, McGraw-Hill.

Hammer, M. (1996). *Beyond Re-Engineering: How the Process-Centred Organisation is Changing Our Lives*. London, HarperCollins.

Moore, K. and Ruddle, K. (2000). *New Business Models – the Challenges of Transition. Moving to E-business: the Ultimate Practical Guide to E-business* (eds. L. Wilcocks and C. Sauer). London, Random House.

Porter, M. E. (1985). *Competitive Advantage: Creating and Sustaining Superior Performance*. New York, Free Press.

Porter, M. E. (2001). Strategy and the Internet. *Harvard Business Review*, **79**(3), 63–78.

Sawhney, M. and Parikh, D. (2001). Where value lies in a networked world. *Harvard Business Review*, **79**(1), 79–86.

Timmers, P. (1998). Business models for electronic marketplaces. *Electronic Markets*, **8**(1), 3–8.

CHAPTER 4

INFORMATION SYSTEMS

Knowledge is of two kinds. We know a subject ourselves, or we know where we can find

information upon it

Samuel Johnson, *Life of Boswell*

If you can fill the unforgiving minute

With sixty seconds worth of distance run...

Rudyard Kipling, *If*

LEARNING OUTCOMES

After reading this chapter, you will be able to:

- Define the concept of information and its relationship to data
- Distinguish between an information system and an ICT system
- Outline some of the key properties of an information system
- Distinguish between the various layers of an ICT system
- Define the term informatics and describe three levels of informatics infrastructure needed for e-business

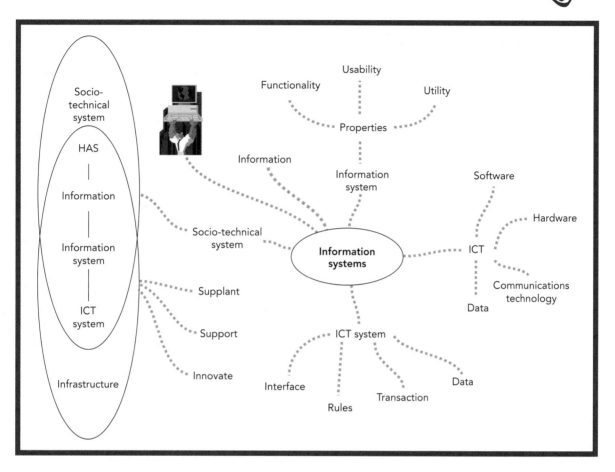

4.1 INTRODUCTION

To review the material of previous chapters, business organisations can be seen to consist of a number of interdependent human activity systems. For the regulation of the effective performance of such human activity systems information as to the current state of the activity systems has to be collected and disseminated. Such information collection and dissemination is undertaken by an organisation's information systems. Therefore information systems are critical to e-business. They mediate between ICT systems and human activity systems and hence are the primary source of information required for the effective coordination of activity.

In this chapter we begin with a definition of data and distinguish this concept from information. This leads us to define the concept of an information system and its key properties. We then distinguish between an information system and an ICT system and outline the fundamental layers of an ICT system. The term informatics is defined to encapsulate considerations of ICT, information systems and information. The human activity systems of the e-business are supported by an informatics infrastructure. We conclude with a review of modelling information systems graphically.

4.2 INFORMATION

Information is data interpreted in some meaningful context. A datum, a unit of data, is one or more symbols that are used to represent something. Information is interpreted data. Information is data placed within a meaningful context. The use of the term information therefore implies a group of people doing interpretation – supplying the context (Kent, 1978).

Example

Take the datum 030500. As a datum it constitutes merely a set of symbols, digits. Given some context we interpret this as a date. However, in Britain we would interpret the significance of the sequence of digits differently from those in the USA. In Britain the first two digits represent the day of the month. In the USA the first two digits represent the month.

Questions

Why is the distinction between data and information important? Can we conceive of any situations in which there is information without people?

4.3 SIGNS AND SEMANTICS

Both data and information are embodied in the concept of a sign.

A sign is anything that is significant. In a sense, everything that humans do is significant to some degree. The world within which humans find themselves is resonant with systems of signs. The linguist and cognitive scientist Steven Pinker (2001) argues that our genetic makeup predisposes humans to be excellent manipulators of sign systems. A sign system is any organised collection of signs. Everyday spoken language is probably the most readily accepted and complex example of a sign system. Signs, however, exist in most other forms of human activity, since they are critical to the process of human communication and understanding (Stamper, 1973).

Example

Humans communicate through non-verbal as well as verbal sign systems. We colloquially refer to such non-verbal communication as 'body language'. Hence humans can impart a great deal in the way of information by facial movements and other forms of bodily gesture. Such gestures are also signs.

The relationship between information and data is located in the area of meaning or, to use its more formal designation, semantics. Semantics is the study of what

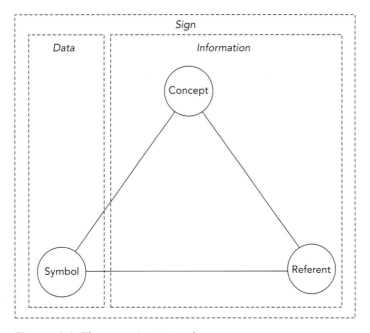

Figure 4.1 The meaning triangle.

signs refer to. Communication involves the use and interpretation of signs. When we communicate the sender has to externalise her intentions in terms of some signs. In face-to-face conversation this will involve the use of linguistic signs. The receiver of the message must interpret the signs. In other words, she must assign some meaning to the signs of the message. Semantics is concerned with this process of assigning meaning to signs.

A simple model of semantics is one in which a sign can be broken down into three component parts, which are frequently referred to collectively as the meaning triangle (Sowa, 1984) (see Figure 4.1):

- The *symbol (or symbols)*, sometimes referred to as the signifier. That which is signifying something.
- The *referent*, sometimes known as the signified. That which is being signified.
- The *concept*. The idea of significance.

Symbols are equivalent to data in the classic language of information systems. A datum, a single item of data, is a set of symbols used to represent something. Information particularly occurs in the 'stands for' relations between the symbol and its concept and the concept and its referent.

Examples

In a manufacturing system the symbols 43 constitute the signifier. A possible referent is a collection of products. The concept may be the quantity of a product sold.

The symbols M and F might be significant in some e-business context. To speak of information we must supply some concept and/or referent for the symbols. M might have as its referent the male population; F might have as its referent the female population. Taken together, the meaning of these symbols is supplied by the concept of human gender.

The meaning triangle should not be taken to mean that signs have an inherent meaning. A sign can mean whatever a particular social group chooses it to mean. Hence the same sign may mean different things in different social contexts. As interpreters of signs humans are extremely proficient at assigning the correct interpretation for a sign in a particular context.

Example

In the Welsh language the same verb *dysgu* (pronounced 'dusgey') is used both for 'to teach' and 'to learn'. Hence the same sentence – *Rydw i'n dysgu* – can mean either 'I am learning' or 'I am teaching', depending on the context supplied, usually by elements such as the rest of the conversation and the background knowledge of both speaker and listener.

Question

In what way is an order number, product number or despatch number a sign?

4.4 INFORMATION SYSTEM

An information system is a system of communication between people. Information systems are systems involved in the gathering, processing, distribution and use of information. Information systems support human activity systems. In a sense they constitute sign manipulation systems and are essential to the coordination of human activity in organisations.

Example

A group has three members. Each member of the group delivers leaflets to houses in specified areas, this is the human activity of the group. To support this activity the group notes on a regular basis which leaflets have been delivered to which houses. They need to do this because they are paid on the basis of how many leaflets they deliver to houses in an area. This comprises their information system. Initially it is a manual information system in that details of leaflet deliveries are noted in a paper file. The signs used in this information system clearly involve written language.

4.5 ⊚ PROPERTIES OF AN INFORMATION SYSTEM

Certain information systems may have evolved within human activity systems over a prolonged period of time. However, in most modern organisations information systems have been rationally designed. Information systems have to be designed in the sense that the key features of such systems need to be determined prior to the construction and implementation of the systems using ICT. Such key features or properties are critical ways in which we can assess the worth or success of some information system (Chapter 27).

Traditionally, the design features of an information system fall into one of two categories: functionality – what the system does; and usability – how the system is used. One should note that both functionality and usability are inherently related to the place of the information system within the context of some human activity system. Hence to functionality and usability we should add utility. Utility is an important but neglected feature of an information system. Utility concerns the contribution that the IS makes to supporting the human activity of an organisation.

Functionality

The functionality of an information system is normally determined by a close examination of organisational requirements. The functionality of an information system is what an information system does or should be able to do. Specifying the core functionality of an information system is a critical aspect of the process of information systems development (Chapter 26). Measures of the functionality of a system are typically measures of an information system's efficacy.

Usability

Usability is evident in the way in which an IS embeds itself within human activity. An information system's usability is how easy a system is to use for the purpose for which it has been constructed. Usability is evident at the human–computer interface – that place where the user interacts with the ICT system. Measures of the usability of a system are typically measures of an information system's efficiency.

Utility

Whereas functionality defines what a system does and usability defines how a system is used, utility defines how acceptable the system is in terms of doing what is needed. Utility refers to the worth of an information system in terms of the contribution it makes to its human activity system and to the organisation as a whole. Measures of the utility of an information system are typically measures of an information system's effectiveness.

Examples
- *Functionality.* Some aspect of the functionality of an IS is normally contained in the name usually given to an IS. For instance, if we describe a system as being an order-processing system, then we are indicating that the system in some way captures,

stores and manipulates data associated with the processing of orders, probably from customers.

- *Usability.* In terms of an order-processing system, the system's usability will be determined by how easy it is for users such as order clerks to input data about orders into the system and to extract data about orders from the system.

- *Utility.* The utility of an order-processing system might be defined in terms of the contribution it makes to the efficient handling of orders made by customers of the organisation. An ICT system may contribute significant cost savings in order processing. It may also contribute to improvements in organisational effectiveness. For instance, it may have positive implications for the level of customer satisfaction experienced.

Question

How would you go about measuring the functionality, usability and utility of some information system?

4.6 INFORMATION AND COMMUNICATIONS TECHNOLOGY

Information and communications technology is any technology used to support information gathering, processing, distribution and use. ICT provides means of constructing aspects of information systems, but is distinct from information systems. Modern ICT consists of hardware, software, data and communications technology.

- *Hardware.* This comprises the physical (hard) aspects of ICT consisting of processors, input devices and output devices.

- *Software.* This comprises the non-physical (soft) aspects of information technology. Software is essentially programs – sets of instructions for controlling computer hardware.

- *Data.* This constitutes a series of structures for storing data on peripheral devices such as hard disks. Such data is manipulated by programs and transmitted via communication technology.

- *Communication technology.* This forms the interconnective tissue of ICT. Communication networks between computing devices are essential elements of the modern ICT infrastructure of organisations.

Examples

- Hardware includes devices such as keyboards (input), processing units and monitors (output).

- Software includes operating systems, programming languages and office packages.

- Data is normally stored in databases managed by a database management system.

- Communications technology includes such components as cabling, transmitters and routers.

It is important to recognise that information systems have existed in organisations prior to the invention of ICT, and hence IS do not need modern ICT to exist. However, in the modern, complex organisational world most IS rely on hardware, software, data and communications technology to a greater or lesser degree because of the efficacy, efficiency and effectiveness gains possible with the use of such technology.

Example Take the leaflet distribution group described in the example above. Eventually, as the business expands in terms of the volume of leaflets handled and the complexity of the instructions for delivery from their customers the manual system becomes cumbersome. They eventually purchase a personal computer and store the delivery information on a database system. This constitutes the ICT in support of the information system. Part of the activity of the information system now involves using the database system. But it still supports a similar human activity system.

Question *What sort of system diagram might be drawn for the typical personal computer?*

4.7 ◎ ICT SYSTEM

An information and communications technology system is a technical system. Such systems are frequently referred to as examples of 'hard' systems in the sense that they have a physical existence and are designed to solve some particular problem. An ICT system is an organised collection of hardware, software, data and communications technology designed to support aspects of some information system. An ICT system has data as input, manipulates such data as a process and outputs manipulated data for interpretation within some human activity system.

Example Take an order-processing ICT system. In such a system the data entered will describe the properties of orders. The manipulation comprises the processing of orders, probably in relation to other data collected such as that on customers. The manipulated data in the system constitutes the processed orders.

The order-processing ICT system will support that activity concerned with the effective sales of products or services to customers. Without effective and efficient performance of this activity the organisation is unlikely to survive in its marketplace.

4.8 ❂ LAYERS OF AN ICT SYSTEM

It is useful to consider an ICT system as being made up of a number of subsystems or horizontal layers (Beynon-Davies, 2002):

- *Interface subsystem.* This subsystem is responsible for managing interaction with the user. This subsystem is generally referred to as the user interface, or sometimes the human–computer interface.
- *Rules subsystem.* This subsystem manages the application logic in terms of a defined model of business rules.
- *Transaction subsystem.* This subsystem acts as the link between the data subsystem and the rules and interface subsystems. Querying, insertion and update activity is triggered at the interface, validated by the rules subsystem and packaged as units (transactions) that will initiate actions (responses or changes) in the data subsystem.
- *Data subsystem.* This subsystem is responsible for managing the underlying data needed by the ICT system.

In the contemporary ICT infrastructure each of these parts of an application may be distributed on different machines, perhaps at different sites. This means that each part usually needs to be stitched together in terms of some communications backbone. For consistency, we refer to this facility as the communication subsystem.

Example

Take the example of an ICT system for storing research publications in a university. One part of the interface will be a data entry form to enter details of a journal publication. One of the rules or constraints used to validate data may be that the date entered for the publication must be less than or equal to today's date. A key transaction will be that update function involved in the entry of new publication data into the system. Part of the data management layer will have data structures for the storage of publication data.

Question *In terms of a business ICT system such as that for managing stock control, what would be a typical business rule?*

4.9 SOCIO-TECHNICAL SYSTEM

Most e-business systems are examples of socio-technical systems (Emery, 1969). A socio-technical system is a system of technology used within a system of activity. Information systems are primary examples of socio-technical systems. Information systems generally consist of ICT systems used within some human activity system. They therefore bridge between ICT and human activity. Part of the human activity will involve the use of the ICT system. Such use occurs at the human–computer interface. It is at this interface that data is interpreted as information. The data provided by the ICT system will also drive decision-making and action within the organisation.

This relationship between the three levels of system is illustrated in Figure 4.2.

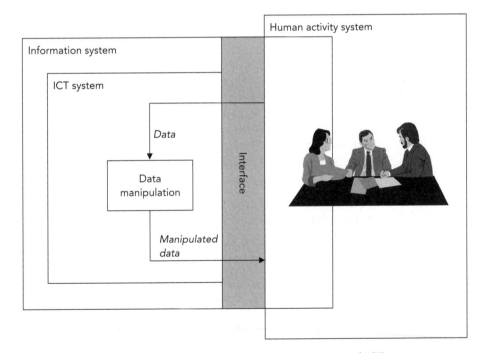

Figure 4.2 Human activity system, information systems and ICT system.

Example   In a video store the human activity system is generally involved in hiring out copies of video cassettes or DVDs. To support hiring activity staff need to have an information system which tells them who are valid members, what copies they have hired out and what copies they have in stock. An ICT system is employed to record details of copies in stock, membership details, details of particular hiring and details of payments made.

Functionality is primarily a feature of the ICT system. It is a property concerned with the performance of the technical artefact. Usability is a feature of the interface between the ICT system and the information system. At its most basic it is an assessment of how easy it is to enter data and retrieve data from the ICT system. Utility is primarily a feature of the relationship between the information system and the human activity system. It constitutes some assessment of the contribution the information system makes to human activity, particularly to improvements in decision-making and action.

Question   *Consider in what ways a typical accountancy package or some other piece of software designed to support business operations constitutes a data manipulation system.*

4.10 ⊚ STAKEHOLDERS

Various social groups within and without an organisation are impacted upon by an information system. We refer to each type of social group as a stakeholder in the information system. We may distinguish between the following major types of stakeholder:

- *Producers*. Producers are the teams of developers that have to design, construct and maintain information systems for organisations (Chapter 26).
- *Clients*. Clients sponsor and provide resources for the construction and continuing use of an information system. Clients normally equate to managerial groups within organisations.
- *End users*. In terms of users, managers are rarely the end users of information systems. Except in the case of so-called management information systems (Chapter 6), most information systems are produced for use by other levels of employee within the organisation.
- *Customers*. Information systems support the customer chain of organisations and hence normally impact upon the customers of organisations. Many front-end information systems in organisations may now be directly accessed by customers (Chapter 6) using remote access mechanisms.

- *Suppliers*. Information systems support the supply chain of organisations and hence are increasingly impacting upon the suppliers of an organisation. Many front-end information systems in organisations may now be directly accessed by suppliers and other partner organisations (Chapter 6).

- *Regulators*. These are groups or agencies that set environmental constraints for an information system. A key regulation agency is typically the national or supra-national government (Chapter 16).

- *Competitors*. Competitors will be impacted upon by information systems, particularly by that group of systems known as strategic information systems (Chapter 24), and may quickly attempt to emulate an organisation's information systems in this area.

- *Partners*. Information systems may be jointly produced by organisations to support key partnership arrangements and facilitate data transfer.

Question   *Who do you think are the regulators of an accounting system?*

4.11 ◎ ORGANISATIONAL INFORMATICS

Informatics is that discipline devoted to the study of information, information systems and ICT applied to various phenomena. The term has been used repeatedly by various branches of the European Union to encompass the application of ICT in support of the information society (Chapter 15). In Germany and France the terms *Informatik* and *informatique*, respectively, are much used.

The term has also been extremely popular within the health and biological sciences fields, as is evident in the common use of such terms as health informatics, medical informatics and bio-informatics. Some have used the term to elevate traditional information management (librarianship) concerns to a new plane founded in ICT. Here we use the term in the sense implied by Kling and Allen (1996). They use the term *organisational informatics* to encompass the application of information, information systems and ICT within organisations (Beynon-Davies, 2002).

We would argue that e-business is an organisational informatics concern. It is concerned both with how business is organised and with the impact of ICT on such organisations. It is particularly concerned with building efficient, effective and efficacious interaction between technology and the organisation.

Having said this, organisational informatics has typically been concerned with the use of ICT to improve the performance of the internal operations of business. E-business has extended this concern to the use of ICT to improve processes that involve interaction with external stakeholders such as customers, suppliers and partners.

4.12 INFRASTRUCTURE

Organised activity of whatever form requires infrastructure. Infrastructure consists of systems of social organisation and technology that support human activity.

Example

A road infrastructure is a supporting infrastructure for travel – the associated human activity system. A road infrastructure enables traffic to get from point A to point B using motorways, carriageways and major or minor roads. This is the technological infrastructure of the transport network. The road infrastructure also needs a corresponding social infrastructure concerned with the planning of new roads, the management of existing roads and the development and maintenance of physical road surfaces.

In terms of e-business we shall argue that there are four layers of infrastructure. Each of these layers is critically dependent on the layer below it:

- Human activity systems infrastructure
- Information infrastructure
- Information Systems infrastructure
- ICT Infrastructure

Organisations can be viewed as complex collections of human activity systems. Information is essential to the effective coordination of activity in organisations and is supplied by information systems. Modern information systems rely on ICT to a greater or lesser extent.

As well as conventional competencies in areas such as sales and production, a specific set of human activity systems will normally be concerned with the critical processes of planning, managing and developing the informatics infrastructure of an organisation. These critical human activity systems are discussed in Part 5.

We have argued previously that ICT plays a primary supporting role in organisations. The focus on infrastructure highlights that ICT has three potentials for change within organisations (Heeks, 1999):

- *Supplant*. ICT can be used to automate major parts of information systems, which involve the collection, storage, processing and dissemination of information. This implies supplanting human agents, particularly control processes, with technology.
- *Support*. ICT can be used to assist human activity through efficient and effective data processing. This implies the use of technology to augment human agents.
- *Innovate*. ICT can be used to stimulate the design and implementation of new human activity systems in organisations.

The traditional role for ICT has been to supplant or automate. More recently the emphasis has been to view ICT as an agency to informate (Zuboff, 1988) and inno- vate. One might argue that this movement towards the innovating potential of ICT is supported by a key principle of systems thinking – sub-optimisation. This states that optimising the performance of a subsystem such as an ICT system independ- ently will not generally optimise the performance of the system as a whole. In fact, it may actually worsen the performance of the whole system. A critical conse- quence of this is that ideally human activity systems and ICT systems should be designed in parallel to achieve optimal performance (Hammer, 1996).

Examples

ICT has been used to automate certain clerical processes in government, such as benefit payments. It has also been used to improve government decision-making, communication and implementation. Finally, new forms of public service delivery are being implemented through the use of ICT.

Question

In what sense can major information systems failures in industry be considered as examples of sub-optimisation?

4.13 ⊚ MODELLING INFORMATION SYSTEMS

To represent the elements and dynamics of an information system and associated elements of human activity we need a graphical notation. This is a model of the information system that we shall refer to as a system diagram. Such a model can be seen as a sign system and is undertaken for three reasons:

- *Communication.* The primary use for a model is as a medium of communication between some group of persons.
- *Representation.* A model is used to represent common understandings about some phenomena among this group of persons.
- *Abstraction.* Modelling generally implies some form of simplification of phenomena. The modeller uses a model to focus on what are seen to be the important features of a situation.

Example

A system diagram may be drawn as a means of representing the primary elements and relationships between elements for some organisational area such as stock control. As such we select from among a large range of possible elements and relationships in this area. We use the model as a means to attempt to communicate this understanding and achieve some agreement about the 'stock control system' among a group of stakeholders within an organisation.

A system diagram can be drawn using four constructs discussed in Chapter 2 with the addition of two other constructs that are particularly useful in analysing current activity within an organisation:

- *Agent.* An agent is something (usually a person, group, department or organisation, but possibly some other information system) that is a net originator or receiver of system data or physical flows. It is represented on a diagram by some form of rounded shape – circle or oval – with an appropriate name. Generally we use agents to indicate something lying outside a system that serve to define the key boundaries of the system.

- *Data flow.* A data flow is a pipeline through which packets of data of known composition flow. Data flow is represented on a system diagram by a labelled directed arrow. Double-headed arrows mean that a process is both passing data to another process or data store and receiving data from another process or data store.

- *Physical flow.* Physical flows are pipelines for the transmission of physical items such as goods between agents and processes. Physical flows are represented as broad, labelled arrows.

- *Document flow.* Many information systems in organisations are paper-based. Such flows can be represented on a system diagram with an arrow plus associated labelled document symbol.

- *Process.* A process is a transformation of incoming data flow(s) into outgoing data flow(s). A process is represented on a diagram by a labelled square or rectangle. The label should obviously be some meaningful encapsulation of the key purpose of the process.

- *Data store.* A data store is a repository of data. For example, in a manual information system this might constitute a filing cabinet or a card index. In an ICT system a data store would probably constitute a database (Chapter 12) of some kind. A data store is represented on a system diagram by an open box.

Figure 4.3 illustrates the graphical notation for each of these information system-modelling constructs.

Most real-life systems are too involved to represent as a single diagram. In representing systems, we therefore usually approach the problem in a top-down manner and decompose a system into subsystems, sub-subsystems, and so on. This is a natural consequence of the hierarchical nature of systems thinking. Hence each process on a system diagram could be considered as a subsystem and at least theoretically could be modelled by its own system diagram.

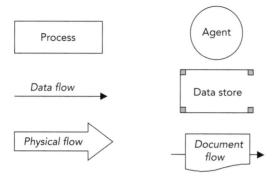

Figure 4.3 IS modelling constructs.

Question How important is effective modelling of systems to effective management of the organisation?

4.14 CASE STUDY: THE BRITISH ELECTORAL SYSTEM

Again we use a non-standard case to illustrate the applicability of systems thinking to modelling an information system necessary to support a key democratic process.

The British electoral system can be modelled as a highly information-intensive human activity system. Interestingly the system has remained relatively unchanged since the Ballot Act of 1872 and hence relies on very little modern ICT. Figure 4.4 represents this system as a diagram. The key activities in the current system are described below:

- *Registration of candidates.* Candidates in a UK general election must be over 21 and must register for election for a given constituency (see Chapter 3).

- *Registration of voters.* Registration used to be done only at set times during the year. Nowadays a person can register to vote at any time prior to the conduct of an election. To vote in a UK general election a person must be a citizen of the UK, be over the age of 18 and not excluded on grounds such as being in prison, detained in a psychiatric hospital or a member of House of Lords. Normally voters would be expected to attend in person at a specified polling booth to vote. If they are able to supply a valid reason a person may be entitled to appoint a proxy (some other person) to attend for them. Postal voting was introduced for the first time in the UK general election of 2001. In that election some 1.4 million people out of a total electorate of 44 million voted in this manner.

- *Production of electoral list and correspondence.* Each local authority in the UK is tasked with maintaining an electoral register. From this register each authority

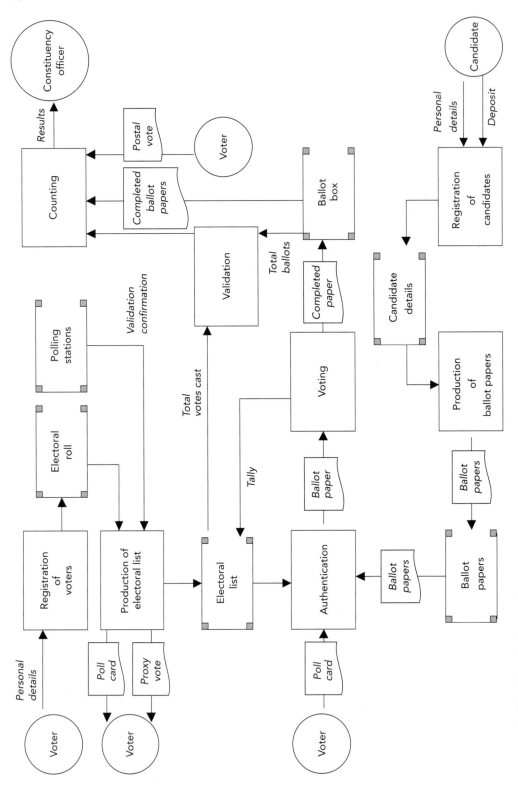

Figure 4.4 The British electoral system.

needs to produce an electoral list for each of the designated polling stations in its area. Electors receive various items of documentation through the post, the main item being a polling card detailing the name and address of the voter plus the date of the election and address of the designated polling station. Interestingly, the poll card also contains a serial number, which can be used to track voters against electoral lists.

- *Authentication.* Voters typically turn up at their indicated polling station. They produce their poll card for inspection and this is checked against the electoral list. If the elector is correctly authenticated in this manner she is handed a ballot paper on which the list of candidates for the constituency is listed. To indicate that it has been issued appropriately a member of polling staff stamps each ballot paper.

- *Voting.* The elector enters a polling booth and chooses one entry against the list of candidates by placing an 'X' in an appropriate box. The ballot paper is then folded and posted in a sealed ballot box.

- *Transfer of ballot boxes.* Most elections in the UK are held during a weekday (typically a Thursday) and voters are only allowed to vote during the set period of 0700 to 2200 hours on that day. At the end of the voting period all ballot boxes are collected and taken to a central counting centre.

- *Validation.* The total number of persons crossed off against the electoral list is usually cross-checked against the total number of ballots cast for each ballot box/polling station.

- *Counting.* A team of workers then count the ballots by hand into piles of 50 by candidate. Recounts are normally only ordered if candidate totals are close. Then only the bundles are normally counted unless candidates request that bundles be checked.

- *Publishing.* Results are announced at each counting centre and communicated to national electoral headquarters.

4.15 ❂ SUMMARY

- Information is data interpreted in some meaningful context.
- Information is fundamentally embodied in the idea of a sign and in the process of semantics.
- An information system is a system of communication between people.
- Information and communications technology provides means of constructing aspects of information systems, but is distinct from information systems. ICT supports information systems.
- Information systems support human activity systems.
- ICT systems can be seen as having four layers: interface management, rules management, transaction management and data management.

- Information systems are socio-technical systems. A socio-technical system is a system of technology used within a system of activity.
- Features of an information system fall into three categories: functionality, usability and utility.
- Informatics is the study of information, information systems and information technology applied to various phenomena. We are primarily interested in the application of informatics in organisations.
- Four layers of infrastructure are critical to e-business: human activity systems, information, information systems and ICT infrastructure.
- ICT can be used to supplant, support or innovate human activity.

4.16   ACTIVITIES

(i) Find one other example of data known to you. Try to separate out issues of data (representation) from information (interpretation).

(ii) Find some visual sign. Try to separate out what the sign is from what it represents. In other words, analyse its semantics.

(iii) Identify some area of human activity known to you. Determine what form of information system there is supporting it.

(iv) Analyse an information system known to you in terms of the properties of functionality, usability and utility.

(v) In terms of an ICT system known to you try to describe it in terms of the four layers of interface, rules, transactions and data.

(vi) In terms of some information system try to identify key stakeholder groups such as producers and users.

(vii) Determine in terms of some organisation known to you the ways in which ICT has been used to supplant, to support or to innovate.

4.17   REFERENCES

Beynon-Davies, P. (2002). *Information Systems: an Introduction to Informatics in Organisations*. Basingstoke, Palgrave.

Emery, F. E. (ed.) (1969). *Systems Thinking*. Harmondsworth, Penguin.

Hammer, M. (1996). Beyond Re-Engineering: How the Process-Centred Organisation is Changing Our Lives. London, HarperCollins.

Heeks, R. (ed.) (1999). *Reinventing Government in the Information Age: International Practice in IT-Enabled Public Sector Reform*. London, Routledge.

Kent, W. (1978). *Data and Reality*. Amsterdam, North-Holland.

Kling, R. and Allen, J. P. (1996). Can computer science solve organisational problems? the case for organisational informatics. In *Computerisation and Controversy: Value Conflicts and Social Choices* (ed. R. Kling). San Diego, CA, Academic Press.

Pinker, S. (2001). *The Language Gene*. Harmondsworth, Penguin.

Sowa, J. F. (1984). *Conceptual Structures: Information Processing in Mind and Machine*. Reading, MA, Addison-Wesley.

Stamper, R. K. (1973). *Information in Business and Administrative Systems*. London, Batsford.

Zuboff, S. (1988). *In the Age of the Smart Machine: the Future of Work and Power*. London, Heinemann.

CHAPTER 5

BACK-END INFORMATION SYSTEMS INFRASTRUCTURE

Our little systems have their day;

They have their day and cease to be:

They are but broken lights of thee,

And thou, o Lord, art more than they.

Alfred, Lord Tennyson, *In Memoriam A. H. H. OBIIT MDCCCXXXIII*

I have not lost my mind – it's backed up on disk somewhere

Anonymous

LEARNING OUTCOMES

After reading this chapter, you will be able to:

- Identify some of the core information systems of business
- Describe some of the functionality of back-end information systems
- Relate the linkage between core information systems and key human activity systems

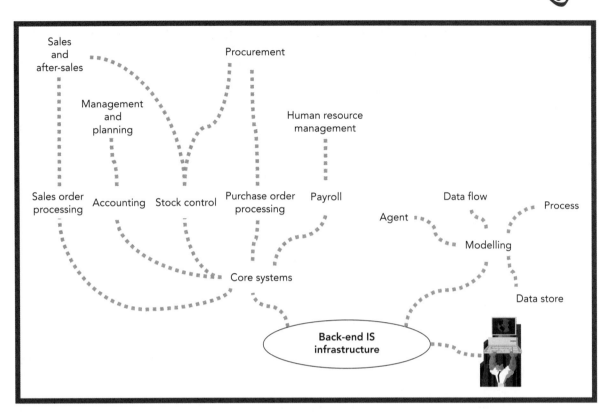

5.1 INTRODUCTION

Human activity systems rely on information for effective performance. Information is provided by information systems. In this chapter we define the core information systems found in business that supply such core information. This is what we refer to as the back-end information systems infrastructure of the business. It is this back-end information systems infrastructure that provides the bedrock for contemporary e-business in the sense of supporting some of the key human activity systems or business processes. Hence, a clear understanding of the workings of such an infrastructure is needed for a true appreciation of the essence of e-business and the place of front-end ICT innovation in the area of e-commerce (Part 4).

5.2 ⊚ INFORMATION SYSTEMS INFRASTRUCTURE OF A TYPICAL COMPANY

Clearly each business is different. This may be partly due to different environments in the sense that obviously different organisations are in different sectors of the economy – retail, manufacturing, education – to name but a few. However, even organisations in the same industrial sector will operate differently. Part of the reason for this may be to achieve something of an advantage over their competitors in the marketplace (Porter, 1985). Competitive advantage may be achieved in a number of ways: through differentiation in human activity, efficiency of human activity and/or effectiveness in human activity (Chapter 22).

The consequence of this is that each company's collection of information systems will necessarily be different. Hence organisations may implement different operational procedures or may parcel up the basic elements of transaction processing in terms of different units. We refer to the entire makeup of an organisation's information systems as its information systems infrastructure (Ciborra *et al.*, 2000).

There are a number of core information systems that, at a high level, most businesses have in common. Financial data is the lifeblood of most business organisations and is subject to a vast range of external regulation in the sense that companies must prepare their financial reports in well-established ways. Therefore it is no surprise to find that, in most business organisations, ICT was first applied in the accounting or finance department and financial information systems form the core around which a number of other information systems are located.

Core information systems constitute the so-called back-end (sometimes referred to as the back-office) systems of some company. They are critical to the performance of core human activity systems of business, such as sales and production. Around this core a number of front-end systems will exist. Such systems face the major stakeholders of the business: managers, employees, customers and suppliers. Hence we refer to such systems in terms of four groups: management information systems, employee-facing systems, customer-facing systems and supplier-facing systems. Such systems are discussed in Chapter 6.

Example

Most companies of whatever size will need an information system for recording orders for products/services from customers, orders made to suppliers for products/services, and the amounts paid or due to employees.

Question

If core information systems tend to have common features across organisations, what potential is there for gaining competitive advantage through information systems?

5.3 CORE INFORMATION SYSTEMS

Many businesses that sell products are founded around the following key information systems:

- *Sales order processing*. The information system that records details of customer orders.
- *Stock control*. The information system that maintains an inventory of raw material and finished goods stored in warehouses.
- *Purchase order processing*. The information system that records details of purchase orders to suppliers.
- *Accounting*. The system that records amounts owed and paid by customers, amounts owed to and paid to suppliers, and amounts paid to and owed to employees.
- *Payroll*. The information system that records details of wages and payments made to employees.

Businesses which sell services will operate differently in the sense of having different human activity systems. Hence, although they will have core information systems in similar areas, these will operate differently from that described in this chapter. We provide such an example in the case study at the end of this chapter.

Figure 5.1 illustrates some of the flows of data (represented by labelled arrows) between these four major back-end information systems.

Example   Because of external regulation most accounting information systems within a country such as the UK will be expected to run in the same way. This offers software suppliers the possibility of building a standard ICT system for supporting accounting activity. Such standardised pieces of software are referred to as software packages.

Question   *In what sense are these core information systems critical for regulating the business organisation?*

5.4 SALES ORDER PROCESSING

Figure 5.2 indicates a decomposition of the elements of the process box 'Sales order processing' on Figure 5.1. Hence sales order processing can be seen to be a subsystem of the transaction processing system of a company and in turn sales order entry can be seen as a subsystem of sales order processing.

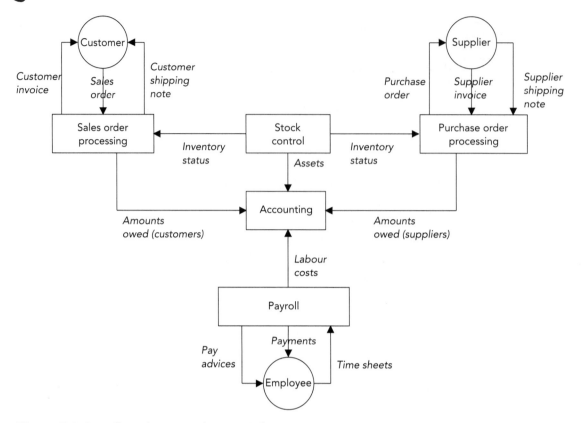

Figure 5.1 Data flows between the core information systems.

Note that this system assumes that goods will be dispatched to customers with an invoice for payment. A payment from the customer will be made to the company at some time after receipt of the invoice. This is the usual state of affairs when the company and its customer are in a so-called trusted relationship. In other words, the company has established in some way that payment will be made at some later date and is therefore willing to effectively award credit to a customer.

In many sectors of business customers are usually members of the general public. In such situations orders and payments are normally expected to arrive at the same time. The customer notification effectively serves as a record of the transaction between the company and the customer.

A suggested decomposition of the order entry subsystem is given in Figure 5.3. Note we have provided data stores on this diagram – a repository of data. This is to indicate the important reliance of actual information systems on organised repositories of data such as that kept on a company's products or customers.

Order entry is a key process that interfaces to the organisation's customers. Order entry captures the key data needed to process a customer order. Traditionally, orders might be expected to arrive through the post or over the telephone line. More recently orders may be sent electronically and come over electronic data interchange (EDI) links (Chapter 8) or via the Internet (Chapter 9).

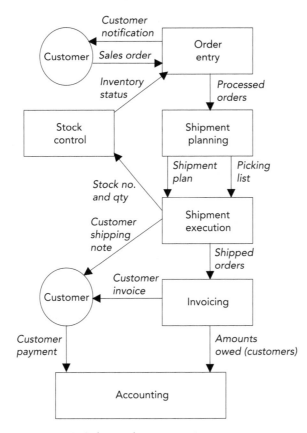

Figure 5.2 Sales order processing.

Normally the order entry system would make an enquiry of the stock control system to check that suitable quantities of the desired item are available. If an order item cannot be filled then a substitute item might be suggested or a back order generated. This back order will be filled later when stock is replenished. A notification of a confirmed, partially filled or back order would be supplied to the customer.

Orders processed by the order entry system will then be passed to a shipment planning system. This is a particularly important system for medium to large companies with lots of customers, minimal stock and many points of distribution. This system determines which orders will be filled and from which location they will be shipped. The system produces two outputs: a shipment plan which indicates how and when each order is to be filled and a picking list which is used by warehouse staff to select the desired goods from the warehouse.

Shipment execution supports the work of the shipping function and is used to coordinate the flow of goods from the business to customers. The system will produce a shipping note that is attached to each despatch of goods. It also passes on details of the shipment to invoicing.

Invoicing systems take the data supplied on shipping and produce invoices to customers using data stored about customers, orders, products and prices. Invoices may be sent at time of shipment or some time thereafter.

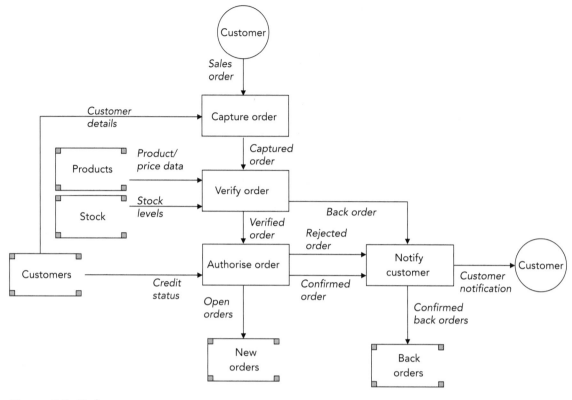

Figure 5.3 Order entry.

Most businesses have several forms of stock or inventory. These include raw materials, materials for packing, finished goods and parts for maintenance of products. Stock control or inventory control systems are designed to manage data about this material. The objective for most businesses is to minimise the amount of stock held while ensuring optimal performance of other systems such as manufacturing.

A simple stock control system is illustrated in Figure 5.4.

When raw materials or finished goods are received by an organisation a check is normally made against the original purchase order made to the supplier. If the goods delivered match that ordered then the stock record can be updated with the quantities supplied. The system then has to determine the optimal place to store the stock in the company's warehouses. Once this is determined a positioning report is generated for use by warehousing staff and the warehousing record updated.

Minimal stock levels are a crucial element of a modern business philosophy known as just in time (JIT) manufacturing. Providing facilities for storing the stock of raw materials needed for manufacture is a critical cost to the business. The more stock that is held the greater the costs incurred. JIT aims to store only enough stock

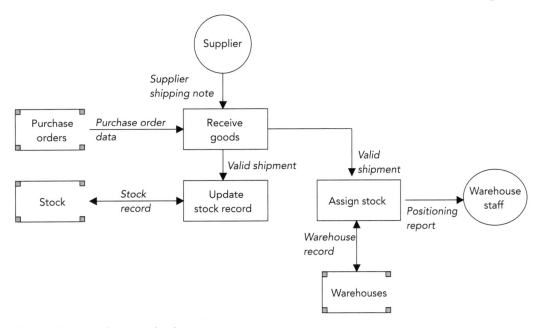

Figure 5.4 Stock control subsystem.

to meet the short-term needs of production. Warehouses are replenished with raw materials just in time to ensure efficient production.

5.6 PURCHASE ORDER PROCESSING

Figure 5.5 represents elements of a standard purchase order processing subsystem.

Purchases may be generated in two ways. The stock control system itself may generate an automatic purchase order if the level of a stock item falls below a certain level. Most medium to large organisations will have a purchasing or procurement unit. Staff in this unit will be generating purchase orders on the basis of orders it receives from the stock control system or from requests from staff for those items not included within the general remit of stock control.

Purchase orders will be produced by purchase order handling and then sent to relevant suppliers. This data will then be used to update a receiving system that will check the data it has on purchase orders against the invoices it receives from suppliers.

If the goods received from suppliers match the purchase order information then financial information about the amounts owed to suppliers is passed on to a major subsystem within accounting – accounts payable.

5.7 ACCOUNTING

Figure 5.6 represents the elements of a standard accounting system.

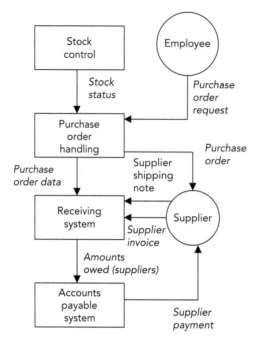

Figure 5.5 Purchase ordering subsystem.

Most accounting systems are divided up into three major subsystems: accounts receivable, accounts payable and general ledger. The data store used by the accounts receivable system is generally called a sales ledger because it records the financial details of all amounts owed by customers to the organisation. The data store used by the accounts payable system is sometimes called the purchase ledger because it stores the details of all monies owed to suppliers by the organisation.

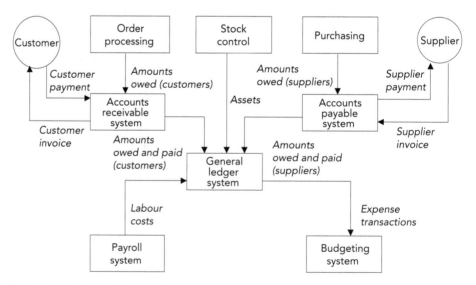

Figure 5.6 Accounting systems.

A third accounting system, called a general ledger system, is used to record details of all the financial transactions relevant to an organisation: income, expenditure and assets. It hence receives data from accounts payable, accounts receivable and stock control systems.

The accounts receivable system is essential for managing the cash flow of the company. When goods are shipped to customers a record of the amount owed by customers is passed on to the accounts receivable system. This leads to the customer's account being updated. When customers send payments to the company the credit balance of the customer is reduced by the appropriate amount. The data about customer credit and amounts paid is regularly used to update the general ledger system.

The accounts payable system is also essential for managing the cash flow of the company. When goods are ordered from suppliers a record of the amount owed to suppliers is passed on to the accounts payable system. This leads to the supplier's account being updated. When the organisation makes payments to its suppliers the credit balance owed to suppliers is reduced by the appropriate amount. The data about credit owed to suppliers and amounts paid is regularly used to update the general ledger system.

The third key input into a general ledger system is a payroll system. The payroll system will regularly update the general ledger with the costs incurred in paying staff. There will also be an input into the general ledger from the stock control system detailing the current financial position of assets held by the company.

5.8 ◎ PAYROLL

Figure 5.7 represents the elements of a standard payroll subsystem.

Payroll produces two primary outputs: a payment to the employee, and a record (payslip or pay advice) of the details of the payment made. The key input into a

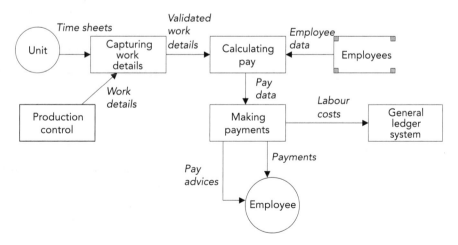

Figure 5.7 Payroll system.

payroll system is some data of the work undertaken during a given time period, such as a week or month. These details may be collected on time-sheets sent on from operational departments or may be automatically generated from a production scheduling and control system. The payroll system will need to access data stored on each employee, such as pay rates and tax details, to produce given pay advices. Periodically, the payroll system will update the general ledger system with the financial costs of labour.

5.9 INFORMATION SYSTEMS AND BUSINESS PROCESSES

As we have indicated in previous chapters, an effective information systems infrastructure is critical to the effective control of human activity within business organisations. One way of looking at this is to say that each of the five information systems described above supports a human activity system or business process in the value chain (Chapter 3):

- *Sales order processing*. This information system is likely to support sales activity as well as possibly after-sales service. Hence it is critical to the goals of gaining and retaining customers.

- *Purchase order processing*. This information system is likely to support major elements of the procurement process; that is, ensuring the effective supply of raw materials into the company.

- *Stock control*. This information system is important for sales activity in providing sales staff with accurate data on quantities and pricing of products. It is also likely to support procurement activity by enabling the identification of stock levels of raw materials. As such it is critical to the effective maintenance of relationships with both suppliers and with customers.

- *Accounting*. Financial data is the lifeblood of most commercial organisations. It is therefore critical for supporting infrastructure activities such as management and planning. Accurate financial data is critical to the performance of management information systems described in Chapter 6.

- *Payroll*. The payroll system is a critical element of any human resource activity in an organisation. For many service organisations labour costs are the primary costs to the organisation. Hence data that enables the effective control of this resource is critical to the organisational mission.

Questions   *How important is it that the information systems in this back-end infrastructure transfer data between systems easily? What potential business problems might arise from poor data transfer between systems?*

5.10 CASE STUDY: THE BACK-END INFORMATION SYSTEMS INFRASTRUCTURE FOR VOTING

Public sector organisations and human activity systems require a back-end information systems infrastructure in a similar manner to private sector organisations. However, the shape of this infrastructure is likely to be critically different from typical manufacturing organisations. Consider the case of the UK electoral system, as discussed in Chapters 2 and 4. The back-end information systems infrastructure supporting this activity currently comprises an information system for registering people entitled to vote – the so-called electoral register.

The current register is organised on constituency lines and each local authority is tasked with maintaining the register(s) in its area. The basic data held within the register comprises personal details of electors such as name, address and date of birth. From this data store an edited register is produced which may be sold on for commercial purposes. Electors have the right to opt out of this edited register.

Details of the candidates for election are also currently organised on constituency lines. However, because of the small number of candidates in each constituency this is unlikely to be organised as a formal information system.

Such a back-end information systems infrastructure is sufficient to manage voting activity that is organised on a constituency basis, since the volume of the data store approximates to thousands of records. However, if electronic voting (see Chapter 7) is to become a reality then registers of electors and candidates will probably need to be managed at a national level. This potentially raises the size of the data store to something approaching 44 million records.

Not surprisingly, the UK government, in association with local authorities, has instituted the Local Authorities Secure Electoral Register (LASER) project which aims to provide electoral registers that are joined up, maintained and managed locally. Such registers will then be accessible on a national level to authorized users. LASER will draw together all of the locally held registers of electors and make them available nationally to support e-voting.

5.11 SUMMARY

- Each business organisation's information systems will necessarily be different. However, there are similarities across organisations in the same business sector. Hence it is possible to develop generic descriptions of a number of key business information systems. This forms the back-end information systems infrastructure for the business.

- Key business information systems include sales order processing, purchase order processing, stock control, accounts and payroll

- Sales order processing is that information system which records details of customer orders. It is likely to support sales activity and after-sales service.

- Stock control is that information system which maintains an inventory of raw material and finished goods stored in warehouses. This information system is important for sales activity in providing sales staff with accurate data on quantities and pricing of products. It is also likely to support procurement activity by enabling the identification of stock levels of raw materials.
- Purchase order processing is that information system which records details of purchase orders to suppliers. It is likely to support major elements of the procurement process.
- Accounting is that system which records amounts owed and paid by customers, amounts owed to and paid to suppliers and amounts paid to and owed to employees. It is therefore critical for supporting infrastructure activities such as management and planning.
- Payroll is that information system which records details of wages and payments made to employees. The payroll system is a critical element of any human resource activity in an organisation.

5.12 ACTIVITIES

(i) Determine why back-end systems are sometimes referred to as back-office systems.

(ii) In a company known to you determine what constitute its core information systems.

(iii) Identify whether there are any software packages in a company known to you used for supporting accounting, sales, procurement or payroll.

(iv) Try to provide more detail on one chosen process from the IS infrastructure such as the receive goods process in the stock control subsystem. Draw a system diagram for this process.

(v) Draw a system diagram of some other system or process known to you such as admissions at a university.

5.13 REFERENCES

Ciborra, C. U., Braa, C., Cordella, A., Dahlbom, B., Falla, A., Hanseth, O., Hepso, V., Ljunberg, J., Monteiro, E. and Simon, K. A. (2000). *From Control to Drift: the Dynamics of Corporate Information Infrastructures.* Oxford, Oxford University Press.

Porter, M. E. (1985). *Competitive Advantage: Creating and Sustaining Superior Performance.* New York, Free Press.

CHAPTER 6

FRONT-END INFORMATION SYSTEMS INFRASTRUCTURE

It's a dangerous business going out your front door

J. R. R. Tolkien, *The Fellowship of the Ring*

LEARNING OUTCOMES

After reading this chapter, you will be able to:

- Define what is meant by a front-end information system
- Describe the differences between transaction processing, management information and decision support systems
- Relate the primary employee-facing information systems in the typical business
- Describe the primary customer-facing information systems in the typical business
- Define the primary supplier-facing information systems in the typical business
- Discuss some of the features of a corporate Intranet

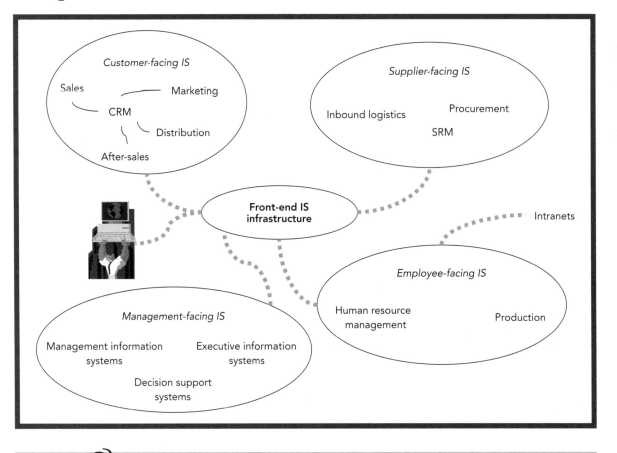

6.1 INTRODUCTION

In Chapter 5 we described the common back-end information systems infrastructure for e-business. In this chapter we describe some of the common elements of the front-end information systems infrastructure of the typical business. Such information systems are critical to maintaining effective relationships between key organisational stakeholders: suppliers, customers, employees and managers. Hence they are critical to supporting the internal value chain as well as the supply and demand chains of the business. A key challenge for the modern organisation is the successful integration of back-end and front-end information systems to support new forms of human activity.

In this chapter we describe some of the functionality of the major front-end information systems. The description is organised in terms of four major stakeholder groups with which these information systems interact: managers, customers, suppliers and employees. For internal stakeholders this front-end information systems infrastructure is likely to be accessed via the corporate Intranet. We conclude with an examination of the role of such information systems in a 'sense and respond' strategy for modern business.

In Chapter 5 we described the typical back-end information systems infrastructure of the business. This infrastructure consists of five major information systems: sales order processing, purchase order processing, stock control, payroll and accounting. Such systems handle most of the essential operational information needed for running the business.

On this foundation a large number of other information systems are normally built. Such systems are front-end systems in the sense that they directly interface to the major stakeholder types of business: managers, employees, suppliers and customers (Chapter 4).

Various information systems may feed off the data provided by core information systems in the back-end infrastructure and summarise such data for effective management and planning. In effect this is a vertical extension to the back-end information systems infrastructure. These are the management-facing information systems of the business.

Extensions may also be made horizontally out from the core information systems of the business. Connections may be made from the core IS infrastructure to other information systems that interface to a company's customers, suppliers or employees. Such are the customer-facing, supplier-facing and employee-facing information systems of the business.

These systems will be accessed by a variety of access mechanisms (Chapter 7), which include:

- Face to face interaction with an organisational representative using a front-end information system.
- Telephone interaction with an organisational representative using a front-end information system.
- Direct customer access through a Web site.

Figure 6.1 illustrates some of the relationships between back-end and front-end information systems in the typical business.

Example	In a university setting, a key back-end information system would be a student information system that would handle data concerned with students, courses and modules. A number of key front-end information systems would run off this back-end information system. For example, academics may use a system to report on students enrolled on a particular module, administrators may use a front-end system to manage student fees and managers may use a front-end system to plan for future intake in the university over a number of years.
Question	*What part do front-end information systems play in organisational performance?*

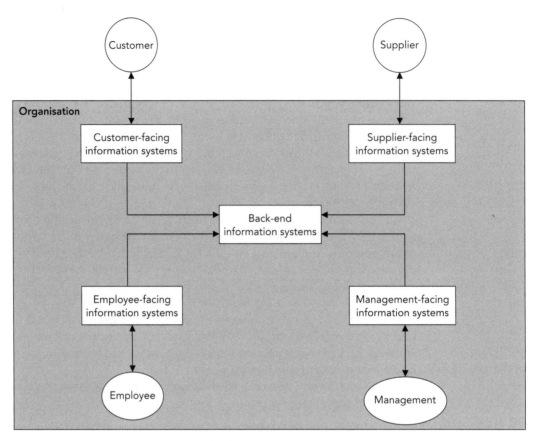

Figure 6.1 Back-end and front-end information systems.

6.3 ⊚ MANAGEMENT-FACING INFORMATION SYSTEMS

In terms of the control processes of organisations we may distinguish between three major types of information system: transaction processing systems (TPS), management information systems (MIS) and decision support systems (DSS)/executive information systems (EIS).

- *Transaction processing systems*. These are the operational information systems of the organisation. In a business organisation examples include order entry, accounts payable and stock control systems. They process the detailed data generated in the operations of the business. The detailed data are normally referred to as transactions and include customer orders, purchase orders, invoices etc. This data is essential to support the day-to-day operations that help a company add value to its products and/or services. TPS are sometimes referred to as the lifeblood of the organisation because they are so critical to effective activity. The key back-end information systems described in Chapter 3 are all TPS.

- *Management information systems*. In Chapter 5 we described management as a key control process for organisations. As a system of human activity management needs information systems to perform effectively. MIS are used particularly by some operational layer of management to monitor the state of the organisation at any one time. From such a system, or level of systems, managers would be expected to retrieve data about current production levels, number of orders achieved, current labour costs and other relevant managerial data.

- *Decision support/executive information systems*. Whereas MIS are generally used to enable effective short-term, tactical decisions about the operation of the organisation, DSS and EIS are generally expected to support longer-term, strategic decision-making. DSS/EIS will utilise the management data generated by MIS to model short-term and long-term scenarios of company performance. These scenarios are used to ask 'What if?' questions of business planning (Chapter 21) and to generate policy decisions in the area of business strategy (Chapter 22). DSS and EIS are therefore critical to effective performance at the strategic level of management and will probably need data from key environmental sensors to function effectively.

In Chapter 5 we identified four major data sets – employees, customers, finance and stock – important to the information systems infrastructure of our model organisation. These four major data sets are likely to form the key inputs into a management information system for an organisation. Using such a system, operational managers can continually monitor the state of the organisation. This is indicated in Figure 6.2 as one large management information system. In practice it may

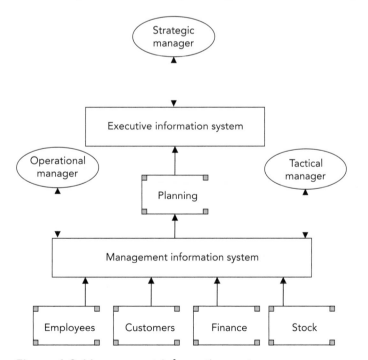

Figure 6.2 Management information systems.

form a number of integrated MIS, perhaps for particular business areas. One of the key outputs from the MIS will be summarised data on major trends affecting the company, such as labour costs, current levels of assets and current levels of spending. This data may be written to a planning data store for use by an executive information system. The EIS is likely to be used to formulate high-level strategic decisions affecting the company (Anthony, 1988).

Examples   In a supermarket chain a management information system will be used to monitor stock in warehouses and cash flow through the company. In a local authority a management information system may be used to monitor fiscal revenues against expenditure.

Question   *What role do management information systems play in the regulation of organisations? What role do DSS and EIS play in strategic planning within organisations?*

6.4 CUSTOMER-FACING SYSTEMS

Customer-facing information systems support demand-chain activities and typically interface between back-end information systems such as sales order processing, stock control and the customer. Traditional customer-facing information systems include sales, marketing and distribution and after-sales systems. Recently, there has been increased emphasis on integrating such systems together to form a customer relationship management or customer chain management system.

6.4.1 SALES

In some companies, particularly those associated with high-value products such as automobile sales or industrial equipment, customers would not normally fill out orders themselves. They are more than likely to interface with a sales force in relation to making orders. Hence a sales system is a common component of the information systems infrastructure of such organisations. This system will record the activities of the sales force in terms of what sales have been made, to whom, by whom and when. This data will frequently be used to calculate commission owed to salespeople on products sold.

6.4.2 MARKETING

Marketing is the organisational process devoted to promoting the products and/or services of some organisation. Good marketing is reliant on good customer information. Marketing is likely to utilise the information held about its existing customers to prepare and manage advertising campaigns for company products and services. A marketing system is likely to store details of various promotions, which customers have been contacted and the results of contacts made.

6.4.3 DISTRIBUTION

Distribution is sometimes referred to as outbound logistics (Chapter 3). Delivering products to customers efficiently and effectively is critical to customer retention. Hence critical aspects of the distribution system will be concerned with optimising the use of delivery channels to customers. Such channels may involve management of intermediaries such as parcel post distributors.

6.4.4 AFTER-SALES

An after-sales system will be involved in tracking customer support and product maintenance activities following a sale and probably on a continuous basis for a number of years. The complexity of this system will probably vary with the type of product or service sold by the company. For low-value goods after-sales may merely track customer complaints and product replacements. For high-value goods after-sales is likely to involve the recording of maintenance or service schedules.

Example

The lift manufacturer OTIS uses an after-sales system which proactively schedules maintenance of lifts by their engineers.

6.4.5 CUSTOMER RELATIONSHIP MANAGEMENT (CRM)

Each of the four systems of sales, marketing, distribution and after-sales interacts with the customer in different ways and record different data associated with each interaction. Customer relationship management (CRM) has become a popular philosophy in the recent management science literature. Winning new customers and keeping existing customers happy is seen to be a key to organisational success (Chapter 18). But effective CRM demands a unified view of the customer. This is provided by a CRM information system.

A CRM system would ideally track all customer interactions with a company from initial enquiries through making orders to the whole range of after-sales services that might be offered to and consumed by the customer. Typically then CRM systems integrate the range of front-end and back-end information systems that have a bearing on the customer.

Some of the relationships between the key customer-facing information systems are illustrated in Figure 6.3.

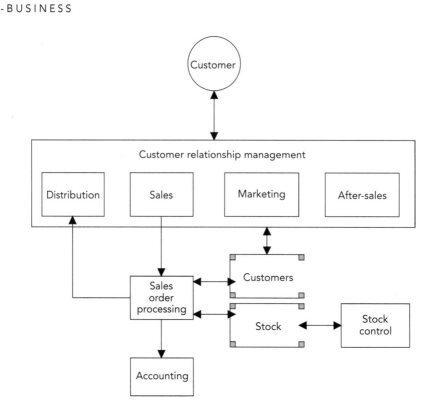

Figure 6.3 Customer-facing information systems.

Example   Many Internet sites maintain forms of CRM system. Such systems log all interactions between an established customer and the site. The data they use may be used for a variety of purposes, such as proactive marketing.

Question   *In what ways may customer-facing information systems contribute to improvements in customer service?*

6.5 ⊚ SUPPLIER-FACING SYSTEMS

Supplier-facing information systems support supply chain activities. Traditional supplier-facing systems include inbound logistics and procurement and typically interface with back-end information systems such as purchase order processing, accounting and stock control. Not surprisingly, given the symmetric nature of buy-side and sell-side activities, there has been increased emphasis on integrating supplier-facing information systems together to form an integrated supply chain system.

6.5.1 INBOUND LOGISTICS

Inbound logistics is that process devoted to managing the material resources entering an organisation from its suppliers and partners. In the retail sector for instance large food retailers are likely to have fleets of vehicles involved in the delivery of goods to stores. These vehicles may have to make up to 100 deliveries in any given working week. Clearly, effective and efficient systems are needed to plan and schedule routes for the vehicles to deliver foodstuffs to stores.

6.5.2 PROCUREMENT

Procurement is that process devoted to the purchasing of goods and services from suppliers at acceptable levels of cost and quality. It can be considered as the sister process of sales. A procurement system will be concerned with managing this process of procuring goods, services and raw materials needed by the company to operate effectively. It is likely to interact with both the purchase ordering system and the stock control system.

6.5.3 SUPPLIER RELATIONSHIP MANAGEMENT (SRM)

This is the sister system to the customer relationship management system. It keeps track of all supplier interactions with the company and integrates the data used by supplier-facing information systems such as procurement and inbound logistics.

Some of the relationships between the key supplier-facing information systems are illustrated in Figure 6.4.

Example   Electronic procurement is the trend for using ICT to integrate many supply chain processes. Procurement systems and SRM systems are important parts of electronic procurement (Chapter 19).

Question   *In what ways may supplier-facing information systems contribute to better management of the supply chain?*

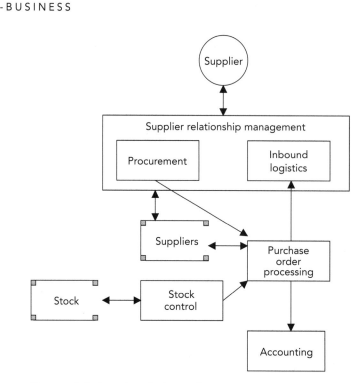

Figure 6.4 Supplier-facing information systems.

6.6 EMPLOYEE-FACING SYSTEMS

Employee-facing information systems support the internal value chain within organisations. Typical employee-facing information systems include human resource management and production control systems and they are likely to interact with key back-end information systems such as payroll.

6.6.1 HUMAN RESOURCE MANAGEMENT

A company is likely to need to build systems to record, process and maintain large amounts of information about its employees. Payroll data is only one facet of this data. Companies will also want to maintain detailed histories of the employment of their employees.

6.6.2 PRODUCTION SYSTEM

This system will be involved in scheduling future production, monitoring current production and interfacing with the stock control system in terms of requisitioning raw material for production and replenishing supplies of finished goods

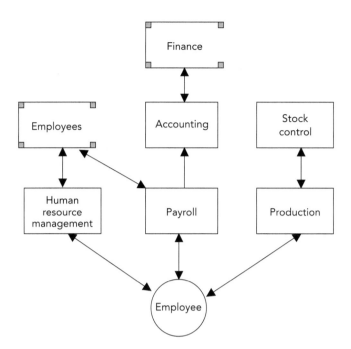

Figure 6.5 Employee-facing information systems.

Some of the relationships between the key employee-facing information systems are illustrated in Figure 6.5.

Example	Human resource management systems and production or manufacturing systems are likely to integrate around activity data. Hence detailed work patterns of employees may be integrated with production scheduling.
Question	*Human resources are now frequently expressed in terms of human capital. How may effective employee-facing information systems contribute to better management of human capital?*

6.7 THE CORPORATE INTRANET

Using a biological analogy, Martin (1996) refers to a corporate Intranet as the internal nervous system of the cyber-corporation. An Intranet can be considered as a special type of overarching front-end information system that can serve to integrate the front-end information systems infrastructure of some organisation.

An Intranet is a corporate local area network or wide area network (Chapter 7) that uses Internet and Web technology (Chapters 9 and 10) and is secured behind firewalls (Chapter 13). The Intranet links various clients, servers, databases and applications together. While using the same technology as the Internet, the Intranet is run as a private network. Only authorised users from within the company are allowed to use it. Such users are normally the internal employees of an organisation.

Companies have implemented Intranets with some of the following expected benefits in mind:

- Better communication
- Access to more accurate information
- Better coordination and collaboration
- Easy to implement and use
- Cheap to implement and use
- Scalable
- Flexible

Examples

- *Better communication*. E-mail, chat and newsgroups may enable more effective communication between organisational members.

- *Access to more accurate information*. Information can be kept more up-to-date on central servers.

- *Better coordination and collaboration*. Workflow can be incorporated into Intranets enabling structured coordination of activities between dispersed organisational stakeholders.

- *Easy to implement and use*. Establishing an Intranet is relatively straightforward technologically speaking. Most people are relatively familiar with using the concept of a Web browser.

- *Cheap to implement and use*. The hardware, software and communication facilities required for constructing a corporate Intranet are relatively inexpensive.

- *Scalable*. A corporate Intranet is easily grown with changes in demand and use.

- *Flexible*. Adaptations in an Intranet are relatively easy to achieve.

Intranets have been used to support the following organisational activities:

- Enhanced knowledge sharing through web pages. For instance, companies are using Intranets to disseminate information in the form of manuals for various company practices.

- Enhanced group decision-making through the use of web-based groupware and workflow systems. Intranets can be used to foster communication and debate on key organisational issues. They may also incorporate business rules that aid the flow of work between dispersed groups in the organisation.

- Distributing software around the organisation from an Intranet server. The informatics service may find an Intranet an invaluable tool for managing the software inventory of a company. Upgrades to clients can be managed more effectively and efficiently from central servers.

- Document management. An Intranet may provide a repository for users to access pictures, photographs or text. The Intranet can be used to manage key organisational resources such as manuals, news feeds, directories, organisation charts, corporate logos and reports.

- Providing a common organisational portal to key information systems. Intranets can offer organisations the possibility of building cross-organisational and uniform access to key organisational systems. Access to the launching of key applications can be more easily controlled.

Examples	The public relations arm of a large telecommunications company uses the corporate Intranet to make sure that its officers are all presenting a consistent message to the external world in relation to issues affecting the company. The Intranet also contains 'best practice' for a number of public relations activities.
	Coopers and Lybrand developed an Intranet to share knowledge among its consultancy employees in the taxation area.
	Many newspapers utilise an Intranet to make the archive of previous stories available to its journalists.
	Compaq uses part of its Intranet to allow staff to access human resources information such as retirement accounts.

Question	*As well as benefits, corporate Intranets are likely to incur costs for the organisation. Can we identify some of these likely costs?*

6.8 ◎ SENSE AND RESPOND

In recent literature (Bradley and Nolan, 1998) there has been much discussion of the e-business as a 'sense and respond' organisation. At heart this is a systems perspective of the business. Sense and respond clearly refers to the components of control within the organisation that enable the various human activity systems making up the organisation to adapt to changes in its environment. Successful adaptation relies on suitable single-loop feedback loops consisting of appropriate sensors, comparators and effectors.

In terms of the model of a control subsystem presented in Chapter 2 the front-end information systems described in this chapter can be seen to be some of the key sensors of the business. Changes in critical data collected by such systems should trigger knock-on changes in other systems within the information systems infra-structure signalling changes to the human activity reliant on such systems. Hence successful organisational adaptation is critically dependent on successful integra-tion of front-end and back-end information systems.

Example	Simplistically, a change in the number of orders being captured by customer-facing information systems should effect a change in back-end systems, such as an increase in the production schedule. This change in back-end data is likely to cause the effect of an increase in the number of purchase requisitions and consequent purchase orders to suppliers.

Successful adaptation is also critically dependent on the double-loop feedback important for effective management. Hence management-facing information systems are critical to the continual development of business plans and strategies (Chapter 24) in the face of environmental change.

Question	A sense and respond perspective on the successful organisation can be said to exploit an open systems viewpoint on the organisation. In what sense is this the case?

6.9 CASE STUDY: CUSTOMER-FACING INFORMATION SYSTEMS IN THE FINANCIAL SERVICES INDUSTRY

ICT and the associated front-end information systems now enable financial services organisations (banks, building societies, insurance companies, share trading agencies) to extend their reach to customers through a number of innova-tive delivery channels, including (Peppard, 2000):

● Internet-enabled PC
● Interactive digital TV
● Mobile phones
● Smart cards

Hence, it is no longer necessary for the banking customer to attend a high street branch to conduct financial transactions. Customers across Europe are able to access 24 hour, 365 day access to banking products and services through remote access devices (Chapter 7). This is having a major impact on the marketing strategies of financial companies and the proliferation of possible distribution channels has placed channel management on the agenda of management within such companies.

For example, prior to setting up the telephone banking operation First Direct, Midland Bank (now HSBC) conducted some consumer research. It found that:

- 20% of customers had not visited a bank in the last month and 10% had not visited a bank in the last six months.
- 51% said that they would prefer to visit their branch as little as possible.
- 48% had not met their bank manager.

Channel management means effective integration of all channels to a business, including call centre, direct mail, branch, head office, Internet and interactive digital TV. This demands effective front-end information systems that are able to capture all customer interactions with a company through all such channels.

6.10 SUMMARY

- The typical back-end information systems infrastructure of the business consists of five major information systems: sales order processing, purchase-order processing, stock control, payroll and accounting.
- Front-end information systems are those that directly interface to the major stakeholder types of business: managers, employees, suppliers and customers.
- Management-facing information systems are built on the foundation of transaction processing systems. Management information systems are used by some operational layer of management to monitor the state of the organisation at any one time. Decision support systems and executive information systems are generally expected to support longer-term strategic decision-making.
- Typical customer-facing information systems include sales, customer relationship management, marketing and distribution systems.
- Typical supplier-facing information systems include procurement and supplier relationship management systems.
- Typical employee-facing information systems include human resource management and production control systems.
- Intranets are used by authorised internal users for specific organisational tasks and to access specific organisational information.
- Intranets are used for knowledge sharing, document management, distributing software and as organisational portals to key systems.
- Front-end information systems enable a sense and respond strategy.

6.11 ACTIVITIES

(i) Identify a management information system in an organisation known to you and try to determine its functionality.

(ii) Take a public sector organisation such as a local authority. Try to identify the key front-end information systems relevant to this organisation.

(iii) Try to identify the types of activity data that might be generated from a production system. In what way might it update a HRM system? What other information systems are likely to feed off a production system?

(iv) Try to identify some of the purposes that the data collected by a CRM system might be used for.

(v) In terms of some organisation known to you, identify which of the benefits of Intranets are most applicable.

(vi) What does your chosen organisation use its Intranet for? If it does not have an Intranet currently, prioritise the key uses in terms of most relevance for the organisation.

6.12 REFERENCES

Anthony, R. A. (1988). *The Management Control Function*. Boston, MA, Harvard Business School Press.

Bradley, S. P. and Nolan, R. L. (eds.) (1998). *Sense and Respond: Capturing Value in the Network Era*. Boston, MA, Harvard Business School Press.

Martin, J. (1996). *Cybercorp*. New York, American Management Association.

Peppard, J. (2000). Customer relationship management in financial services. *European Management Journal*, **18**(3), 312–327.

THE TECHNICAL INFRASTRUCTURE FOR E-BUSINESS

Technology... the knack of so arranging the world that we need not experience it

Max Frisch, *Second Stop*

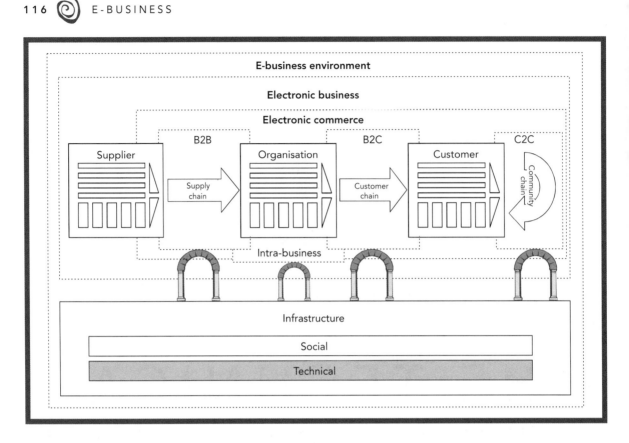

In our model of the e-business domain presented above we have indicated the key relationship between infrastructure and e-business. Social and technical infrastructure is critical to supporting effective e-business in general and e-commerce in particular. Social infrastructure refers to the processes or human activity systems of planning, management, development and evaluation. Technical infrastructure refers to the necessary ICT base on which e-business and e-commerce is built. Hence it is difficult to understand the importance and practicalities of e-business without some understanding of the technologies on which this phenomenon is founded. It is impossible to understand e-business without some understanding of the 'e'.

Part 2 is designed to provide a key overview of the key technical infrastructure components. The relationships between these components are illustrated in Figure P2.1. The key message being promoted is that ICT is an enabler for organisational change focused on the redesign of the delivery of services and products to key stakeholders – customers, suppliers, partners and employees. Hence ICT is seen to offer the potential for more effective and efficient delivery of value along supply, customer, internal and potentially community value chains. The chapters within this part are presented in terms of this organising framework, the essence of which is summarised below.

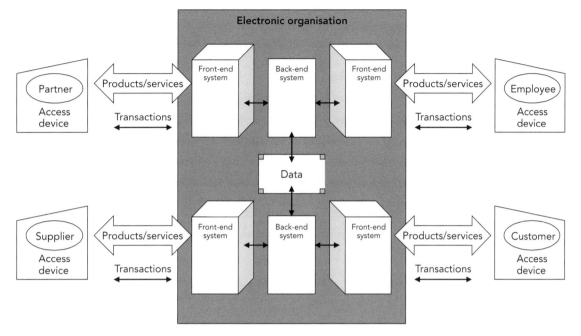

Figure P2.1 The technical infrastructure for e-business.

ICT is being promoted within both the public and private sectors as a means of improving the efficiency and effectiveness of the delivery of services and goods to internal and external stakeholders. A key distinction is essential between goods, services and transactions. Goods and services are end points of processes or human activity systems undertaken by organisations. Information is needed to support most human activity systems particularly in terms of transactional data. Transactions are ways of recording activities associated with the delivery of goods and services and hence are the essential raw data for modelling and evaluating organisational performance. Performance management systems cannot work effectively within organisations without transactional data. Reducing the costs associated with the administration of transactions is also seen as the typical way of introducing cost savings with ICT.

The objective of redesigning organisational processes around ICT to support electronic delivery will typically involve:

● *Investigating and implementing various access mechanisms for different stakeholders*
In terms of interaction with the customer, face-to-face contact and telephone conversations are two of the most commonly used mechanisms for accessing company services and products. However, with an eye on the longer term, most companies are either implementing or investigating access mechanisms that allow customers to interact with the organisation using devices such as the Internet-enabled personal computer (PC) and even interactive digital television (iDTV).

The aim is to provide access to company services and products 24 hours a day, 365 days a year. This is the topic of Chapter 7.

● *Providing effective delivery of intangible goods and services*
Certain goods and services are information-based or intangible. As such they are prime candidates for electronic delivery. Other goods and services are tangible in nature, and while not being amenable to electronic delivery still rely on information-based activity to record transactions. In Chapter 8 we examine these distinctions in more detail and discuss some of the standards supporting the electronic delivery of goods and services, particularly electronic payment systems.

● *Re-engineering or constructing front-end ICT systems to manage customer interaction.*
The technological infrastructure for modern front-end systems relies on two critical technologies: the Internet and the Web.

Currently the Internet is a set of interconnected computer networks distributed around the globe. The Internet can be considered on a number of levels. The base infrastructure of the Internet is composed of packet-switched networks and a series of communication protocols. On this layer runs a series of applications such as electronic mail (e-mail) and more recently the World Wide Web – the Web for short. The Web is effectively a set of standards for the representation and distribution of hypermedia documents over the Internet. It has become a key technology for constructing the front-end ICT systems of organisations through Web sites.

Because of the increasing use of technologies such as the Internet and the Web, major investment is currently being undertaken by companies to increase levels of interactivity on their Web sites. The aim for many companies is to provide fully transactional Web sites in which customers can undertake a substantial proportion of their interaction with a company online.

In Chapters 9 and 10 we examine these important technological foundations for the electronic delivery of goods and services.

● *Re-engineering or constructing back-end ICT systems*
A key focus within the e-business agenda is on re-engineering service delivery around the customer. Hence, for example, when a customer enters personal details such as their name and address into one system this information should ideally be available to all other systems that need such data. Such a customer-focused strategy demands integration and interoperability of ICT systems. This is the topic of Chapter 11.

● *Ensuring front-end/back-end ICT systems integration*
To enable fully transactional Web sites, the information presented needs to be updated dynamically from back-end databases. Also, the information entered by customers needs to update
company information systems effectively. This is the topic of Chapter 12.

● *Ensuring secure data and transactions along communication channels*
For effective e-commerce people must trust electronic delivery. A major part of such trust is
focused on the privacy of electronic transactions, particularly payments. In Chapter 13 we examine
the issues of securing data in ICT systems and ensuring secure electronic transactions along
communication channels.

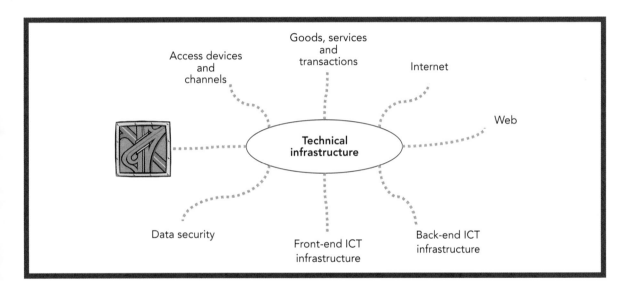

ACCESS DEVICES AND CHANNELS

A fo ben, bid bont

(I will be a bridge for my people)

Welsh Aphorism

You never know till you try to reach them how accessible men are; but you must approach each man by the right door.

Henry Ward Beecher

LEARNING OUTCOMES

After reading this chapter, you will be able to:

- Describe a range of mechanisms for accessing electronic organisations
- Outline some of the major characteristics of communication channels
- Describe some of the links between access devices, channels and front-end ICT systems

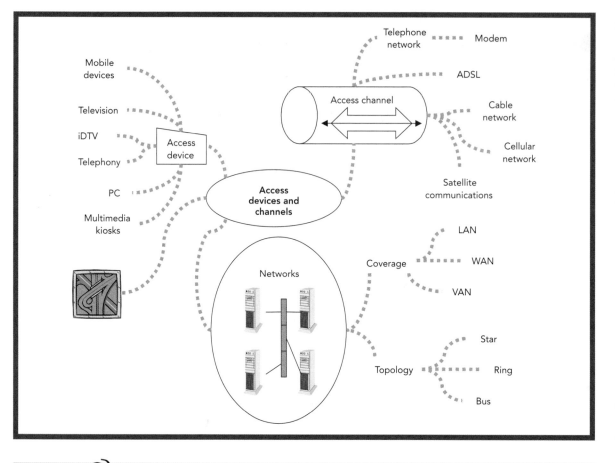

Organisations in both the private and public sectors can be seen as systems for the provision of value – typically the provision of goods and services to definable populations. However, an organisation's services or products may be accessed in a number of different ways. Each way we might describe as a mode or mechanism of access. Traditionally, such services or products would be accessed through:

- Face-to-face communication
- Postal channels
- Telephone communication

More recently, with the rise of the e-business, different modes that involve remote and interactive electronic access to products and services are becoming popular. This phenomenon is frequently referred to as electronic delivery. Certain products, such as digitised music, will be accessible directly via remote access mechanisms. For other more physical products organisations are likely to provide information and ordering services but distribute the products to customers through conventional channels.

In this chapter we consider the various forms of remote access mechanism currently available. We also discuss the corresponding communication channels that connect such access devices to the front-end ICT systems of the business.

Example

New Brunswick in Canada was the first jurisdiction in the world to establish an information highway secretariat (IDEA, 2002). The Canadian province has also established Service New Brunswick (SNB), an agency responsible for building a 'single window' access to government services. To achieve this, SNB operates a three-pronged approach to access:

- A network of one-stop shop service centres located in 35 New Brunswick communities. In 2002 3.5 million transactions were completed at such service centres and $319 million was collected on behalf of government departments.

- An integrated call centre offering 15 services over the phone, such as motor vehicle registration renewals, disability permit applications and property tax accounts.

- SNB supports SNB online, a Web portal to electronic services available from the public sector in New Brunswick.

7.2 ⊚ A MODEL OF COMMUNICATION

Remote access to services and products is a form of communication. Generally speaking we can distinguish between three component elements of any communication:

- A *sender* that transmits some message as a signal.
- A *communication channel* or medium along which the message is transmitted.
- A *receiver* which interprets the signal as a message.

In normal face-to-face conversation both sender and receiver are humans and the communication channel is air. The signal involves the transmission of sound through air. For ICT systems telecommunications are more relevant. This refers to the electronic transmission of signals for communications, usually at a distance. In fact, ICT systems generally utilise a subset of telecommunications known as data communications. Data communication refers to the electronic collection, processing and distribution of data over telecommunication networks.

The basic model of communication (Figure 7.1) above can be modified for data communication:

- A *sender unit* formulates a message and transmits it as a signal to a...
- *Telecommunication device*, which is a piece of hardware that performs a number of functions on the signal and then transmits the signal along a...

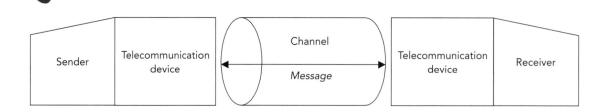

Figure 7.1 Data communication.

- *Communication channel* to another...
- *Telecommunication device*, which reverses the process performed by the sending telecommunications device and passes the signal on to a...
- *Receiving unit*, which interprets the signal as a message.

For convenience we shall combine the idea of a sender unit and telecommunication device into the concept of an access device. The telecommunication device and receiving unit at the organisation end of the communication we shall refer to as a front-end ICT system (see Chapter 12).

Question   *What are the component elements of a communication conducted by post and by telephone?*

7.3 ACCESS DEVICES AND CHANNELS

For remote access to the products or services of some organisation access mechanisms are needed. Any mode or mechanism for access consists of an access device and associated access channel. The access device is used to formulate, transmit, receive and display messages. The access channel is used to carry the message between external stakeholders (customers, suppliers, partners, employees) and the organisation (see Figure 7.2).

In the modern electronic organisation various remote access mechanisms can be used (Whyte, 2001). Generally there is an interdependence between certain access devices and channels. Access channels are conduits for the delivery of certain goods and services as well as for the transmission of transactional data (see Figure 7.3). Access mechanisms are not mutually exclusive. Certain access devices and channels can be used in correspondence with traditional face-to-face access and certain organisations may wish to keep open traditional access channels for reasons of effectiveness. However, in terms of a cost reduction strategy, many organisations are likely to wish to reduce the number of traditional access mechanisms and increase the number of remote access mechanisms (Norris and West, 2001).

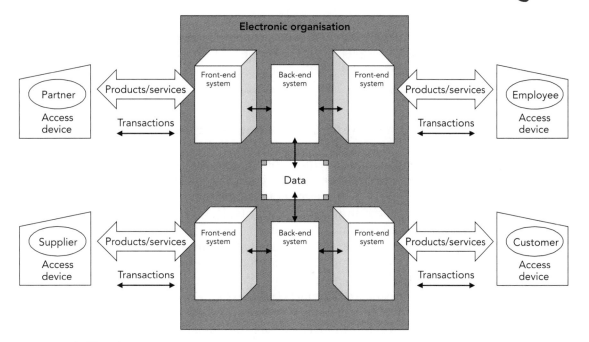

Figure 7.2 The electronic organisation.

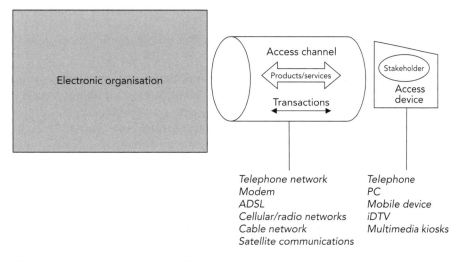

Figure 7.3 Access devices and channels.

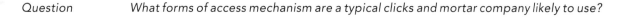

Question	*What forms of access mechanism are a typical clicks and mortar company likely to use?*

Example	The cost of a typical high street banking transaction such as a credit or debit to a bank account over the counter costs a few pence for each bank to undertake. The cost of an online credit or debit to a bank account is a fraction of a penny.

In this chapter we consider the various devices and channels that enable access to be made to electronic organisations.

The computer systems in a contemporary computer network will be generally be organised into two types: clients and servers. Clients request services from server systems. Servers supply services to clients.

The concept of an access device is a typical example of a client system. The access device is used to formulate, transmit, receive and display messages. Front-end ICT systems would typically be regarded as the servers in a telecommunications network. Front-end ICT systems supply the data services and/or products for clients. The access channel is used to carry the message between users of access devices – customers, suppliers, partners and employees – and the organisation's front-end ICT systems.

This partnership arrangement may be emulated within the ICT infrastructure of an organisation. Hence front-end ICT systems may act as the clients of back-end ICT systems (Chapter 11).

7.4 ⊚ STAKEHOLDER ACCESS DEVICES

Electronic business relies on individuals, groups and organisations (or what we have called stakeholders – see Chapter 4) being able to access electronic networks and systems. Four main types of stakeholder are of interest to the business: customers, suppliers, partners and employees (Chapter 4). Each type of stakeholder will have a variety of access devices and channels open to it. Each stakeholder type will also interact with different front-end and back-end systems in the organisation. We particularly focus on the customer and the type of devices available to e-tailing (electronic retailing) in this chapter. Access by suppliers, employees and partners are considered in subsequent chapters.

A number of options exist for remote stakeholder access devices. These include telephones, television, personal computers, multimedia kiosks and mobile devices.

7.4.1 TELEPHONY

Telephony includes conventional audio telephones, modern video telephones and the use of fax/telex for data transmission. Telephones have been used for a number of years as a form of retail access device. In more recent times a number of trends have enabled a growth in the use of such devices for the ordering of products and services. Of these the most significant are the development of touch-tone services, intelligent networks and the growth of call centres. Telephony can be effectively combined with other access mechanisms such as interactive television (see below) to provide a more complete e-tailing experience.

7.4.2 TELEVISION

Currently television is provided as an analogue terrestrial channel to most domestic customers in the UK. Television is already used as a form of e-commerce channel through terrestrial broadcasting in the sense that commercial advertising is piped into the home using this medium. With the emergence of satellite and more lately digital broadcasting, a number of pay-per-view channels have emerged. Retailing already occurs via the medium of pay-per-view television through specialist shopping channels.

Because service providers in the area of pay-per-view need a mechanism for extracting payments from their customers, the broadcasting signal is usually encrypted. This means that service providers normally have to provide some form of decryption equipment or set-top box for each customer. Such a device can easily be converted to provide a backward channel to the service provider through conventional telephony services (using modems) to enable interaction.

Conventional television of both the terrestrial and the satellite variety suffers from lack of personalisation and interactivity. This is likely to change with the possibilities offered by digital television. In a sense, the only thing that changes with the advent of digital television is the way in which the television signal is encoded. However, with digital television it becomes possible to deliver not only traditional television channels but also Web content. This further opens up the possibility of interactive digital television (iDTV), in which handheld devices or other input devices allow the customer to navigate through online material and also to input data.

iDTV offers similar e-commerce capability as the Internet-enabled PC (see below). However, it perhaps offers a lower level of actual content, reflecting the lower bandwidth (see below) of this access mechanism. The high start-up costs for companies also mean that there tend to be fewer service providers than are available in the area of Internet service provision.

7.4.3 PERSONAL COMPUTERS

Personal computers are currently the preferred mode of access to the Internet (Chapter 9). The vast majority of domestic users and small businesses connect to the Internet via standard analogue telephone lines. Since such lines were originally designed to handle analogue speech transmission, a device known as a modem is needed. This converts the digital data transmitted by a computer into a series of analogue tones of varying pitch and amplitude that can be transmitted over the analogue network. A capacity of up to 56 kbits/sec is available using this approach.

Telephone lines to date have been the key technology supporting access to electronic organisations from personal computers in the home. Currently a key constraint is the bandwidth that can be delivered into the home using a conventional modem. Broadband technologies are beginning to impact on this market through technologies such as ADSL (see below).

A key problem with this access channel is the variable penetration of this technology into the home from various regions within countries and between different social classes. Generally speaking penetration varies between 20% and 50% of households in the UK compared to almost 100% penetration of television.

A significant degree of standardisation of the home personal computer has been achieved over the last decade. This has encouraged a degree of domestication in its use. However, a key problem still remains. Average home users have to upgrade their hardware and software on a frequent basis, thus increasing the general cost of ownership above other technologies such as television.

7.4.4   MULTIMEDIA KIOSKS

Personal computers are designed for use from the home or office. Multimedia kiosks are specialist access points to services provided on the Internet. Generally such kiosks are specifically designed for certain forms of access and normally placed in public places. Thus they are frequently referred to in European literature on the information society as public Internet access points (PIAPs).

Examples   A multimedia kiosk situated in a shopping mall is likely to permit access to a range of shopping services, while that sited in a hotel lobby is likely to offer tourist information.

7.4.5   MOBILE DEVICES

Mobile devices include mobile phones, palmtops and laptops. Here the mobile computer appears either in its general-purpose or 'fat' form (the laptop) or in more dedicated or 'thin' devices, such as palmtops or wireless application protocol (WAP) enabled mobile phones. The main difference with conventional PC access is that the access channel is likely to be the cellular phone network. WAP servers have enabled access to the Internet from mobile devices such as mobile phones. However Web provision currently has to be adapted to the limited capability of the current generation of mobile phones.

Examples   Workers in many gas supply companies now use mobile devices to access corporate systems. Generally, such devices are used to enter data such as meter readings and to update customer-billing services online.

The Thomas Cook group services 3.5 million passengers per year, employs over 16,000 staff and operates a branch network of over 1,050 in the UK and overseas. The travel company produced its first Web site, Thomas Cook Online, in 1995. It was one of the first UK travel agencies to offer customers services such as holiday bookings, ordering of travellers' cheques and flight availability information via a Web site. It decided to engage in significant investment in a new Internet strategy and relaunched its online operations in 1999 as thomascook.com. The company has based its strategy around multi-channel operations allowing customers to access its services on the high street, by phone, over the Internet using a PC or mobile phone and through interactive digital television.

Woolworth is installing wireless handheld tills at its 826 stores in the UK to cut customer queuing times. This access channel allows staff to process credit and debit card sales transactions quickly. It also enables staff to look up product pricing and stock information from anywhere in the store.

7.4.6 MULTI-CHANNEL ACCESS CENTRES

One should not assume that 'bricks and mortar' organisations, whether in the private or the public sector, can entirely switch over to one or more remote access mechanisms. This may prove a risky strategy in the sense of excluding particular customer segments. It is more than likely that at least in the medium term organisations will wish to maintain traditional access mechanisms such as face-to-face contact and telephone access. Some 'clicks-only' companies are beginning to establish a physical presence in an attempt to differentiate the quality of their service. Many organisations are also attempting to integrate various access mechanisms in multi-channel access centres. Here the organisation establishes a common entry point for all customer interaction.

Example   Cardiff City Council has created C2C – Connect to Cardiff. This consists of a large call centre capable of handling telephone and Web based enquiries. However, it also has established a number of 'one stop shops around the capital to handle all customer queries to the local authority in a face-to-face manner.

Question   *Dreyfus (2001) questions the richness of experience possible through remote access mechanisms and as a consequence questions the viability of using such to access services of public and private organisations in and of themselves. For instance, he questions whether e-learning will ever substitute for traditional face-to-face forms of learning. Given this line of argument, will remote access to government services be a viable strategy for improving the efficiency of public service provision?*

7.5 🌀 CHARACTERISTICS OF AN ACCESS CHANNEL

Access devices presume an access channel for communication to occur between stakeholders and the systems of the organisation. A signal must be sent along this communication channel.

We may describe a communication channel in various ways. Some relevant properties are the capacity of the channel, the synchronisation, the modulation and the direction of the channel:

- *Capacity*. Generally speaking this refers to the amount of data that can be transmitted along the channel in some given period of time. The bandwidth of a channel refers to the minimum and maximum frequencies allowed along a channel. Bandwidth is related to baud rate, which is a measure of the amount of data that can be transmitted along a channel in a unit of time. In a digital channel baud rate corresponds to bit rate: the number of bits we can transfer per second between sender and receiver. This is typically measured in terms of kilobits per second (kbits/sec) or megabits per second (Mbits/sec). A communications channel in the kbits/sec range is frequently referred to as a narrowband channel, whereas a channel in the Mbits/sec range is typically called a broadband channel.

- *Synchronisation*. This refers to whether the messages between sender and receiver are synchronised. In an asynchronous channel the sender and receiver are not synchronised. Hence a message may be sent at any time. In a synchronous channel the receiver has to wait to receive the message from the sender before it can respond with its message.

- *Modulation*. Generally speaking there are two types of signal: digital and analogue. A digital signal has a small number of possible values – two for a binary digital signal. An analogue signal has values drawn from a continuous range. The value of the signal varies over this range.

- *Direction*. This refers to the data flow between sender and receiver. In a simplex channel the flow is in one direction only. In a duplex channel data may flow in both directions simultaneously. In a half duplex channel flow can occur in both directions but not at the same time.

Example

The human voice uses sound as its access channel. Human communication through voice is analogue, half duplex and synchronous.

The capacity of a communication channel will inherently determine the type of e-business activity that can occur. For instance, downloading a Web page of text with associated still images demands only a few kbits/sec of capacity, as does real-time audio and animated graphics. In comparison, the transmission of high-quality, seductive moving images demands as much as 2 Mbits/sec capacity.

Question   *Why is bandwidth important for business?*

7.6 ⊚ CONSTRUCTING AN ACCESS CHANNEL

The options for access channels include:

- *Twisted pair cable*. This consists of pairs of twisted wires, usually of copper, and offers a cheap communication solution but with low transmission rates.

- *Coaxial cable*. This consists of an inner conductor wire surrounded by insulation called the dielectric. The dielectric is in turn surrounded by a conductive shield usually made of a layer of foil or metal braiding. The conductive shield is in turn covered by a layer of non-conductive insulation known as the jacket. This medium is more expensive than twisted pair cable but is subject to fewer transmission problems.

- *Fibre-optic cable*. This consists of many thin strands of glass or plastic bound together in a sheath. Signals are transmitted using high-intensity light beams generated by lasers. Fibre-optic cable is capable of very high transmission rates in the range 2.5 Gbits/sec (billion bits per second).

- *Microwave transmission*. This is a form of 'wireless' medium. It involves high-frequency radio signals sent through the air. For it to work effectively microwave transmitting and receiving stations have to be in line of sight.

- *Communication satellites*. These are basically microwave stations placed in low Earth orbit. The satellite receives a signal from Earth and re-broadcasts it either to some other satellite or to an Earth-bound microwave station. Thus it can be used to transmit signals over large geographic areas.

- *Cellular transmission*. This medium involves a local area being divided up into a number of cells. As a cellular device such as a mobile phone moves between cells the cellular system passes the connection from one cell to another. The signals from the cells are transmitted to a receiver and integrated into the regular phone system. This is the fundamental technology underlying the recent growth in mobile communication.

- *Infrared transmission*. This involves sending signals through the air using light waves. It requires line of sight transmission and short distances to be effective.

Generally speaking particular access channels are heavily associated with particular access devices. Access channels are converging around digital standards. This means that at the basic level voice, video and data communications are becoming interchangeable.

Example	Most mobile devices use cellular radio networks or for short distances infrared transmission. Most local area networks are wired using coaxial cable of some form.

Question	*Why is the provision of an effective telecommunication infrastructure including all the options above important to national and international trade?*

7.7 COMMUNICATION NETWORKS AND COVERAGE

Access devices and channels are generally organised into arrangements called communication networks. A network is any set of computer systems joined by some communications technology. Networks can be described in terms of their coverage:

- *Local area network (LAN).* A type of network in which the various nodes are situated relatively close together, usually in one building or buildings in close proximity. The most common use of LANs is to link a group of personal computers together sharing devices such as printers.
- *Wide area network (WAN).* A type of network in which the nodes are geographically remote. WANs may consist of a mix of dedicated and non-dedicated communication lines as well as microwave and satellite communications.
- *Value added Network (VAN).* A type of network in which a third-party organisation sets up and maintains a network and sells on the use of the network to other organisations.

Example	Figure 7.4 illustrates the components of a typical LAN. The personal computers and the printer are linked to the cable forming the network by interface cards. These are

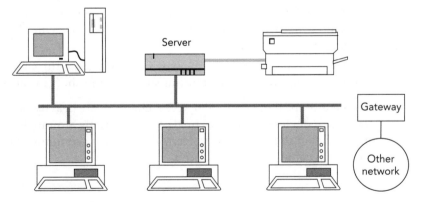

Figure 7.4 A local area network.

pieces of firmware (a combination of hardware and software), which specify the data transmission rate, the size of message packets, the addressing information attached to each packet and the network topology. The cabling is likely to consist of coaxial or fibre optic cable. The server is likely to be a powerful PC, which acts as a resource for programs and data used by other PCs in the network. The server will also run the network operating system that operates the server facilities and manages communication on the network. The gateway connects the LAN to other networks and consists of a processor that translates between the communication protocols of different networks.

7.8 ⊚ NETWORK TOPOLOGIES

A topology is a physical arrangement of objects. The topology of a data communications network refers to the arrangement of computing devices around the network. There are generally three main types of topology for a communication network (Figure 7.5):

- *Star network*. In this form of network devices are all connected to a central computer. The central computer acts as a form of traffic controller for all the other devices on the network. All data communication between devices must pass through the central computer, which periodically polls other devices on the network.

- *Ring network*. In this form of network hardware devices are connected in a loop. When a particular computer wants to send a message it grabs a special bit pattern known as a token which is recognisable as a carrier of a message by all devices on the network. Hence this type of network topology is also known as a token ring.

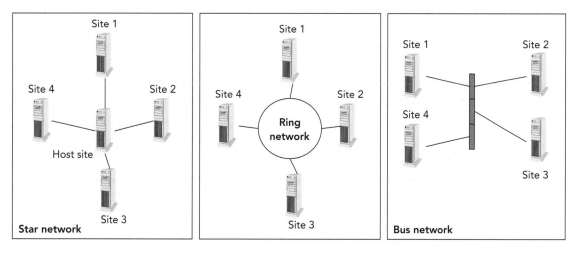

Figure 7.5 Network topologies.

The message along with the address of the destination computer is added to the token. Messages are transmitted from computer to computer flowing around a closed loop in a single direction. Since each computer operates independently, if one fails the network is able to continue uninterrupted.

● *Bus network*. In this form of network – also known as the Ethernet model – devices are connected to a main communication line called a bus along which messages are sent. Messages can be broadcast to the entire network through a single circuit and messages may travel in both directions along the bus. Each computer checks the message and accepts it if it is meant for itself.

Practical networks will be hybrids of these topologies. Parts of the network may, for instance, have a star topology while other parts utilise a ring topology. Generally speaking most LANs tend to route messages to destinations in terms of broadcasting messages across the entire network to all computers. Each site checks the messages and only receives the message if the destination address matches its own. Clearly for WANs this approach would be extremely inefficient. WANs therefore tend to use point-to-point protocols. This means that if a site wishes to send a message to all sites on the network it must send one for each destination computer.

Question
: *Sawhney and Parikh (2001) argue that intelligence and hence the value in networks is being pushed towards the core and periphery of such networks. What consequences might this have for business?*

7.9 CONNECTING ACCESS DEVICES TO FRONT-END ICT SYSTEMS

In this section we consider the major current alternatives for connecting the home or office personal computer to organisations' front-end ICT systems.

7.9.1 TELEPHONE NETWORK

The telephone network in the UK is a wide area telecommunications network. Conceptually the design of this network is that of a tapered star. There are a relatively small number of main exchanges connected by long-distance trunk cables. Main exchanges are connected to a much larger number of local exchanges. These local exchanges connect directly to customers in the home or the office. This is illustrated in Figure 7.6.

Because the connections between main exchanges and local exchanges are much fewer in number than the cables that connect local exchanges to customers, the cables are designed for high performance of data transmission. These cables are

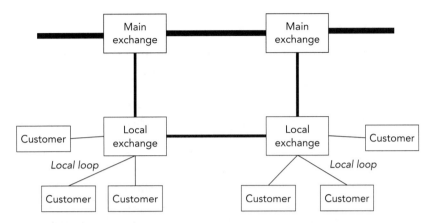

Figure 7.6 The telephone network.

typically of optical fibre and can handle transmission of many Mbits/sec. Such cabling can also be much more easily upgraded than the cabling to customers.

The performance of the telephone network as a medium for data transmission is therefore heavily reliant on the performance of the so-called local loop – the physical characteristics of the communication medium between local exchange and customer. The typical capacity of the local loop is in the kbits/sec range, a typical maximum being 56 kbits/sec.

7.9.2   DIGITAL TRANSMISSION

Telephone companies are interested in increasing the speed of data transmission over the telephony local loop. Digital services have been developed that allow the simultaneous transmission of multiple voice circuits into business premises. This allows the business to treat its local telephone network as subsumed under the integrated services digital network (ISDN). The data rates available can be as large as the business requires.

For smaller businesses and domestic users there is also what is known as basic rate ISDN. This offers customers a two-way digital communication over existing copper wires for usually twice the price of analogue telephony. The business gets two independent fully duplex 64 kbits/sec channels. These can be combined for certain applications such as downloading higher quality video at 128 kbits/sec.

ISDN is now under threat from the new technology of the digital subscriber loop (DSL). Asymmetric Digital Subscriber Loop (ADSL) was originally developed as a means of providing video-on-demand services over the conventional copper telephony infrastructure. It is now proposed as an effective means of providing fast, very high quality, access to the Internet. The technology relies on short transmission distances between a local exchange and a domestic customer or business (typically 10 km). Capacity between 2 Mbits/sec and 51 Mbits/sec is available using this technology. Some of the main advantages of ADSL are lower cost than ISDN and permanent connection to the Internet.

7.9.3 RADIO NETWORKS

Point to point networks using radio communication have been attempted but have not achieved a sizable penetration of the market. Radio networks are currently dominated by the use of cellular mobile phones. Such phones were originally analogue devices and were capable of carrying only voice traffic. However, in Europe the development of digital standards has enabled the development of integrated voice/data communications. Data can be transmitted by these means between 9.6 and 28 kbits/sec. With associated data compression capacity as much as 57.8 kbits/sec can be achieved.

Radio services will be extended in the short-term future with the introduction of General Packet Radio Service (GPRS). Under this system, the base radio station makes available eight radio channels for data transmission. Aggregated together these channels make available to customers a total capacity of approximately 114 kbits/sec. Any customer within range can send traffic to this channel (possibly in the form of text messages) in terms of data packets and receive data from this data channel. It thus behaves like a slow Ethernet and has the major advantage that since the data is transmitted in bursts the costs to the customer are cheaper than a conventional mobile telephone call.

Question *What are the problems typically associated with dial-up connections over the local loop to the Internet?*

7.10 CASE STUDY: E-VOTING

The human activity system underlying the current approach to electoral voting in the UK was described in Chapter 4. There are a number of problems with this current system, many of which are associated with the traditional way in which its associated information system is organised. These problems include:

- *Problems of registration.* Ensuring that a person is registered on one and only one register is a difficult process given social mobility. Ensuring that all persons are registered is even more difficult. It is estimated that as many as 9% of the UK population (3 million people) were not registered for the 2001 general election.
- *Access.* The requirement to visit a polling station during a set period frequently disadvantages certain groups such as the elderly, disabled and shift workers.
- *Time.* Currently voting only occurs on weekdays between 0700 and 2200. This can lead to queuing at peak periods at polling booths. Because of the manual nature of processing it can also take an inordinate time to process votes in a general election; 36 hours is typical.

- *Authentication.* Frequently people are allowed to vote without an appropriate polling card.
- *Error-prone.* Spoiled ballot papers are a regular occurrence – 0.26% of papers in the 2001 election were spoiled. Such errors are primarily due to lack of validation at point of entry. Errors are also frequent in the processing of votes leading to a need for recounts.
- *Cost-intensive.* The current electoral system involves employing many staff in polling booths and counting centres. The estimated cost of the 1997 general election was £52 million, which represents £1.19 for each elector. Such costs mean that polling of citizen opinion is not normally conducted outside of periodic elections.

For such reasons the UK government has considered introducing various forms of e-voting. Figure 7.7 illustrates the fundamental processes of such an e-voting system. Two such processes fall within the remit of various forms of remote access device: authentication and the act of voting itself. The other processes are likely to run on one or more voting servers. Particular access devices presuppose particular communication channels. Such access mechanisms include:

- Specialised electronic voting machines placed within polling booths. Communication with back-end ICT systems may be through the physical transfer of

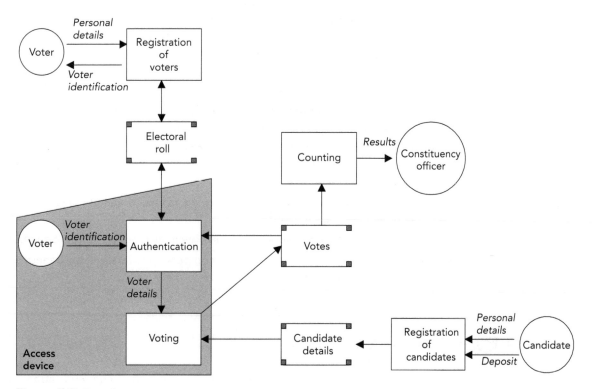

Figure 7.7 E-voting.

storage media such as removable disks or CD-ROMs. It may also occur through transmission across public or private WANs.

- Voting kiosks placed within public spaces such as libraries and supermarkets. Again, transfer of data may occur through physical transfer or over WANs.
- Personal computers based in the home. Here the communication channel is likely to involve the use of modems and the public telephony network.
- Interactive Digital Television. Here the communication will involve digital broadcasting and a telephony up-channel.
- Mobile devices such as WAP-enabled mobile phones. Here the communication channel is likely to be the cellular radio network.
- Commercial access devices such as lottery machines and Automatic Teller Machines (ATMs). These devices will be hooked up to dedicated private Wide Area Networks.

7.11 SUMMARY

- An organisation's services or products may be accessed in a number of different ways. Each way we might describe as a mode or mechanism of access.
- Any mode or mechanism for access consists of an access device and associated access channel. The access device is used to formulate, transmit, receive and display messages. The access channel is used to carry the message between customers, suppliers, partners and employees and the organisation's ICT systems.
- Stakeholder access devices come in many forms, including telephones, interactive digital television, personal computers and mobile devices.
- Major ways of connecting access devices to front-end ICT systems access include telephone networks, digital transmission and radio networks.
- Access channels include twisted pair cable, coaxial cable, fibre-optic cable, micro-wave transmission, infrared transmission, communication satellites and cellular transmission.
- Communication networks tend to get organised as local area networks, wide area networks or value-added networks.
- The topology of a network generally follows three main models: star, ring and bus.
- The computer systems in a contemporary computer network will be generally be organised into two types: clients and servers.

7.12 ACTIVITIES

(i) In terms of traditional access modes such as face-to-face communication, what represents the access device and channel?

(ii) In terms of some remote access mechanism investigate the key costs for the stakeholder of maintaining such an access mechanism.

(iii) Does a company known to you use any mobile devices to access systems? What types of system are accessed through such devices?

(iv) Attempt to determine the current penetration of iDTV into the nation's homes.

(v) In terms of some access channel known to you, investigate the precise media used for data transmission.

(vi) Investigate the communication networks used by an organisation known to you and determine whether there are elements of LANs, WANs and VANs in their communication infrastructure.

7.13 REFERENCES

Dreyfus, H. L. (2001). *On the Internet*. London, Routledge.

IDEA (2002). *Local E-government Now: a Worldwide View*. Improvement and Development Agency/Society of Information Technology Management.

Norris, M. and N. West (2001). *eBusiness Essentials*. Chichester, BT/John Wiley.

Sawhney, M. and D. Parikh (2001). Where value lies in a networked world. *Harvard Business Review*, **79**(1), 79–86.

Whyte, W. S. (2001). *Enabling E-business: Integrating Technologies, Architectures and Applications*. Chichester, John Wiley.

8

ELECTRONIC DELIVERY OF GOODS AND SERVICES

Dyfal donc a dyrr y garreg

(A gentle tapping breaks the stone)

Welsh aphorism

Be silent as to services you have rendered, but speak of favours you have received.

Seneca (5 BC–AD 65)

LEARNING OUTCOMES

After reading this chapter, you will be able to:

- Describe the differences between tangible and intangible goods
- Describe the differences between tangible and intangible services
- Define the concept of a transaction
- Outline some of the major transaction flows between organisations
- Discuss some of the key technologies underlying electronic transaction flow

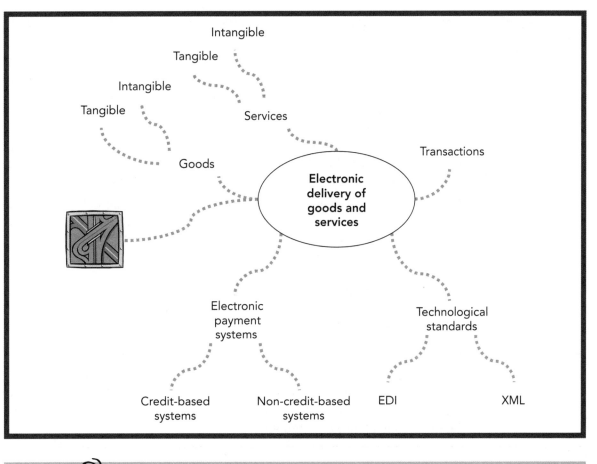

In Chapter 7 we considered the access devices and channels of the technical infrastructure for e-business. In this chapter we consider the nature of the 'stuff' that flows between access devices and ICT systems – the electronic delivery of goods and services and accompanying transactional data. One of the key issues we wish to address is what sort of goods and services are amenable to electronic delivery. Also, we need to know what key standards are in place to enable the effective flow of transactional data both within and between organisations.

We begin with a discussion of the differences between tangible and intangible goods and between tangible and intangible services. The flow of goods and services in a market is normally matched with associated transaction flows. We define the concept of a transaction and outline some of the major transaction flows between organisations. This leads us to discuss some of the key technologies underlying electronic transaction flow, such as EDI and XML. We conclude with an examination of one of the most critical forms of transaction flow for commercial organisations – monetary flows – and consider some of the technology underlying electronic payment systems.

8.2 GOODS AND SERVICES

As we defined it in Chapter 7, electronic delivery refers to remote access to goods and services. A consideration of the different types of goods and services contributes to a greater understanding of the relevance of electronic delivery to business. Also the design and use of certain access mechanisms will depend on the type of product or service being accessed.

We may distinguish between two types of goods: physical or tangible goods and non-physical or intangible goods, corresponding to the idea of physical and non-physical system flows introduced in Chapter 2 (Anthony, 1988).

- *Tangible goods* have a physical form and hence cannot be delivered to the customer electronically. Nevertheless, the customer may be able to inspect images of the product, order the product and pay for the product using forms of electronic service delivery.

- *Intangible goods* may be fundamentally represented as data. They are hence amenable to digitisation (sometimes called digital goods) and thus may be delivered to the customer electronically. The customer may also, of course, inspect, order and pay for such intangible goods electronically.

Examples

Examples of tangible goods are mechanical goods such as automobiles, electrical goods such as DVD players, and perishable goods such as foodstuffs. Examples of intangible goods are music, text (as in books, magazines and academic papers) and images such as in prints or photographs.

Digital convergence is the capture, storage and dissemination of media of various types in a digital format. Traditional forms of content provision such as radio and television are now all moving over to digital transmission. This increases the number of intangible goods available for transmission over standard access channels. It also allows a convergence with various media stored in ICT systems.

Example

The British Broadcasting Corporation (BBC) has initiated a considerable reinvestment of its strategy into offering its material as digital media. Its conventional television and radio programmes are now offered digitally as well as via a number of specialist channels, particularly its 24-hour news channel. Each conventional channel is supported by a parallel Internet presence.

The inspection of goods, the ordering of such goods and the delivery of goods are information-based services that support the sale of tangible and intangible products. However, certain services are tangible in nature and hence not amenable to electronic service delivery. Other services are intangible by nature and thus primarily constitute information services. They are hence open to delivery through electronic channels.

Examples   Tangible services include health treatments such as operations and beauty treatments such as hairdressing. Intangible services include legal advice, news reports and monetary transfers.

Question   *The degree of tangible and intangible goods and services in a market sector will determine the likely impact of electronic delivery. What do you feel is the likely impact in a sector such as financial services?*

Hiu and Chau (2002) propose a framework for intangible goods and services (they refer to them as digital products) based on two dimensions: product category and product characteristics. In this framework they distinguish three major categories of digital product:

- Tools and utilities that assist users in accomplishing specific goals and tasks.
- Content-based products where the value lies in their information content.
- Online services that provide access to useful resources.

Example   Examples of tools and utilities include Adobe Acrobat and RealPlayer. Examples of content-based products include online newspapers and journals such as the *Wall Street Journal* (http://www.wsj.com/), research reports or databases and online entertainment such as music. Examples of online services are Internet telephony or consultant search services.

Such product types may be distinguished in terms of three product characteristics:

- *Delivery mode.* This refers to the delivery mechanism between buyers and sellers. Generally the delivery mode is either by one-time download or interactively.
- *Granularity.* This refers to the divisibility of the digital product. Generally speaking the more highly divisible the product the more opportunity is provided to the seller for vertical differentiation.
- *Trialability.* This refers to the ability to preview the whole or part of the product before purchase.

The relationship between product category and product characteristics is presented in the table below:

	Tools and utilities	Content-based products	Online services
Delivery mode	Download	Download	Interactive
Granularity	Low	High	Medium
Trialability	High	Low	Medium

Question

Media companies such as the BBC are making inroads into digital products and services. To what extent is the framework proposed by Hiu and Chau useful in understanding business strategy in this market sector?

8.3 TRANSACTIONS

Transactions record events within a human activity system. They are hence critical to recording a history of the behaviour of a human activity system – past, current and future activity. Transactions typically write data to the data stores of an information system and such data is important to performance measurement within organizations.

Example

A customer order is a crucial transaction for most commercial organizations. An order will record data in the company's order processing system. It will establish facts such as who made the order, when and for what goods or services. Such data is critical to measuring the sales performance of the company.

Commerce involves the trade in goods and services (Chapter 17). Accompanying such trade there will be a two-way flow of transactions. In any regular trading relationship four main packages of transaction flow between buyer and seller (Figure 8.1):

- The buyer sends an order to the seller.
- The seller sends the goods and an accompanying delivery note at some later time to the buyer.
- The seller follows up the delivery note with an invoice that is sent to the buyer.
- The buyer makes payment against the invoice to the seller and sends a payment advice to the seller.

Order, delivery note, invoice, payment and payment advice are all sets of transactions flowing between buyer and seller.

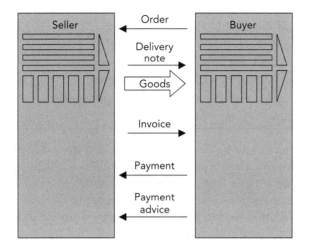

Figure 8.1 Major transactions between buyer and seller.

Example	In a supermarket chain an order might be made for a quantity of potatoes from some agricultural producer. The delivery note would detail the actual number of sacks of potatoes delivered to the distribution warehouse of the supermarket chain.
Question	*To what extent may an analysis of transactions impacting upon an organisation provide it with a better understanding of value chain issues?*

8.4 ⊚ DATA AND DOCUMENT FORMATS

To enable the effective flow of transactions between organisations certain standards have to be defined for the format and the transmission of electronic messages. For any transactional flow along electronic channels three conditions must be satisfied:

- The electronic message comprising the transaction must have a defined format.
- The receiver and sender of the message must agree the format of the message.
- The message must be able to be sent and read by electronic devices.

Electronic messages are forms of data transmission. Hence, for effective transfer of such data between sending and receiving systems some format must be declared for data. In general any data format can be considered as a hierarchy of data items, data elements and data structures:

- A data item is the lowest level of data format. Much of the meaning of a given data item is embodied in its data type. A data type declares the range of valid operations that are possible on a data item.
- A data element is a logical collection of data items.
- A data structure is a logical collection of data elements.

Example

A typical data structure to be found in a database system (Chapter 11) is a table. A table is made up of a number of rows and columns. Rows constitute the data elements and columns the data items. Each data item is defined in terms of a standard data type such as integer or character. Hence defining a data item such as the column *age* to be of an *integer* data type means that it is valid to add, subtract and multiply the datum assigned to this particular data item.

Historically, a standard for transactional flow has been based in something known as Electronic Data Interchange (EDI). More recently, standards have been defined using a Web-based technology known as eXtensible Markup Language (XML). Both EDI and XML are attempts to define standard ways of defining data formats for the transmission of electronic messages between organisations.

Question

To what extent do you think common data formats influence trading relationships between companies?

8.5 ◉ ELECTRONIC DATA INTERCHANGE (EDI)

Electronic Data Interchange (EDI) provides a collection of standard message formats and an element dictionary for businesses to exchange data through an electronic messaging service (Norris and West, 2001). EDI mainly supports the execution and settlement phases of a commercial transaction (Chapter 17).

Effectively, EDI allows documentation such as orders, delivery notes, invoices and payment advices that have traditionally constituted paper documents to be coded up as EDI messages. Each message would be made up of a number of data segments and each data segment is made up of a tag and a number of data elements. The tag identifies the data segment and the data elements include the codes and values required in the message.

Example	In a purchase order we might have a data element for detailing shipment dates and times. The code used for this data element might be DTM, short for Date/Time reference.

EDI has been in existence for over twenty years and has been used by major companies such as Ford to link suppliers tightly into their business processes. EDI typically run over VANs. There are in fact four main standards for EDI:

- *UN/EDIFACT*. This is the main standard supported by the UN. EDIFACT stands for EDI for Administration, Commerce and Industry and is the only EDI standard that is truly accepted worldwide.
- *ANSI X12*. This is an EDI standard developed by the American National Standards Institute (ANSI) separately from Europe. It is commonly used in the USA and Canada, and to a lesser degree in Australia.
- *TRADACOMS*. This is an EDI standard developed by the Article Numbering Association in 1982 for the UK retail industry. It is currently the most widely used standard in the UK in this market sector.
- *ODETTE*. An EDI standard developed in the UK for use in the motor industry for supporting just-in-time manufacturing.

Each standards body publishes definitions of the documents that may be exchanged electronically. Due to the vast number of segments associated with each standard, most industries have appointed bodies that generate subsets of their chosen EDI standard. These standard subsets adhere to the parent standard but remove conditional segments within each message that are not required by a particular industry.

Example	This subsetting is particularly common for EDIFACT because this standard was originally created to enable trading for all types of EDI scenario. For example, EDIFICE is an EDIFACT subset created for the computing, electronics and telecommunications industry.

The main benefits of EDI arise from its ability to streamline key business processes, particularly those associated with the management of external stakeholders (Mukhodadhyay, 1993). For instance, EDI can be used to introduce more rapid fulfilment of purchase orders (Chapter 19). Reductions in placing and receiving orders and fewer errors in the entry and transmission of purchase order data are likely to reduce staff time devoted to this activity and improve other processes such as inventory control.

The main problems with EDI are that standardisation has never been sufficiently broad and technical implementation has proven expensive. For this reason organisations are looking to the next generation of business documentation standards based on Internet technology. Standards are developing in Internet EDI that enable EDI to be implemented at lower cost through VPNs (Chapter 13) or over the public Internet.

Example

Flymo, the largest lawnmower manufacturer in the UK, has used EDI for a number of years to link to its largest retailers such as DIY superstores. The company has recently introduced Internet EDI to enable its smaller retailers to communicate effectively with the company.

Question

Why are data standards such as EDI important for modern business and what implications do multiple competing standards have?

8.6 STANDARD GENERALIZED MARKUP LANGUAGE (SGML)

Electronic documents (such as invoices and delivery notes) are made up of two forms of data, the first representing content and the second data that describes to ICT applications how the document is to be processed. Typical processing involves formatting the document on such media as the printed page and the PC screen. In terms of electronic documents content normally comprises text and graphics. Process information is normally represented by a set of embedded tags that indicate how the content is to be presented. This process of tagging text with extra information is known as *marking up*, and the set of tags for doing this a *markup language*. In the 1960s work began on developing a generalised markup language for describing the formatting of electronic documents. This work became established in a standard known as the Standard Generalized Markup Language or SGML.

SGML in fact constitutes a meta-language – a language for defining other languages. Hence SGML can be used to define a large set of markup languages. Tim Berners-Lee used SGML to define a specific language for hypertext documents known as hypertext markup language (HTML). HTML (Chapter 10) is a standard for marking up or tagging documents that can be published on the Web, and can be made up of text, graphics, images, audio clips and video clips. Web documents also include links to other documents stored on either the local HTML server or remote HTML servers and are frequently referred to as 'pages' because of their historical association with printed documents.

Example

Below we include a very simple document expressed in HTML

```
<HTML>
<TITLE>E-Business</TITLE>
<H1>E-Business</H1>
<H2>Paul Beynon-Davies</H2>
</HTML>
```

The text between angle brackets constitutes tags. Each piece of text is preceded by a start tag and succeeded by an end tag. A forward slash precedes an end tag. The HTML tags indicate the start and end of the document. The tag TITLE provides a name for the page. The tags H1 and H2 indicate that first- and second-level headings should be displayed respectively.

8.7 ⊚ EXTENSIBLE MARKUP LANGUAGE (XML)

One of the main advantages of HTML is its simplicity. This enables it to be used effectively by a wide user community. However, this simplicity is also one of its disadvantages. Sophisticated users want to define their own tags particularly for functionality involved with the exchange of data. The World Wide Web Consortium developed eXtensible Markup Language (XML) in 1998 (W3C, 2000). The key feature of XML is that it is extensible, which means that new markup tags can be created by users for the exchange of data.

Like HTML, XML is another restricted descendant of SGML. Whereas HTML is used to define how the data in a document is to be displayed, XML can be used to define the content of a document. XML can be used to specify standard templates for business documents such as invoices, shipping notes and fund transfers. Hence, XML has been seen as a major way in which EDI may be replaced for electronic document transmission between organisations.

8.7.1 OVERVIEW OF XML

An XML document consists of a set of elements and attributes.

Elements or tags are the most common form of markup. The first element in an XML document must be a root element. The document must have only one root element, but this element may contain a number of other elements.

Example

Suppose your company is a coffee wholesaler. You might wish to create XML documents for the exchange of shipping information to your customers. An appropriate root element might therefore be the tag <PRODUCTDETAILSLIST>.

An element begins with a start tag and ends with an end tag.

Example

The start tag in our document for the root element would be `<ProductDetailsList>`. The corresponding end tag would be `</ProductDetailsList>`. Note that tags are case-sensitive in XML. Hence `<PRODUCTDETAILSLIST>` is a different tag from `<ProductDetailsList>`.

Elements can be empty, in which case they can be abbreviated to `<EmptyElement/>`. Elements must be properly nested as subelements within a superior element.

Example

The following XML element might be used to define a particular coffee product.

```
<ProductDetails ID='1234'>
    <ItemName>Kenya Special</ItemName>
    <CountryOfOrigin>Kenya Special</CountryOfOrigin>
    <WholeSaleCost>20.00</WholeSaleCost>
    <Stock>4000</Stock>
</ProductDetails>
```

Here we have a `ProductDetails` element with a number of subelements. Subelements such as `ItemName`, `CountryOfOrigin`, `WholeSaleCost` and `Stock` are properly nested within `ProductDetails`.

In traditional database terms this would constitute a row in a products table (Chapter 11). This row is made up of a number of columns including an identifier for the product, the name of the item, the country of origin of the product, the cost of the product and the number of product items in stock.

Attributes are Name–Value pairs that contain descriptive information about an element. The attribute is placed inside the start tag for the element and consists of an attribute name, an equality '=' sign and the value for the attribute placed within quotes.

Example

In our coffee producer example the tag `<ProductDetails ID='1234'>` contains the attribute ID and the value '1234'.

Within XML the ordering of elements is significant. However, the ordering of attributes is not significant.

Example The two orders for the product information below would be regarded as different elements:

```
<ProductDetails ID='1234'>
    <ItemName>Kenya Special</ItemName>
    <CountryOfOrigin>Kenya Special</CountryOfOrigin>
    <WholeSaleCost>20.00</WholeSaleCost>
    <Stock>4000</Stock>
</ProductDetails>

<ProductDetails ID='1234'>
    <ItemName>Kenya Special</ItemName>
    <WholeSaleCost>20.00</WholeSaleCost>
    <Stock>4000</Stock>
    <CountryOfOrigin>Kenya Special</CountryOfOrigin>
</ProductDetails>
```

However, we might have represented this information as attributes of the element Product.

```
<Product ID="1234" ItemName="Kenya Special" CountryOfOrigin="Kenya" Stock = "400" WholeSaleCost="20.00"/>
```

In this case the following element is regarded as being identical:

```
<Product ID="1234" ItemName="Kenya Special" WholeSaleCost="20.00" Stock = "400" CountryOfOrigin="Kenya"/>
```

Two other mechanisms are important for an XML document:

- A *document type definition (DTD)*. This defines the valid syntax for an XML document. It lists the names of all elements, which elements can appear in combination and what attributes are available for each type of element.
- An *extensible style sheet (XSL)*. A style sheet is a definition that is used by a browser for the rendering of a document. XSL allows the developer to specify the appropriate rendering for a given XML document.

8.9 ELECTRONIC PAYMENT SYSTEMS

Payments are a special form of transactional data. Any payment system is effectively a mechanism for recording exchanges of value.

In earlier times goods and services were exchanged using the principle of barter. In other words, in a barter system goods themselves are exchanged or goods are exchanged for services. A major characteristic of this form of economic exchange is that the value of an item or a service varies with the negotiated basis of the exchange.

A leap forward occurred with the invention of tokens that held their own intrinsic value. Such tokens are generally referred to as money. This meant that tokens could be exchanged in lieu of goods and services. Money performs four functions. It is:

- A medium of exchange.
- A means of accounting for amounts owed by actors in an economic exchange.
- A standard of deferred payment.
- A defined store of value.

Money has traditionally taken a tangible, physical form, first in terms of coinage and second in terms of banknotes. In the electronic world money assumes an intangible form. Money is essentially data held in the information systems of financial institutions. Money is transferred between such systems electronically and accompanies the exchange of goods and services.

E-commerce relies on the concept of an electronic market (e-market) (Bakos, 1998). By an e-market we mean one in which economic exchanges are conducted between businesses using ICT. In an e-market, electronic transactions between buyers and sellers enable the efficient and effective flow of goods and services through internal, supply and customer chains (Malone *et al.*, 1989).

The essential features of an e-market are illustrated in Figure 8.2. The e-market is the domain in which buying companies and selling companies meet. The exchange of goods and services is enabled through electronic transactions between both buyer and seller and the financial institutions of each. The market handles all

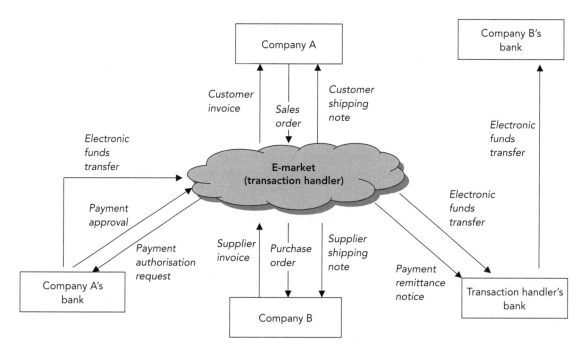

Figure 8.2 Electronic markets.

the transactions between companies, including the transfer of money between banks. Banks are effectively intermediaries in any trading relationship in the e-market.

Electronic funds transfer (EFT) and electronic funds transfer at the point of sale (EFTPOS) are electronic mechanisms for the monetary flows accompanying the exchange of goods and services. EFT uses ICT to supply and transfer money between financial repositories (such as banks or bank accounts). EFTPOS is a form of EFT where the purchaser is physically at the point of sale, such as at a super-market checkout.

Question	*Why are financial information systems critically important to the performance of business organisations?*

8.10 🌀 FORMS OF ELECTRONIC PAYMENT SYSTEM

Electronic markets are reliant on efficient and effective e-payment systems. Such systems effectively constitute information systems for monetary exchange.

The forms of electronic payment system tend to vary between forms of e-commerce (Chapter 17). In terms of B2C and C2C e-commerce (Part 4), electronic payment systems can be divided into two types: credit-based systems and non-credit-based systems.

8.10.1 NON-CREDIT-BASED SYSTEMS

Most non-credit-based systems are designed to encourage the exchange of micropayments – small amounts of money used for the purchase of goods such as access to online newspapers. Such non-credit-based systems use a pre-paying principle. A purchaser must have a ready supply of funds built up in some mechanism that she can use to buy goods and services. Such funds are effectively electronic tokens and can be purchased using traditional payment mechanisms such as credit cards or funds transfer from a personal bank account.

Example   Examples of non-credit-based systems include:

- *Digital or electronic cash.* Companies have attempted to establish payment systems that emulate the anonymity of traditional cash payment (Clemons *et al.*, 1996). These systems have suffered from poor take-up.

- *Micro-transactions or micropayments.* Such systems permit the transfer of small amounts of money between the accounts of buyers and sellers. Because the amounts transferred are small, levels of electronic security can be less. Ecoin (http://www.ecoin.net/) is one such micropayment system.

- *Debit cards*. Cards issued in association with conventional bank accounts can be used for cash e-commerce.

- *Smartcards*. These are physical cards with embedded chips that allow the storage of significant amounts of data. Because such cards demand the use of card readers sited at stores or connected to PCs in the home the use of smartcards for electronic cash has been restricted currently to some major experiments. One of the most notable was the trial of the Mondex card in the city of Swindon in the UK.

8.10.2 CREDIT-BASED SYSTEMS

Credit-based systems are modelled on conventional payment mechanisms, such as the cheque and credit card, except that signatures are digital rather than physical. The most popular method of paying for goods and services in B2C e-commerce is currently the credit card. Secure payment systems are required for this (Chapter 13).

In terms of traditional forms of B2B e-commerce no standard payment mechanisms exist. This is because businesses tend to engage in repeat commerce in which purchases are repeat orders, frequently complex (having many items), and frequently highly specialised or bespoke. Also, the value of payments is likely to be significantly larger than for B2C transactions and hence associated levels of security must be higher.

8.11 BUSINESS IMPLICATIONS OF ELECTRONIC DELIVERY OF GOODS AND SERVICES

The e-business as a system is critically reliant on an effective technical infrastructure. Traditionally the importance of this technical infrastructure lies in the role it plays in capturing data about the performance of the business. Much of such data is transactional in nature. Hence to be a viable system – that is, to survive in its environment – the typical business need to have data which tells it how many orders it has received, how many products it has produced and how many finished goods it has despatched.

ICT has enabled organisations to capture, store and disseminate transactional data efficiently (Bakos, 1997). However, it has also enabled the electronic delivery of services and goods. The convergence of many intangible goods and services around digital standards has meant that companies may not only use the technical infrastructure as a control mechanism for the business, but may also use it as their major delivery mechanism. Hence, the electronic delivery of goods and services has key potential for transforming particular market sectors.

8.12 CASE STUDY: MP3

One of the most significant forms of intangible good to benefit from digitisation is music. The digitisation of music is most readily associated with a file format known as MP3. Developed by the Fraunhofer Institute in Germany in 1992, MP3 stands for Motion Picture Experts Group-1 Level 3. This format employs an algorithm to compress a music file, achieving a significant reduction of data while retaining near CD-quality sound. This means that a three-minute song, which would normally require 32 Mbyte of disk space, can be compressed to 3 Mbyte without significant reduction in sound quality. Hence, using a standard 56K modem, the song can be transmitted over the Internet in a matter of a few minutes rather than the two hours required if the file had not been compressed.

MP3 is not the only compression format available for digital music, but it has become something of a *de facto* standard. Its success is frequently attributed to the fact that it is freely available and costs users nothing. The algorithm also employs an extremely efficient method of data compression.

MP3 technology enables individuals to download and upload music to and from servers over the Internet efficiently and effectively (see the Napster case study in Chapter 14). Individuals can 'rip' (duplicate) MP3 files from CDs easily and can exchange such files using technology such as e-mail or more sophisticated peer-to-peer applications (see the Napster case study). Hence it is relatively easy for users to build virtual libraries of music and listen to it either from their hard drives on their PC or from a growing range of portable MP3 players.

8.13 SUMMARY

- We may distinguish between two types of goods: physical or tangible goods and non-physical or intangible goods.
- We may also distinguish between two types of services: physical or tangible services and non-physical or intangible services.
- Commerce involves the trade in goods and services. Accompanying such trade there will be a two-way flow of transactions.
- To enable the effective flow of transactions between organisations certain standards have to be defined for the format and the transmission of electronic messages.
- In general any data format can be considered as a hierarchy of data items, data elements and data structures.
- Both EDI and XML are attempts to define standard ways of defining formats for electronic messages.

- E-commerce relies on the concept of an electronic market (e-market).
- E-markets rely on effective electronic payment systems that come in two forms: credit-based systems and non-credit-based systems.

8.14 ◉ ACTIVITIES

(i) E-medicine is a developing area of medical practice and involves the remote treatment of patients using ICT. Experiments have even been undertaken in performing surgical operations using robotic devices controlled across communication networks. How would you class this form of service – tangible or intangible?

(ii) Find an example of the use of EDI in a key industrial sector.

(iii) Find an example of the use of XML in a key industrial sector.

(iv) Try to determine the volume of monetary transactions occurring within a nation such as the UK in any one day.

(v) Investigate the degree to which media such as television will be delivered over the Internet in the next decade.

(vi) Investigate the uptake of non-credit-based payment systems in an area of interest to you.

8.15 ◉ REFERENCES

Anthony, R. A. (1988). *The Management Control Function*. Boston, MA, Harvard Business School Press.

Bakos, J. Y. (1997). Reducing buyer search costs – implications for electronic marketplaces. *Management Science*, **43**(12), 1676–1692.

Bakos, J. Y. (1998). The emerging role of electronic marketplaces on the Internet. *Communications of the ACM*, **41**(8), 35–42.

Clemons, E. K., Croson, D. C. and Weber, B. W. (1996). Reengineering money: the Mondex stored value card and beyond. *International Journal of Electronic Commerce*, **1**(2), 5–31.

Hiu, K. L. and Chau, P. Y. K. (2002). Classifying digital products. *Communications of the ACM*, **45**(6), 73–79.

Malone, T. W., Benjamin, R. I. and Yates, J. (1989). The logic of electronic marketplaces. *Harvard Business Review*, **67**(3), 166.

Mukhodadhyay, T. (1993). Assessing the economic impacts of electronic data interchange technology. *Strategic and Economic Impacts of Information Technology Investment* (eds. R. Banker, R. J. Kauffman and M. A. Mahmood). Middletown, PA, Idea Publishing, pp. 241–264.

Norris, M. and N. West (2001). *eBusiness Essentials*. Chichester, BT/John Wiley.

W3C (2000). *XML 1.0 2nd Edition*. World-Wide-Web Consortium.

THE INTERNET

It shouldn't be too much of a surprise that the Internet has evolved into a force strong enough to reflect the greatest hopes and fears of those who use it. After all, it was designed to withstand nuclear war, not just the puny huffs and puffs of politicians and religious fanatics.

Denise Caruso (digital commerce columnist, *New York Times*)

My favorite thing about the Internet is that you get to go into the private world of real creeps without having to smell them.

Penn Jillette

LEARNING OUTCOMES

After reading this chapter, you will be able to:

- Relate some of the history of the Internet
- Describe some of the key technological infrastructure of the Internet
- Distinguish between the Internet, an Intranet and an Extranet

---

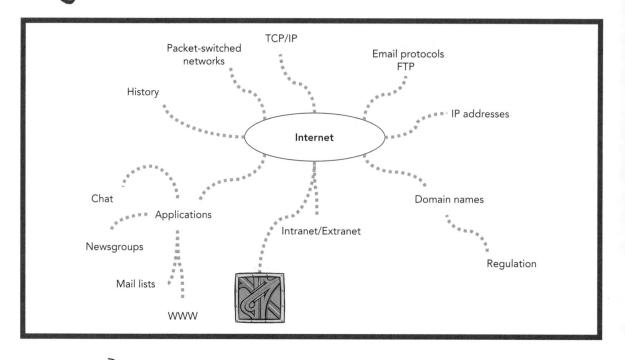

Packet-switched
networks
TCP/IP
Email protocols
FTP
History
IP addresses
Internet
Chat
Applications
Domain names
Newsgroups
Intranet/Extranet
Mail lists
Regulation
WWW

9.1 INTRODUCTION

The most prevalent current example of the application of communications technology is the Internet (Whiteley, 2000). The Internet – short for inter-network – began as a Wide Area Network in the USA funded by its Department of Defense to link scientists and researchers around the world (see below). It was initially designed primarily as a medium to exchange research data, but it has now become an essential part of the technological infrastructure of modern organisations in both the public and private sectors. Some have even claimed it to be the fundamental basis of a global information society (Currie, 2000).

Currently the Internet is a set of interconnected computer networks distributed around the globe. The Internet can be considered on a number of levels. The base infrastructure of the Internet is composed of packet-switched networks and a series of communication protocols. On this layer runs a series of applications such as electronic mail (e-mail) and more recently the World Wide Web (Chapter 10).

9.2 HISTORY OF THE INTERNET

In August 1962 J. C. R. Licklider (the first head of the computer research programme at DARPA – the Defence Advanced Research Projects Agency in the USA) wrote a series of memos discussing his concept of a 'Galactic Network'. This constituted a global interconnected set of computers through which any person from any site in the network could quickly access data and programs.

Lawrence G. Roberts at ARPA (DARPA changed its name to ARPA and back again a number of times) took up the idea and published his initial plan for the ARPANET in 1967. This exploited the development of appropriate routing hardware using the proposed theory of packet-switching networks (see below). In 1969 the ARPANET was created by linking four university computers together in the USA.

In October 1972 the first large demonstration of the ARPANET was made by Bob Kahn at an academic conference to the public. Also in 1972 the idea of electronic mail (e-mail) was introduced for the first time as a viable application running on this network.

The original ARPANET grew into the Internet, based around the idea that multiple independent networks of differing architectures could be made to work together through an open network architecture. Critical to this idea was the formulation of a meta-level 'Internetworking Architecture' that specified the interfaces required between networks. Also critical to the development of the Internet was Bob Kahn's development of a protocol that enabled end-to-end network communication in the face of environmental problems causing transmission error. The robustness and survivability of the network was critical to its design, including the capability to withstand losses of large portions of the underlying networks. The eventual protocol, which became known as TCP/IP (see below), enabled effective error control across an open network architecture.

Four principles were critical to Kahn's thinking:

- That each distinct network must remain autonomous and that no internal changes should be required to enable any such network to connect to the Internet.

- That communications would be on a best effort basis. If a data packet did not make it to the final destination, it would shortly be retransmitted from the source.

- That 'black boxes' would be used to connect the networks. These would later be called gateways and routers. There would be no information retained by the black boxes about the individual flows of packets passing through them, thereby keeping them simple and avoiding complicated adaptation and recovery from various failure modes.

- There would be no global control of the Internet at the operations level.

Part of the motivation for the development of ARPANET and TCP/IP was to enable the sharing of computer resources across a network. These were referred to as time-sharing computers. When desktop computers first appeared, it was thought by some that TCP was too big and complex to run on a personal computer. A research group at MIT set out to show that a compact and simple implementation of TCP was possible. They produced an implementation, first for the Xerox Alto (the early personal workstation developed at Xerox PARC) and then for the IBM PC.

Widespread development of local area networks (LANS), PCs and workstations in the 1980s allowed the Internet to flourish. Ethernet technology, developed by Bob Metcalfe at Xerox PARC in 1973, is now probably the dominant network technology in the Internet. PCs and workstations are the dominant forms of computer on the Internet.

A major shift occurred as a result of the increase in scale of the Internet and its associated management issues. To make it easy for people to use the network, host computers were assigned names, so that it was not necessary to remember the numeric addresses or so-called IP addresses. Originally, there were a fairly limited number of hosts, so it was feasible to maintain a single table of all the hosts and their associated names and addresses. With the invention of LANs the shift to having a large number of independently managed networks meant that having a single table of hosts was no longer feasible. Hence the Domain Name System (DNS) was invented by Paul Mockapetris. The DNS permitted a scalable distributed mechanism for resolving hierarchical host names (e.g. www.acm.org) into an Internet address (see below).

Thus, by 1985, the Internet was already well established as a technology supporting a broad community of researchers and developers, and was beginning to be used by other communities for daily computer communications. Electronic mail was being used broadly across several communities, often with different systems, but interconnection between different mail systems was demonstrating the utility of broad-based electronic communications between people. In 1984 the British JANET and in the following year the US NSFNET programmes explicitly announced their intention to serve the entire higher education community, regardless of discipline. This was a major stimulus to the idea of inter-networking.

On 24 October 1995, the Federal Networking Council (FNC) unanimously passed a resolution defining the term Internet. This definition, given below, was developed in consultation with members of the Internet and intellectual property rights communities.

> RESOLUTION: The Federal Networking Council (FNC) agrees that the following language reflects our definition of the term "Internet". "Internet" refers to the global information system that – (i) is logically linked together by a globally unique address space based on the Internet Protocol (IP) or its subsequent extensions/follow-ons; (ii) is able to support communications using the Transmission Control Protocol/Internet Protocol (TCP/IP) suite or its subsequent extensions/follow-ons, and/or other IP-compatible protocols; and (iii) provides, uses or makes accessible, either publicly or privately, high level services layered on the communications and related infrastructure described herein.

Example

From initially connecting a handful of nodes on the ARPANET the Internet has grown astronomically. Some estimates for this growth are included below:

- 1997 – 100 million users worldwide

- 1998 – 200 million users worldwide

- 2001 – 390 million users worldwide

- 2003 – 640 million users worldwide

Questions   *Do you think we would have the Internet today without defence spending? In what respect do you feel the Internet is creating a global information society?*

9.3 ⊚ TECHNICAL INFRASTRUCTURE

The section on the history of the Internet has raised a number of technical concepts that we now consider in more detail. The technical infrastructure of the Internet consists of a number of components. These include:

- Packet-switched networks
- TCP/IP
- E-mail protocols, FTP and HTTP
- IP addresses
- Uniform Resource Locators (URLs)
- Domain names

9.4 ⊚ PACKET-SWITCHED NETWORKS

The early computer networks were modelled on the local and long-distance telephone networks that dated back to the early 1950s. Computer networks during the period tended to be composed of leased telephone lines. In these traditional telephone networks a connection between a caller and the receiver was established through telephone switching equipment (both mechanical and computerised) selecting specific electrical circuits to form a single path. Once the connection was established data travelled along the path. This is known as a circuit-switching network.

The process of circuit-switching works well for voice communication but proves expensive for data communication because of the need to establish a point-to-point connection for each pair of senders/receivers. Most computer networks therefore use a form of network technology known as packet-switching. In such a network the data in a message or file is broken up into chunks known as packets. Each packet is electronically labelled with codes that indicate the sender (origin) and receiver (destination) of the packet. Data travels along the network from computer to computer until they reach their destination. Each computer in the network determines the best route forward for the packets it receives and must transmit. Computers that make these decisions are known as routers. The destination computer reassembles the packets into the original message.

There are a number of advantages to packet-switching networks for data communications. Long streams of data can be broken up into small, manageable chunks.

This means that the packets can be distributed efficiently to balance the traffic across a wide range of possible transmission paths in a communications network.

9.5 ⊚ TCP/IP

One of the key objectives of most computer networks is to achieve high levels of connectivity. Connectivity is the ability of computer systems to communicate with each other and share data. To achieve such connectivity, standards must be defined to enable communication between sender and receiver. Such standards are embodied in communication software.

One approach to developing higher connectivity among systems is by using the idea of open systems. Open systems are built on public domain operating systems, user interfaces, application standards and networking standards. One of the oldest examples of an open systems model for communications is the Transmission Control Protocol/Internet Protocol (TCP/IP). This was developed by the US Department of Defense in 1972. TCP/IP is the communications software model underlying the Internet. A protocol is a statement that explains how a specific networking task such as the transmission of data should be performed. TCP/IP divides the communication process into five layers of networking tasks:

- *Application.* The application layer is that closest to the network user. The application layer provides data entry and presentation functionality to the end user of the network.
- *Transport/TCP.* This layer breaks application data up into TCP packets known as datagrams. Each packet consists of a header comprising the address of the sending computer, data for reassembling the data and error-checking data.
- *Internet Protocol.* This layer receives datagrams from the TCP layer and breaks the packets down further. An IP packet contains a header with an address and carries TCP information and data in the body of the packet. The IP layer routes the individual packets from the sender to the receiver.
- *Network.* This handles addressing issues usually within the operating system as well as providing an interface between the computer and the network. Each device on a network will normally have a unique ID (an IP number) assigned to it – represented in the network interface of each device.
- *Physical.* Defines the basic characteristics of signal transmission along communication networks.

Two different computer systems using TCP/IP are able to communicate with each other even though they may be based on different hardware and software platforms. Data sent from one computer passes down through the five layers of the protocol. Once the data reaches the receiving computer it travels up through the layers. If the receiving computer finds a damaged data packet it requests the sending computer to send again. This process is illustrated in Figure 9.1.

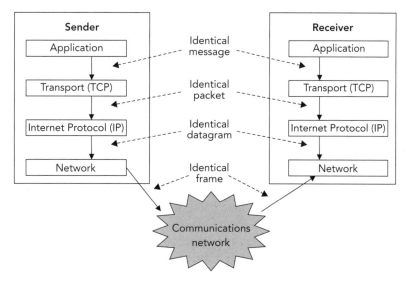

Figure 9.1 TCP/IP layers.

9.6 E-MAIL PROTOCOLS, FTP AND HTTP

In addition to the TCP/IP protocol, other protocols are used to provide file, e-mail and Web applications on the Internet:

- *File Transfer Protocol (FTP)* enables the transfer of files between computers.
- *Simple Mail Transfer Protocol (SMTP)* enables mail transfer between computers.
- *Multi-purpose Internet Mail Extensions (MIME)* enables mail transfer in complex organisations. It is particularly used by the Web to specify the media type contained in a message such as text, images or video.
- *Hypertext Transfer Protocol (HTTP)* is an object-oriented protocol that defines how information can be transmitted between Web clients and Web servers in a network.

9.7 IP ADDRESSES

An IP address is the fundamental way of uniquely identifying a computer system on the Internet. An IP address is constructed as a series of up to four numbers each delimited by a period. It is hence called a dotted quad. In a 32-bit IP address each of the four numbers can range from 0 to 255. Generally the first of the four numbers identify a computer network. The remaining numbers usually identify a node on this network.

Because of the explosion in Internet usage more computers are being added to the global network. Hence the 32-bit IP address will eventually run out of unique addresses. To offset this a 128-bit IP address will be introduced globally.

Example   126.203.97.54 may be an IP address for a computer on the local area network at my university.

9.8 UNIFORM RESOURCE LOCATORS (URLS)

Internet users generally find IP addresses difficult to remember. Hence more memorable identifiers have been introduced which map to IP addresses.

Computers attached to the Internet and the HTML documents (Chapter 8) resident on such computers are identified by Uniform Resource Locators (URL). URLs can thus be used to provide a unique address for each document on the Web. Links between documents are activated by 'hotspots' in the document: a word, phrase or image used to reference a link to another document.

The syntax of a URL consists of at least two and as many as four parts. A simple two-part URL consists of:

- the protocol used for the connection (such as HTTP)
- the address at which a resource may be located on the host

Example   In the URL below, the protocol – HTTP – is placed before the symbols ://. The address after these symbols identifies a specific web page on the host computer, in this case the home page of the University of Wales, Swansea.

HTTP://www.swansea.ac.uk/

9.9 DOMAIN NAMES

The swansea in the URL in the previous example is short for 'The University of Wales, Swansea', the ac for academic and the uk for United Kingdom. This constitutes a so-called domain name, an agreed string of characters that may be used to provide some greater meaning to a URL. In practice, a domain name identifies and locates a host computer or service on the Internet. It often relates to the name of a business, organisation or service and must be registered in the same way as a company name.

A domain name is actually made up of three parts:

- *Subdomain*. This constitutes a provider of an Internet service. In this case it is University of Wales, Swansea.

- *Domain type*. This suggests the type of provider. In this case it is ac – indicating an academic institution based in the UK. The string edu (short for education) is used more generally for an educational institution internationally.
- *Country code*. Every country has its own specific code. For instance, au is the code for Australia. If no country code is specified then the organisation is more than likely based in the USA, although an increasing range of companies internationally are using simply the .com domain type to indicate a global presence.

9.10 THE REGULATION OF DOMAIN NAMES

Internet Protocol addresses are mapped to domain names by domain name servers. These are computer systems in the inter-network that perform this transformation. For such domain servers to work effectively standardisation is needed in domain names.

Such standardisation has traditionally been in the hands of the US government. During the late 1980s and early 1990s, the responsibility for allocating domain names was given to the Internet Assigned Numbers Authority (IANA). Then a company – Network Solutions inc. (NSI) – was set up and started charging customers for the registration of domain names. In 1997, IANA and a number of other organisations advocated self-governance in the domain name service and a year later the Internet Corporation for Assigned Names and Numbers was created. Its main role is to oversee the allocation of domain names and the distribution of addresses by domain name registrars. Domain name registrars are public and private organisations that exist within countries tasked with maintaining registries (databases of names and addresses).

At the end of 2000 a new set of domain names were approved and are currently available for use. These include:

- .name
- .info
- .pro
- .aero
- .biz
- .museum
- .coop

Question   *What effect does the global regulation of domain names have on business practices?*

Long-range data communications are rapidly moving off conventional telephony-based architectures to those based on the architecture the Internet (Chapter 7).

Layer 3 of the TCP/IP communications model described above – the transport layer – utilises the Internet Protocol (IP) (Norris and West, 2001). Using this protocol data is split up into autonomous packets each carrying the address of the sender and receiver. The packets find their way across a range of interconnected subnetworks. Each subnetwork may constitute a local area network (LAN) or wide area network (WAN) and is connected to other networks by routers. The routers manage naming conventions for the sending and receiving units. This is illustrated in Figure 9.2.

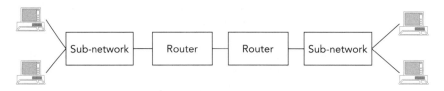

Figure 9.2 Subnetworks and routers.

This situation has to be modified for connection from a domestic user or small business. In this case it is unlikely that the domestic user will be using a LAN. Instead, the customer PC is likely to be connected via a modem and a conventional telephone line to an Internet Service Provider (ISP). The customer achieves connection as a standard telephone call to a bank of modems held at the ISP. For the duration of the call the ISP provides a unique but temporary IP address to the customer's computer. It informs the computer of this address, which is used by the customer's browser in any communication with the Internet during the duration of the connection. This temporary binding of IP address to computer is typically achieved through a so-called point-to-point protocol (PPP). This situation is illustrated in Figure 9.3.

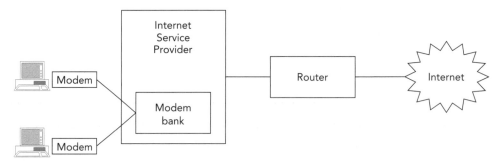

Figure 9.3 Connection to an ISP.

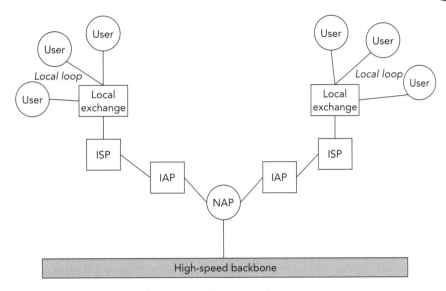

Figure 9.4 Primary architecture of the Internet.

Figure 9.4 displays graphically the primary architecture of the Internet. The Internet is supported by a high-speed communications backbone. Users access the Internet by connecting to an ISP via the local telephone loop. The ISP is connected to an Internet Access Provider (IAP), which has permanent access to a Network Access Point (NAP). This is an interconnection point that exchanges data traffic from a number of IAPs at high speed. Smaller ISPs may connect to the backbone via larger ISPs.

Question
> *One of the most important factors for business is the reach of the Internet into their potential customer population. Is it likely that we will ever achieve 100% penetration of the Internet into people's homes?*

9.12 INTERNET, INTRANET AND EXTRANET

Internet technology is now being used to enable the major value chains of organisations. The terms Intranet and Internet are frequently used in this context.

The Internet, an Intranet and an Extranet can be distinguished in terms of the type of user, the level of access and the type of information supplied. The main differences are summarised below.

- *Internet.* This is a public and global communication network that provides direct connectivity to anyone who has access to a local access provider such as through a LAN or ISP. The local access providers are connected to Internet access providers and eventually to the Internet backbone. The information available is unconstrained. Hence the control of information and access to such information on the Internet is unrestricted.

- *Intranet.* This is a corporate LAN or WAN that uses Internet technology and is secured behind firewalls. The Intranet links various clients, servers, databases and applications together. While using the same technology as the Internet, the Intranet is run as a private network. Only authorised users from within the company are allowed to use it.

- *Extranet.* This is an extended Intranet. It uses Internet technology to connect together a series of Intranets, in the process securing communications over the Extranet. This it does by creating tunnels of secured data flows using cryptography and authorisation algorithms (Chapter 13). The Internet with tunnelling technology is known as a virtual private network (VPN). Data on the Extranet is shared between partners and enables collaboration between such partners. Access to the Extranet is therefore restricted by agreements among the parties to the Extranet.

The differences between Internet, Intranet and Extranet are illustrated in Figure 9.5.

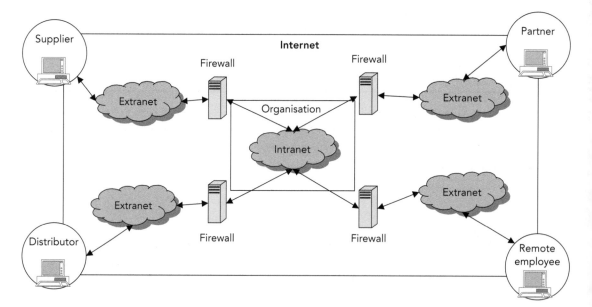

Figure 9.5 Internet, Intranet and Extranet.

9.13 APPLICATIONS THAT RUN ON THE INTERNET

The Internet is an inter-network on which a number of applications currently run. Examples of some of these applications are included below:

- *World Wide Web (WWW)*. Effectively a client–server application that allows the use and transmission of hypermedia documentation over the Internet (Chapter 10).
- *E-mail*. Electronic mail was one of the first applications to run on the Internet. It utilises both e-mail servers and e-mail software to enable organisational members to communicate primarily through the asynchronous one-to-one transmission of text messages. Electronic mail is reliant on the assignment of e-mail addresses to users.
- *Mail lists and list servers*. A mail list is a collection of e-mail addresses. Using this technology the same message can be distributed precisely to the persons that need the information. Mail lists are therefore important for enabling one-to-many asynchronous communication. List servers permit the easy maintenance of mail lists.
- *Newsgroups*. Newsgroups consist of threaded discussions and enable many-to-many asynchronous communication. Participants can post messages to the newsgroup using e-mail. Other participants can then thread comments or replies to each message. Bulletin boards and online fora are variants of the newsgroup idea.
- *Chat*. This enables people to engage in synchronous many-to-many communication in approximate real-time using text messaging over the Internet.

Question   *What is the business opportunity afforded by chat as a technology?*

9.14 SUMMARY

- The most prevalent current example of the application of communications technology is the Internet. The Internet – short for inter-network – began as a Wide Area Network in the USA funded by its Department of Defense to link scientists and researchers around the world.
- The technical infrastructure of the Internet consists of a number of components that include packet-switched networks, TCP/IP, HTTP, e-mail protocols, FTP, IP addresses, Uniform Resource Locators (URLs) and domain names.
- Packet-switching networks employ protocols in which data in a message or file is broken up into chunks known as packets and distributed around the network using.

- TCP/IP is an open systems model for communications that employs a number of layers.
- In addition to the TCP/IP protocol, other protocols are used to provide file and e-mail applications on the Internet including FTP, SMTP, MIME and HTTP.
- Computers attached to the Internet and the HTML (Chapter 8) documents resident on such computers are identified by Uniform Resource Locators (URLs).
- A domain name provides more meaning to a URL and identifies and locates a host computer or service on the Internet.
- Internet Protocol addresses are mapped to domain names by domain name servers.
- Individuals and small businesses are likely to connect to the Internet using a PC/modem and an Internet Service Provider.
- A variety of applications run on the Internet and include WWW, e-mail, mail lists, newsgroups and chat.

9.15 ACTIVITIES

(i) Find one other protocol for the transmission of data over communication networks.

(ii) If you use a computer on some network try to determine the IP address of the computer.

(iii) Determine the entire range of domain names currently available for use.

(iv) Determine the precise technological infrastructure for an Intranet known to you.

(v) Determine the precise technological infrastructure for an Extranet known to you.

9.16 REFERENCES

Currie, W. (2000). *The Global Information Society*. Chichester, John Wiley.
Norris, M. and N. West (2001). *eBusiness Essentials*. Chichester, BT/John Wiley.
Whiteley, D. (2000). *E-commerce: Strategy, Technologies and Applications*. Maidenhead, McGraw-Hill.

THE WORLD WIDE WEB

Man did not weave the web of life, he is merely a strand in it. Whatever he does to the web, he does to himself.

Attributed to Chief Seattle, 1854

LEARNING OUTCOMES

After reading this chapter, you will be able to:

- Relate the history of the Web in the technology of hypertext/hypermedia
- Describe the key technological components of the Web
- Outline some of the applications that enhance use of the Web

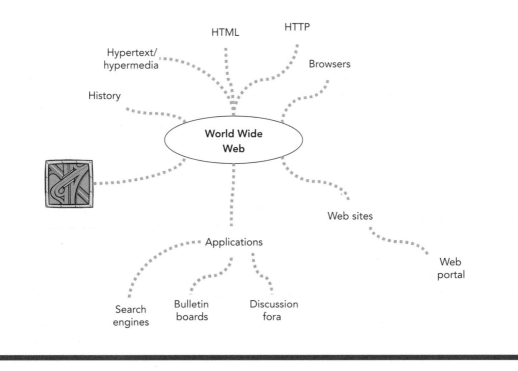

10.1 🌀 INTRODUCTION

The World Wide Web, or the Web for short, dominates any discussion concerning the technical infrastructure for e-business and e-commerce. Frequently people confuse the Internet with the Web. The Internet is the backbone communications infrastructure for e-business (Chapter 9). The Web is effectively an application that runs on the Internet and forms a set of core standards for most contemporary front-end ICT systems (Chapter 12).

In this chapter we consider some of the history for the Web in the technology of hypertext and hypermedia. We then describe some of the contemporary component elements of Web-based systems: hypermedia, HTML, Web sites and portals.

10.2 🌀 HISTORY OF THE WEB

Tim Berners-Lee (1999), the creator of the concept of the Web, has claimed that a major motivation for the invention was the fact that computers have not been able to store random associations between disparate things for organisations – something the human brain does effectively for the individual. A number of researchers in the academic community had proposed that networks of loosely connected nodes of textual material – referred to as Hypertext (Conklin, 1987) (see below) – might emulate the brain's associative capacity. In 1989, while working at the European particle physics laboratory (CERN), Berners-Lee proposed that a global hypertext space might be created in which any information on the network could be accessed by a single 'Universal Document Identifier' or UDI. Given time by his laboratory, Berners-Lee wrote a program in 1990 called 'WorlDwidEweb'. This constituted a point and click hypertext editor which ran on the 'NeXT' machine – a hardware platform of the time. This hypertext editor and an associated specification for a Web server were released to the high-energy physics community at first. In the summer of 1991 the technology together with an early browser (see below) written by a student was released to the hypertext and NeXT communities. The specifications of UDIs (now URIs), HyperText Markup Language (HTML) and HyperText Transfer Protocol (HTTP) (see below) were also published on the first server in order to promote widespread adoption.

Between the summers of 1991 and 1994, the load on the first Web server (info.cern.ch) rose steadily by a factor of 10 every year. The first three years of the development of the Web were devoted to attempting to get the technology adopted first by academia and then by industry. For this to prove successful Web clients were needed for other hardware platforms (as the NeXT computer was not commonplace) and eventually an array of browsers – Erwise, Viola, Cello and Mosaic – emerged.

Berners-Lee was under pressure to define the future evolution of the Web. After much discussion he decided to form the World Wide Web Consortium (W3C) in September 1994, with bases at MIT in the USA, INRIA in France, and now also at Keio University in Japan. W3C has taken on the responsibility for evolving the various protocols and standards associated with the Web.

10.3 COMPONENTS OF THE WWW

The World Wide Web, or Web for short is the application (or set of applications) which is associated most readily with the Internet at the current time. Figure 10.1 illustrates the primary components of the Web:

- Hypertext/hypermedia
- HTTP
- HTML
- Web browsers
- Web sites
- Web portals

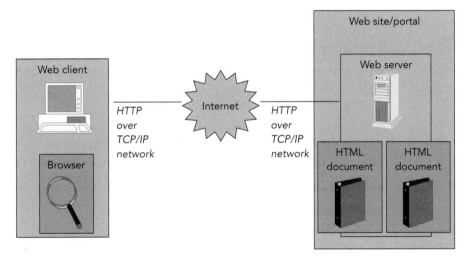

Figure 10.1 Components of the Web.

The Web is effectively a client–server (Chapter 7) application running over the Internet (Chapter 9). Web clients effectively run pieces of software known as a browser. This enables connection to Web servers using two communication protocols – HTTP and TCP/IP. Web servers deliver hypermedia documents in HTML format over the Internet to Web clients.

10.4 HYPERTEXT/HYPERMEDIA

Vannevar Bush (1945) envisaged hypertext/hypermedia systems in the 1940s. In a ground-breaking paper Bush discussed the concept of a memex (memory extender), a device capable of storing and retrieving information on the basis of content. In 1968, Douglas Englebart demonstrated the Augment system. Augment was an online working environment designed to augment the human intellect. It could be used to store and retrieve memos, research notes and other forms of documentation. Ted Nelson extended Bush's original idea in his Xanadu environment. Xanadu was designed to be an ever-expanding workspace that could be used to create and interconnect documents containing text, video, audio and graphics. Nelson actually coined the term *Hypertext* and described it as being 'nonlinear reading or writing'. A number of prominent hypermedia prototypes were developed during the 1980s. However, a software tool (HyperCard) bundled with the Apple Macintosh computer did most to popularise the concept. In recent times hypertext and hypermedia form the bedrock for the Web.

Text can normally be organised in three major ways:

- *Linear text.* Linear text is exemplified in the format of the conventional novel. The reader is expected to start at the beginning and progress to the conclusion via a sequential reading of chapters.
- *Hierarchical text.* Most textbooks and reports are organised hierarchically in terms of chapters, sections, subsections etc. The reader is able to access the text at various points in the hierarchy.
- *Network text.* The dictionary or the encyclopaedia exemplifies network text. In a dictionary each entry has an independent existence but is linked to a number of other entries via references.

Hypertext is an electronic or online version of network text. A hypertext document is made up of a number of textual chunks connected together by associative links called hyperlinks. Hypermedia is a superset of hypertext. Here the nodes of the network may be various media including text, graphics, audio and video.

10.5 HYPERTEXT TRANSFER PROTOCOL (HTTP)

HTTP is an object-oriented protocol that defines how information can be transmitted between Web clients and Web servers typically over a TCP/IP network (Chapter 9). An HTTP transaction consists of the following phases:

- *Connection.* The client establishes a connection with a Web server.
- *Request.* The client sends a request message to a Web server.
- *Response.* The Web server sends a response to the client.
- *Close.* The connection is closed by the Web server.

HTTP is said to be a stateless protocol. This means that when a server provides a response and the connection is closed, the server has no memory of any previous transactions. This has the advantage of simplicity in that clients and servers can run with simple logic and there is little need for extra memory.

10.6 HYPERTEXT MARKUP LANGUAGE (HTML)

The WWW can be thought of as a collection of hypermedia documents residing on thousands of servers or Web sites around the world. Each such document contains content such as text and a set of embedded tags that indicate how the content is to be presented. This process of tagging text with extra presentational information is known as marking-up and the set of tags for doing this a markup language. In the 1960s work began on developing a generalised markup language for describing the formatting of electronic documents. This work became established in a standard known as the Standard Generalized Markup Language or SGML.

SGML in fact constitutes a meta-language – a language for defining other languages. Hence SGML can be used to define a large set of markup languages. Tim Berners-Lee used SGML to define a specific language for hypertext documents known as hypertext markup language (HTML). HTML is a standard for marking up or tagging documents that can be published on the Web (W3C, 1999), and can be made up of text, graphics, images, audio clips and video clips. Documents also include links to other documents stored on either the local HTML server or remote HTML servers.

Example

Below we include a very simple document expressed in HTML

```
<HTML>
<TITLE>E-Business</TITLE>
<H1>E-Business</H1>
<H2>Paul Beynon-Davies</H2>
</HTML>
```

The text between angle brackets constitutes tags. Each piece of text is preceded by a start tag and succeeded by an end tag. A forward slash precedes an end tag. The HTML tags indicate the start and end of the document. The tag TITLE provides a name for the page. The tags H1 and H2 indicate that first- and second-level headings should be displayed respectively.

10.7 WEB BROWSER

To access the Web one needs a browser. These are essentially programs that let the user read Web documents, view any in-built images or activate other media and hotspots. After the invention of the concept of the Web the idea became established quickly in the scientific community. However, few people outside this community had software capable of reading HTML documents. In 1993 the first program that could read HTML documents and display them on a graphical user interface was written at the University of Illinois. It became known as Mosaic.

The commercial opportunities afforded by browsers soon became apparent and members of the Illinois team joined with one other to form the company Netscape Communications. Their key product, Netscape Navigator, became an immediate success. Microsoft soon entered the market with its Internet Explorer product and these two browsers still dominate this niche in the software market.

10.8 VERSIONS OF HTML

HTML has undergone a number of versions since it was first introduced in 1991. The W3C (see above) was founded to serve as a focus for the development of Web standards. A major part of its work has been to produce standard versions of HTML with increased functionality. A summary of the major versions, with a brief description of the functionality of each version, is included below:

- Version 2.0 was released in 1995. It included support for in-line graphics and fill-out forms.
- Version 3.0 was released shortly after version 2.0. Version 3.2, released in 1997, included support for tables, complex numbers and text flow around images.
- Version 4.0 was released in December of 1997. This included support for the OBJECT tag and cascading style sheets. The OBJECT tag allows the developers of Web sites to embed scripting language code directly into HTML pages. Scripting language code allows a downloaded HTML page to execute programs on the user's computer. Cascading style sheets allow Web developers to separate out formatting information from the content in HTML documents. Effectively they act as presentation templates that can be applied a number of times to a given HTML document.
- Version 4.01 was released in December 1991. It corrected errors in version 4.0 and defined a new semantics and some new data types for HTML. This is still the current version of HTML.

10.9 THE STRUCTURE OF HTML

An HTML document contains both content and tags. The document content consists of what is displayed on the computer screen. The tags constitute codes that tell the browser how to format and present the content on the screen.

The general form of this relationship between tags and content is:

```
<tagname properties> content </tagname>
```

The tagname is taken from a set of keywords established in the particular version of HTML. Certain tagnames have associated with them a number of properties that serve to refine the meaning of a tag to a browser.

Example

In the tag <P align="right">, P is the tagname and acts as an abbreviation for the word *paragraph*. Consequently this tag is designed to be placed at the start of a chunk or paragraph of text. The word align is a property which can be assigned a number of values from a limited list. Here the value right specifies that the paragraph in question should be right-justified on the screen. An end tag </P> will be placed at the end of the chunk of text.

The hyperlinks between pieces of text are established using anchor tags. The link can be to a textual element in the same document or to another document. This anchor tag has the form:

```
<A HREF="address">visible link text</A>
```

The letter A stands for *anchor*. HREF is a property that is used to specify the address of the document or piece of text to be linked to. The visible link text establishes what is displayed on the screen as a so-called hot spot. When you move the cursor over a hot spot the cursor typically changes from an arrow to a pointing hand. This indicates that a click on the hot spot will transfer you to the text specified in the address.

Example

The following tag embedded in an HTML document will establish a hyperlink to the author's current place of work:

```
<A HREF="http://www.swan.ac.uk">The University of Wales, Swansea</A>
```

In Table 10.1 we list some of the commonly used tagnames. Note that most such tags demand a corresponding end tag.

Question

How significant do you think HTML is to business communication and why?

10.10 ◎ WEB SITES

The term *Web site* is generally used to refer to a logical collection of HTML documents normally stored on a Web server.

We can distinguish between the content and presentation on a Web page. The content consists of the text and other media bundled in terms of HTML documents. The presentation concerns the way the content is displayed on the user's

Table 10.1 Common HTML tagnames.

Tag name	Functionality
<HTML>	Start of an HTML document
<HEAD>	Establishes the header of the page
<BODY>	Establishes the body of the page
<TITLE>	Can be used within the page header to indicate the text to appear in the title bar of the browser
<H1>, <H2> ...	Used to establish various levels of headings within the text
<P>	Start of a paragraph
<B>	Embolden text
<I>	Italicise text
<U>	Underline text
<LI>	An item in a list
<CENTER>	Centre text
<FONT>	Used to establish the font, size and colour of text
<IMG>	Short for image – used to refer to a graphics file for insertion within the text
<A HREF>	A tag for linking to parts within or without a document
<UL>	Start of an unordered list
<OL>	Start of an ordered list
<TABLE>	Start of a table definition
<FORM>	Start of a form definition

access device. The presentation is controlled by HTML. Frequently people refer to the items on a Web site as Web pages to describe the presentational aspect of an HTML document.

Typically a Web site will be organised hierarchically. The user enters at the site's home page. This usually establishes the range of products and services available from a particular company. From the home page the user may select a particular product or service by clicking on a hotspot, causing navigation typically to another page on the Web site. From here the user may be able to drill down to further detail or perhaps order from the Web site.

Web sites are typically classified in terms of the functionality they provide:

- *Information content.* These sites merely provide information for the user.
- *Query content.* Such sites allow the user to search for certain information via the Web sites, perhaps in coordination with back-end systems.
- *Transactional.* Such sites allow the user to update the data held in back-end systems.

Example

Suppose a company sells toy soldiers. An information site will provide simple details of the company and perhaps indicate how order should be made. A query site would allow the user to search an online catalogue of toy soldiers for sale. A transactional Web site would allow the user to place an order online – perhaps even to pay for the order online.

Web sites that primarily only offer information content typically use static Web pages. A static Web page is primarily produced as a standalone HTML document. Any changes to the page demand posting a new version of the page to the Web site. In contrast, a dynamic Web page consists of both HTML code and calls to some back-end ICT systems such as database systems. A certain amount of the content may be retrieved from such back-end systems and displayed to the user.

For both static and dynamic Web pages the process of content management and the associated content management systems are critical to the effective maintenance of Web sites. We discuss content management in Chapter 25.

Example

The functionality of a Web site used for teleshopping or e-tail has been defined by the Digital Audio Visual Council (DAVIC) (DAVIC, 2002). This is an industry body primarily concerned with specifying the services to be delivered through iDTV. Such online shopping services are likely to be common to a range of access mechanisms. Some of these requirements for an e-tail site are presented below:

- The system should permit a content provider to create a virtual store.
- The system should enable a content provider to determine the layout of the virtual store.
- The content provider should be able to assign products to virtual departments.
- The system should permit multiple items to be displayed simultaneously.
- The user should be able to place selections in a virtual shopping basket prior to committing to purchase these items, maintain a record of total cost, and be able to adjust contents as better alternatives are found in other virtual stores or departments.
- The system should enable a transaction to take place between a user and a product supplier.

- A user, within a teleshopping environment, should be able to request exchange or return of goods.

- The user should be able to store and readily retrieve product information from one store for comparison with offers found elsewhere (a virtual shopping list).

- The user should be able to commit to purchase items in a virtual shopping basket using a choice of methods of payment.

- The user should be able to amend an order already placed, or enquire of the status of an existing order.

- The system should enable an order placed by a user to be processed and for the status of an order to be reported.

- The system should permit collaborative (group) shopping.

- The system should facilitate the use of intelligent agents (aware of user preferences and parameters) to locate items matching needs.

Question

Estimate the percentage of Web sites in the food retail sector you think fulfil the majority of the DAVIC criteria? Run through some reasons to substantiate your estimate.

10.11 WEB PAGE LAYOUT

The discussion above makes clear that Web pages can be used both to display information and as sophisticated data entry and query interfaces to back-end ICT systems. Therefore, in many ways Web page design is a hybrid activity. On the one hand the design of Web pages can be considered to be in many ways similar to the design of physical media such as newspaper pages or magazine pages. Hence Web page design demands an appreciation of the principles of good graphic design. On the other hand Web pages are now used as interfaces to both the front- and back-end ICT systems of the organisation. As such, an understanding of good user interface design is required.

We limit ourselves here to a discussion of some of the main technical options involved in the layout of Web pages:

- *Tables*. Tables are used both for formatting data into a two-dimensional presentation and for layout of larger elements of pages.

- *Frames*. Frames were introduced as a means of providing a straightforward way of parcelling up the page into distinct areas each with their own functionality. Hence, for instance, a Web page might be divided into two frames: one concerned with displaying a menu; the other concerned with displaying main content. When a user selects a menu option this will cause the content in the mainframe window to be updated. Although widely used because of their convenience frames suffer a number of problems in relation to the indexing of sites by search engines, the bookmarking and printing of pages by users and the measurement of user activity against Web sites. For these reasons many developers prefer to use tables as their main way of handling page layout.

- *Forms and menus*. Forms and menus form interdependent lower-level component elements of Web page layout. Forms are used to enable interaction through a number of named data entry fields. Menus are ways of presenting a list of items to the user for selection.

Question	*How important is it for a company to have a well-designed Web site and why?*

10.12 WEB PORTALS

A portal is defined in the *Oxford English Dictionary* as 'a door, gate or entrance, especially one of imposing appearance'. Web portals are specialised Web sites designed to act as an entry point for users into the Web. Portals can be seen as a form of electronic reintermediation (Chapter 14). A portal tries to attract users through a range of value-added services such as information, news, e-shopping, directories and searching, making it an anchor site for such users. We may distinguish between two major types of portal:

- *Horizontal portals*. These portals attempt to serve the entire Internet community, typically by offering search functions and classification for the whole of Web content.
- *Vertical portals*. These normally provide the same functionality as horizontal portals but for a specific market sector. They attempt to target a niche audience – providing access to a multitude of organisations, products and services via a Web site.

Examples	Typical examples of horizontal portals are Lycos and Yahoo. Examples of vertical portals are the ones supplied by Dell and Cisco.

Question	*Some pundits have predicted that we are likely to see a rationalisation of portals over the next decade. Why might this occur?*

10.13 APPLICATIONS THAT ENHANCE THE WEB

A number of software applications, although independent of the Web, are now heavily associated with the Web and its use. Such applications enhance the functionality of the Web experience and include:

- *Search engines*. Because of the information explosion experienced on the Web a key problem that a user has is finding relevant information. A search engine allows the user to specify a combination of keywords with logical operators such as AND, NOT and OR. The search engine then looks up the keyword combinations in what is effectively a large index linking keywords to URLs and displays results for the user to select from. Search engines are typically offered by information intermediaries or infomediaries, which normally are organisations maintaining horizontal portals.

- *Bulletin boards*. These constitute virtual versions of the physical bulletin boards and permit users to post news of events, products or services.

- *Discussion fora*. These are sites typically attached to a Web site that allow users to add comments to long threads of discussion about diverse topics. Each topic is normally given a distinct forum.

Question   *Have bulletin boards and discussion fora any business applications? If so, what?*

10.14 BUSINESS IMPLICATIONS OF THE INTERNET AND THE WEB

Much has been written on the business implications of the Internet ranging from predicting its effect in totally transforming market structures to equating it with the very idea of e-business itself. Porter (2001) has sensibly argued that such extreme positions are untenable. The Internet and the Web are enabling technologies for business. They have created a set of key standards for communication both within the organisation and in terms of communication with external stakeholders.

As such both the Internet and the Web are opportunities for establishing new patterns for business activity, but they are unlikely to change the fundamental principles of business. The failure of many clicks-only or dotcom companies during the late 1990s demonstrated the truth of this position. As a consequence, many clicks and mortar companies are now establishing a balanced portfolio of physical and online presence.

10.15 CASE STUDY: FREESERVE

Freeserve is one of the major ISPs in the UK. The company initially pioneered the free Internet access model in the late 1990s and experienced phenomenal growth as a result. This has now become a standard offering with numerous competitors in the marketplace. Freeserve has therefore redirected its strategy to attempt to become a valued source of customer information and services – a Web portal. In fact, it aims to develop a range of specialist portals – for example, an Internet auction site and one specialising in women's products. In support of this strategy the company has deployed customer and site tracking software. This, the company believes, will provide it with invaluable management information such as the 'stickiness' of its Web site, seasonal trends and online purchasing behaviour.

10.16 SUMMARY

- The World Wide Web, or Web for short, is an application that runs on the Internet.
- The primary elements of the Web include the concept of hypertext/hypermedia, its implementation in HTML and the use of Web browsers.
- Hypertext is an electronic or online version of network text. A hypertext document is made up of a number of textual chunks connected together with associative links called hyperlinks. Hypermedia is a superset of hypertext.
- HTTP is an object-oriented protocol that defines how information can be transmitted between clients and servers in a network.
- HTML is a standard for marking up or tagging documents that can be published on the Web, and can be made up of text, graphics, images, audio clips and video clips.
- To access the Web one needs a browser. These are essentially programs that let the user read Web documents, view any in-built images or activate other media and hotspots.
- The nodes of the Web are generally made up of Web sites and Web portals.
- The term *Web site* is generally used to refer to a logical collection of HTML documents normally stored on a Web server.
- The design of Web pages demands an appreciation of graphic design and user interface design.
- Web portals are specialised Web sites designed to act as an entry point for users into the Web.
- Software applications that enhance use of the Web include search engines, bulletin boards and discussion fora.

10.17 ⊚ ACTIVITIES

(i) Investigate some of the other common tags used in an HTML document.

(ii) Investigate how academic material such as a textbook may be presented via the Web.

(iii) HTTP is a stateless protocol. Determine some of the problems of the stateless nature of this protocol.

(iv) Determine how many distinct browsers there are in existence and how they differ in terms of their functionality.

(v) Classify a Web site known to you in terms of whether it solely provides information content, allows querying or enables transactions.

(vi) Access a teleshopping Web site and score it in terms of the DAVIC functions.

(vii) Compare two or more Web portals known to you in terms of functionality and usability.

(viii) Compare the functionality and usability of two or more search engines known to you.

10.18 ⊚ REFERENCES

Berners-Lee, T. (1999). *Weaving the Web: the Past, Present and Future of the World Wide Web by its Inventor*. London, Orion Business Publishing.

Bush, V. (1945). As we may think. *Atlantic Monthly*, **176**, 101–103.

Conklin, E. J. (1987). Hypertext: an introduction and survey. *IEEE Computer*, **2**(9), 17–41.

DAVIC (2002). http://www.davic.org/.

Porter, M. E. (2001). Strategy and the Internet. *Harvard Business Review*, **79**(3), 63–78.

W3C (1999). *HTML 4.01*. World-Wide Web Consortium.

BACK-END ICT INFRASTRUCTURE

Life can only be understood backwards; but it must be lived forwards

Sören Kierkegaard

Never grow a wishbone, daughter, where your backbone ought to be

Clementine Paddleford

LEARNING OUTCOMES

After reading this chapter, you will be able to:

- Describe the three layers of an informatics infrastructure
- Outline the key functionality of some key technologies for the back-end ICT infrastructure
- Define the importance of integration of ICT systems
- Discuss the important place that ERP systems have in fulfilling the objective of integration

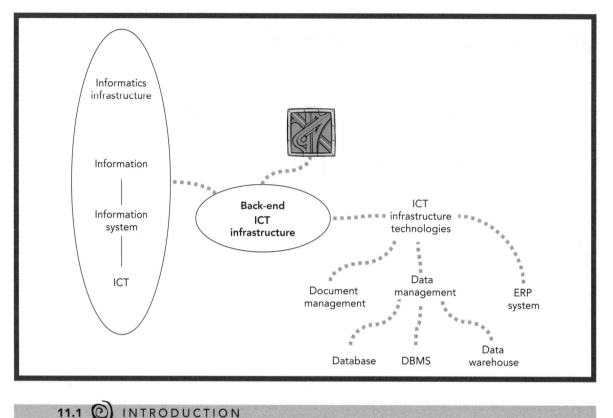

The fundamental thread running through this part of the book is that the e-business agenda for many companies is focused on re-engineering service delivery around the customer. Hence, for example, when a customer enters personal details such as their name and address into one system this information should ideally be available to all other systems that need such data. Such customer-focused strategy demands integration and interoperability of the ICT infrastructure of the business.

Hence the information systems infrastructure of an organisation will be supported by a range of ICT systems. Just as we made a distinction between some of the front-end and back-end information systems of business, we can equally refer to the front-end and back-end ICT systems in a typical business. In this chapter we look at some of the common components of this back-end ICT infrastructure and consider the differences between an information systems infrastructure and an ICT infrastructure.

ICT infrastructure can be viewed horizontally or vertically. Horizontally, we may describe the key functionality provided by ICT systems (Chapter 4). Vertically, we may describe some of the key information and communication technologies making up such systems. The back-end ICT infrastructure of the organisation will particularly manage the operational data of the organisation. Hence we consider the critical technologies associated with data management: databases, DBMS and data warehouses. The degrees of integration and interoperability associated with

ICT systems are key measures of the effectiveness of an organisation's back-end ICT infrastructure. For this reason we briefly review the approach of employing ERP systems for back-end integration and supply of operational data needed by the key activity systems in the business.

11.2 ⊚ INFORMATICS INFRASTRUCTURE

E-business relies on informatics infrastructure. The human activity systems of an organisation rely on three mutually interdependent layers or levels of informatics infrastructure:

- *Information infrastructure*. This layer consists of definitions of information need and activities involved in the collection, storage, dissemination and use of information within the organisation.
- *Information systems infrastructure*. This layer consists of the information systems needed to support organisational activity in the areas of collection, storage, dissemination and use.
- *Information and communication technology infrastructure*. This layer consists of the hardware, software, data and communication facilities as well as the ICT knowledge and skills available to the organisation.

Figure 11.1 can be considered as a high-level map of the information systems likely to be found in a typical commercial organisation. It represents a composite of the systems considered in Chapters 5 and 6. The information systems typically emulate some standard human activity systems, such as sales, accounting, stock control and procurement, that they support. From such a map it is possible to infer some of the information needs of the typical organisation. For example, most organisations need to store data about their employees, customers, suppliers, stock and finance. This constitutes a typical information infrastructure for a commercial organisation.

An ICT infrastructure will consist of the ICT systems that support information systems. It is likely that the organisation may adopt significant standardisation in the areas of hardware, software, data and communications technology to facilitate integration and interoperability of ICT systems.

A possible map of an ICT infrastructure corresponding to the information systems infrastructure illustrated in Figure 11.1 is given in Figure 11.2. Note that the data stores of the information systems infrastructure have been replaced by a number of database systems (see below). Hence the Customers data store has been replaced by a Customers database. Also, the information systems in Figure 11.1 have been replaced by a number of ICT systems. However, not all the ICT systems directly correspond to the information systems. More than one information system may be supported by one ICT system and vice versa. Hence the supplier relationship management ICT system on Figure 11.2 combines the functions of the procurement, inbound logistics and purchase order processing information systems on Figure 11.1.

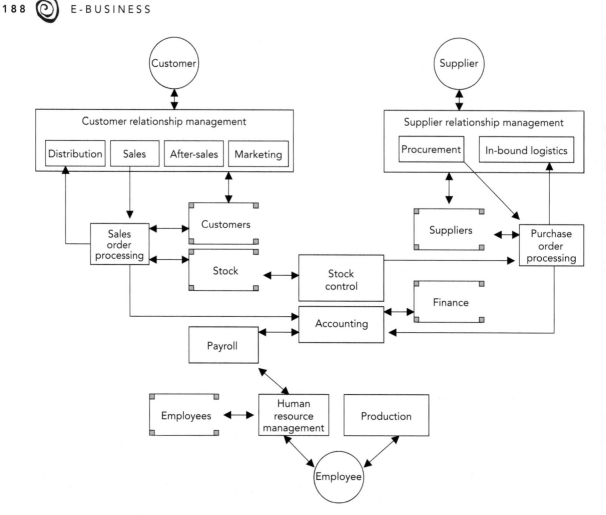

Figure 11.1 An information systems infrastructure.

| Example | In a university, an informatics infrastructure would contain: |

- *Information infrastructure.* A university needs to collect and store data pertaining to teaching, research and consultancy. Information is essential to the effective performance of these three organisational processes. For instance data about students and their progression is essential to the teaching process.

- *Information systems infrastructure.* On a very broad level a university needs information systems to support the teaching, research and consultancy processes. In terms of teaching, for instance, a university needs to record data about its student population, the courses and modules students are currently taking and the grades that students have achieved. Hence some form of integrated student management

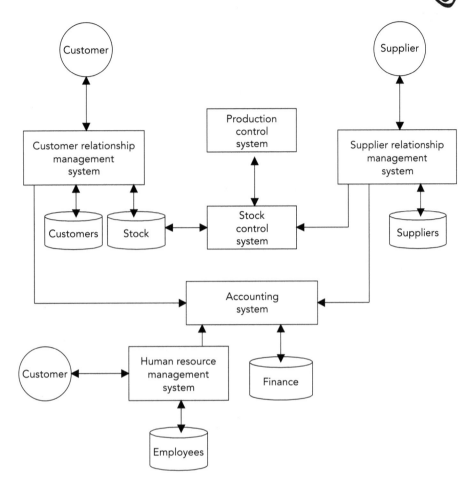

Figure 11.2 An ICT infrastructure.

information system is an essential part of the organisation's information systems architecture.

- *ICT infrastructure.* A university needs an integrated communications infrastructure enabling technology such as e-mail and the Internet. It also needs standards established in terms of hardware and software for both administrative and teaching purposes. Most universities will also maintain some form of informatics service.

Question   *Can the performance of an organisation be determined by the degree to which its information systems infrastructure is enabled with ICT?*

11.3 ICT INFRASTRUCTURE

In a horizontal sense, back-end ICT systems form the core ICT systems of the organisation, such as accounting, sales order processing and payroll. These collect the operational data from transactions impacting upon the front-end ICT systems of the organisation.

A number of technologies are critical to the back office. These include:

- Data management technologies such as databases, DBMS and data warehouses
- Document management technologies
- Enterprise Resource Planning systems

11.4 DATA MANAGEMENT

Traditionally data management in ICT systems has been the domain of the file system managed by the operating system. During the 1970s a type of software started being used for the higher-level management of data – the database management system (DBMS). DBMS are software systems for managing databases and constitute the fundamental technology in the data management layer of most contemporary ICT systems (Figure 11.3). A database system is composed of a database and a database management system (DBMS). Both database and DBMS must conform to a given data model (Beynon-Davies, 2003). In this section we define these three terms in greater detail.

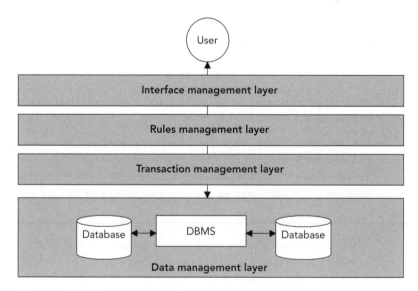

Figure 11.3 Data management.

Question	*In what way does Figure 11.3 relate to Figure 4.2?*

11.4.1 DATABASE

A database is an organised repository for data having the following properties:

- *Data sharing.* A database is normally accessible by more than one person, perhaps at the same time.

- *Data integration.* One major responsibility of database usage is to ensure that the data is integrated. This implies that a database should be a collection of data that has no unnecessarily duplicated or redundant data.

- *Data integrity.* Another responsibility arising as a consequence of shared data is that a database should display integrity; in other words, that the database accurately reflects the universe of discourse that it is attempting to model.

- *Data security.* One of the major ways of ensuring the integrity of a database is by restricting access; in other words, securing the database. The main way this is done in contemporary database systems is by defining in some detail a set of authorised users of the whole, or more usually parts, of the database.

- *Data abstraction.* A database can be viewed as a model of reality. The information stored in a database is usually an attempt to represent the properties of some objects in the real world.

- *Data independence.* One immediate consequence of abstraction is the idea of buffering data from the processes that use such data. The ideal is to achieve a situation where data organisation is transparent to the users or application programs that feed off data.

11.4.2 DBMS

A database management system (DBMS) is an organised set of facilities for accessing and maintaining one or more databases. A DBMS is a shell which surrounds a database and through which all interactions with the database take place. The interactions catered for by most existing DBMS fall into four main groups:

- *Structural maintenance.* Adding new data structures to the database; removing data structures from the database; modifying the format of existing data structures.

- *Transaction processing.* Managing logical units of work: inserting new data into existing data structures; updating data in existing data structures; deleting data from existing data structures.

- *Information retrieval.* Extracting data from existing data structures for use by end users; extracting data for use by application programs.
- *Database administration.* Creating and monitoring users of the database; restricting access to data structures in the database; monitoring the performance of databases.

11.4.3   DATA MODELS

Any database or DBMS adheres to a particular data model. A data model is an architecture for data. It describes the general structure of how data is organised. A data model is generally held to be made up of three components:

- *Data definition.* This comprises a set of data structures.
- *Data manipulation.* This comprises a set of data operators for the insertion of data, the removal of data, the retrieval of data and the amendment of data in data structures.
- *Data integrity.* This comprises a set of integrity rules that must form part of the database. Integrity is enforced in a database through the application of integrity constraints or rules.

Example

One of the most popular forms of data model is that of the relational data model. The one and only data structure in a relational database is the table. Each table is made up of a number of data elements called rows and each row is made of a number of data items known as columns. Each row in the table is identified by values in one or more columns of the table and is called the table's primary key. Values in columns may also act as links to data contained in other tables. Such columns are called foreign keys. In the relational data model there are three types of integrity rule: entity integrity rules (concerned with primary keys), referential integrity rules (concerned with foreign keys) and domain integrity rules (concerned with data items).

Two tables are contained in the database below. Both the Modules and the Lecturers tables have two columns each. ModuleName is the primary key of the Modules table and staffNo is the primary key of the Lecturers table. The Modules table contains a foreign key staffNo that references the primary key of the Lecturers table.

Modules

moduleName	staffNo
Relational Database Systems	234
Relational Database Design	234
Relational Database Design	234
Deductive Databases	345

Lecturers

staffNo	staffName
234	Davies T
345	Evans R

Question   *Databases have been seen to be perhaps the central technology for modern business. Why do you think this might be the case?*

11.5 TYPES OF DATABASE SYSTEM

As we have indicated above, databases are arguably the most important contemporary component of an ICT system. In such systems databases serve three primary purposes: as operational tools, as tools for supporting decision-making and as tools for deploying data around the organisation.

11.5.1 OPERATIONAL DATABASES

Such databases are used to collect operational data. Operational databases are used to support standard organisational functions by providing reliable, timely and valid data. The primary usage of such databases includes the creating, reading, updating and deleting of data – sometimes referred to as the CRUD activities.

Example   In terms of a university, an operational database will probably be needed to maintain an ongoing record of student progression. This will involve creating student records, reading such records, updating records and deleting records.

11.5.2 DECISION SUPPORT DATABASES

Such databases are used as data repositories from which to retrieve information for the support of organisational decision-making. Such databases are read-only databases. They are designed to facilitate the use of query tools or custom applications. Decision support databases tend to be critical components of Management Information Systems (Chapter 5).

Example	In terms of a university, a decision support database may be needed to monitor recruitment and retention patterns among a student population.

11.5.3 MASS DEPLOYMENT DATABASES

Such databases are used to deliver data to the desktop. Generally such databases are single-user tools running under a PC-based DBMS. They may be updated on a regular basis from either operational or decision support databases.

Example	In terms of a university, a mass deployment database is likely to be needed by each lecturer to maintain an ongoing record of student attendance at lectures and tutorials.

11.5.4 INTEGRATION OF DATABASES

Ideally we would like any database system to fulfil each of these purposes at the same time. However, in practice, medium- to large-scale databases can rarely fulfil all these purposes without sacrificing something in terms of either retrieval or update performance. Many organisations therefore choose to design separate databases to fulfil operational, decision support and mass deployment needs and build necessary update strategies between each type (Figure 11.4).

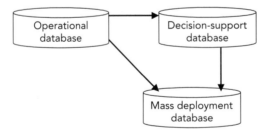

Figure 11.4 Links between the types of database system.

Question	*Which type of database would be used typically by employees and which by managers?*

11.6 〇 DATA WAREHOUSING

A data warehouse is a type of contemporary database system designed to fulfil decision support needs (Anahory and Murray, 1997). However, a data warehouse differs from a conventional decision support database in a number of ways:

- A data warehouse is likely to hold far more data than a decision support database.
- The data stored in a warehouse is likely to have been extracted from a diverse range of ICT systems, only some of which may utilise database systems.
- A data warehouse is designed to fulfil a number of distinct ways (dimensions) in which users may wish to retrieve data.

This latter characteristic of a data warehouse is important in supporting two related technologies:

- *OLAP*. Modern database applications such as market analysis and financial forecasting require access to large databases for the support of queries that can rapidly produce aggregate data. Such applications are frequently called online analytical processing applications, or OLAP for short. OLAP systems use multi-dimensional data structures to store data and relationships (Berson and Smith, 1997).
- *Data mining*. To gain benefit from a data warehouse the data patterns resident in the large data sets characteristic of such applications need to be extracted. As the size of a data warehouse grows the more difficult it is to extract such data using the conventional means of query and analysis. Data mining involves the use of automatic algorithms to extract such data (Witten and Frank, 2000).

Example

Consider the case of a supermarket chain. At the operational level sales data is recorded in each supermarket in the chain at checkouts using electronic point of sale devices. This data allows administrative staff to record the amount of each type of product sold and, in turn, triggers decisions as to the amount of stock to reorder.

This sales data may be a major data source for a data warehouse, perhaps sited at the headquarters of the supermarket chain. This enables headquarters staff to monitor nationally or perhaps internationally their sales performance in certain areas. This helps them to make decisions as to what they should be selling and for what price.

However, the sales data is likely to be combined with data from other sources such as customer data, collected perhaps through the supermarket's loyalty card scheme. Associating sales data with customer data in their data warehouse may provide the chain with important information about the purchasing patterns of their customers. This may enable the chain to proactively plan activities in relation to particular customer groups or in terms of new business opportunities such as financial services.

11.7 ⊚ DOCUMENT MANAGEMENT

The data held within databases and data warehouses is said to be structured data. By this we mean that it is organised in terms of data structures, data elements and data items. However, much data collected, disseminated and used within organisations is unstructured or semi-structured. Typically such data comprises data contained in physical documents of various types. Database systems have typically not been good at handling such unstructured data. Hence a type of system known as a document management system is frequently used for this purpose.

A document management system typically comprises:

- An input device such as a scanner that produces a digital image of the document.
- A processing module that normally allows the user to index the document in various ways.
- A storage module consisting of some specialised hardware and software for storing large amounts of images.
- A retrieval module allowing the user to retrieve a particular document quickly.

Example

Any UK citizen who is self-employed, a company director, or has more complicated tax affairs is required each year to fill out a Self Assessment Tax Return and send it to the Inland Revenue by a specified deadline. The process of Self Assessment affects more than 8 million individuals, 700,000 partnerships and 300,000 trusts. Although this government department has introduced an electronic submission service, most tax returns are filled out in paper-based form. The organisation faces a mammoth task of storing and retrieving this documentation. Document management is hence one solution to this problem.

Question

The introduction of document management systems could contribute a great deal to effective performance of the National Health Service. Why do you think this might be the case?

11.8 ⊚ ENTERPRISE RESOURCE PLANNING (ERP) SYSTEMS

The layered model of an ICT system discussed in Chapter 4 can be considered as the vertical integration, interoperability and distribution of ICT systems. Generally such integration can be described as cooperative and distributed processing. Integration, interoperability and distribution can also be considered in a horizontal sense. The aim of many strategies is to integrate ICT systems across the organisation. Generally speaking such integration is focused around issues of integrated and distributed data.

Traditionally integration has been achieved by effective planning and management of ICT systems built internally within organisations. More recently many organisations have chosen to buy in large suites of ICT systems with in-built integration. This is the enterprise resource planning (ERP) package or mega-package (Davenport, 1998). The strategy of purchasing enterprise resource planning (ERP) systems can be seen as an attempt to buy in a complete ICT infrastructure (Shields, 2001).

An ERP system integrates a number of different organisational functions under the umbrella of one system. An ERP system typically consists of a series of packaged software modules feeding off a central database of organisational data. Many such packages originally developed from manufacturing resource planning (MRP) systems.

Figure 11.5 illustrates the typical suite available in a mega-package. Such ICT systems promise the seamless flow of information through an organisation – financial and accounting information, human resource information, supply chain information and customer chain information (Davenport, 2000).

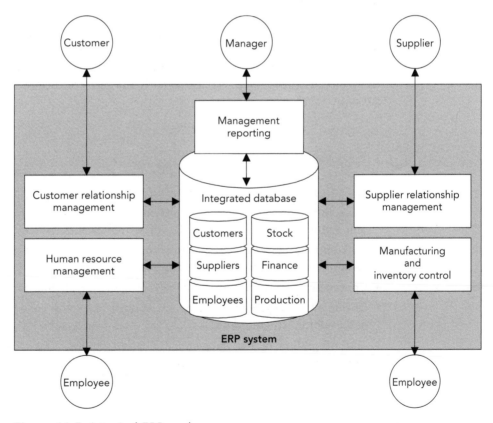

Figure 11.5 A typical ERP package.

Example	Leading vendors in this segment of the software industry are SAP, BAAN, PeopleSoft, J.D. Edwards (now merged with PeopleSoft) and Oracle. There is evidence of significant acquisitions of such packages among organisations in Europe and the USA.

Question	*What sort of problems are businesses likely to meet in implementing ERP systems?*

11.9 CASE STUDY: NECTAR

The importance of effective back-end ICT infrastructure to business performance is demonstrated by the case of the company Nectar. In the autumn of 2002 a number of companies participated in the establishment of an organisation known as Nectar. Nectar offered various products and services for bonus points collected via purchases made with companies such as Barclaycard, Sainsbury's and Debenhams. Existing customers with the bonus schemes of these companies or new customers wishing to participate were offered the incentive of 200 points to register online with the Web site. Within the first couple of days of operation the company had to take its online registration offline. Unprecedented demand for registration using the Web caused the site to crash. Nectar temporarily withdrew its registration Web site from service.

11.10 SUMMARY

- The informatics infrastructure of an organisation can be considered as consisting of three mutually interdependent layers or levels: information infrastructure, information systems infrastructure, and ICT infrastructure.
- Back-end ICT systems include the core systems of the business. They tend to be located around databases storing important corporate data.
- Contemporary data management involves databases, DBMS and data warehouses.
- Document management systems are important for the collection, dissemination and use of unstructured data.
- The integration of the back-end ICT infrastructure is now frequently achieved through the purchase of ERP systems.

11.11 ACTIVITIES

(i) Identify core database systems in an organisation known to you.

(ii) Attempt to distinguish between operational and decision support database systems in an organisation known to you.

(iii) Investigate technologies for contemporary document management.

(iv) Investigate the penetration of ERP systems into a particular industrial sector.

11.12 ☺ REFERENCES

Anahory, S. and Murray, D. (1997). *Data Warehousing in the Real World: a Practical Guide for Building Decision-Support Systems*. Harlow, Addison-Wesley.

Berson, A. and Smith, S. J. (1997). *Data Warehousing, Data Mining and OLAP*. New York, McGraw-Hill.

Beynon-Davies, P. (2003). *Database Systems*, Basingstoke, Palgrave.

Davenport, T. H. (1998). Putting the enterprise into the enterprise system. *Harvard Business Review*, July/Aug, 121–131.

Davenport, T. H. (2000). *Mission Critical: Realising the Promise of Enterprise Systems*. Boston, MA, Harvard Business School Press.

Shields, M. G. (2001). *E-business and ERP: Rapid Implementation and Project Planning*. New York, Wiley.

Witten, I. H. and Frank, E. (2000). *Data Mining*. San Francisco, CA, Morgan Kaufmann.

FRONT-END ICT INFRASTRUCTURE

Teachers open the door. You enter by yourself

Chinese proverb

Still round the corner there may wait,

A new road or a secret gate.

J. R. R. Tolkien, *The Return of the King*

LEARNING OUTCOMES

After reading this chapter, you will be able to:

- Describe the key options for distributing the layers of an ICT system
- Describe the three-tier client–server architecture
- Define the concept of an Intranet and an Extranet in terms of technology
- Describe some of the ways of integrating database systems and Web sites

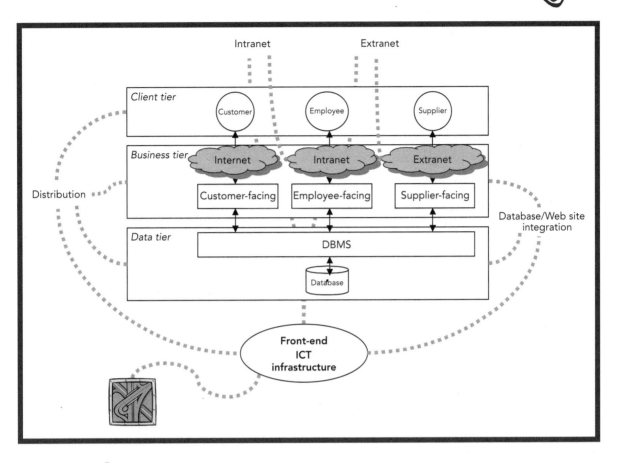

12.1 INTRODUCTION

Electronic delivery of goods and services demands effective ICT systems that interface directly with the key stakeholders of the business – customers, suppliers, employees and partners. These are the front-end ICT systems of the business. In this chapter we describe the typical technologies common to contemporary front-end ICT. Such front-end ICT systems will work in collaboration with a number of core back-end ICT systems (Chapter 11). Such collaboration is characteristic of the distributed processing in the contemporary ICT infrastructure (Markus, 2000).

Front-end ICT systems are likely to work in the modern business using Internet and Web technologies. Hence the effective integration of front- and back-office systems is key to organisational effectiveness. For instance, to enable fully transactional Web sites, the information presented needs to be updated dynamically from back-end databases. Also, the information entered by customers needs to update company information systems effectively. For this reason we particularly focus on a discussion of the technology of Intranets and Extranets within this chapter and provide an overview of how integration of these front-end technologies with back-end database systems is possible.

We begin with a review of the options for distributing processing power around the organisation. This is followed by a review of the technology of front-end ICT systems. Intranets and Extranets are key ways in which front-end interaction is currently organised in businesses. This leads us to conclude with a consideration of Web site database integration.

12.2 DISTRIBUTION

In Chapter 4 we discussed the four main layers of an ICT application: interface management, rules management, transaction management and data management. In the contemporary ICT infrastructure each of these parts of an application may be distributed on different computer systems, perhaps at different sites. This means that each part usually needs to be connected together in terms of some communications backbone or subsystem.

Figure 12.1 illustrates a number of different distribution patterns for ICT systems. The diagram is divided vertically into client computers and server computers. Clients request services from server computers.

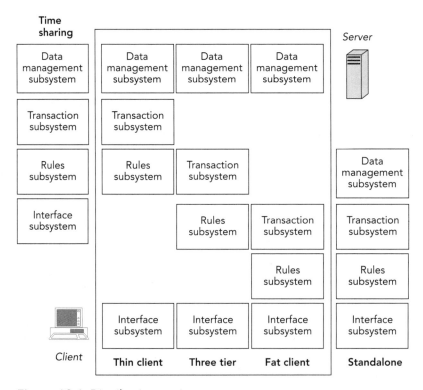

Figure 12.1 Distribution options.

12.2.1 TIME-SHARING

In the first phase of ICT systems, each of the component layers of such a system was located on one machine. Large mainframe systems ran the data management, transaction management, rules management and much of the interface management functions of an application. Connection to such systems was via so-called 'dumb' terminals. They were referred to as 'dumb' because they contained very little inherent functionality and primarily enabled users to control systems via character-based interfaces – interfaces demanding users to type in commands. Most of the processing on such systems was conducted in batch mode, i.e. the processing of vast amounts of transactions in sequence with very little direct user input. Specialist data entry staff conducted data entry. Retrieval of information was available through paper reports produced from the system.

12.2.2 FAT CLIENTS

Over time, more and more functionality has been placed on the clients within a computer network. Technological developments enabled the interface management layer and some of the rules management layer to be located on so-called 'intelligent' terminals. They were referred to as 'intelligent' because they were able to take some of the processing off of the centralised mainframe or mini-computer. This advance enabled the development of online systems. Such systems enabled users in the workplace to enter data directly into the information system and in certain respects to query the data in the system. The rise of online systems enabled the development of Management Information System (MIS) and decision support system (DSS) applications (Chapter 6).

With the rise of personal computers much more of the functionality of the ICT system began to be placed on desktop machines. The sophistication of graphical user interfaces meant that more power needed to be available on the desktop to run such interfaces effectively. With the rise of software for the desktop, slices from the total functionality of an ICT system could be built using application development tools available for the desktop.

12.2.3 THREE-TIER ARCHITECTURE

Many current applications run on three-tier client–server architectures. The first tier runs the user interface layer, the second tier runs the business rules and the third layer runs the transaction and data management functions. In a Web-based approach the client will run a browser and the middle tier will comprise a Web server that will interact with a database server (see below). Modern systems may extend this three-tier architecture to an *n*-tier architecture – meaning that more than three layers may be involved in the distribution of processing.

12.2.4   THIN CLIENTS

Some discussion has occurred within the computing fraternity over the way in which Internet technology may cause a profound change from 'fat' clients to 'thin' clients. The corporate PC is currently a fat client. It requests information from a server and then processes and presents it at the client end using software resident on the PC. The network computer or NC is a thin client. In its extreme form, only a minimum of software (usually a Web browser) will be resident on the client. Applications will be resident on and accessed from the server. This means that each user will have a desktop system that looks like a PC but which has no secondary storage devices. Consequently, NCs, or so the argument goes, are likely to be considerably less expensive than PCs. Also, the network administrator will only need to buy and maintain one copy of each software application on the server.

Example

Consider an ATM (automated teller machine) run by a consortium of high street banks. The client end comprises the ATM itself. The ATM is effectively a specialised computer system running a number of screens with associated dialogue and controlling the operation of a cash dispenser and other devices. At the server end there is likely to be a series of large banking databases storing data about customers and accounts. The mediating application layer is likely to consist of a business rules layer containing rules such as 'a customer should not be able to go overdrawn to a degree greater than his or her overdraft limit'. It will also contain a transaction layer implementing transaction types such as 'check an entered customer identifier against a recorded identifier for the customer in the customer database' and 'update the account balance of a customer by crediting or debiting a given account'.

In the remaining sections of this chapter we particularly concentrate on explaining a typical three-tier model for the ICT infrastructure in which the infrastructure relies heavily on Web technology in association with databases.

Question

The trend towards distributed processing within organisations has led many to suggest that the network is now the computer. To what extent do you think this is the case and what business implications arise from this?

12.3 THE TECHNOLOGY OF FRONT-END ICT SYSTEMS

The typical ICT infrastructure of the modern organisation will therefore tend to be built as a three-tier client–server architecture with either thin or fat clients. In such an architecture the three tiers will typically consist of:

- *The client tier*. Most contemporary front-end ICT systems within organisations have been designed to be accessed through various access devices running a Web browser (Chapter 10). Access channels may be over a local area network or over a wide area network.

- *The business tier*. The front-end ICT infrastructure of the typical contemporary organisation is likely to consist of a series of Web servers. Such Web servers are likely to provide electronic services to the major stakeholders of the organisation: customers, suppliers, managers and employees.

- *The data tier*. Operational data in back-end ICT systems will be made available in response to requests from the business layer. Data will typically be stored in large corporate databases (Chapter 11)

Internet and Web technologies are being used to produce standard interfaces to front-end ICT systems in organisations (Figure 12.2). Front-end ICT systems will vary with the type of stakeholder.

- Customers are likely to access services through some Internet-enabled device to a general Web site on the Internet.

- Internal stakeholders such as employees and managers are likely to access front-end ICT systems through some form of corporate Intranet run on the organisation's LAN.

- External stakeholders such as suppliers and partners are likely to access front-end ICT systems through some form of Extranet.

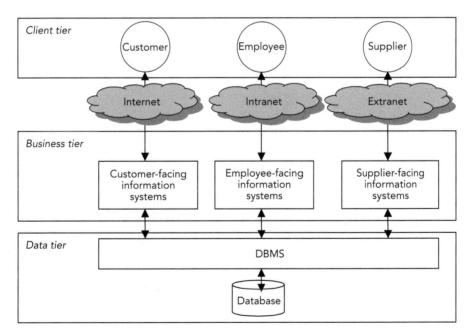

Figure 12.2 Access to front-end ICT systems.

Question *What advantages do you think arise from organisations maintaining n-tier architectures for their ICT systems?*

12.4 INTRANETS

An Intranet involves using Internet and Web technology within the context of a single organisation. At its most basic it involves setting up a Web service for internal communications and coordination. At its most sophisticated, it involves using Web interfaces to core corporate applications such as corporate-wide database systems.

An Intranet can be considered as a special type of ICT system. As such, we can consider it in terms of its horizontal components or in terms of its vertical components. Horizontally an Intranet will be made up of (Figure 12.3):

- *Hardware*. Computers acting as both clients and servers will be required as well as communication lines between such machines.

- *Software*. Web browser software will be required on client machines and Web server software on server machines. The role of the Web server software involves processing requests from the client browser software and returning documents to the clients. An Intranet may also have a domain server. This system translates between the numeric addresses assigned to each machine in the network under TCP/IP and more meaningful names for servers.

- *Communications*. An Intranet relies on some form of communications infrastructure. This may be a LAN, a WAN or a combination of both (Chapter 7). Hardware and software will be required to run the TCP/IP communications protocol.

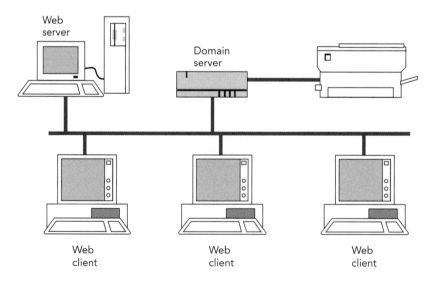

Figure 12.3 Horizontal components of an Intranet.

- *Data*. Data will primarily be held in the form of HTML documents held on the servers in the network. Some data may be held in database systems accessible from the Web pages.

Vertically, we can consider an Intranet in terms of a series of typical applications such as:

- *E-mail*. Most Intranets utilise both e-mail servers and e-mail software to enable organisational members to communicate.
- *Internal Web*. An Intranet will use Internet technology such as browsers, HTML and TCP/IP to produce and disseminate information throughout the organisation.
- *Mail lists and list servers*. A mail list is a collection of e-mail addresses. Using this technology the same message can be distributed precisely to the persons that need the information. List servers permit the easy maintenance of mail lists.
- *Newsgroups*. Newsgroups consist of threaded discussions. Participants can post messages to the newsgroup using e-mail.
- *Chat*. This enables people to communicate in approximate real time using Internet technology.
- *FTP*. File Transfer Protocol enables users to download large files from servers.
- *Firewalls*. Typically an Intranet is connected to the wider Internet through a so-called firewall (Chapter 13). The firewall consists of hardware and software placed between an organisation's internal network and an external network such as the Internet. The firewall is programmed to intercept each message packet passing between the external and internal networks, examine its properties and reject any unauthorised messages. Hence the firewall constrains the types of information that can be passed into and out from an organisation's Intranet.

Example   Schlumberger is the world's largest oil service company. In the late 1990s it introduced a Web-based procurement system into its largest division. The system consists of two parts. The first part enables company employees to search online catalogues of common products such as office supplies using the company Intranet. Once the employee has chosen an item the system automatically creates a requisition, routes the order to the appropriate person for approval and transforms the requisition into a purchase order. The second part of the system provides access for employees to a marketplace of hundreds of suppliers. Each buyer is able to customise this marketplace of products and prices to their needs.

Question   *What do you feel is the most important application of an Intranet within business?*

12.5 EXTRANETS

An Extranet is an extended Intranet. It uses Internet technology to connect together a series of Intranets, in the process securing communications over the Extranet. This it does by creating tunnels of secured data flows using encryption and authorisation algorithms (Chapter 13). The Internet with tunnelling technology is known as a virtual private network (VPN). Data on the Extranet is shared between partners and enables collaboration between such partners. Access to the Extranet is therefore restricted by agreements among the parties to the Extranet.

Whereas an Intranet is only accessible to the members of an organisation, an Extranet provides a certain level of access to an organisation's Web-based information to outsiders. Extranets are becoming particularly popular as a way of enabling electronic connections to be made to an organisation's established customers and suppliers. The organisation will utilise firewalls to ensure that outside access is secure.

Example | Dulux trade, a division of ICI Paints, has created an Extranet that enables professional decorators to select the right paint for the particular job. The system includes a facility that shows the user a building or room painted in the selected colour. It also produces a technical specification of the paint and directs the user to a suitable merchant.

Question | In what ways may Extranets be used to more tightly integrate the activities of partner organisations?

12.6 DATABASE/WEB SITE INTEGRATION

A typical Web page on a company's Internet, Intranet or Extranet will be a static Web page. A static Web page is one that consists of HTML and associated graphics. The key problems of constructing Web sites with static Web pages is that whenever a change needs to be made to the content the page has to be manually amended and republished to the Web site. For large and complex Web sites such an amendment process can be time-consuming and error-prone.

For this reason, core technologies have been developed which enable application developers to create linkages between the data held in corporate databases and the information published on Internet, Intranet or Extranet Web pages. We can distinguish between three main ways in which a database system may interact with Web-based services on a Web server (Beynon-Davies, 2003):

- *Static report publishing.* In this type of application the DBMS generates a report, static form (a display only form), or response to a query in HTML format and posts this to the Web site automatically.

- *Query publishing.* In this type of application an HTML form is generated containing text boxes in which the user may enter criteria for a query. Once the form is submitted a request is made to the DBMS that returns matching data or an error.

- *Application publishing.* In this type of application the interfaces (both data entry and reports) are all Web-based. This is clearly a Web-based emulation of the traditional ICT system architecture.

Each of the applications described above demands the use of dynamic Web pages. Traditionally an HTML file stored as a document is an example of a static Web page. The content of the page only changes if a change is made to the document. In a dynamic Web page the content is dynamically generated each time the page is accessed.

Example

An example of a static report application is a university Web site that updates the timetable from a timetabling system with a core database. A query-publishing application in this domain would allow the user to enter enquiries concerning, for instance, the timetable of a specific room on campus.

There are a number of approaches to building database/Web site integration including:

- *Common Gateway Interface (CGI).* This constitutes a specification for how scripts communicate with Web servers. Scripts are programs stored on the Web server which are executed by the server and the results of the execution are returned to the browser. Parameters can be passed to the script using the query string part of a URL.

- *Server-Side Includes.* Normally Web servers do not examine the files it sends to browsers. Some servers are able to examine the files for so-called server-side includes. Such includes may command the server to execute some program and include the results within the document before returning it to the browser.

- *JDBC, JSQL.* The popular programming language Java can be used in association with a number of defined application programming interfaces (APIs). An API enables connection between an application written in some programming language and a database. For instance, Java Database Connectivity (JDBC) is modelled on the Open Database Connectivity (ODBC) API that enables connection to a variety of DBMS. JSQL is an extension to a standard query language for database systems known as Structured Query Language (SQL) – proposed for use with Java.

- *Scripting languages such as JavaScript and VBScript.* Scripting languages enable the specification of functions within HTML documents. JavaScript is an object-based scripting language originally developed by Netscape and Sun. VBScript is a Microsoft scripting language whose functionality is similar to JavaScript but which more closely resembles Microsoft's Visual Basic in terms of syntax.

- *Vendor initiatives such as Microsoft's Active Server Pages.* Active Server Pages (ASP) is a Microsoft specific model for building Web pages on Web servers. An ASP can contain a combination of text, HTML tags and script commands and output expressions. ASP files are requested using the `.asp` extension from the server. The Web server reads through the requested file, executes any commands, and returns the dynamic HTML page to the browser.

12.8 CASE STUDY: DELL

Michael Dell, the founder of Dell Computer Corporation is often credited with creating a revolution in the personal computer industry. Dell's business model, built around direct selling to the customer and managing its inventory and distribution processes effectively, is credited with a rapid growth in the business.

The idea for the company originated in a business run from Michael Dell's parents home when he was a teenager. From here he originally sold memory chips and disk drives for IBM PCs. Michael Dell was able to sell his products through newspapers and magazines at 10–15% below retail prices. He dropped out of college in 1984 and started assembling his own IBM clones selling direct to customers at 40% below retail price. In 1988 his company went public. Having experienced some problems in 1990 the company re-established its position through selling its PCs via mail order through Soft Warehouse/CompUSA superstores. In 1994 the company abandoned superstores to return to its mail order/direct retail roots. Dell is now a worldwide business based around integrated manufacturing and supply of hardware.

Dell's mission is to be the most successful computer company in the world at delivering the best customer experience in the markets it serves. In doing so, Dell aims to meet customer expectations of:

- Highest quality
- Leading technology
- Competitive pricing
- Individual and company accountability
- Best-in-class service and support
- Flexible customisation capability
- Superior corporate citizenship
- Financial stability

Dell originally started its Internet initiative in the late 1980s to attempt to increase its level of customer support. The company traditionally provided such customer support using a call centre. At the call centre Dell customer care representatives normally advised customers to obtain software updates either sent on disks or as software downloads from a site run by CompuServe. By 1989 Dell began online distribution of software updates.

In 1996 the company launched www.dell.com to provide technical support online. Initially the Web site was used to provide technical information to customers. Later, customers were able to order through a Web site that provided an online catalogue of products. Customers can now also enter details of specific configurations of hardware they require and hence configure systems online.

Build-to-order retail requires assembly plants close to suppliers Intel (chips), Maxtor (hard drives) and Selectron (motherboards). Dell has assembly plants in Austin, Texas; Limerick, Eire; and Penang, Malaysia. At such plants order forms follow each PC across the factory floor.

Dell put in back-end software which enabled integration of order processing with production. Orders coming in via the Web site were downloaded every hour. A software package was then used to generate a new production schedule every two hours. In turn the software informed suppliers in real time what materials were required for production.

In 1997 Dell launched Premier Pages, an electronic catalogue that allowed corporate customers a value-added online purchasing function. By 2000 there were approximately 40,000 Premier Pages that contained purchase order processes and information pertaining to each corporate account. This facility allowed the company to more closely interact with its customers. The facility gave customers access to automated paperless purchase orders, predefined configuration, order tracking and status, a worldwide view of customer assets and customised service tools.

In 1998 Dell launched Valuechain@Dell.Com. This facility offered the same services to the company's suppliers as Premier Pages offered to its corporate customers. The site let the suppliers know Dell's component requirements at any given moment. This enabled them to plan their production schedules appropriately. Such supply chain management at Dell reduced planning cycles for new product development. It also reduced inventory to two to three days for some parts.

The benefits of e-business for Dell are various. For instance:

- Faster order–delivery cycle
- Lower inventory causing reduced working capital requirements
- Outsourcing of subassemblies leading to reduced fixed costs
- All contributing to sustained financial performance

12.9 SUMMARY

- Processing in the contemporary ICT infrastructure is likely to be distributed in terms of a three-tier client–server architecture.
- Front-end ICT systems will vary with the type of stakeholder and will involve the use of Internet, Intranet and Extranet sites.
- An Intranet involves using Internet technology within the context of a single organisation.
- An Extranet is an extended Intranet. It uses Internet technology to connect together a series of Intranets, in the process securing communications over the Extranet.
- Database systems are important in the context of managing large-scale Web applications through the use of dynamic pages.
- Three types of application for the use of database systems within Web applications are report publishing, query publishing and application publishing.
- Different approaches for building database-enabled Web applications include CGI, JDBC and Active Server Pages.

12.10 ACTIVITIES

(i) Determine whether an application known to you uses a three-tier client–server architecture.

(ii) Investigate the penetration of thin client technology into organisations.

(iii) Try to find an organisation that maintains both an Internet and Intranet Web site and determine how these two sites differ.

(iv) Determine whether an organisation known to you uses an Extranet. Attempt to determine the functionality of the Extranet.

(v) In terms of one Web site known to you attempt to determine whether database integration is used and in what way.

12.11 REFERENCES

Beynon-Davies, P. (2003). *Database Systems*, Basingstoke, Palgrave.

Markus, M. (2000). Paradigm shifts: e-business and business/systems integration. *Communications of the AIS*, **4**(10).

CHAPTER 13

DATA SECURITY

There is no security on this earth, there is only opportunity.

General Douglas MacArthur

Better be despised for too anxious apprehensions, than ruined by too confident security.

Edmund Burke

LEARNING OUTCOMES

After reading this chapter, you will be able to:

- Describe the importance of data security particularly for e-commerce
- Distinguish between securing stored data and securing transactional data
- Outline some of the approaches to securing stored data
- Outline some of the approaches to securing transactional data

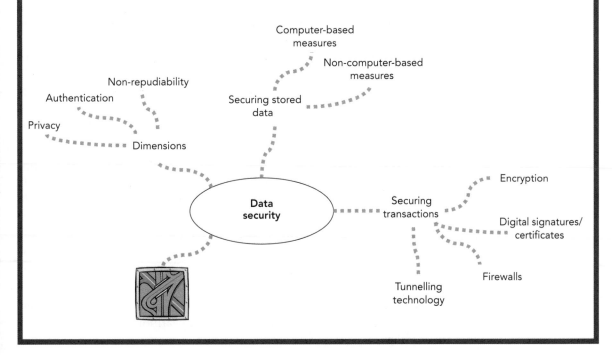

13.1 INTRODUCTION

One of the major barriers to the utilisation of e-commerce by customers has been the expressed concern over the lack of security associated with such systems. This concern has meant that whereas customers might be prepared to inspect online catalogues of products and services, they have been reluctant to release credit card details over the Internet. Over the last few years there has been a growing attempt to offer secure e-commerce sites to customers and other organisational stakeholders in an attempt to encourage uptake of electronic delivery of goods and services.

In this chapter we consider two major technological dimensions to the issue of security (Greenstein and Vasarhelyi, 2002): securing stored data and securing transactional data. The data in an organisation's ICT systems is a valuable resource and must be protected. We consider both computer-based and non-computer-based ways of achieving this. Likewise, the privacy of data transmitted between external stakeholders such as customers and suppliers and the organisation as well as between parts of the organisation itself should also be maintained. As ways of achieving this we provide an overview of the technologies of encryption and digital certificates.

13.2 THE DIMENSIONS OF DATA SECURITY

Data is an increasingly valued resource and forms the lifeblood of much modern business and commerce (Stamper, 1985). It is therefore no surprise to find an increasing level of computer-related crime and an increasing number of technological reactions to such increase. Data security is becoming a critical issue for most businesses and involves a vast range of technical and non-technical solutions. In this chapter we limit ourselves to a consideration of ensuring the security of stored data and to securing transactions between access devices and ICT systems or between ICT systems themselves.

To provide a secure environment for the conduct of e-business three conditions must be satisfied (Schneier, 2000):

- *Privacy*. Only those persons who can demand access to data as a right or in terms of use should be given access to stored data. In terms of data transmission only the parties to the e-commerce transaction should have access to the data held about the transaction.
- *Authentication*. Users of ICT systems need to be authenticated as well as the parties to an e-business transaction. In general messages should only be exchanged between parties whose identity has been certified by a reputable organisation.
- *Non-repudiability*. A user of an ICT system should not be able to deny that they have used the systems and the sender of a message cannot deny that they have sent the message.

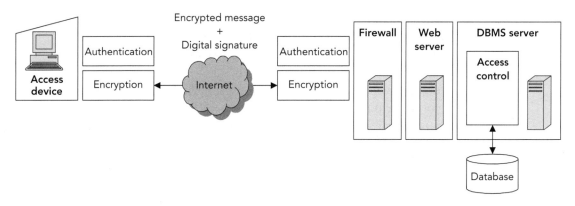

Figure 13.1 The components of data security.

Some of the major components of the technical infrastructure for ensuring data security between and within the ICT infrastructure are illustrated in Figure 13.1.

Suppose we consider an individual user wishing to access her bank account details in order to transfer monies between her bank accounts. In a simple model of secure electronic service delivery a particular access device such as a PC will attempt to connect to a secure Web server resident in the banking organisation. Depending on the activity, messages from the access device will be encrypted and bundled with a form of identification known as a digital signature. The message will be sent over the Internet. Messages will be decrypted and unbundled at the organisation end and examined by a system known as a firewall. This will validate the message in various ways and only allow access to particular Web servers once certain security rules are satisfied. It is likely that personal bank account details will be held in some form of database managed by a DBMS server. Further levels of security control may be required for access to this data such as user names and passwords checked against an access control list.

Question	Are the issues of trust and security two sides of the same coin or is the relationship more complex?

13.3 SECURING STORED DATA

Data security is the process of protecting stored data from external threats. Data security is of primary concern because of the key value that data holds for modern organisations.

Threats include possibilities of theft and fraud, loss of confidentiality, loss of privacy, loss of integrity and loss of availability. Examples of each type of threat are given below:

- *Theft and fraud*. Examples here include a person not authorised to do so updating corporate data with the aim of defrauding their employer. Another example is that of a hacker making an illegal entry into a database system and extracting corporate data without permission.
- *Confidentiality*. An unauthorised person viewing information on confidential corporate policies and disclosing it to outside agencies.
- *Privacy*. An unauthorised person viewing data on persons held by an organisation.
- *Integrity*. A software virus causing corruption of data or loss of integrity caused by software or hardware failure.
- *Availability*. A database system becoming unavailable because of natural disasters such as fire and flood or disasters initiated by humans, such as bomb attacks.

The organisation will need to plan a number of computer-based and non-computer-based measures for countering threats such as those encountered above.

Example

Meerkanten (Cabinet Office, 2002) was the first of 9 psychiatric and 16 general hospitals in the Netherlands to use a database system specifically designed to enhance privacy of data. Patient data in the database is divided into three domains:

- Identification data, such as patient name and address
- Carer information, such as the name and local carer number
- Clinical data such as symptoms, diagnosis and treatment plans

Each patient in this psychiatric hospital has a lead psychiatrist who is the only person able to access all the data stored about a patient by merging these three domains. Linking the domains is also possible by others in the case of an emergency. In such cases an entry is written to an audit file.

13.3.1 COMPUTER-BASED SECURITY MEASURES

Computer-based measures include implementing a suitable authorisation strategy in relation to a number of key technologies such as operating systems, ICT systems and database systems. This normally involves assigning user names and passwords to various individuals and groups in the organisation. When a user logs into a system using an access device a user name and password are typically requested. The authentication items will have been assigned to her previously by system administrators. Such authorisation tokens are typically checked against an access control list held in encrypted form by the relevant system.

Extensions to authentication of this nature include the issuing of physical tokens such as a card with an electromagnetic strip or a smartcard with an embedded chip to each valid user. Such security mechanisms require a specialised input device connected to an access device in order to read the card. Biometric systems are being introduced for extremely secure systems. These constitute specialised authentication systems, again connected to appropriate access devices, which are able to validate access on the basis of input such as an image of a person's face, iris or fingerprint.

Example

The Nationwide Building Society plans to implement biometric signature verification technology. The aim is to combat fraud and reduce reliance on paper-based processes for authentication. An electronic pad on the counter records a profile of the customer's signature, which is then embedded in an electronic document. The signature profile includes not only the physical characteristics of the signature but other variables such as the speed and acceleration of writing. The electronic document produced by such a system is intended to be used to authenticate customer transactions.

13.3.2 NON-COMPUTER-BASED MEASURES

Security is a larger issue than merely technology. Non-computer-based measures include:

- Establishing a security policy and plan and enforcing such a policy.
- Putting suitable personnel controls in place, such as separation of duties.
- Positioning computer hardware in secure environments through physical access controls.
- Securing copies of data and software in off-site, fireproof storage.

Question

Why is a separation of duties important to security? Can you provide some example of a separation of duties?

13.4 ◎ SECURING TRANSACTIONS

An increasing amount of data is now transmitted between organisations as electronic transactions. Key technologies for ensuring privacy and authentication of transactional data include:

- Encryption
- Digital signatures and certificates
- Firewalls
- Tunnelling technology

13.5 ENCRYPTION

The encryption and decryption of messages is a human activity system that has been undertaken in human societies for many thousands of years to ensure the privacy of such messages (Singh, 2000). Figure 13.2 illustrates the essential elements of this process that accompanies communication activity. An unencrypted message is normally referred to as a plain text message because of its historical association with the written word. This plain text message is first encrypted using a particular algorithm – a method for producing something – and an appropriate key that specifies the exact details of a particular encryption. At the receiver end the algorithm is applied as a decryption method using another key. This reveals the plain text message to the receiver.

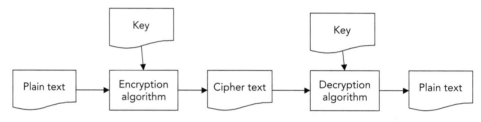

Figure 13.2 Coding of messages.

Example

One of the simplest forms of encryption employs the substitution of letters of the alphabet with the letters from a cipher alphabet. The cipher alphabet is the key to a message. The encryption and decryption algorithms involve the mere substitution of symbols between alphabets. For instance, suppose we have the plain alphabet and cipher alphabets below:

Plain: abcdefghijklmnopqrstuvwxyz

Cipher: jlpawiqbctrzydskegfxhuonvm

Hence, the plain text message 'et tu brute?' would be encrypted as 'wx xh lghxw?'.

Encryption ensures the privacy of transactions because the encryption and decryption of the message is dependent on the key that is issued to authorised actors in the communication.

Two basic algorithms for encryption are normally employed in commercial data transmission known as symmetric and asymmetric key encryption.

- *Symmetric key encryption.* In this type of encryption, sometimes known as private key encryption, the same key is applied at both ends of the encryption process. The key is agreed in advance between the sender and receiver of the message. This introduces the main problem with symmetric key encryption – messages can only be transmitted between parties known to each other and trusted to hold the private key.
- *Asymmetric key encryption.* Sometimes known as public key encryption, this technique uses a pair of keys: one private and one public. A user with a private key can give a corresponding public key to anyone she wishes. This then allows the user to send a message encrypted with the private key safe in the knowledge that only users with a corresponding public key can decrypt the message. There is no requirement for the sender to agree the keys in advance of sending a message since the user can place the public key in a register of selected users via encrypted messages.

Question	Can you think of any limitations in terms of relying on encryption to ensure security of transactions?

13.6 ⊚ DIGITAL SIGNATURES AND CERTIFICATES

Public key encryption provides the foundation for digital signatures. Digital signatures are important in authenticating the senders of messages and for ensuring a degree of non-repudiability. The sender transmits a message using a private key. If the receiver of the message is able to decrypt the message successfully using the public key then this automatically acts as a way of authenticating the sender.

The management of encryption and digital signatures requires an infrastructure that includes ensuring that keys are used only by legitimate holders and procedures for managing the assignment and storage of keys. This is referred to as the public key infrastructure (PKI) and is provided by a trusted certification authority (CA). All legitimate users are required to register with the CA to use public key encryption. The CA issues a digital certificate sometimes called a digital passport to the user. This consists of an electronic document that keeps a record of users and their public keys.

13.7 ⊚ SECURE SOCKET LAYER

Public key encryption is also important to securing data transmission over the Internet. Secure Sockets Layer (SSL) is Netscape's attempt to offer a secure channel of communication. It is a framework for transmitting sensitive information such as credit card details over the Internet. It involves using a sophisticated protocol between client and server systems that is transparent to the user and provides a secure connection. It involves the exchange of digital signatures between a client (such as an individual using an Internet-enabled PC) and a server (an organisation's front-end ICT system).

Leading vendors of Internet browsers such as Netscape and Microsoft use standards for digital certificates to implement SSL. Figure 13.3 illustrates the process of using digital certificates. The customer first has to request a digital certificate from the certification authority. She provides details of herself plus evidence of her identity to the certification authority. She also sends her public key to the certification authority (i.e. the key provided to her by the organisation she is trying to access). The certification authority produces a digital certificate and includes her public key within it. When she later wants to engage in e-commerce she uses her digital certificate to prove her authenticity to the participating organisation.

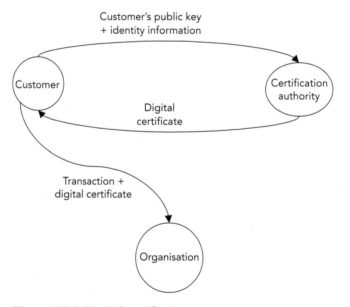

Figure 13.3 Digital certificates.

Question   The take-up of digital certificates and the associated public key infrastructure has been relatively slow in most countries. Why do you think this might be the case?

13.8 ⊚ FIREWALLS

A firewall is a system that attempts to protect a private network from hackers, software viruses, data corruption or unauthorised access. Effectively it restricts access to the private network by external users and may also be used to prohibit internal users from accessing selected parts of the private network.

Example | A typical use of a firewall would be to prevent unauthorised Internet (public network) users from accessing the Intranet of an organisation (private network).

Firewalls can be implemented in hardware or software or both. It typically comprises a proxy server, which examines all messages entering or leaving the private network, and blocks those that do not match particular security criteria. In a Web environment a proxy server is a computer system that sits between a web browser and a web server. Such a proxy server is likely to run routers, other communications software and special programs known as proxies. One proxy is normally assigned for each Internet service, such as HTTP and FTP. When data packets from the external environment reach the firewall it checks the packets for details of their source and destination. It then makes a decision to accept or reject the packet depending on an inspection of an access control list and a set of associated security controls.

13.9 ⊚ TUNNELLING TECHNOLOGY

Tunnelling technology involves the transmission of data over the Internet using leased lines to the local ISP. With the use of encryption, authentication and other security technologies such an approach can be used to produce a Virtual Private Network (VPN) over a wide area network. In this approach data packets are encrypted and encapsulated into IP packets and then transmitted over the Internet using routers. At the receiver end the packet is decrypted and authenticity checks are made. Thus secure data tunnels are created between an organisation's systems and key external stakeholders such as suppliers and partners. This approach offers an inexpensive way for an organisation to extend the reach of its information systems and is the key technology underlying Extranets (Chapter 12).

13.10 ⊚ CASE STUDY: ELECTRONIC VOTING

Authentication of electors in the current human activity system of voting (Chapter 4) consists of the production of a valid polling card by the elector. This is used to check the elector's details, such as name and address, against an electoral list by a polling officer.

Security of voting transactions is assured through the following manual procedures. A line is drawn through the elector's details on the electoral list to indicate that a ballot paper has been issued to the elector. The ballot paper is stamped to indicate that a polling officer has issued it and voting is undertaken in a booth under the supervision of the polling officer.

Security of voting date is assured through votes being posted in a sealed ballot box that is transferred to a counting centre at the close of voting. The ballot boxes are opened under the supervision of a presiding officer for the constituency.

In a situation in which remote electronic voting is introduced (Chapter 7), various other forms of authentication and security must be employed. This might include posting a Personal Identification Number (PIN) to each elector on the electoral roll. In the case of using a government Web site to vote this may be accompanied by an appropriate password. In the case of using an electronic voting machine or kiosk to vote the elector might be sent a smart card for use in an authentication device attached to the voting machine. This might be taken to its logical extreme in employing some biometric device to perform authentication.

The security of transactions may be assured in various ways such as in the case of voting over the Internet using encryption and issuing some form of digital certificate to each elector that registers to vote in this way. If voting were conducted using private networks such as the ATM or National Lottery network, security would be assured through the use of a dedicated communications network or possibly by employing tunnelling technology.

The security of data is likely to involve various computer-based and non-computer-based measures employed against the voting server. Computer-based measures are likely to employ authorisation control lists and use of firewalls.

13.11 SUMMARY

- To provide a secure environment for the conduct of e-commerce over the Internet three conditions must be satisfied: authentication, privacy and non-repudiability.

- We may distinguish between ensuring the security of stored data and securing transactions between access devices and ICT systems or between ICT systems.

- Key approaches to ensuring the security of stored data include the use of authorisation schemes such as user names and passwords.

- Key technologies for ensuring privacy and authentication of transactional data include encryption; digital signatures and certificates; firewalls; and tunnelling technology.

13.12 ⊚ ACTIVITIES

(i) Determine how privacy is handled in a system known to you.

(ii) Investigate more systematically the relationship between trust and security.

(iii) Determine how authentication is handled in a system known to you.

(iv) Determine how non-repudiability is handled in a system known to you.

(v) Determine the sort of access controls used in an ICT system known to you.

(vi) Determine the range of approaches to establishing firewalls.

13.13 ⊚ REFERENCES

Cabinet Office (2002). *Privacy and Data Sharing: the Way Forward for Public Services.* London, Cabinet Office.

Greenstein, M. and Vasarhelyi, M. (2002). *Electronic Commerce: Security, Management and Control.* New York, McGraw-Hill.

Schneier, B. (2000). *Secrets and Lies: Digital Security in a Networked World.* Chichester, John Wiley.

Singh, S. (2000). *The Science of Secrecy.* London, Fourth Estate.

Stamper, R. K. (1985). Information: mystical fluid or a subject for scientific enquiry? *The Computer Journal,* 28(3).

PART **3**

THE ENVIRONMENT OF E-BUSINESS

Grace is given of god, but knowledge is bought in the market

Arthur Hugh Clough, *The Bothie of Toper-na-Vuolich*

A verbal contract isn't worth the paper it is written on.

Samuel Goldwyn

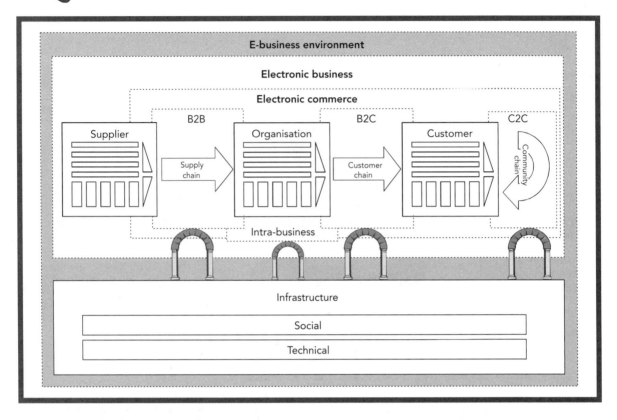

An organisation can be considered as a human activity system, or more accurately as a series of human activity systems. An organisation is an open system. As represented in the model of the e-business domain illustrated above, an organisation is surrounded by its environment. It receives inputs from its environment and outputs into its environment. A commercial organisation, for instance, may be conceived of as a unit which takes resources from its environment and processes them to produce products or services which it supplies back to its environment. Capital and labour are the two types of resources provided by the environment. The environment consumes the products and services produced by the organisation and supplies additional capital and labour to the organisation.

The environment allows an organisation to grow in various ways. It also constrains what an organisation is able to do in terms of its human activity. Hence, by *environment* we mean anything outside of the organisation with which it interacts. The environment of most organisations can be considered in terms of the interaction between three major overlapping environmental systems: an economic system, a political system and a social system. The environment of an organisation comprises a complex network of relationships and activities between the organisation and other agencies in the social, political and economic spheres.

An open systems model of the organisation emphasises that the relationship between the environment and an organisation is a dialectical one. In other words, organisations are both affected by and affect environments. Hence the external systems in each area of the environment will exert an impact on the e-business activities of an organisation. Likewise, the e-business activities of organisations are likely to impact on other agencies in the social, economic and political spheres.

Beer (1985) argues that this dialectical relationship between environment and organisation is characterised by processes of amplification and attenuation that have a critical bearing on the viability of an organisation (Chapter 3). It is always true to say that the variety (Chapter 2) in the environment of an organisation is inherently greater than the variety in the organisation itself. Because of this an organisation must continually react to its environment in terms of a cycle of attenuation and amplification.

Attenuation is the process of reducing variety. In terms of the relationship between an organisation and its environment, attenuation refers to the process by which an organisation reduces the variety inherent in its environment as a means of understanding and reacting to environmental change. An organisation is continually attenuating the high variety in its environment to the possible number of states that it is able to handle. Information systems are critical both in terms of defining the variety an organisation is able to handle and in terms of managing such variety.

Amplification is the process by which an organisation attempts to increase its variety within the environment. The comparatively low variety within an organisation compared to its environment means that it must amplify its variety to the number of possible states that the environment needs if it is to remain regulated. Again, information systems are critical to this amplification process.

Both attenuation and amplification are strategies by which organisations adapt to their environments while also influencing change within the environment. Hence the e-business is both affected by and affects its environment. For instance:

● In terms of the economic environment information systems are key to organisational performance within economic markets. Recently, growth has been experienced in specialised markets focused on the use of electronic networks. Electronic business and electronic commerce have become significant strategies for modern organisations. However, the utility of conducting business electronically is determined by the shape of the economic environment, both nationally and globally. Indeed, the globalisation of economic activity is a significant feature of the contemporary economic environment for business and a significant driving force behind e-business. This is the topic of Chapter 14.

- The social system concerns ways in which people relate to organisational activity. The social attitudes to issues such as data protection and privacy, as well as the trust in e-commerce systems, affects the practicality of e-business long-term. A number of preconditions exist for the successful take-up of electronic delivery of services and products, including awareness, interest, access, skills, use and impact. The increasing use of ICT for private and public sector transactions is seen as potentially creating a 'digital divide' between those who have access to technology and those who do not. This is the topic of Chapter 15.

- The political environment is particularly concerned with government and legal frameworks within nation states. The practice of government determines policy and regulation in the e-business and e-commerce areas. However, e-business is also a significant force in government. The political environment of Western countries has been much subject to the influence of ICT in the areas of electronic government and electronic democracy in recent times. This is the topic of Chapter 16.

We will argue in Chapter 23 that an understanding of the economic, social and political environment surrounding an organisation and its activities is critical to organisational success. Organisations continually need to scan their environment in all three areas for threats and opportunities. Such monitoring will contribute to the development and implementation of effective e-business strategy (Chapter 24).

REFERENCE

Beer, S. (1985). *Diagnosing the System for Organisations*. Oxford, Oxford University Press.

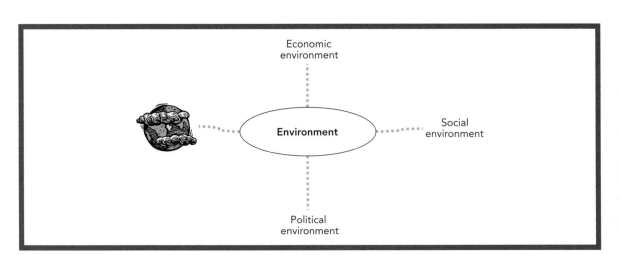

14

THE ECONOMIC ENVIRONMENT FOR E-BUSINESS

There can be no economy where there is no efficiency

Benjamin Disraeli

Economics is the science which studies human behaviour as a relationship between ends and scarce means which have alternative uses

Lord Lionel Robbins, *An Essay on the Nature and Significance of Economic Science*

LEARNING OUTCOMES

After reading this chapter, you will be able to:

- Discuss the economic environment of e-business
- Define the concepts of a market and hierarchy and outline the major elements of these economic forms
- Describe the different types of economic actor
- Outline the major economic relationships a business has to deal with and how this affects the competitive position of the company
- Define the concept of an electronic market and electronic hierarchy

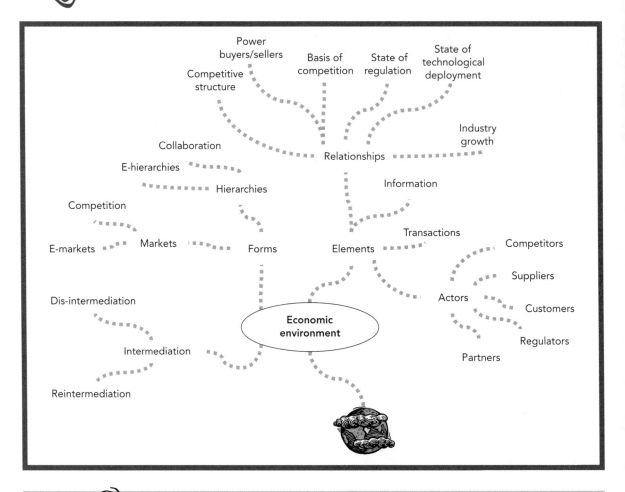

14.1 INTRODUCTION

Any organisation works within the constraints and opportunities afforded by its environment. For commercial organisations the economic environment of the organisation is probably the most important. The economic environment is typically organised in terms of systems of markets and hierarchies. Markets are systems of competition. Hierarchies are systems of collaboration. Increasingly economic markets and hierarchies worldwide have been subject to the influence of ICT (Turner, 2000). Hence many contemporary markets are electronic markets (e-markets) and many contemporary hierarchies are electronic hierarchies (e-hierarchies). Such economic systems constitute markets and hierarchies in which economic exchanges are conducted using ICT.

In this chapter we define more precisely the concepts of markets and hierarchies. We examine the economic actors and relationships contributing to such economic systems. We then define the concepts of an electronic market and an electronic hierarchy and make reference to the ways in which such economic systems affect the competitive position of organisations. We conclude with a brief review of the issue of globalisation of economic activity and its effect on e-business.

14.2 ⊚ THE ECONOMIC ENVIRONMENT

An organisation exists within some economic system. At the level of the nation state we speak of such an economic system as being an economy. An economic system is the way in which a group of humans arrange their material provisioning. It essentially involves the coordination of activities concerned with such provisioning.

Two major processes are relevant to economic systems: production and distribution. Production is that set of activities concerned with the creation of goods and services for human existence. Distribution is the associated process of collecting, storing and moving goods into the hands of consumers and providing services for consumers.

Production and distribution are activities that deliver value. Hence economies can be seen as consisting of a multitude of chains of value both within and between organisations (Chapter 3): the internal value chain, supply chain, customer chain and community chain.

Example
Agriculture is that part of the economy which produces basic foodstuffs. Various other companies may process such foodstuffs to produce processed foods. Retailers such as supermarket chains will then collect, store and sell such goods on to the customer.

Questions
It is probably more accurate to describe modern economic systems as being composed of complex networks of organisations. What forms of value transmit along such networks? Can such complex systems be controlled?

14.3 ⊚ MARKETS AND HIERARCHIES

Malone *et al.* (1987) insist that economies have two basic mechanisms for controlling the flow of goods and services in such chains of value: markets and hierarchies. Markets coordinate flow through forces of supply and demand and external transactions between individuals and firms. Hierarchies coordinate flow by controlling and directing it at a higher level in management hierarchies. In a sense, markets and hierarchies constitute types of economic control system.

According to Malone *et al.* (1987) markets and hierarchies can be distinguished in terms of:

- The balance of production costs to coordination (transaction) costs.
- The balance of asset specificity to the complexity of product description.

Production costs include the processes necessary to create and distribute goods and services. Coordination costs or transaction costs include the costs of information processing necessary to coordinate the work of people and machines (Bakos, 1997). Markets are generally characterised by low production costs and high coordination costs. Hierarchies are typically characterised by high production costs and low coordination costs.

Malone *et al.* (1987) argued in the 1980s that the increase in ICT use would stimulate a trend towards electronic markets and electronic hierarchies. They also argued for the dominance of market forms because ICT will decrease the costs of coordination and will enable companies to increase the personalisation of goods and services – thus enabling them to better handle issues of product complexity and asset specificity.

Asset specificity refers to inputs that are specific to a firm. A company input is asset-specific if it cannot be readily used by another firm. This may be because it is specific in terms of its location, human knowledge or physical attributes. Complexity of product description refers to the amount of information needed to specify the attributes of a product in enough detail to allow buyers to make a selection. Generally speaking, markets are good for low product complexity and low asset specificity, whereas hierarchies are good for high asset specificity and high product complexity.

Examples

A specialised tool such as a machine tool is physically specific if it is designed for a specific purpose. Coal produced by a coal mine located close to some power station is site-specific. A service provided by a consultant with specific knowledge of a company's processes would be said to be knowledge specific.

Questions

In what respect is it appropriate to describe both the idea of a market and hierarchy as being forms of control mechanism? Have Malone et al.'s predictions for the dominance of market forms come true?

14.4 MARKETS

Markets are systems of competition. A market is a medium for exchanges between many potential buyers and many potential sellers. A market, or for larger companies a series of markets, forms the immediate environment of a company. Markets form the competitive environment of the organisation and because of their many-to-many nature they are heavily reliant on large volumes of information flow.

Example
One of the crucial markets for financial companies is the stock market. The stock market is a market for the exchange of shares and other forms of securities.

14.5 HIERARCHIES

Hierarchies are systems of cooperation. A hierarchy is a medium for exchanges between a limited number of buyers and sellers. The buyers and sellers exchange goods and services within established patterns of trade. Hierarchies form the cooperative environment of organisations and typically, because of the established nature of relationships, they rely on smaller volumes of information flow than for markets.

Example
Most companies have established trading relationships with a limited number of suppliers. Such relationships are fundamentally exercised in terms of hierarchies. Hence an automobile manufacturer is likely to build established trading relationships with a limited range of component suppliers. It is also likely to distribute its products through a specialised network of dealerships.

14.6 ELEMENTS OF MARKETS AND HIERARCHIES

Both markets and hierarchies can be seen to be composed of:

- *Economic actors*. Economic activity occurs between organisations, groups and/or individuals.
- *Relationships*. A market is fundamentally a series of relationships between defined economic actors, whether they be individuals, groups or organisations. The relationships are fundamentally located around forms of exchange.
- *Information*. Information is essential to the coordination of activity in markets and hierarchies between buyers and sellers.
- *Transactions*. Economic exchanges within markets are bundled in terms of defined transactions between buyers and sellers.

Example
Consider two organisations in which organisation A is the buyer of goods from organisation B. The relationship between organisation A and B is therefore one of trade. Organisations A and B are both economic actors. Along with the flow of goods

between these two organisations there is a flow of information. Such information is normally bundled in terms of defined transactions such as invoices, shipping notes and payments.

Question

What actors, relationships, information and transactions make up the stock market?

14.7 ⊚ ECONOMIC ACTORS

It is convenient to consider an organisation's economic environment as defined by activities and relationships between four main types of economic actor and the organisation (Figure 14.1). These activities and relationships define a particular market.

- *Competitors*. Other organisations in the same fundamental area of business.
- *Suppliers*. Those organisations providing resources to the organisation.

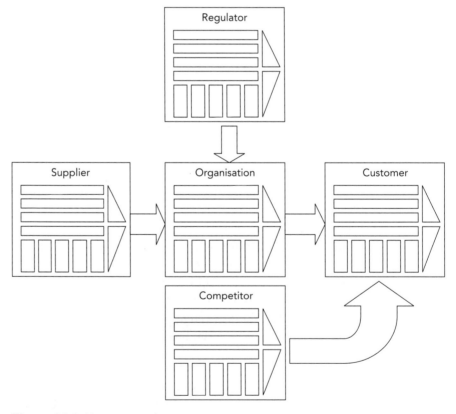

Figure 14.1 Key economic actors.

- *Customers*. Those individuals, groups or organisations purchasing products or services from the organisation.

- *Regulators*. Groups or organisations which set policy for appropriate activities in a particular market. Effectively these are groups which attempt to control behaviour in economic systems.

A fifth type of economic actor, namely partners, is important in the context of hierarchies.

Organisations may take on the role of different actors at different times in an economic environment. Organisations may be both buyers of goods and services and sellers of goods and services. Organisations may compete with other organisations in the sale of particular goods and services. Organisations may also set policy for the supply of particular goods and services from other, perhaps smaller, organisations and hence act as regulators.

Example

Take the case of an organisation such as a supermarket chain. The economic environment of this organisation could be described as food retail. In the UK this economic environment is characterised by the dominance of four major competitors: Tesco, Asda, Sainsbury and Safeway. Each supermarket chain has many suppliers ranging from farms providing fresh foodstuffs to factories providing processed foods and other products. The customers of the supermarkets are the general public. Food retail is heavily regulated by bodies such as the Food Standards Agency within the UK.

Question

What sort of economic actors exist in the financial services industry?

14.8 ECONOMIC RELATIONSHIPS

Michael Porter (Porter and Millar, 1985) defines an economic environment in terms of the following factors that involve relationships between the four main types of economic actors described above (Figure 14.2):

- *Competitive structure of the industry*. This really defines the relative power of competitors to determine things like the pricing policy in the economic environment.

- *Relative power of buyers and sellers*. This highlights the important position that customers and suppliers play in markets.

- *Basis of competition*. This means describing the main products or services sold and the main ways in which organisations compete in the economic environment.

- *State of regulation in the economic environment*. Regulation can crucially determine the activities that companies may perform in particular markets or hierarchies.

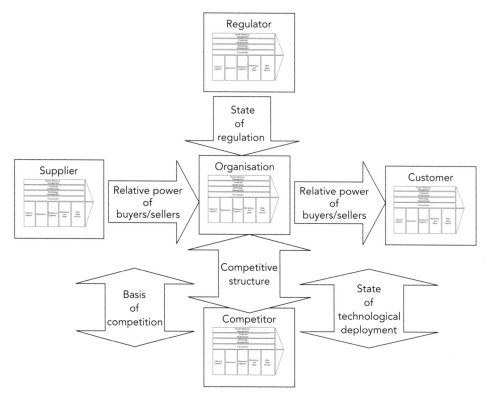

Figure 14.2 Actors and relationships in a market.

- *State of technological deployment in the environment.* In certain markets the use of technology is essential to competitiveness and/or cooperation.
- *Industry growth.* Whether the industry is growing, shrinking or stable; this is a reflection of the state of regulation, competition and demand in a particular market.

Examples | In food retail in the UK the dominance of big supermarkets means that they have enormous power in determining pricing levels for key foodstuffs from their suppliers. However, the food retail industry is subject to quite heavy degrees of regulation in such areas as environmental health legislation. The food retail sector is still growing in the UK. In recent years the major supermarkets have increased their levels of technological deployment quite dramatically and have utilised their information systems in new areas such as financial services. The basis of competition has traditionally been on matters of pricing although other bases such as the quality of foodstuffs (particularly in relation to organic foodstuffs) have recently come into play.

The use of ICT to support the modern information-based economy is normally given the label of the New Economy. Coyle and Quah (2002) argue that consumers are now the critical drivers of the innovation and change in advanced economies. For them, understanding the New Economy means understanding how technology and consumerism interact. A critical aspect of this is the growing use of electronic delivery of products and services as described in Chapter 7.

14.9 ◎ COMPETITIVE POSITION

An organisation takes up a particular position in an economic system defined by its activities and relationships with its competitors, suppliers, customers and regulators (Porter, 2001). The strategy of a business is normally developed with the objective of at least maintaining and more usually improving the competitive or market position of some company. In systems terms strategy is a weapon of viability.

E-business strategy (Chapter 22) is a specialised form of business strategy. An e-business strategy attempts to influence an organisation's position and relationships through its relative technological capability.

Example   Consider a major book retailer. Part of its business strategy may be to increase the coverage of its marketing campaigns for new books. Part of this business strategy may be fulfilled by an e-business strategy that produces a marketing Internet site for the company. This will be expected to improve the position of the retailer in relation to its competitors.

Question   *What is the relationship between the notion of competitive position and that of the viability of an organisation?*

14.10 ◎ ELECTRONIC MARKETS

Many contemporary markets are electronic markets (e-markets) (Malone *et al.*, 1989). By an e-market we mean one in which economic exchanges are conducted using ICT. In an e-market, electronic transactions between employees, buyers and sellers enable the efficient and effective flow of goods and services through internal, supply, customer and community chains (Means and Schneider, 2000).

The e-market is the domain in which buying companies and selling companies meet. The exchange of goods and services are enabled through electronic transactions between both buyer and seller and the financial institutions of each. In its most comprehensive form the market handles all the transactions between companies and individuals, including the transfer of money between banks.

Examples

The stock market within the UK is now an electronic market. Shares can be traded between companies using ICT. There is hence no longer a need for a physical stock exchange in central London. The stock exchange is now a virtual entity.

Gatetrade.net (Brunn, *et al.*, 2002) is a public e-marketplace founded in October 2000 by a consortium of the four large Danish corporations (TDV, Post Danmark, Danske Bank and Maersk Data) on behalf of the A. P. Møller group. The aim of this initiative is to become the leading horizontal e-marketplace in the Nordic region. Each of the four companies initially invested €3.4 million in the venture. In the short term gatetrade.net has focused its sales effort on a few key buyers and sellers in the Danish market, particularly the Danish State. In March 2001 it was awarded the contract for the Danish public purchasing portal by the Danish State. This ensures that public purchasing to the potential value of €27 billion over a five-year period could flow through the operation.

Question

Electronic payment systems are critical to the operation of electronic markets. Why?

14.11 INTERMEDIATION, DISINTERMEDIATION AND REINTERMEDIATION

Aspects of the external value chains of organisations have been critically affected by the creation of electronic markets. The traditional retail chain is one of wholesalers, distributors and retailers. However, by using the Internet, producers can now sell directly to their customers. This process is known as disintermediation in the sense that intermediaries are removed in the customer chain. But the Internet suffers from being a large and complex medium for supporting a market. Potential customers for particular products and services frequently find it difficult to find the precise company meeting their needs. Hence in recent times a new breed of intermediaries – electronic intermediaries – has emerged. Such organisations reimpose middlemen between the producers of products and services and the consumers of such products and services. They supply a service to the consumer in locating companies fulfilling their needs and they supply a service to the producer in identifying potential customers. This process is known as reintermediation. Figure 14.3 illustrates these three processes of intermediation, disintermediation and reintermediation.

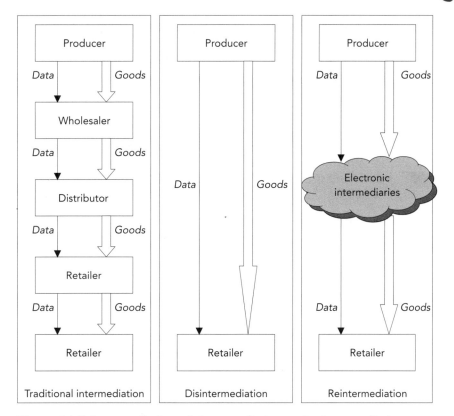

Figure 14.3 Intermediation, disintermediation and reintermediation.

Question   *Disintermediation has been happening in industries such as travel and insurance. Explain why?*

14.12   ELECTRONIC HIERARCHIES AND INTER-ORGANISATIONAL INFORMATION SYSTEMS

E-markets are founded on competition. A market is a network of interactions and relationships by which products and services are negotiated and exchanged. However, business can also be founded on cooperation and collaboration. Electronic hierarchies are ways of managing such cooperation and collaboration.

Malone *et al.* argued in the 1980s that electronic hierarchies will tend towards forms of inter-organisational information system (IOS) (Barrette and Konsynski, 1982). An IOS is an information system developed and maintained by a consortium of companies for the mutual benefit of member companies. Generally such systems provide an infrastructure for sharing an application. IOS can prove a particularly effective way of sharing the costs of developing and maintaining large and complex information systems.

Examples

The automatic teller machine (ATM) networks run by major building societies and banks in the UK are key examples of business-to-consumer IOS. These networks are constructed and maintained by consortia of these financial institutions. This enables them to distribute the large costs of running such networks among the participating members.

Autobytel Nederland's Web site (De man *et al.*, 2002) offers a complete solution for automobile purchasers and owners. The site integrates four main services for this market:

- *New car purchases.* Customers may select a car on the site. Autobytel then e-mails the nearest dealer to the customer for a price. Dealer and buyer are then left to conclude a deal.

- *Buying and selling used cars.* Both dealers and private persons may offer used cars for sale via the Web site. Private persons pay a fee to do so.

- *Insurance products.* Insurance companies are able to offer products such as car insurance through the Web site.

- *Financial products.* Clients can obtain financial products through the site such as loans for car purchase.

Autobytel Nederland is made up of four main partners: Autobytel Europe (a subsidiary of Autobytel US), De Telegraaf (a Netherlands newspaper with expertise in second-hand car advertisements), PON Holding (an international trading group) and Achmea (a financial conglomerate). The company has negotiated deals with a number of contractual partners, such as car dealership networks and financial corporations. Such contractual partners pay membership fees to Autobytel Nederland and incur fees against each sale made via the site.

Question

Are Extranets forms of IOS or not?

 14.13 ⦿ GLOBALISATION

It is important to emphasise that the movement towards electronic markets and to a certain extent electronic hierarchies is a global phenomenon. Companies can trade electronically with customers and suppliers situated in almost any country and hence the economic environment becomes worldwide. Companies can also choose to site their operations in the most advantageous regulatory regime. Competition in this economic environment is not solely from local competitors but from global competitors. This means that pricing policy in particular markets will be affected by global competition.

Many of these trends are encapsulated in the term globalisation (Castells, 1996). For large companies the term *globalisation* frequently has a number of positive connotations, such as the ability to reduce costs and increase flexibility of business operation. For many nation states the term *globalisation* has a series of negative connotations, such as increasing Americanisation and Westernisation. They see globalisation as causing a loss of national identity and national control over economic activity.

Because of its critical role in supporting both competitive and collaborative systems between organisations and between organisations and individuals, ICT can be seen as an enabler of globalisation. One particular example of this is the degree to which Western governments have felt it important to stimulate e-commerce among their small and medium sized enterprises (SMEs). The rationale is that SMEs must compete on the global scale, and effective use of ICT is critical to achieving this.

Example

Larger organisations have clearly been involved in e-business and e-commerce for several years, notably by trading electronically using electronic data interchange (EDI). Such large companies have had ample opportunity to assess the relative benefits of implementing such technology into their business process. However, developments under the Internet umbrella are offering increasingly affordable technologies that permit e-commerce to reach the smallest businesses as well. Hence e-business and e-commerce as a form of technological innovation has been seen as critical to stimulating growth in the Small and Medium-sized Enterprise (SME) sector. Such innovation has been seen as particularly significant for disadvantaged regions of the European Union.

There is no universally accepted definition of an SME. The main feature of an SME is that it is 'not large', in the sense that an SME is not in the core of the largest 10% or 20% of enterprises in the market or industry (OECD, 2000). In February 1996, the European Commission (EC) set out a single definition of SMEs (EC, 1996), as enterprises employing fewer than 250 employees, with an annual turnover of less than €40 million or an annual balance sheet of no more than €27 million.

SMEs are the most significant sector of the UK economy, accounting for 99.8% of all UK enterprises and 99.9% of total Welsh enterprises. Moreover the 'size class zero' enterprises – those made up of sole traders or partners (e.g. two people) without employees (DTI, 2000) account for 63% of all UK enterprises. In contrast, medium-sized (50 to 249 employees) and non-SME classified enterprises constitute only 0.7% and 0.2% of total UK enterprises respectively.

A conference by the Organisation for Economic Co-operation & Development (OECD) identified that governments worldwide recognise the importance of SMEs and their contribution to economic growth, social cohesion, employment, and regional and local development (OECD, 2000). Globalisation and technological change bring new opportunities for SMEs to enter foreign markets and to reduce business costs, but there are also transition costs, new competitive challenges and risks that have to be met. It has therefore been seen as vital that governments encourage the development of innovation in the SME sector.

14.14 ꩜ CASE STUDY: NAPSTER

The software application Napster is an important example of the way in which ICT impacts upon economic structures in an established industry. In Porter's terms such applications have begun to affect the competitive structure of the music industry.

Napster was created by Shawn Fanning when he was a freshman student at the NorthEastern University in Boston, Massachusetts in the summer of 1999. It was initially produced as a fun application and Fanning originally released it to 15 fellow students, swearing them not to release it to others.

Effectively Napster is a software application that enables users to locate and share digital music in MP3 format (Chapter 8). It combined features of existing programs such as search engines, file-sharing systems and instant messaging. It is generally regarded as a pioneer in what has become known as P2P (peer-to-peer) Internet software. This form of software architecture is predicted to have an increasing impact on both B2B and B2C trading (McAfee, 2000).

By August 2000 Napster had been used in a total of 6.7 million homes. By February 2001 Napster had 45 employees and by September 2002 it had 60 million devotees worldwide.

Napster threatened the traditional value chain and business model of the music industry. Traditionally musical artists record for a recording company which then mass produces and markets the musical material on media such as compact discs (CDs). Such material is then sold by a number of retail outlets. The consumer has to purchase material from the retailer, plus an appropriate means of playing the material, such as a CD player. In this chain artists get paid royalties on the sale and use of their musical material and therefore get a return on their creative investment.

By using MP3 and Napster individuals could bypass recording companies and retailers – a form of disintermediation. Music can be quickly copied from CDs and stored as MP3 files. Such files can then be freely distributed around the Internet using the Napster application.

The music industry responded on two fronts. First, the Recording Industry Association of America (RIAA) created the Secure Digital Music Initiative (SDMI). This was an industry group which attempted to create a secure form of digital music format. The intention was to attempt to prevent copying of digital music from CDs. Second, litigation was undertaken by various actors within the music industry which attempted to prove that the existence of Napster infringed US copyright law (Chapter 16).

In 2002 Napster had to close down because of a judicial ruling in favour of the music industry. However, many P2P applications are still impacting upon sales of CD music.

14.15 SUMMARY

- The primary environment of a commercial organisation is the economy.
- Economies are systems for coordinating the production and distribution of goods/products and services.
- Economic activity is organised in terms of markets or hierarchies.
- Markets are systems of competition. They are media of exchange between buyers and sellers.
- Hierarchies are systems of cooperation. Exchange is conducted on the basis of established trading arrangements.
- Both markets and hierarchies can be seen to be composed of actors, relationships, information and transactions.
- There are four main types of economic actor in a market: competitors, suppliers, customers and regulators.
- The shape of an economic environment can be seen to be determined by six major forces: competitive structure of the industry, relative power of buyers and sellers, basis of competition, state of regulation in the economic environment, state of technological deployment in the environment, whether the industry is growing, shrinking or stable.
- An organisation takes up a particular position in an economic system defined by its activities and relationships with its competitors, suppliers, customers and regulators.
- An e-market is a market in which economic exchanges are conducted using information technology and computer networks.
- Electronic hierarchies tend towards inter-organisational information systems. This is an information system developed and maintained by a consortium of companies for the mutual benefit of member companies.

14.16 ACTIVITIES

(i) Identify the production and distribution processes in an industry known to you.

(ii) Identify the internal and external value chains relevant to a company or organisation known to you.

(iii) Consider a company which produces trucks for haulage contractors. Determine whether this business sector would be arranged as a market or a hierarchy.

(iv) Provide one other example of a market and describe what is exchanged.

(v) Provide one other example of an economic hierarchy and determine what established trading relationships exist in this hierarchy.

(vi) Describe the actors, relationships, information and transactions in a segment of a market or hierarchy known to you.

(vii) Identify the competitors, customers and suppliers of an organisation known to you.

(viii) Describe some of the relationships between competitors, suppliers, customers and regulators in an industrial sector known to you. Determine the basis of competition and the state of technological deployment. Identify whether the industry is growing, shrinking or stable.

(ix) Jot down some brief notes on the business strategy of an organisation known to you and examine whether this strategy includes any consideration of the strategic implications of ICT.

(x) In a trading relationship known to you identify some common transactions and information flows.

(xi) Many travel companies are now offering holiday products over the Internet. Determine to what degree such business is becoming an electronic market.

(xii) Another example of an inter-organisational information system is the limited number of airline reservation systems run by the consortia of the major airlines. Determine some of the reasons such systems are managed as IOS.

14.17 REFERENCES

Bakos, J. Y. (1997). Reducing buyer search costs – implications for electronic marketplaces. *Management Science*, **43**(12), 1676–1692.

Barrette, S. and Konsynski, B. R. (1982). Inter-organisational information sharing systems. *MIS Quarterly* (Fall).

Brunn, P., Jensen, M. and Skovgaard, J. (2002). e-Marketplaces: crafting a winning strategy. *European Management Journal*, **20**(3), 286–298.

Castells, M. (1996). *The Rise of the Network Society*. Massachusetts, Blackwell.

Coyle, D. and Quah, D. (2002). *Getting the Measure of the New Economy*. London, The Work Foundation.

De man, A.-P., Strenstra, M. and Vallenda, H. W. (2002). e-Partnering: moving bricks and mortar online. *European Management Journal*, **20**(4), 329–399.

DTI (2000). *Statistical News Release, Small and Medium Enterprise (SME) Statistics for the UK, 1999*, Department of Trade and Industry.

EC (1996). *Commission recommendation of 3 April 1996 concerning the definition of small and medium-sized enterprises*, European Commission: 4–9.

Malone, T. W., Yates, J. and Benjamin, R. I. C. (1987). Electronic markets and electronic hierarchies. *Communications of the ACM*, **30**(6), 484–497.

Malone, T. W., Benjamin, R. I. and Yates, J. (1989). The logic of electronic marketplaces. *Harvard Business Review*, **67**(3), 166.

McAfee, A. (2000). The Napsterization of B2B. Harvard Business Review 2000(November-December): 18–19.

Means, G. and Schneider, D. (2000). *MetaCapitalism: the E-business Revolution and the Design of 21st-Century Companies and Markets*. New York, John Wiley.

OECD (2000). The Bologna Charter on SME policies: enhancing the competitiveness of SMEs, In *The Global Economy: Strategies and Policies*. Bologna, OECD.

Porter, M. E. (2001). Strategy and the Internet. *Harvard Business Review*, **79**(3), 63–78.

Porter, M. E. and Millar, V. E. (1985). How information gives you competitive advantage. *Harvard Business Review*, **63**(4), 149–160.

Turner, C. (2000). *The Information E-Conomy*. London, Kogan-Page.

THE SOCIAL ENVIRONMENT OF E-BUSINESS

He who is unable to live in society, or who has no need because he is sufficient for himself, must be either a beast or a god.

Aristotle, *Politics*

LEARNING OUTCOMES

After reading this chapter, you will be able to:

- Describe some of the major indicators of the information society
- Outline some of the preconditions for the electronic delivery of goods and services
- Define the digital divide and its relationship to social exclusion
- Outline how concerns of privacy and trust may affect the uptake of e-commerce

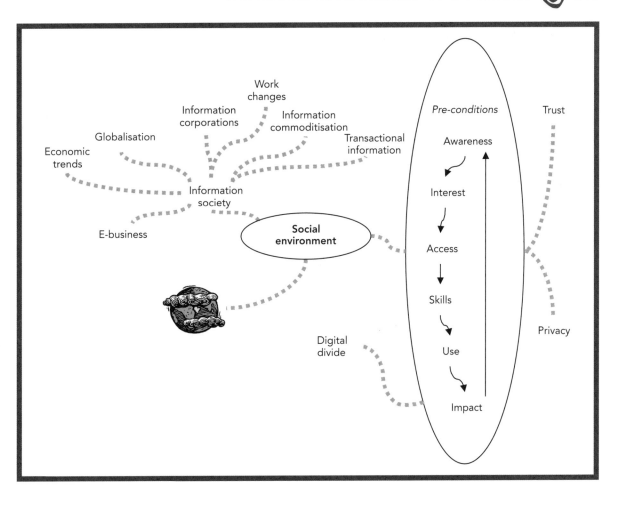

INTRODUCTION

In recent times it has become popular to speak of the information society, thus identifying the important impact of information, information systems and ICT upon modern social systems. In this chapter we examine this issue of the information society and consider a number of indicators for its existence among Western nations. We use a model of the preconditions for the electronic delivery of services and products to structure our discussion of a number of issues present in the social environment that critically affect both current and future e-business activity. Three factors are particularly considered as important to consider as key constraints on business activity: the emergence of a digital divide, concerns over the privacy of data and the trust placed in e-commerce transactions.

15.2 INFORMATION SOCIETY

In the 1970s Daniel Bell, a US sociologist, wrote an influential book entitled *The Coming of Post-Industrial Society* (Bell, 1972). In this work, Bell made a series of predictions about the state of Western societies. His major premise is now generally accepted: that Western societies are becoming information societies. He maintained that whereas the revolution of the latter part of the 19th century was an industrial revolution, the revolution of the latter part of the 20th century was an information revolution.

Since the publication of Bell's seminal work a great deal of debate has ensued over the question of whether the concept of an information society is a reality. We would argue that a number of indicators of changes in Western societies might be used to provide evidence for the information society:

15.2.1 ECONOMIC TRENDS

Over the last half-century significant change has occurred in the structure of Western economies. These economies have changed from goods-producing economies to service economies. Many more people are now employed in service industries than in agricultural, tertiary and manufacturing industries in the USA and the EU. Information, information systems and ICT are particularly important to the service industries.

15.2.2 GLOBALISATION

The structural forms that emerged in Western economic markets have now diffused throughout the world. There is significant evidence that many commercial organisations work or must work within global rather than local markets. This process has been referred to as globalisation. Information is essential to the management of organisations in global markets (Castells, 1996).

15.2.3 INFORMATION CORPORATIONS

Many organisations in economic systems now devote most of their activities to information-related activities. They are information corporations. For instance, one of the fastest growing industrial sectors has been the media in Western economies.

15.2.4 CHANGES TO WORK

Information and communications technology has caused changes to the way in which work is conducted. One significant phenomenon is the degree to which individuals now work from home or on the move and utilise ICT to maintain their connection to an organisational hub.

15.2.5   INFORMATION COMMODITISATION

Much discussion has been made of the commoditisation of information. In information societies information is seen to be a commodity itself. However, information is an intangible commodity (Chapter 8). For commercial organisations there is a key use-value in the transactional data they can collect on their customers.

15.2.6   TRANSACTIONAL INFORMATION

Companies collect significant amounts of transactional data about their activities, suppliers and customers (Burnham, 1983). Transactional data is data that records events taking place between individuals, groups and organisations. Transactional data is essential to the effective running of most organisations and markets.

15.2.7   E-BUSINESS AND E-COMMERCE

Despite the recent obsession, we would argue that e-business and e-commerce are not new phenomena. The current interest in e-business and e-commerce is merely indicative of the level to which modern societies are information societies. Since the use of ICT to transform internal and external business processes has been ongoing for at least three decades, one might argue that much of the discussion surrounding e-business and e-commerce is an acknowledgement of the centrality of information systems to the effective performance of the internal processes of modern organisations and the external processes of trading.

Examples   The Lisbon European Council set the objective for Europe to become the most dynamic knowledge-based economy by 2010. The eEurope action plan (EC, 2002a) is a central part of this strategy and was endorsed at the Feira European Council in 2000. The overall objective of eEurope 2002 was to 'bring Europe online as fast as possible'. The action plan targeted three areas:

- Cheaper, faster and secure Internet.

- Investing in people and skills.

- Stimulating the use of the Internet.

The eEurope 2002 action plan was built upon three prongs of measures: accelerating legal measures, re-focusing existing financial support programmes and benchmarking. Sixty-four targets were established in this action plan, together with 23 performance indicators. The rationale for benchmarking is that the Lisbon European Council established that progress towards the knowledge-based economy should be monitored through an 'open method of coordination'.

The Barcelona European Council called on the European Commission to establish an eEurope action plan. This states that by 2005 the EU should have:

- Modern online public services: eGovernment, eHealth, eLearning.
- A dynamic e-business environment.
- Widespread availability of broadband access at competitive prices.
- A secure information infrastructure.

The eEurope 2005 action plan (EC, 2002b) is designed to replace the eEurope 2002 action plan and is based on four prongs:

- Policy measures to review and adapt legal frameworks to improve competition and interoperability.
- The exchange of good practice.
- Benchmarking of progress.
- Coordination of existing policies.

Many national governments in the EU have initiated their own policies for the information society which complement that at the European level. For instance, the Federal Republic of Germany has established a five year €5.9 billion programme, Innovation and Jobs in the Information Society of the 21st Century (IDEA, 2002). This programme is designed to modernise government, promote the use of ICT in all areas of society and make Germany one of the ICT sector leaders in Europe.

Question
Which of the trends described above do you regard as the most significant indicator of the information society and why?

15.3 PRECONDITIONS FOR ELECTRONIC DELIVERY OF SERVICES AND PRODUCTS

The section above provides some evidence that modern Western societies are information societies. At its heart, however, the definition of the information society relies on a critical mass of the populace using what we have called electronic delivery (Chapter 7) as their preferred method of accessing the services and products of public and private sector organisations.

Although organisations are producing strategies (Chapter 24) to encourage their external stakeholders, such as customers to use remote modes of access to their services and products, a number of preconditions exist for the successful uptake of such access mechanisms. These preconditions represent the interaction of a range of social factors likely to affect take-up of remote access mechanisms and include:

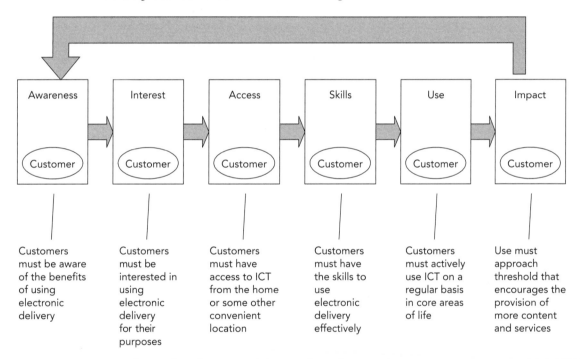

- *Awareness*. Stakeholders must be aware of the benefits of using various remote access mechanisms.
- *Interest*. Stakeholders must be interested in using various remote access mechanisms for their purposes.
- *Access*. Stakeholders must have access to remote access devices from the home or some other convenient location.
- *Skills*. Stakeholders must have the skills necessary to use access mechanisms such as the Internet-enabled PC effectively.
- *Use*. Stakeholders must actively use remote access mechanisms on a regular basis in core areas of life.
- *Impact*. Use of various access mechanisms must approach a threshold that encourages the provision of more content and services delivered electronically. These preconditions are illustrated in Figure 15.1.

Awareness	Interest	Access	Skills	Use	Impact
Customer	Customer	Customer	Customer	Customer	Customer
Customers must be aware of the benefits of using electronic delivery	Customers must be interested in using electronic delivery for their purposes	Customers must have access to ICT from the home or some other convenient location	Customers must have the skills to use electronic delivery effectively	Customers must actively use ICT on a regular basis in core areas of life	Use must approach threshold that encourages the provision of more content and services

Figure 15.1 Preconditions for electronic delivery of products and services.

15.4 AWARENESS

Stakeholders must be aware of the benefits of using various remote access mechanisms. Such benefits must outweigh the costs of using electronic delivery in people's minds.

Example

Crabtree *et al.* (2002) argue that there are three useful stereotypes of people's reactions to ICT:

- *Enthusiasts*. These are people who are naturally enthusiastic about ICT and hence are usually early adopters of most innovations in this area.

- *Aversives*. These are people who are naturally averse to any new technology.

- *Pragmatists*. These are people who are likely to be adopters of a technology once a critical mass of users have become established and the benefits of a particular technology have been suitably proven.

The typical diffusion of awareness of any innovations is likely to be through enthusiasts through pragmatists to aversives. However, awareness in and of itself is not guaranteed to affect take-up.

A big promotional push has been made by suppliers of telecommunications services to households in order to encourage the adoption of broadband technologies such as ADSL (Chapter 7). Broadband is promoted purely in terms of its technical features, such as being fast and being always available as compared to dial-up technology. However, research by Crabtree *et al.* has shown that broadband is not an isolated technology in people's minds. Hence speed is typically not an important issue for consumers because the typical applications used by pragmatists do not demand high bandwidth. Also, broadband does not mean 'always on' in people's minds, because the PC is typically placed in isolation away from most household activity.

Even for enthusiasts, two interrelated features of electronic delivery are of concern to potential entrants: the trust placed in electronic transactions and the privacy of electronic transactions. Evidence suggests that low levels of trust and concerns over the privacy of information are critically affecting the take-up of electronic delivery in certain sectors (see below).

Questions

Are you personally able to list the benefits of electronic delivery? What strategies are needed to raise the awareness of such benefits? Are low levels of awareness a concern for business and why?

15.5 ⊚ INTEREST

Stakeholders must be interested in using remote access mechanisms for their purposes. Margetts and Dunleavy (2002) argue that for people to change their conventional way of interacting with organisations over to new technology mechanisms there is a substantial and immediate set of transaction costs, which include the costs of finding relevant information, the costs of learning new ways of conducting interaction and the costs of correcting mistakes. These are typically referred to as switching costs. Evidence suggests that small, up-front transaction costs of this nature may discourage people from making a commitment to electronic delivery. To outweigh such transaction costs, interest from customers is likely to depend on substantial and perceived added value offered by using electronic access over traditional modes of access.

Example   The consulting organisation KPMG has conducted an annual benchmarking survey of e-government that measures the UK public's access to the Internet and its appetite for accessing government services online. Recently, public awareness and interest have shown a significant increase, with two in three people now wanting access to at least one government service online and over one sixth of the population accessing six or more services electronically (KPMG, 2002).

Question   *How would you persuade a customer of your organisation that there is significant added value in electronic delivery to your products and services? What is the added value?*

15.6   ACCESS

Stakeholders must have access to remote devices from the home or some other convenient location. Measures of such access are frequently expressed in terms of forms of connectivity to the Internet.

Example   The percentage of a population which have Internet access varies between countries and within countries. In Europe this approached over 15% of the population in 2000. In Asia the figure is closer to 1%. Within a country such as the UK access varies among different demographic characteristics, such as gender, age and socio-economic class. Currently only 7% of those in the lowest economic group in the UK have home Internet access compared to 71% of those on higher incomes (National Audit Office, 2002).

Access can be determined by a whole number of factors, particularly income, since the money available to an individual or household will determine whether or not a computer and Internet access (as well as their associated costs) are affordable.

There is no such thing as 'free' access to the Internet. All those who enjoy 'free' access do so because the university, organisation or other institution in which they work pays the costs (Sardar and Ravetz, 1996). For those who cannot enjoy this luxury, Internet access can include the costs of the hardware and software and payments to the Internet Service Provider (ISP), as well as telephone bills for those with dial-up Internet access. The cost of upgrading equipment and replacing obsolete software compounds the financial burden imposed on many individuals with Internet access.

Example

Many of the heaviest users of local authority services are the disadvantaged groups in the community. Hence such groups may be excluded economically from having access to devices such as personal computers in the home. Therefore, to widen access many initiatives have been undertaken in the UK to position personal computers with broadband access in public spaces such as libraries, community halls, job centres and even supermarkets.

Questions

At what level do you think that access to the Internet will stabilise among the general population? Do you think that public Internet access points actually increase levels of access?

15.7 SKILLS

Stakeholders must have the skills to use access mechanisms such as the Internet-enabled PC effectively. This is frequently cast as the problem of e-literacy – the low-level skills required to use ICT effectively. Such low-level skills include:

- Being able to use a keyboard and a computer mouse.
- Being able to conduct basic operations with operating systems such as Microsoft Windows effectively.
- Being able to use productivity packages such as office software effectively.
- Being able to use Internet and Web tools such as browsers.

Clearly there are a number of transaction costs for the individual associated with learning to use new access devices effectively.

Example

Most local authorities in the UK have produced Web sites and most offer various forms of content through such sites. Clearly, to access this information effectively local authority customers need to be able to use a PC and a Web browser.

Various subsidised courses have been offered throughout the UK in basic e-Literacy skills. Some such courses are built around a European-accredited qualification known as the European Computer Driving Licence (ECDL).

Question | *Are there any specific skills associated with using transactional Web sites? Is it easy to switch between using say one flight booking service on the Internet and another?*

15.8 USE

Stakeholders must actively use remote access mechanisms on a regular basis in core areas of life. Margetts and Dunleavy (2002), for example, argue that e-government initiatives have to be capable of domestication. In other words, people accept technological innovations if such innovations become domesticated into personal, everyday routines, as telephones, televisions, fridges, washing machines and microwave ovens have done.

The Internet-enabled personal computer has certainly made an impact in many homes in First World countries. However, there is little evidence yet to suggest that people are turning to this access device as their first point of call for doing things such as:

- Accessing bank account details.
- Registering a birth.
- Taking an educational course.

Example | Major investment is currently being undertaken by local authorities in the UK to increase levels of interactivity on their Web sites. The aim for many authorities is to provide fully transactional Web sites designed around so-called life episodes such as registering births and deaths and adding names to an electoral register.

Questions | *Have you engaged in any of the online activities listed above? If so, what persuaded you to use such services? If not, consider some of the personal reasons for not engaging with these online services?*

15.9 IMPACT

The use of various access mechanisms must approach a threshold that encourages the provision of more content and services delivered electronically. The hope for many organisations is that a virtuous cycle is established in which better content and services, perhaps directed at particular social, economic or political groups, will encourage greater awareness, or interest in and use, of remote access mechanisms as the preferred method of contact with organisations.

Example

Take the case of local authorities in the UK. In terms of service delivery to the customer of local government, face-to-face contact with authority staff and telephone conversations are two of the most commonly used mechanisms for accessing authority services. Consultations recently conducted by authorities suggest that relatively low levels of uptake of electronic service delivery are to be expected in the short term. However, with an eye on the longer term, most authorities are either implementing or investigating multiple-channel access centres that allow customers to interact with the authority using devices such as the Internet-enabled personal computer (PC) and even interactive digital television (iDTV). The aim is to provide access to authority services 24 hours a day, 365 days a year.

Questions

Attempt to access one of the many government Web sites. What did you think of the content? Do you regard it is useful? How might it be improved?

15.10 DIGITAL DIVIDE

Much publicity has been given to a range of concerns associated with the information society that has taken on the label of the *digital divide*. We would argue that the digital divide fundamentally refers to the phenomenon of differential rates of awareness, interest, access, skills and use of ICT among different groups in society. There is substantial evidence to suggest that the lower socio-economic groups in society are the least aware, are the least interested, have the least access to ICT, have the lowest levels of e-literacy and use electronic services the least.

The digital divide is fundamentally related to issues of social exclusion – processes by which certain social groups are excluded from participation in key activities of society. The potential for ICT to improve economic, social and political processes is limited by a number of major forces of such social exclusion present in Western societies. Particular sectors in society may be excluded economically, socially and politically from effective communication and participation in the information society (Tapscott, 1998). On the economic front the cost of ICT equipment and maintaining a connection to the Internet may prove prohibitive for many disadvantaged groups. Socially, low levels of e-literacy may exclude certain sectors from participation. Finally, politically government institutions may wish to impose levels of political/state control of the network infrastructure that prohibit or discourage certain opinions from being aired or activities undertaken through electronic channels.

Example | In the UK a Regulation of Investigatory Powers Act took a number of years to enact because companies such as ISPs were concerned about the powers given to security agencies to monitor traffic passing through these providers. A human rights organisation – The Freedom House (http://www.freedomhouse.org/) – believes that countries around the world are increasingly censoring content on the Internet. In a large list of countries access to the Internet is tightly controlled by governments.

A key concern is that information elites will be able to exploit economic, social and political advantages of the information society. For business a key concern is that major sectors of a potential customer base will miss out on electronic delivery of services and products.

Question | How extensive do you think the digital divide is at the moment? What policies might have an impact on the digital divide?

15.11 ◎ PRIVACY

Transactional data is data that records events taking place between individuals, groups and organisations. Transactional data is essential to the effective running of most organisations and markets. However, the increase in transactional data has potentially insidious consequences. Burnham (1983) illustrates the way in which transactional information can be used to record the daily lives of almost every person in the USA. This information can be combined with more traditional kinds of information, such as people's age and place of birth, to permit organisations to make decisions about the planning of their work.

Example | Within the UK the Driver and Vehicle Licensing Agency (DVLA) collects details of car ownership within the country. The UK supermarket chain Safeway pays the DVLA for address details of persons illegally parked at their stores. It uses such information to collect parking fines.

Therefore some key privacy concerns associated with e-commerce include:

- The collection and storage of personal data by companies.
- The disclosure of such data to third parties.
- The use of such information by companies or other agencies to impact upon personal space.

Examples

Cookies are data files placed on an Internet user's machine by a Web browser. Such cookies are typically used to identify the user to the Web site visited and the date of the last visit to a site. This is particularly useful to companies because they can identify particular customers, monitor their surfing behaviour and tailor interaction with their own particular site in terms of the data collected about the customer. However, many regard the use of cookies for the collection of data in this manner as an invasion of privacy. This is mainly because cookies are passed surreptitiously between Web server and user.

Spamming – the sending of unsolicited e-mails to large numbers of people whose data is held on address lists of various forms – is seen by many to be an invasion of privacy. During the 1990s thousands of Usenet newsgroups were spammed by the US legal firm Canter and Siegel offering to help US immigrants get US green cards.

Such concerns have brought to the fore the issue of ensuring the privacy of data held about an individual. In the UK the Data Protection Act of 1984 laid down a number of principles that enforce good practice in the management of personal data by organisations. In 2000 the UK government implemented new legislation to bring the act in line with the data protection directive of the European Union.

According to the act, anyone processing personal data must comply with eight enforceable principles of good practice. Data must be:

- *Fairly and lawfully processed.* Individuals must be informed who will process their details.
- *Processed for limited purposes.* Individuals must be informed of the precise purposes to which the data will be put.
- *Adequate, relevant and not excessive.*
- *Accurate.* Individuals have the right to access any data held about them to check its accuracy.
- *Not kept longer than necessary.* Individuals can require businesses to stop direct marketing activities which involve them.
- *Processed in accordance with the data subject's rights.*
- *Secure.*
- *Not transferred to countries without adequate data protection.* Before sending data outside the EU the organisation must ensure it is permitted to do so

Personal data covers both facts and opinions about the individual. Processing incorporates the concepts of collecting, storing and disseminating data about individuals. Both manual data and computerised data are covered by the act.

Example

European countries have generally enacted legislation to attempt to regulate data protection and privacy. In the US the strategy has been to rely more on self-regulation by organisations. This makes it difficult for many multinational companies to transfer data across the globe. In order to ease such data transfer the US Department of Commerce and the European Union have created the Safe Harbour Framework. Companies which sign up to this framework, such as Microsoft, are seen as having adequate data protection procedures for cross-border data transfer.

Within the UK, all organisations that maintain personal data must register the data held with the Data Protection Register and are obliged to ensure that their use of such data conforms to the principles above. Many other European countries, such as those in Scandinavia, also have data protection legislation in place.

Questions

How concerned are you over the privacy of data held about yourself? Would you be in favour of or against a national identity card in the UK?

15.12   TRUST

Trust is the glue that binds organisations together into a single cohesive unit and keeps them functioning. Trust is also critical to economic transactions between buyers and sellers. Trust is defined in the *Oxford English Dictionary* as 'a firm belief that a person or thing may be relied upon'. Key concerns have been expressed over the trust placed in electronic transactions (Bryant and Colledge, 2002). A number of technical solutions have been proposed for addressing some of these concerns (Chapter 13). However, trust is still very much a social concern and is embodied in factors such as:

- *Need*. Need is a crucial element of trust. In an organisational transaction between actors, one actor may believe that he or she can trust the other because the actor knows that the other actor needs the transaction to take place. In the traditional relationship between a customer and some organisation there is an inherent need to satisfy the requirements of the customer because of the relatively low volume of transactions. Over the Internet the volume of transactions between individuals and organisations means that there is a clear perception that organisations do not need to build long-term relationships with customers.

- *Identification.* Trust is critically based on easy identification of parties and clear similarities between persons in some relationship. In other words, I trust you because I believe we share a common set of values, mission, vision, roles, culture etc. The stateless nature of Internet transactions is a key problem because it is in practice extremely difficult to identify the parties in a transaction.

- *Competence.* Trust is also based in competence. I trust you because your competence is visibly good since your ability to provide some product or service is accredited in some way. Competence-based trust can be established through qualification from recognised bodies or agencies, supervision by a recognised body or agency, and knowledge of the business process and value chains that are at work within the organisation. It is extremely difficult to judge the competence of a provider of some good or service on the Internet. Because of its unregulated nature it is easy for any person or group to set themselves up with little or no accreditation for the delivery of some service or good.

- *Evidence.* Evidentially based trust is based upon an individual having evidence to support the assertion that they or another individual are trustworthy. People have varying degrees of evidence of transactions by telephone and Internet. Most people have ordered over the telephone or through the post, but few have ordered over the Internet. Hence there is very little accumulated experience among the network of consumers about the trustworthiness of Internet commerce.

Example   Since trust is primarily a social phenomenon, the degree of trust placed in electronic delivery is likely to be relative to different cultures. Mäori culture in New Zealand is based on collective strength and includes ideals of nurturing, supporting and empowering interdependent groups. Hence, Mäori tend to help and trust people within their in-group. Not surprisingly, research (Peszynski and Thanasankit, 2002) has shown that the main way in which individuals decide to visit a particular Web site is based on positive word-of-mouth reports from in-group members. Technical solutions such as customer testimonials on Web sites have little influence on this culture's online consumer behaviour.

Questions   *How much trust do you place in e-commerce? Do you release your credit or debit card details in e-commerce transactions currently? Have you had any adverse experiences with e-commerce?*

15.13 CASE STUDY: THE DIGITAL DIVIDE IN LONDON

Foley *et al.* (2002) report on features of the digital divide in the Greater London Authority. Household connectivity to the Internet was 45% in 2001, the highest figure of any region of the UK. Average UK connectivity in 2001 was 37%. However, the overall high connectivity figure hides a dimension of exclusion. The three most connected boroughs in the authority – Kingston upon Thames, Richmond upon Thames and the City of London – are some of the most affluent boroughs in the capital. The least connected boroughs of Barking and Dagenham, Hackney and Islington are three of the most disadvantaged.

Therefore, not surprisingly, barriers to use of ICT are generally related to socio-economic factors. Use of ICT by socially excluded groups on housing estates with high-levels of unemployment was only 16% in 2001.

Socio-personal factors such as awareness and understanding of ICT are also key barriers to adoption by socially excluded groups. Of the 49% of UK adults who have never used the Internet, just under half reported that they had not done so because of lack of interest. Of non-users, 39% stated that nothing would encourage them to use the Internet.

The consequence of this is that providing greater access to the information highway – such as in public places – is unlikely to decrease the digital divide beyond a certain level. Other activities aimed at raising awareness and raising the level of ICT-related skills amongst socially disadvantaged groups are likely to be equally significant.

15.14 SUMMARY

- There is clear evidence that modern Western societies are information societies.
- The definition of the information society relies on a critical mass of the populace using what we have called electronic service delivery as their preferred method of accessing the services and products of public and private sector organisations.
- A number of preconditions exist to the successful uptake of electronic service delivery: awareness, interest, access, skills, use and impact.
- The digital divide fundamentally refers to the phenomenon of differential rates of awareness, interest, access, skills and use among different groups in society.
- Evidence suggests that low levels of trust and concerns over the privacy of information are critically affecting the take-up of electronic service delivery.

15.15 ACTIVITIES

(i) In terms of an electronic service known to you, use the model of preconditions to analyse some of the barriers to effective take-up of such a service.

(ii) Find evidence of social exclusion experienced in relation to electronic service delivery.

(iii) Find evidence of economic exclusion experienced in relation to electronic service delivery.

(iv) Find evidence of political exclusion experienced in relation to electronic service delivery.

(v) Investigate data protection legislation in two countries.

15.16 REFERENCES

Bell, D. (1972). *The Coming of the Post-industrial Society.* Reading, MA, Addison-Wesley.

Bryant, A. and Colledge, B. (2002). Trust in electronic commerce business relationships. *Journal of Electronic Commerce Research*, **3**(2), 32–39.

Burnham, D. (1983). *The Rise of the Computer State.* New York, Random House.

Castells, M. (1996). *The Rise of the Network Society.* Massachusetts, Blackwell.

Crabtree, J., Nathan, M. and Reeves, R. (2002). *Reality IT: Technology and Everyday Life.* London, The Work Foundation.

EC (2002a). *eEurope Benchmarking Report.* Brussels, European Commission.

EC (2002b). *eEurope 2005: an Information Society For All.* Brussels, European Commission.

Foley, P., Ximena, A. and Shazad, G. (2002). *The digital divide in a world city: a literature review and recommendations for research and strategy development to address the digital divide in London.* London, Greater London Authority.

IDEA (2002). *Local E-government Now: a Worldwide View.* Improvement and Development Agency/Society of Information Technology Management.

KPMG (2002). *Is Britain on Course for 2005?* London, KPMG Consulting.

Margetts, H. and Dunleavy, P. (2002). *Cultural Barriers to E-government: Academic Article in Support of Better Public Services Through E-government.* London, National Audit Office.

National Audit Office (2002). *Better Public Services Through E-government.* National Audit Office.

Sardar, Z. and Ravetz, J. R. (eds.) (1996) *Cyberfutures: Culture and Politics on the Information Superhighway.* New York University Press.

Tapscott, D. (1998). *Growing up Digital: the Rise of the Net Generation.* London, McGraw-Hill.

16

THE POLITICAL ENVIRONMENT FOR E-BUSINESS

Modern politics is, at bottom, a struggle not of men but of forces

Henry Brooks Adams, *The Education of Henry Adams*

Politics is the art of the possible.

R. A. Butler, *The Art of the Possible*

LEARNING OUTCOMES

After reading this chapter, you will be able to:

- Describe some of the issues surrounding the difficulties of legislating for e-business
- Describe how law is adapting to the world of electronic business
- Distinguish between e-government and e-democracy
- Distinguish between internal and external e-democracy

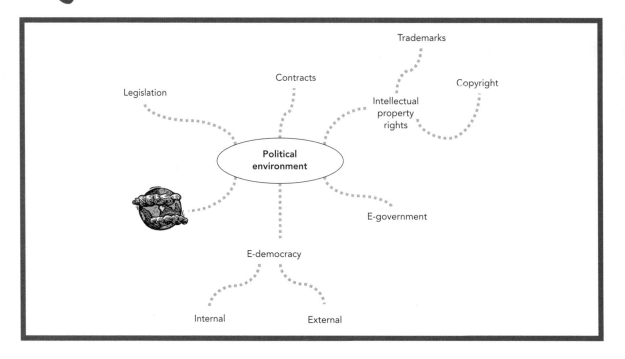

The political environment or system concerns issues of power. Political systems are made up of sets of activities and relationships concerned with power and its exercise. A polity is a political system centred on some geographical area in the modern world. The central idea of a polity is a political system centred on the nation state.

The shape of a polity will clearly be different depending on the country to which it refers. Some polities such as the European Union may be supra-national polities in the sense that they impose a certain level of communality among the political systems of the member states of the union.

Generally speaking a polity will consist of a structure of governance, usually some form of parliamentary democracy in the Western world. Polities generate processes of governance. Legislation is the major instrument of such governance processes. In systems terms legislation and agencies of enforcement can be viewed as the major control system of the contemporary nation state. Governance is fundamentally the process by which a polity controls a nation state.

Therefore, any organisation works within a political environment of legal regulation. Political systems exert considerable pressure on the development and use of ICT systems in organisations. Most polities require that commercial organisations behave in certain ways and enact law to attempt to ensure this. The rise and continued growth of e-business has raised the stakes in this process of regulation. A fundamental problem exists in that most legislation is enacted by national governments, whereas the phenomenon of e-business and particularly e-commerce is a global phenomenon.

However, e-business is not only affected by polities but also has an influence on the shape of modern polities. In this chapter we review definitions of e-government and e-democracy and provide examples of e-business issues in these critical areas of modern life.

16.2 LEGISLATION

Political systems can exert significant pressure on the development and use of information systems in organisations. This normally occurs through the requirements of particular aspects of national and supra-national legislation. Most polities require that commercial organisations behave in certain ways. Legislation is enacted to ensure this and an organisation's information systems are normally critically shaped by such legislation.

There are fundamentally two viewpoints on the relationship between e-business and legislation (Singleton, 2001).

- Some legal commentators suggest that the world of e-business raises challenging questions about the effectiveness of law, which in the non-electronic world has evolved over centuries to reach its current form. This school of thought argues that although the goals of law remain the same when applied to e-business, it often falls short of meeting these goals. Hence new forms of legislation designed to cope with the practicalities of e-business are inevitable.

- The other school of thought argues that concerns over the role of technology in undermining current legislation are not new. Each new form of remote communication – including surface mail, telegraph, telephone, and fax – has brought with it a new set of legal concerns about, for instance, forming contracts and fulfilling their terms. However, the law has evolved appropriately to cope with the exigencies of each case. Those espousing this view argue that the law will evolve as it has done before, and although some new legislation may be required in response to the rapid change in social and business practices brought about by the Internet, the existing body of law, perhaps modified in places, will largely suffice.

Regardless of the relative merits of the arguments presented by these schools of thought, it cannot be disputed that the rate of development of the Internet as a tool for conducting business has brought challenges to legal systems at a greater rate than previously experienced with the advent of other innovative forms of remote communication.

Example | For instance, conventionally law involves a centralised sovereign actor such as a nation state exerting power within its territorial boundaries. This traditional concept of law is challenged by Internet commerce since it lacks geographical boundaries and there is no centralised authority controlling the Internet.

Some of the key areas of concern for e-business in the area of regulation include:

- The use and enforcement of contracts.
- The use and enforcement of intellectual property rights, particularly in the area of domain name registration, use of data from Web sites and the establishment of new Internet brands.
- Laws enacted by nation states to enforce advertising standards.
- Data protection and privacy legislation (Chapter 15).
- Collection of sales tax from customers.

Example

Guidance on UK legislation affecting e-business can be found at `http://www.itcompliance.com/`.

Question

Which do you think is the most appropriate position – that existing law may be adapted to cope with e-business and e-commerce or that new forms of legislation will need to be invented to cope with this phenomenon?

16.3 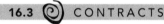 CONTRACTS

Contract law defines the use and nature of contracts between individuals and business organisations. A contract is an agreement between parties which is enforceable in law. Such legislation defines valid business activity between customers, suppliers and organisations. Hence the design of trading systems between customers, suppliers and organisations will be heavily affected by contractual regulation.

A contract defines an agreement between parties over business activity. The basic elements of a valid contract in the UK are offer, consideration, intention to create legal relations, and acceptance (compared with offer, consideration and acceptance in the USA).

Example

In terms of a sale of goods, for instance, a contract details the precise nature of the sale, including the price of goods and delivery conditions. When making a purchase in person, opportunities exist to raise questions about the goods, the price and other concerns. If parties have doubts about the integrity of the product, are concerned about whether the parties have authority to make the transaction, or if the payment is suspect, again opportunities exist to ask questions in order to obtain further information. If anything goes wrong with the sale then either party has recourse to the law.

In the world of e-commerce a number of difficulties emerge with contracts:

- Because a sale is made through the exchange of electronic messages it is frequently difficult to determine the precise nature of contractual obligation. Some commentators question whether an electronic communication can be considered a 'writing' that will be accepted in a court of law.
- There is a lack of opportunity for parties to evaluate the goods being sold before purchase.
- It is frequently difficult for parties to authenticate each other.
- Because a sales transaction may be conducted across national borders it is frequently difficult to determine which nation's contractual law applies in a particular case. This is expressed as the problem of jurisdiction.

Example	In the UK, commercial contracts do not generally have to take written form and hence the law is generally favourable to electronic contracts. However, some types of contract (particularly those relating to property) do have to be in writing. Interestingly, the content of a Web site (which may include price information) is not viewed as a contractual obligation, but as an advertisement, the content of which is covered by the code of the Advertising Standards Authority (ASA).

At the international level, there is no consensus on contractual law. However, the United Nations Commission on International Trade Law (UNCITRAL) has, in its Model Law on Electronic Commerce, attempted to establish an international standard. Although this law has no authority until individual countries adopt it through their respective legislative processes, it does represent an effort to bring clarity to electronic contracts in the international environment. The UNCITRAL Model Law adopts a minimalist approach, recognising that contracts may be made and signed in an electronic environment, and that electronic transmissions may satisfy signature requirements. Similarly, the European Union (EU) has issued a Directive on Electronic Signatures (1999/93/EC) that requires member states to enact legislation pertaining to the authentication and recognition of electronic signatures (Chapter 13).

Question	*Which of the above problems with the contractual basis of e-commerce transactions is the most important to deal with and why?*

16.4 INTELLECTUAL PROPERTY RIGHTS

Another key aspect of the law which has been significantly affected by e-commerce is that of intellectual property rights. The nature of e-commerce is such that it is constantly involved in the production and transfer of information. It is the information-based nature of e-commerce that brings the phenomenon into direct confrontation with intellectual property law (Chen, 2001).

Intellectual property rights emerged as a means of ensuring that creators are able to benefit from their intellectual accomplishments. Two types of intellectual property rights are commonly recognised: those which are protected by patents, trademarks and design rights, and those which are protected by copyright.

16.4.1 TRADEMARKS

A trademark is a sign (Chapter 4) that distinguishes the goods or services of one business from another, and should be registered with the appropriate authorities (Chen 2001). A trademark may consist of a company logo, a name or even a sound or tune. Indeed, anything which serves to identify an organisation can be registered as a trademark.

In the UK, trademarks are registered at the Trade Marks Registry. Once in possession of a trademark, the owner is in a strong position to prevent a third party from using that mark. Unfortunately, trademarks can only be registered in terms of a particular country. Hence protecting a trademark on the Internet is made difficult because a user of a trademark registered in one country is not guaranteed use of that trademark in another country.

Examples

In the world of e-commerce companies often register their domain names as trademarks in an attempt to prevent what is called cyber-squatting – the use of a popular name by another company to attract customers. There have been a number of cases in the UK where domain name registrations have been challenged in court.

For instance, the retail store Harrods obtained an injunction requiring the holders of the domain name Harrods.com to transfer all rights to Harrods.

Perhaps the best known case of this type was the 1998 Court of appeal decision in favour of British Telecom and others who had mounted a legal challenge to the activities of the One-in-a-Million organisation. One-in-a-Million had registered domain names of a number of well known entities including marksandspencer.com, sainsbury.com, BT.com, virgin.com and spicegirls.com. These domain names contained the names and/or trademarks of those involved, and were judged to constitute an instance of trademark infringement. The view of the court was that there was clear evidence of systematic registration of well-known names in order to prevent their registration by their authorised owners, and that even though the names had not been used online, the law had been infringed. The judgement against One-in-a-

Million effectively ended the practice of domain name grabbing or cyber-squatting in the UK.

Questions

Why are trademarks and domain name registration such a significant problem for modern business? Have you ever typed in a Web address on the basis of some expected company name and found yourself in a surprising place? What were your reactions to this?

16.4.2   COPYRIGHT

Copyright law enables authors of an intellectual property to prevent unauthorised copying of such material. The law applies to physical transactions of written material regardless of its country of origin. The law applies equally to digital products such as computer programs and documents published on the Internet. The difficulty lies in the enforcement of copyright law between countries. Also, copyright law is unclear over the precise nature of links from Web sites to other material.

The ease with which digital material placed on the Internet may be copied, altered, and redistributed poses obvious intellectual property problems. Although copyright laws suggest that use of material is only lawful with the consent of the copyright holder, once material is placed on the Internet the copyright holder effectively loses all control of the material. The material may be downloaded, printed, distributed, altered or even sold for profit without the consent of the copyright holder. The ease with which material may be purloined from Internet sources has resulted in numerous legal disputes.

The key lesson for business is that careful thought should be given to possible repercussions when any material is placed on a Web site. This extends to the use of material for which a license is already held, as licenses are generally granted to use copyrighted works for a specific and limited purpose and this purpose may not extend to use of that material in electronic form on a Web site.

Example

Copyright may also be breached by the use of hypertext links on Web sites. In a well known case (*Shetland Times* v. Wills and Zetnews Ltd), the Outer House Court of Session in Scotland ruled that the defendant's use of hypertext links to point directly to news stories in the plaintiff's Web site (bypassing the plaintiff's home page), coupled with their copying of the plaintiff's headlines in their Web site, constituted an infringement of the Copyright, Designs and Patents Act, 1988. Part of the settlement entitled the defendant to continued use of the headlines, provided that they displayed the *Shetland Times* logo on their homepage, and acknowledged that the headlines referred to *Shetland Times* news stories.

Question	*How significant do you think is plagiarism from Web content in relation to student course works? Is this a copyright problem?*

16.4.3   TAXATION

The Internet facilitates the creation of global electronic marketplaces. This causes key problems in taxation which affect commercial activity such as transactions affecting the sale of goods. The establishment and enforcement of taxation in such areas is typically an issue for a nation state. However, companies trading over electronic markets can typically choose to set up operation where the costs of taxation are the lowest.

Example	The UK bookmaker William Hill has set up an Internet-based betting operation in Gibraltar where there are lower duties on betting than in the UK. Such movement to 'offshore' operations has caused significant loss of revenue to the UK government.

Supra-national governments such as the European Union are attempting to establish policy that will cross national boundaries and cope with some of these problems of e-commerce.

Example	A radical position has been taken by the US government, which in its Framework for Global Electronic Commerce has proposed that the Internet be declared a tariff-free zone.

Questions	*If the Internet became a tariff-free zone, what consequences might this have for conventional forms of trade? What consequences would this have for e-commerce?*

16.5 INFORMATION SYSTEMS AFFECT THE POLITICAL ENVIRONMENT

Polities not only regulate e-business. E-business influences the shape of modern polities in the sense that the use of information systems and ICT affects both the smooth operation and shape of modern polities. Information systems support political systems in the sense that they are relevant to the operation of the political system itself. Information is essential to the relationship between the citizen of a nation state and the government of that nation state.

- *Democratic representation.* The process of democratic representation relies on information for effective functioning. For instance, governmental representatives have to be voted into power at various times. Referenda, which are effectively large-scale surveys of opinion from a national population, may be held on various issues at various times. Also, government representatives will wish to communicate information to their constituents at various times.

- *Tax collection.* Government demands financial support from the citizen and from the business organisation in the form of taxation. The assessment of levels of taxation and the effective collection of fiscal revenue relies heavily on large and complex information systems.

- *Benefit payment.* Payment of monies and other forms of support are made to citizens by government agencies as part of welfare programmes. The effective identification of people in need and the timely payment of benefits to such people are heavily reliant on effective information systems.

- *Pressure groups.* Pressure groups in democracies maintain information systems for effective operation. They may also use information systems to help organise forms of protest. Extreme deviant groups such as terrorist organisations have also used media like the Internet to publicise their activities and organise terrorist action.

- *Social control.* The use-value of some types of information as a commodity for social control has caused concern amongst civil liberties groups in many countries. Modern ICT permits organisations to collate information from various sources to form profiles of people and their behaviour. Such information may be used by enforcement agencies such as the police to detect and punish any behaviour seen to be deviant.

Questions   *To what degree is the modern welfare state dependent on information systems? Could the modern welfare state operate effectively without ICT? Can you provide examples?*

16.6 ⊚ E-GOVERNMENT AND E-DEMOCRACY

ICT and information systems are being used to re-engineer aspects of governmental processes and the relationship between government and the citizen. The interface between government and citizen in terms of services such as tax collection and benefit payment and the associated use of ICT systems to deliver these

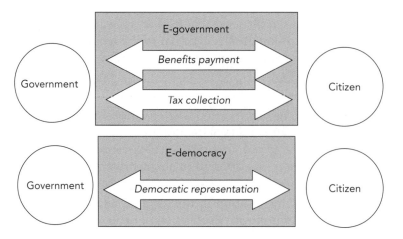

Figure 16.1 E-government and e-democracy.

services via government agencies is typically referred to as electronic government (e-government). The term *e-democracy* may be restricted to the use of ICT in the service of democratic representation between government and citizen and the associated use of ICT within democratic processes in government. This is illustrated in Figure 16.1.

Example

In the words of a recent UK government paper:

> The Government is committed to ensuring that the UK is placed to become a world leader in the new electronic age. It is essential that public services play a full part in this digital transformation. All tiers of government must be able to provide services that take advantage of the improved speed and efficiency of new methods of delivery in line with heightened customer expectations (Department of the Environment Transport and the Regions, 2001).

It is clear that policymakers see new technologies as the key both to re-engineering internal business processes and to reshaping the relationship between citizens and service providers. Ministers believe that ICT can facilitate service improvement by reconfiguring frontline services in ways that match the needs of service users rather than the organisational convenience of producers. They expect services to become both more 'joined up' and more accessible – for example enabling them to operate outside of traditional 'office hours'. They also anticipate that electronic voting, combined with new methods of communicating with and consulting local people, will help to reinvigorate local democracy, increasing turnout in local elections and enabling more direct public participation in local decision making.

The UK Prime Minister announced in 1997 that by 2002, 25% of dealings with government should be able to be carried out by the public electronically. These targets were later revised in the Modernising Government White Paper that initially set a target of 100% electronic service delivery by 2008. In March 2000 the Prime Minister Tony Blair announced that this target was to be brought forward. The government has now set a target that by 2005 all (100%) of government services that can be delivered electronically will be delivered electronically.

Questions   *Is e-government a good thing? If so, why? If not, why not?*

16.7 E-DEMOCRACY

E-democracy can be defined in broad or narrow terms. In narrow terms e-democracy can be used to refer solely to the enablement of democratic processes between members of some political grouping and their governmental representatives. This we call external e-democracy. In a sense, external e-democracy can be seen to be an attempt to introduce elements of direct democracy into situations of representative democracy.

Examples   External e-democratic initiatives include:

- The provision of Web sites for governmental units allowing the publication of debates and the schedule of governmental proceedings.

- The provision of e-mail addresses for governmental members to improve the efficiency and effectiveness of communications between constituents and representatives.

- The running of the electoral process through ICT systems which can capture votes and process results in the fraction of time of conventional paper-based ballot approaches.

- The provision of video-conferencing facilities which enable citizens to contribute directly to the formation of legislative policy in particular areas.

On the other hand e-democracy can serve to refer to the way in which ICT can be used to improve internal democratic processes within government. This we call internal e-democracy.

Examples   Internal e-democratic initiatives include:

- The provision of ICT to democratic representatives in order to improve the efficiency of the transfer and storage of governmental documentation.

- The provision of a secure government Intranet enabling the efficient and effective transfer of government information between departments.

- The integration of government information systems to provide effective up-to-date statistics on the population of a nation state, essential to the effective formulation of legislative policy.

There is also the notion of local e-democracy. Local e-democracy occurs where local groups use ICT to create democratic forms, fora and processes to facilitate political interaction within the community itself. This form of e-democracy is seen as particularly critical for producing effects such as a reduction in social exclusion and increasing levels of community action. Local e-democracy is e-democracy in the community and in civil society. Civil society is the zone between the state and private life in which citizens interact with other citizens to pursue a common purpose or goal (UK Online, 2002).

Internal e-democracy is fundamentally what we would call an intra-business e-business issue. External e-democracy can be seen as a public sector variant of a B2C e-commerce issue (Chapter 18). Local e-democracy is a special instance of a C2C e-commerce issue (Chapter 20). These distinctions are illustrated in Figure 16.2.

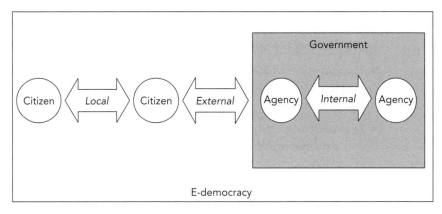

Figure 16.2 Internal and external e-democracy.

Question   Which of the three forms of e-democracy will be the most successful in the short term: external, internal or local?

16.8 ⊚ CASE STUDY: ONLINE CONSULTATION AT THE NATIONAL ASSEMBLY FOR WALES

The UK government has recently published a consultation document on e-democracy (UK Online, 2002) describing it as 'using new technology to energise the democratic and political life of the nation'. The consultation document also admits that e-democracy is still a relatively untested concept and describes two tracks of e-democracy – what they refer to as e-participation and e-voting. E-participation is defined as the use of ICT to open new channels of participation in the democratic process between elections. E-voting is defined as the use of ICT to facilitate participation in elections or other ballots under statutory control (see Chapter 7). A major facet of e-participation is e-consultation. E-consultation is the use of ICT to enable online interaction with the citizen on matters of policy and decision-making. The key aims of this technological innovation are to improve the effectiveness of policy formulation and the engagement of a greater proportion of the populace in this process.

It is possible to define government in terms of democratic structures or institutions or in terms of democratic processes. Using this e-business perspective government is concerned with the processes of the policy cycle (Jones *et al.*, 2000). This systemic view of government, illustrated in Figure 16.3, focuses on the development of policy and its implementation. Policy can be defined as a set of ideas and proposals for action culminating in a decision. The policy process takes demands from the social/economic/political environment and resources available in these domains as inputs. Policy is the key output which inputs into the implementation

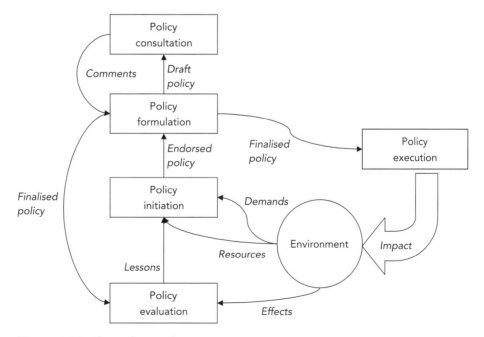

Figure 16.3 The policy cycle.

process. Implementation of policy has a key impact on the social/economic/political environment and forms the starting point for the reformulation of policy.

One of the recently devolved regional assemblies in the UK, the National Assembly for Wales (NAfW), has initiated a major e-consultation programme. As a refinement of the policy cycle, democratic processes within and without the NAfW include:

- *Policy initiation*. The Welsh Assembly Government (WAG), the political arm of the NAfW, develops specific policy as it relates to Wales taking into account existing political demands and resources such as funding and personnel as well as lessons and evidence established from previous policy exercises.

- *Policy formulation*. Once a policy has received political endorsement it is fed into the NAfW's structures for detailed consideration. Meetings of the NafW chamber and committees agree, modify and ratify policy.

- *Policy consultation*. Various divisions within the NAfW consult with various partner organisations and citizenry on specific policy. Policy may be reformulated on the basis of input from such consultation.

- *Policy execution*. Various organs of the NAfW and its sponsored bodies implement and monitor the execution of programmes arising from key policy areas.

- *Policy evaluation*. The NAfW has a remit to evaluate the impact of policy initiatives in particular areas. This involves attempting to relate issues of policy to impacts upon the social/economic/political/environmental landscape of Wales.

The NAfW is currently in the process of implementing an e-consultation system consisting of a collection of databases and ICT systems closely integrated with the policy process described above. Four databases exist storing data about consultees, documents, events and external parties. The content of these databases is managed by Assembly officials through a secure administration facility, and is accessible internally through the various policy tools and/or a guidance wizard. Parts of the data are also accessible externally through the consultations Web site. These databases are used by the following ICT tools:

- *Document management and publication tool*. This system provides Assembly staff with templates for the production of policy documents. Policy documents can then be published via a secure document management system to the Assembly Web site. The document management system stores planned, current and archived policy documents and may be searchable via the Internet.

- *Contacts tool*. This system allows consultees to register to receive notification of new consultations. They are able to specify which type and subject areas are of particular interest to them. The consultees are contacted automatically once every six months by the system to encourage them to keep their records up to date.

- *Dissemination tool*. This is a system for managing the dissemination of consultations through block e-mail and/or mail-merge. It also enables the creation of reminders at pre-set dates.

- *Event organiser.* This tool is used for managing a database of events and venues. Assembly staff can define events and search the database for an appropriate venue. A number of venue suggestions are shown prior to selection. The tool invites venue managers to keep the information held about their venue up to date via a secure Extranet.

- *Response collection tool.* This system is used for managing the collection of responses and acknowledging receipt of the same. Responses are collected in a number of ways – via the provision of a preformatted online response question-naire, a free format text uploading facility, or the invitation to send a paper-based response. Automatic acknowledgements are sent to all respondees.

- *Voting tool.* In addition to the classic feedback collected in text format, in some instances it is appropriate to ask for numerical voting feedback. For some consul-tations an online voting form is provided. The tool is capable of counting and analysing the various contributions. As above, the system generates an auto-matic acknowledgement of receipt to the consultee.

- *Response analysis tool.* This system is used for analysing responses received. Feed-back is received in a variety of formats: set answers to a row of specific questions in small paragraph format; free-form additional information in conjunction with the answers to the specific questions asked within the consultation; free-format texts, received in digital or paper-based format. In the latter case, a manual qualitative analysis is conducted aided by the provision of preformatted response evaluation forms. When the feedback is collected via voting forms the feedback is analysed automatically and presented via a data visualisation tool.

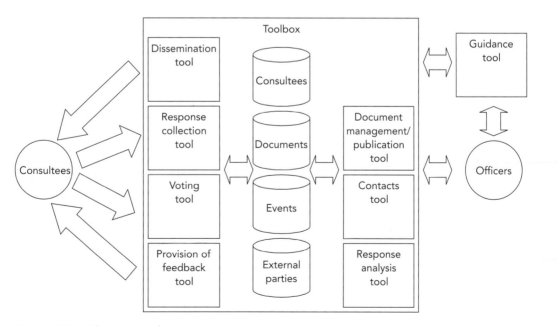

Figure 16.4 The e-consultation system.

- *Provision of feedback tool.* This system is used for informing consultees of the outcome of the consultation. Feedback is provided in terms of the final policy text together with a clear indication of which sections were altered as a result of the responses to the consultation. For consultees that have access to the Internet, and whose preference it is to exchange information with the NAfW in digital format, these documents are made available on the Internet. For the consultees that prefer to communicate with paper-based media, the feedback is made available in printed form.

The various tools are accessible via a general toolbox or through a guidance facility. This latter facility is meant to shepherd inexperienced policy officers through the early stages of the policy cycle, from policy initiation through to issuing the policy into implementation. As such, it constitutes a simple form of workflow system. The relationships between the tools, databases and guidance facility are illustrated in Figure 16.4.

16.9 SUMMARY

- Traditional conceptions of law are being challenged by Internet commerce. Some of the key areas of concern for e-business include the use and enforcement of contracts and intellectual property rights.

- Contract law defines the use and nature of contracts between individuals and business organisations. In the world of electronic commerce a number of difficulties emerge with contracts, such as a lack of opportunity for parties to evaluate the goods being sold and the fact that it is frequently difficult for parties to authenticate each other.

- Another key aspect of the law which has been significantly affected by e-commerce is that of intellectual property rights.

- Two types of intellectual property rights are commonly recognised: those which are protected by patents, trademarks and design rights, and those which are protected by copyright.

- ICT and information systems are being used to re-engineer aspects of governmental processes and the relationship between government and the citizen.

- The interface between government and citizen in terms of services such as tax collection and benefit payment and the associated use of ICT systems to deliver these services via government agencies is sometimes referred to as electronic government (e-government).

- The term *e-democracy* may be restricted to the use of ICT in the service of democratic representation between government and citizen and the associated use of ICT within democratic processes in government.

16.10 ⊚ ACTIVITIES

(i) Investigate some of the debate concerning the way in which e-business is impacting on the concept of law. Come to a conclusion as to whether you believe new forms of legislation are required for e-business or not.

(ii) Investigate the UNCITRAL Model Law on e-commerce or the EU Directive on Electronic Signatures. Determine how successful these are likely to be in handling some of the problems of contractual law as it concerns e-commerce.

(iii) Investigate copyright law and its capability for coping with the increasing demands of digital convergence.

(iv) Investigate the prevalence of the activity of cyber-squatting.

(v) Investigate one or more e-government initiatives in a government organisation known to you.

(vi) Investigate one or more e-democracy initiatives in a nation state known to you.

16.11 ⊚ REFERENCES

Chen, S. (2001). *Strategic Management of E-business*. Chichester, John Wiley.

Department of the Environment Transport and the Regions (2001). *Delivering Local Government Online*. London, HMSO.

Jones, B., Gray, A., Kavanagh, D., Moran, M., Norton, P. and Seldon, A. (2000). *Politics UK*. Cambridge, Cambridge University Press.

Singleton, S. (2001). *Ecommerce: a Practical Guide to the Law*. Burlington, VT, Gower.

UK Online (2002). *In the Service of Democracy: a Consultation Paper on a Policy for Electronic Democracy*. HM Government.

E-COMMERCE

I dread success. To have succeeded is to have finished one's business on earth, like the male spider, who is killed by the female the moment he has succeeded in his courtship. I like a state of continual becoming, with a goal in front and not behind.

George Bernard Shaw

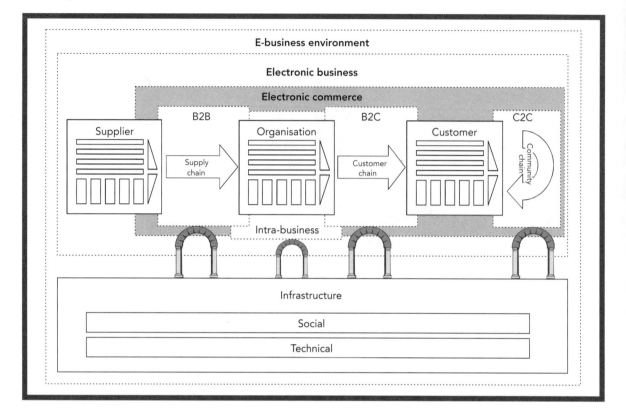

Kalakota and Whinston (1997) define at least four perspectives on e-business. Each perspective effectively provides a different definition for this phenomenon:

- *Communications perspective*. The delivery of information, products/services, or payments via communications networks.

- *Business perspective*. The application of technology toward the automation of business transactions and workflows.

- *Service perspective*. A tool that addresses the desire of firms, consumers and management to cut service costs while improving the quality of goods and increasing the speed of service delivery.

- *Online perspective*. Providing the capability of buying and selling products and information on the Internet and other online services.

In a sense these correspond to the distinctions between human activity systems, information systems and ICT systems made in Chapter 4. Electronic business can be viewed in terms of the changes to organisational structures made possible by ICT (business/service perspective), in terms of the extension of information systems into the environment of organisations (online perspective) or in terms of innovations in technology making inter-organisational communication easier (communications perspective). In the chapters in this part of the book we concentrate on the online perspective. In terms of the figure above, e-commerce is located as an important subset of e-business. Chapter 17 is devoted to elaborating on the system of commerce and differences between various forms of e-commerce. Commerce constitutes the exchange of products and services between businesses, groups and individuals. Commerce or trade can hence be seen as one of the essential activities of any business. Commerce of whatever nature can be considered as a system of exchange between economic actors with the following generic phases or states: pre-sale, sale execution, sale settlement and after-sale. The precise form of the system of commerce will vary in terms of the nature of the economic actors involved, the frequency of commerce and the nature of the goods or services being exchanged.

E-commerce refers to the use of ICT to enable aspects of this system of exchange. E-commerce focuses on the use of ICT to enable the external activities and relationships of the business with individuals, groups and other businesses. Internet commerce is a subset of e-commerce focused on the use of Internet and Web technologies to enable e-commerce.

Generally we may distinguish between three distinct forms of e-commerce:

● *B2C e-commerce*. Business to consumer e-commerce is sometimes called sell-side e-commerce and concerns the enablement of the customer or demand chain with ICT. Customers or consumers will typically be individuals, sometimes other organisations and B2C commerce normally follows a cash commerce model for low and standard-priced goods. For medium- to high-priced items some form of credit commerce will operate. In other words, organisations will search for a product, negotiate a price, order a product, receive delivery of the product, be invoiced for the product, pay for the product and receive some form of after-sales service. Typically, B2C e-commerce will utilise a market model of economic exchange. B2C e-commerce is the topic of Chapter 18.

● *B2B e-commerce*. Business to business e-commerce is sometimes called buy-side e-commerce and typically involves supporting the supply chain with ICT. B2B commerce clearly concerns exchanges between organisational actors – public and/or private sector organisations. This form of e-commerce invariably involves the use of ICT to enable forms of credit commerce between a company and its suppliers or other partners. For high-priced and customised goods traded between organisations some form of repeat commerce model operates. In other words, the same processes occur as for credit commerce, but the processes cycle around indefinitely in a trusted relationship between producer and consumer. Hence typically some form of managerial hierarchy is employed to control the operation of the commercial relationship between supplier and consumer, although many developments in this area are assuming market forms. B2B e-commerce is the topic of Chapter 19.

- *C2C e-commerce.* Consumer to consumer e-commerce concerns the enablement of the community chain with ICT. C2C e-commerce occurs primarily between individuals and typically involves forms of cash commerce generally for low-cost services or goods. Consequently, it tends to follow a market model for the economic exchange. Other forms of value may be generated in the communities or social networks engaged in C2C e-commerce. Of particular interest is the degree of social capital that may be located in such social networks. Social capital is the productive value of people engaged in a dense network of social relations. Social capital consists of those features of social organisation – networks of secondary associations, high levels of interpersonal trust, reciprocity – which act as resources for individuals and facilitate collective action. C2C e-commerce is the topic of Chapter 20.

Two key sub-processes of B2C and B2B e-commerce are considered in more detail as separate chapters. This is because of their contemporary significance as key process strategies for improving organisational performance. In the case of B2C e-commerce we consider the issue of electronic marketing (e-marketing) in Chapter 21. In the case of B2B e-commerce we consider the issue of electronic procurement (e-procurement) in Chapter 22.

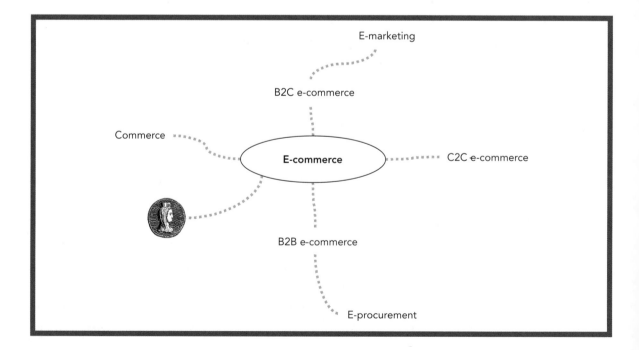

REFERENCE

Kalakota, R. and Whinston, A. B. (1997). *Electronic Commerce: a Manager's Guide*. Harlow, UK, Addison-Wesley.

CHAPTER 17

ELECTRONIC COMMERCE

...Saw the heavens fill with commerce, argosies of magic sails

Pilots of the purple twilight, dropping down with costly bales;

Alfred, Lord Tennyson, *Locksley Hall*

LEARNING OUTCOMES

After reading this chapter, you will be able to:

- Define the four phases of commerce
- Distinguish between various types of commerce in terms of actors, frequency and the nature of products and/or services
- Distinguish between cash, credit and repeat commerce
- Define the key features of electronic commerce
- Describe the three major forms of electronic commerce
- Outline some of the benefits and some of the problems associated with e-commerce
- Relate some of the characteristics of consumer behaviour

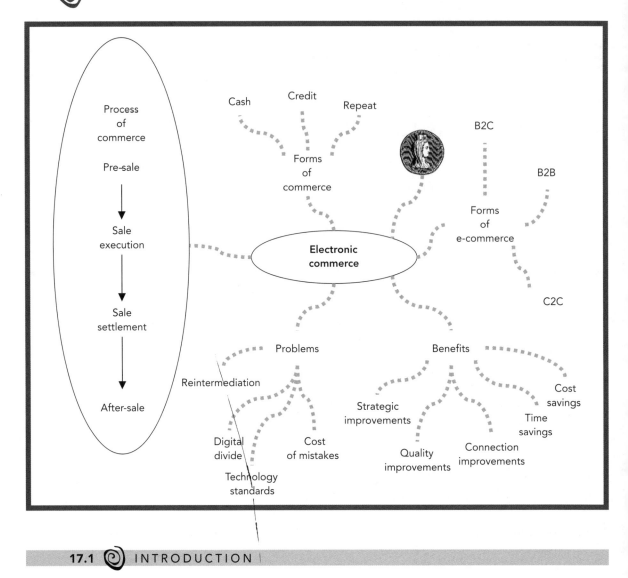

Commerce constitutes the exchange of products and services between businesses, groups and individuals. Commerce or trade can hence be seen as one of the essential activities of any business. E-commerce focuses on the use of ICT to enable the external activities and relationships of the business with individuals, groups and other businesses (Turban and King, 2003). As such, e-commerce is a subset of e-business. Internet commerce is the use of Internet technologies to enable e-commerce. Such technologies are becoming the key standards for intra- and inter-organisational communication, and therefore i-commerce is a subset of e-commerce.

In this chapter we define a model of commerce based on a number of key stages and the types of economic actor, frequency of commerce and nature of the goods and services exchanged. We then define three forms of e-commerce in terms of this model and consider some of the major potentialities and pitfalls of e-commerce.

We conclude with an examination of consumer behaviour and its importance for e-commerce strategy.

17.2 (🌀) COMMERCE

Commerce of whatever nature can be considered as a system or process with the following generic phases:

- *Pre-sale*. This involves activities occurring before a sale occurs.
- *Sale execution*. This comprises the activities of the actual sale of a product or service between economic actors.
- *Sale settlement*. This involves those activities that complete the sale of product or service.
- *After-sale*. This involves those activities that take place after the buyer has received the product or service.

Each of these activities generates a range of transactions (Chapter 8). As well as the transfer of goods and services one of the most prominent of such transaction types is that of payments.

Example	Consider the process of buying a book from a bookseller. Pre-sale activity ht include the marketing of particular books by inclusion in various catalogues. e execution clearly involves the purchase of the book by a customer. The customer n be an organisation, in which case, it is likely that sale settlement will occur through process in which the bookseller invoices the organisation and the purchaser makes payment at some later date. After-sale service may include site visits by sales personnel to particular institutions and perhaps initiatives such as discounting partic-ular book lines.
Question	*Can a model of exchange on the lines of the above be used to help understand the relationship between a public sector organisation and its customers?*

17.3 (🌀) ACTORS, FREQUENCY AND NATURE

The precise form of this process of commerce will vary depending on:

- *The nature of the economic actors involved*. Generally speaking we may distinguish between organisational actors and individual actors. In terms of organisational actors we may distinguish between private sector or commercial organisations, public sector organisations, and other not-for-profit organisations such as voluntary organisations.

- *The frequency of commerce between the economic actors.* Whiteley (2000) distinguishes between three major patterns of frequency. Repeat commerce is the pattern in which regular, repeat transactions occur between trading partners. Credit commerce is where irregular transactions occur between trading partners and the processes of settlement and execution are separated. Cash commerce occurs when irregular transactions of a one-off nature are conducted between economic actors. In cash commerce the processes of execution and settlement are typically combined.

- *The nature of the goods or services being exchanged.* Generally the most important feature of the product or service is its price. Hoque (2000) distinguishes between low-priced items in a standard configuration and quantity, low- to medium-priced items, medium- to high-priced items and high-priced customised items. Another important distinction of relevance to e-business is whether the goods are tangible or intangible. Tangible goods are those that have a physical existence. Intangible goods are those that are fundamentally information-based (Chapter 8).

Examples

Various agencies of government are examples of public sector organisations. Such organisations still have defined customers and suppliers and hence electronic government – the application of e-business principles to government processes – is relevant.

Low-priced items in a standard configuration and quantity include envelopes; low- to medium-priced items include such items as personal computers; medium- to high-priced items include items such as office furniture; and high-priced customised items include bulk industrial components such as aero engines.

Foodstuffs and electrical goods are classic examples of tangible goods. Recorded digital music and software are classic examples of intangible goods.

Question

What relationship is there between credit commerce and the issue of trust?

17.4 CASH COMMERCE, CREDIT COMMERCE AND REPEAT COMMERCE

Cash commerce for low- and standard-priced goods typically follows the four stages of the generic commerce model quite closely. It typically involves a see/buy/get sequence. For medium- to high-priced items some form of credit commerce will operate. In other words, organisations will search for a product, negotiate a price, order a product, receive delivery of the product, be invoiced for the product, pay

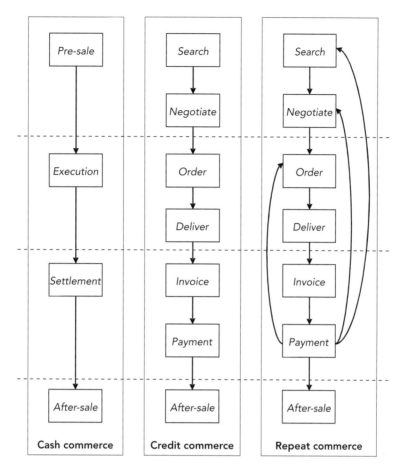

Figure 17.1 Cash, credit and repeat commerce.

for the product and receive some form of after-sales service. For high-priced and customised goods traded between organisations some form of repeat commerce model operates. The same processes occur as for credit commerce but the processes cycle around indefinitely in a trusted relationship between producer and consumer. These three forms of commerce are illustrated in Figure 17.1.

Example   Most purchases of small items over the Internet occur in cash commerce mode. For example, the purchase of foodstuffs from an online supermarket chain generally occurs as a form of cash commerce. Companies in established relationships tend to work with either a credit or repeat commerce model.

Question   *Why is a repeat commerce model typically associated with an electronic hierarchy?*

17.5 ☺ E-COMMERCE

Electronic commerce (e-commerce) is the use of ICT to enable the external activities and relationships of the business with individuals, groups and other businesses (Laudon and Traver, 2002). E-commerce supports the supply chain (a series of interdependent activities by which an organisation sources products or services from other individuals, groups or organisations), customer chains (a series of interdependent activities by which an organisation sells its products or services to customers) and community chains (a series of activities by which the business interacts with its surrounding community) of business.

E-commerce is also usually conducted in terms of e-markets (a many-to-many medium in which economic exchanges are conducted using ICT) or e-hierarchies (a one-to-many medium in which economic exchanges are conducted using ICT) (Chapter 14).

Example

Much hype has been associated with e-commerce, particularly that experienced during the 'dotcom' boom. This refers to the investment bubble that became associated with Internet start-up companies during the late 1990s. Cassidy (2002) has made the analogy between the 'irrational' investment behaviour associated with dotcom companies and other financial boom and bust periods such as the South Sea Bubble that occurred in the 18th century.

Much of the Dot Com phenomenon was directed at B2C e-commerce, probably because it is the most visible form of e-commerce. However, analysts predict that the majority of business to be conducted electronically over the next decade will be B2B e-commerce.

Questions

What percentage of commerce is conducted electronically? Will all commerce eventually become electronic?

17.6 ☺ FORMS OF E-COMMERCE

Generally we may distinguish between three major forms of e-commerce. These forms are primarily distinguished in terms of the value chain supported, the economic actors involved, the direction of transactional/informational flow between economic actors, the frequency of commerce, the nature of goods or services exchanged, and the typical model of economic exchange utilised (Figure 17.2). These distinctions are summarised in Table 17.1.

Table 17.1 Forms of e-commerce.

	B2C e-commerce	B2B e-commerce	C2C e-commerce
Value chain	Customer chain	Supply chain	Community chain
Economic actors	Company/consumers	Company/suppliers	Consumers/consumers
Direction of transactional flow	Consumer–customer	Company–supplier	Consumer–consumer
Nature of goods/services	Standard-priced items	Customised/high-priced items	Negotiated/low-priced items
Form of commerce	Cash/credit commerce	Credit/repeat commerce	Cash commerce
Model of economic exchange	Markets	Hierarchies	Markets

17.6.1 BUSINESS TO CUSTOMER (B2C) AND CUSTOMER TO BUSINESS (C2B) E-COMMERCE

These forms of e-commerce invariably concern the use of ICT to enable forms of cash and credit commerce between a company and its customers/consumers. Hence B2C e-commerce generally supports the customer chain in that it focuses on sell-side activities. The primary difference between B2C and C2B e-commerce is in terms of the transactional/informational flow. In B2C e-commerce the primary direction of such flow is from business to consumer. In C2B e-commerce the primary direction of such flow is from consumer to business. To avoid confusion we use the term B2C e-commerce to refer to both directions of flow in this text.

Customers or consumers will typically be individuals, and sometimes other organisations. Cash commerce for low- and standard-priced goods typically follows the four stages of the generic commerce model quite closely. It typically involves a see/buy/get sequence.

For medium- to high-priced items some form of credit commerce will operate. Typically, B2C e-commerce will utilise a market model of economic exchange in which economic actors freely exchange goods and services in many-to-many interaction.

17.6.2 BUSINESS TO BUSINESS (B2B) E-COMMERCE

B2B e-commerce supports the supply chain of organisations since it focuses on buy-side activities. B2B commerce is clearly between organisational actors – public and/or private sector organisations. This form of e-commerce invariably concerns the use of ICT to enable forms of credit and repeat commerce between a company and its suppliers or other partners.

For high-priced and customised goods traded between organisations some form of repeat commerce model operates. Hence typically some form of managerial hierarchy is employed to control the operation of the commercial relationship. The use of inter-organisational information systems such as Extranets are becoming popular as a technological vehicle for supporting B2B e-commerce.

17.6.3 CONSUMER TO CONSUMER (C2C) E-COMMERCE

C2C e-commerce supports the community chain surrounding the organisation (Figure 17.2). C2C e-commerce can be seen as a commercial extension of community activities. It typically occurs between individuals and involves forms of cash commerce generally for low-cost services or goods. Consequently, it tends to follow a market model for the economic exchange. Other forms of value may be generated in the communities or social networks engaged in C2C e-commerce. Of particular interest is the degree of social capital (Chapter 20) that may be located in such social networks. Social capital is the productive value of people engaged in a dense network of social relations. Social capital consists of those features of social organisation – networks of secondary associations, high levels of interpersonal trust, reciprocity – which act as resources for individuals and facilitate collective action.

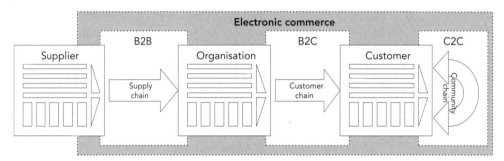

Figure 17.2 B2C, B2B and C2C e-commerce.

Examples

A typical B2C i-commerce application is the e-shop. Here the company sells its products or services through a transactional Web site.

A typical B2B i-commerce application is the vertical Web portal. This is a Web site which connects the buyers and sellers of products and services in particular market sectors.

C2C applications are typically 'exchange and mart' applications. In other words, persons put up goods for sale or exchange and contact details on some organised Web site. Some sites of this nature also manage the transfer of payments/exchanges between users of the site.

It is important to recognise that there are certain areas of overlap between these forms and in some instances distinctions between for instance B2C and B2B e-commerce are largely a matter of presentational convenience. However, they are useful ways for organisations to understand trends in information economies and they constitute useful conceptual tools for the construction and implementation of e-business strategy.

Example

Many companies will engage in B2C e-commerce for buy-side activities, particularly for the purchase of low-priced items such as office stationery.

Question

Which form of e-commerce will be the most significant in the future and why?

17.7 BENEFITS OF E-COMMERCE

The literature identifies a large volume of potential benefits from the adoption of e-commerce. Such benefits are typically factored into a strategic evaluation of e-commerce systems and can help define key performances measures for e-business (Chapter 25). The benefits may be divided into five main areas:

- *Cost savings*. These are efficiency gains that include lower logistic costs, lower postal costs, lower storage costs and lower personnel costs.
- *Time savings*. These are efficiency gains that include quicker response time to markets, customers and suppliers; higher flexibility; and a reduction in the delivery time and processing of payments.
- *Connection improvements*. These include benefits such as disintermediation – the process by which mediating organisations are removed in the customer chain or the supply chain. As such they may impact on both efficiency and effectiveness.
- *Quality improvements*. These improvements include access to new markets, innovative ways of marketing new products and services, and the general improvement in customer relations. Again, they primarily constitute efficiency and effectiveness improvements.
- *Strategic improvements*. These include more efficient and effective organisational forms and doing business on the global scale.

Examples

An example of cost savings may be the reduction in transaction costs associated with orders and payments. A time saving will accrue if e-commerce systems make it quicker to capture a customer order. An example of a connection improvement is that associated with the closer integration of suppliers into inventory systems, enabling just-in-time manufacturing.

Question   *Which of the above benefits is the most significant for the typical business?*

17.8 PROBLEMS WITH E-COMMERCE

There are also a number of current problems and issues with e-commerce:

- *Trust*. Many people do not trust e-commerce in the sense that they will refrain from purchasing high-value goods or services using this medium. Such mistrust seems to be focused around issues such as the perceived difficulties of securing electronic transactions and the reluctance to release personal information over the Internet (Chapter 15). The first is an issue of information security; the second is an issue of information privacy.
- *Reintermediation (brokerage)*. One of the problems with the Internet is the difficulty of finding exact/precise suppliers of goods and services. Organisations have arisen in electronic markets (frequently known as e-brokers or information brokerages) trying to satisfy this need.
- *Information rich and poor*. Concerns have been expressed over differential access to electronic markets afforded to different economic groups in society. This was referred to as the digital divide in Chapter 15.
- *Technological standards*. Technological standards develop rapidly in support of electronic markets. Some of these standards are not particularly secure or have trouble integrating with standards in other areas.
- *Cost of computer-related mistakes and errors*. The visibility of mistakes made with customers and suppliers is much more prominent within electronic markets.

Examples   Much work is being undertaken worldwide to create effective security standards for the transmission of electronic transactions. For instance, progress is being made in the determination of electronic signatures to provide means of authentication for electronic transactions (Chapter 13).

Concern has been expressed over the growing digital divide – those who have access to electronic goods and services and those who do not. Clearly, for many lower income families the cost of PC purchase and maintaining an Internet connection is prohibitive. Such groups may hence be excluded from the digital economy and the benefits thereof (Chapter 15).

The Singapore share trader Nick Leeson used the information systems utilised by his financial house to hide many millions of pounds sterling that had been lost in his financial deals.

Barclays Bank apologised to customers when early in its implementation of an online banking facility customers found they were able to access other customers' financial details.

Question   *Which of the above problems is the most significant for the typical business?*

17.9 CONSUMER BEHAVIOUR

Commerce is fundamentally a process that connects buyers to sellers or producers to consumers. The concept of a producer or consumer is a role that a particular economic actor plays in the commercial process. Economic actors may be individuals, groups or organisations. A particular economic actor may be a producer in one relationship and a consumer in another relationship. Hence the terms B2C, B2B and C2C e-commerce are somewhat arbitrary and constitute stereotypes of forms of commercial activity undertaken in electronic markets and hierarchies.

For the business, serving the needs of your consumers or customers is clearly critical to success. But how do we define the e-commerce consumer?

A narrow definition would include as the e-commerce consumer any economic actor that makes a purchase online for tangible goods (Chapter 8). Clearly, this definition would exclude a great deal of commercial activity that is important for e-commerce. A broader definition of the consumer would include any actor consuming products or services, whether tangible or intangible, using e-commerce. This definition allows us to include:

- Readers of Web pages.
- Online subscribers to mail lists.
- Direct purchasers of intangible goods such as software and graphic art.
- Indirect purchasers of tangible goods such as books and CDs.

Question   *In what ways do you think the online consumer is different from the traditional consumer?*

But how does a consumer decide what to consume and from whom? This is a question of consumer behaviour. A starting point is to assume that consumption is a rational decision-making process on the part of the consumer based fundamentally in processing information. Simon argues that there are four general stages in any decision-making process (Simon, 1976):

- *Intelligence*. In this phase a problem is recognised and information in the decision-making area is searched for and examined. In rational decision-making the decision-maker must gather all relevant information and interpret it in an unbiased manner.

- *Design*. The problem is formulated or specified in greater detail; solutions are developed and tested for feasibility. In rational decision-making the decision-maker must identify all feasible alternatives and identify an explicit set of criteria for selecting between them.

- *Choice*. Selection is made among alternatives. In rational decision-making the decision-maker should choose among alternatives based on a systematic assessment using explicit weightings of the importance of key criteria.

- *Implementation*. The chosen alternative is implemented and substantiated.

Example

In terms of consumption the intelligence phase means that the consumer establishes a goal and searches for information to aid in achieving her goal. Suppose that the goal is to purchase a new car. The consumer is likely to gather various information resources (newspaper advertisements, Web sites, catalogues, visits to showrooms) to help establish her goal more clearly. Design means that the parameters of the intended purchase are established more clearly. This may be in terms of maximum price, fuel consumption, warranty arrangements, exchange terms and so on. Choice in rational terms would involve the consumer in tabulating various models of car against the established criteria and scoring the models to select a winner. Implementation involves the purchase of the automobile and any post-purchase evaluation that might occur.

These phases can clearly be mapped onto the key phases of commerce described above or models such as the customer resource life cycle described in Chapter 23. This model also favours the online consumption experience. The ability to collect information about products and services easily from different providers on a global scale and to evaluate the features of products quickly are seen to be key advantages of online shopping.

However, close studies of actual human decision-making reveal that human behaviour diverges substantially from this rational ideal. This is not surprising when one realises that rational decision-making requires unlimited time within which to make a decision, all the information relevant to the problem and an information processor that is able to handle all of the information and alternatives.

Therefore most human decision-making appears to be satisficing rather than rational behaviour. Satisficing decision-making describes how humans make decisions in a limited amount of time, based on limited information and with limited ability to process information.

- *Limited time.* Most decision-making has to be done in a finite amount of time.
- *Limited information.* In most practicable situations it is impossible to gather all the possible information relevant to the problem because of limited resources.
- *Limited information-processing capability.* The decision-making process is constrained by the limitations of human information processing. For instance, information is interpreted and human interpretation is subject to non-rational emotive influences. Also, human beings display limitations of short-term memory. Most humans can handle on average only seven items of information at any one time.

Shopping is also a much more complex behaviour than a focus on the decision-making characteristics of consumption would suggest. Shopping is frequently a leisure experience for many consumers and is associated with a range of other activities, such as eating and drinking, sightseeing and even walking. Much consumer behaviour is also not particularly goal-directed and may involve browsing or grazing through shops, catalogues and Web sites with no particular purpose in mind.

An understanding of some of the complexities of consumer behaviour, particularly as it affects the industrial sector within which the organisation lies, is critical input into:

- the overall definition of e-business strategy (Chapter 24)
- the shape of e-marketing (Chapter 21)
- the nature of customer relationship management (Chapter 18)
- the design of particular e-commerce sites (Chapter 10)

Critical to this will be the nature of the consumer. There are likely to be major differences in the consumer behaviour in a B2C rather than a B2B context. B2C e-commerce typically involves large numbers of relatively small buyers making low-volume, low-value orders. In contrast, B2B e-commerce typically involves far fewer numbers of larger buyers, frequently organised in teams and making high-volume, high-value orders.

| Example | Clearly it makes little sense to employ e-marketing techniques such as banner advertising on B2B sites because of the scale of numbers involved. It does make sense to perhaps provide higher levels of customisation of orders and perhaps heavier discounting of products. |

The stock market is a classic example of an economic market. It is a market for the purchase and sale of securities – intangible products. Securities come in two major forms: stocks and shares. A stock, sometimes known as a gilt-edged security or gilt, is a security with an associated interest rate. The most important type of stock is the government bond. Shares are a type of security that pay no interest, but pay a dividend to shareholders at regular intervals. Shares are normally issued by companies to raise financial capital for investment.

The modern UK stock market is an e-market. No physical Stock Exchange exists any longer. The Stock Exchange is therefore a network of economic actors that exchange securities using ICT. Persons or institutions that deal in securities on the stock market are known as financial intermediaries. There are two main types of financial intermediary: brokers and market makers. Securities are bought from certain registered market makers. Market makers are normally financial institutions that opt to deal in a limited number of securities. The collection of such securities held by a market maker is known as the market maker's 'book'. Nowadays financial intermediaries tend to engage in e-commerce in order to trade securities. Trade between financial intermediaries themselves can be seen as a form of B2B e-commerce. Trade between financial intermediaries and investors can be seen as a form of B2C e-commerce.

All securities are initially placed on the stock market at an issue price: a price in pence per share. Once a share has been issued it can be traded: that is, bought and sold on the stock market.

Stocks can have variable interest rates or fixed interest rates. Fixed interest rate stock is sometimes called debenture or loan capital. Similarly, shares can offer fixed or variable dividends. Fixed dividend shares are sometimes known as preference capital; variable dividend shares are known as equity capital.

Each market maker will define the state of each type of share it holds in terms of two prices: the offer price and the bid price. The offer price is the price at which a market maker is willing to sell a share – the price at which an investor will buy. The bid price is the price that a market maker is willing to pay for a share – the price at which an investor can sell to him. The difference between the two prices is known as the market maker's 'spread'. Different market makers will quote different spreads on shares depending on the state of their book.

Example	Allied Metals	

	Marketmaker A	MarketMaker B
Offer	102	103
Bid	100	101

Brokers act as intermediaries between investors and market makers. Market makers act as intermediaries between corporations and brokers. Brokers purchase securities on behalf of investors, and/or sell securities to market makers on behalf of an investor. On both such transactions brokers normally charge a commission, normally a percentage of each share price. Under the recent reorganisation of the market, market makers may also act in the capacity of brokers. However, if a market maker deals with itself, in its role as market maker it must equal the best price offered on the market.

To conduct a deal, an investor issues a broker with an order specification. Such a specification normally includes:

- The name of the security.
- Whether the order is to purchase or sell securities.
- The size of an order.
- The time for which the order is to remain outstanding. Day orders should terminate at the end of day's trading; open orders remain in force until filled by a broker or cancelled by an investor.
- Type of order. A market order indicates that the broker should get the best price at the time; a limit order specifies a price below which the broker should buy or above which the broker should sell; a stop order is the reverse of a limit order.

17.11 ◎ SUMMARY

- Commerce of whatever nature can be considered as a process with the following phases: pre-sale, sale execution, sale settlement, after-sale.
- The precise form of the process of commerce will vary in terms of the nature of the economic actors involved, the frequency of commerce, the nature of the goods or services being exchanged.
- Electronic commerce (e-commerce) is the use of ICT to enable the external activities and relationships of the business with individuals, groups and other businesses.
- Generally we may distinguish between three major forms of e-commerce: B2C e-commerce, B2B e-commerce, C2C e-commerce.
- Some of the benefits of e-commerce include cost-savings, time savings, and connection improvements.
- Some of the problems of e-commerce include security concerns, the digital divide and technological standards.
- Consumer behaviour can be considered as a decision-making process involving the stages of intelligence, design, choice and implementation.
- Consumption is more complex than a rational decision-making model of this process would suggest.

17.12 ACTIVITIES

(i) In relation to the commercial activities associated with a product or service known to you, jot down what the four phases of commerce represent.

(ii) Choose a particular example of a commercial activity known to you. List the economic actors involved, the frequency of the activity and the type of product or service offered.

(iii) Attempt to access the Web site of a major large equipment manufacturer. Determine whether the site offers any large-scale goods for sale. If it does, determine what sort of commerce model is expected.

(iv) If you have ever purchased goods or services over the Internet, list the things you have purchased. If not, try to identify the reasons why not.

(v) Identify a C2C site. What sort of items are sold or exchanged on this site? Does the site manage the process of payment and exchange?

(vi) Determine whether some organisation known to you uses e-commerce. If so, attempt to determine the benefits it derives from e-commerce. If not, determine what benefits it might derive.

(vii) If you have made any payments online, determine how sites inform you that they are secure. Determine the confidence you place in the security of such sites.

(viii) Try to analyse a particular purchasing decision you have made recently in terms of the four phases of decision-making described in this chapter.

17.13 REFERENCES

Cassidy, J. (2002). *Dot.con: the Real Story of Why the Internet Bubble Burst*. London, Allen Lane/Penguin Press.

Hoque, F. (2000). *E-enterprise: Business Models, Architecture And Components*. Cambridge, Cambridge University Press.

Laudon, K. C. and Traver, C. G. (2002). *E-commerce: Business, Technology, Society*. Boston, Addison-Wesley.

Simon, H. A. (1976). *Administrative Behavior: a Study of Decision-making Processes in Administration*. New York, Free Press.

Turban, E. and King, D. (2003). *Introduction to E-commerce*. Upper Saddle River, NJ, Prentice Hall.

Whiteley, D. (2000). *E-commerce: Strategy, Technologies and Applications*. Maidenhead, McGraw-Hill.

CHAPTER 18

BUSINESS TO CONSUMER (B2C) ELECTRONIC COMMERCE

Business today consists in persuading crowds

Gerald Stanley Lee, *Crowds*

Your most unhappy customers are your greatest source of learning

Bill Gates, *Business @ The Speed of Thought*

LEARNING OUTCOMES

After reading this chapter, you will be able to:

- Outline the major elements of the customer chain
- Describe the key forms of B2C e-commerce
- Define customer relationship management
- Understand some of the key benefits and problems of B2C e-commerce
- Outline some key B2C business models

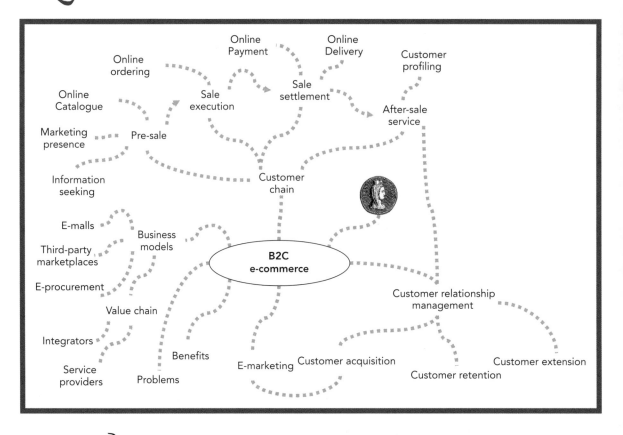

18.1 INTRODUCTION

In earlier chapters we defined B2C e-commerce as concerned with the use of ICT to enable and transform the customer or demand chain of business. Traditional business processes involving relationships between businesses and customers include sales, marketing and after-sales (Chapter 6). All such processes have been amenable to ICT innovation for a number of years. However, two trends explain the current explosion of interest in ICT-enablement of the customer chain:

- The infiltration of ICT infrastructure into the home and public spaces stimulated by the rise of the Internet and the Web. This technological innovation has increased the variety of access channels to business products and services open to the potential consumer (Chapter 7).

- Postal and telephone services have enabled customers to access services and products remotely for a number of years. Changes to the ICT infrastructure worldwide have opened up increasing opportunities for organisations to extend the realms of remote access by implementing efficient and effective electronic delivery systems. It is only comparatively recently, with the rise of such technologies as the Internet, that direct connections between customers and businesses have been made possible.

In this chapter we describe some of the major ways in which the customer chain is being supported and restructured using ICT (De Kare-Silver, 2000). The use of such technology has stimulated interest in integrating all aspects of the relationship with the customer. This is known as customer relationship management. In Chapter 21 we also describe how electronic marketing is a critical part of this customer focus.

18.2 ⊚ THE CUSTOMER CHAIN

Business to customer/consumer (B2C) e-commerce refers to the attempt to support the organisation's customer or demand chain (Chapter 14) with ICT. B2C focuses on the ICT-enablement of the key processes in the customer chain. Key efficiency, effectiveness and strategic gains are possible through such activity. The most common form of such e-commerce currently is the replacement of traditional retail channels with forms of e-tailing.

Example

Blackwell's, established in 1879, is one of the world's largest independently held academic publishers. Although one of the oldest of the UK's publishers it was the first to trade online, launching its Web site one month before Amazon's in June 1995. Initially the Web site was conceived of as effectively adding a new front-end to the company's already established mail order business. However, growing user demand eventually led to the establishment of a separate division: Blackwell's Online. In 2000 the company launched headfiller.com, a site specifically targeting a student customer base. Headfiller offers discounts on publications of up to 30%, credits on future purchases and a scheme that allows students to sell their books back to the company at the end of the academic term.

The company is attempting to offer the same standards of customer service both in terms of its bookshops and in terms of its online channels. The Web sites are also being integrated with the high street service. For instance, customers making orders through their Web sites have the option of collecting books from their stores.

When an order is placed on any of the group's Web sites the publication required is automatically located either in the warehouse or in one of its many stores. If the book is not in stock it is placed on order. When it arrives it is identified as an online, mail or store order and automatically sent to the appropriate destination within 24 hours.

The headfiller site cost some £5 million to develop and took some 22 weeks to construct. The company has committed £10 million to developing the site over a three-year period, of which £1 million is devoted to marketing.

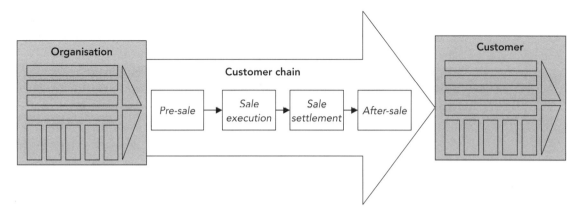

Figure 18.1 The customer chain.

The customer chain generally uses either a cash or a credit model of commerce (Figure 18.1). E-commerce applications can be used to support most of these stages of the customer chain. For instance:

- *Pre-sale.* On the Web, product identification can be enabled through banners on Web sites, inclusion in search engines and personalised marketing based on customer profiling. Online catalogues and portals may also enable product comparison between vendors.
- *Sale execution.* Web sites permit online ordering of products and services.
- *Sale settlement.* Online payment can be made through secure B2C sites and integration with back-end information systems such as accounting and distribution.
- *After sale.* Various forms of customer profiling and preferencing systems may be used to encourage further purchases from customers.

Example   In terms of an online seller of art prints, pre-sale involves activities such as e-mailing past and potential customers with details of products and discounts. Sale execution is conducted through online ordering. Sale settlement is conducted through online payment. After-sale service runs off a customer profiling system which automatically e-mails previous customers with details of upcoming prints in their indicated areas of preference.

Question   *Which of these four activities within the customer chain has the most potential for being affected by ICT?*

We may think of an organisation's experience of B2C e-commerce as moving through a number of distinct stages of increasing ICT infrastructure complexity, which support the various activities of B2C e-commerce. These can be seen to be extensions of the customer-facing information systems described in Chapter 6.

- Information-seeking and communication
- Marketing presence
- Online catalogue
- Online ordering
- Online payment
- Online delivery
- Customer profiling and preferencing

Examples

Small enterprises will probably first use a computer and an Internet connection to seek out information about potential competitors. It will also probably use this facility to e-mail suppliers. The more sophisticated it gets, and depending upon its business strategy, the SME may eventually reach the stage at which most of its business with customers is conducted electronically.

In Australia the use of the Internet for business activity is more prevalent among the larger organisations. The most recent survey by the Australian Bureau of Statistics found that the majority of businesses with Web sites used their site to display company information (88%) or advertise their goods and services (79%). Only 5% had an online payments facility (ABS, 2000).

Recent research conducted on 107 Australian Web sites indicates (Hawking and Fisher, 2002) that 11% of companies primarily use their Web site as a basic marketing presence; 47% of companies have moved beyond this to provide some interactivity via e-mail communication, online forms and configurations for products; 24% of companies provide more detailed product details and pricing and provide a basic online ordering facility; and 18% of companies conduct mature e-commerce activity including online payment and delivery.

Each of these stages supports parts of the model of commerce described in Chapter 17 (Figure 18.2). Pre-sale activities include information seeking and communication, marketing presence and online catalogue. Sale execution activities are online ordering and potentially online delivery. Sale settlement activities equate to online payment, and after-sales activities equate to customer profiling and preferencing.

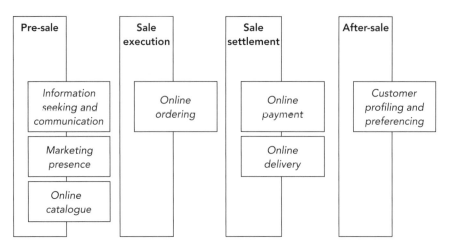

Figure 18.2 Stages of B2C e-commerce systems.

Question   *In what way is it appropriate to use a growth model such as this to plan e-business strategy?*

Here the company is beginning to engage with the Internet, probably using it primarily for information seeking and communication via e-mail (Figure 18.3).

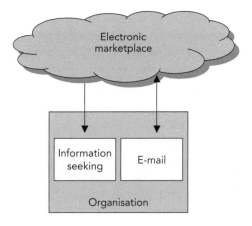

Figure 18.3 Information seeking and communication.

The Internet and the Web have enabled more effective and efficient information-seeking behaviour on the part of individuals. Many software tools exist (such as search engines) to support such behaviour.

Electronic mail is a significant technology for business because it allows asynchronous communication between stakeholders. It also enables easy transfer of electronic files around computer networks. In terms of B2C e-commerce the availability of an e-mail address for a company makes it easy for customers to make enquiries and even to transfer details of an order.

Example

Many small and medium-sized enterprises (SMEs) (those with less then 250 employees) are at this stage in the adoption of e-commerce, particularly so-called micro-enterprises (those with fewer than 10 employees). Such businesses use the Internet primarily as a tool for gathering information about organisations in the same market segment as themselves, receiving e-mails from customers and e-mailing suppliers.

18.5 ⊙ MARKETING PRESENCE

Marketing is a key customer-focused process for business and is discussed more fully in Chapter 21. Initially, companies typically consider establishing a marketing presence on the Internet through producing a corporate Web site with details of the company profile on it (Figure 18.4). This will most likely include a description of the main activities of the company, its location and some contact details. Potential customers may use the Web site only to contact the company, probably through interaction with e-mail systems.

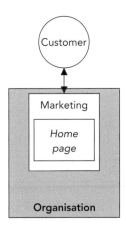

Figure 18.4 Marketing presence.

Example

Some SMEs have produced their own Web sites or have had a Web site produced for them. Within the UK a number of portals have been produced specifically to act as gateways to the Web sites of regional SMEs.

18.6 ◎ ONLINE CATALOGUE

Here the company provides an online catalogue of its products or services available for inspection by potential customers. The catalogue may amount to a series of static Web pages or may be dynamic in the sense that it is updated from a database of products (Chapter 12). More sophisticated sites of this nature will allow dynamic pricing of product information perhaps for different types of market segment. Customers still have to place orders through traditional channels such as over the telephone, through the post or potentially through e-mail (Figure 18.5).

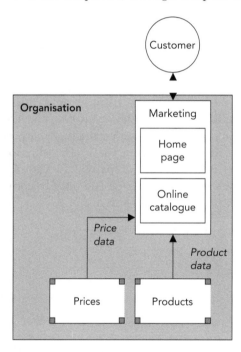

Figure 18.5 Online catalogue.

Example

A specialist publisher produces an online catalogue of its limited range of specialist publications. The catalogue contains a cover image, a short synopsis of the contents of each publication, details of the cost of each publication and delivery charges. To order publications customers have to ring a telephone line or send an order form through the post with the appropriate payment.

The UK music retailer HMV created its first Web site (hmv.com) in 1997 in response to continuous customer requests for such a facility. Initially produced as a pilot it has now been upgraded to incorporate an online catalogue of over a quarter of a million products.

18.7 ◎ ONLINE ORDERING

The next logical step is to enable customers to place orders online for products or services. This is a key transition point for most businesses, since it involves the integration of Web sites with back-end information systems. In a credit commerce model (Chapter 17) the company will invoice the customer for payment after delivery. This situation demands integration between the Web site and the sales order information system. The sales order information system will trigger the distribution information system that manages the delivery of goods and services. Payment details will also be passed to the organisation's accounting system that will send an invoice to the customer and receive payment from the customer (Figure 18.6).

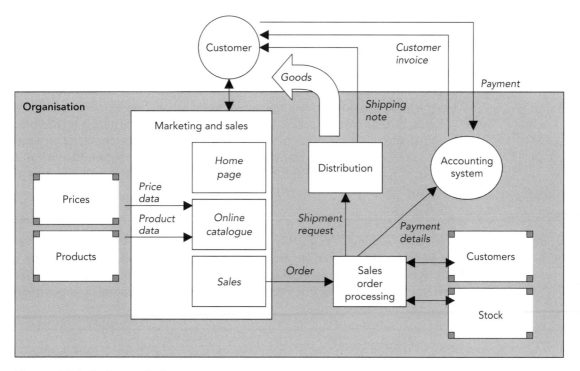

Figure 18.6 Online ordering.

Examples	A bulk supplier of stationery provides an online catalogue of its most popular range of office products. Certain volumes of this material can be ordered via the Internet site for established customers. The traditional distribution, invoicing and accounting systems of the supplier are used to support the B2C process.
	The MH900e is a high-performance, handcrafted motorcycle. It was produced as a limited edition by Ducati Motorcycles, an Italian motorcycle manufacturer. Selling at a premium price of €15,000 it was sold only through the company's Web site on the 1 January 2000. Within 31 minutes of release the first year's production was sold. With its online sales of the MH900e Ducati established a position as one of Italy's largest e-tailers.

18.8 ONLINE PAYMENT

In this scenario the customer both orders and pays for the goods using the Web site. This is more usual for cash commerce, in which the customer is an individual and the goods are standardised and relatively low in price, such as CDs or books. However, this form of B2C e-commerce demands close integration between an organisation's front-end and back-end information systems (Chapter 11).

We describe here a scenario available in many sites offering online ordering and payment. Clearly the details of the specific functionality of each site will vary. The customer may first order goods using an electronic shopping facility in the sales system. The shopping facility calculates the total cost of the order for the customer and includes the delivery charge. The customer enters her credit or debit card details to complete the purchase. For such payment details to be entered the organisation provides a secure payment system (Chapter 13).

Payment details are checked with a financial intermediary such as the customer's bank. If the customer has sufficient funds available the financial intermediary makes an electronic funds transfer (Chapter 8) to the company's bank account and details of the transfer are recorded in the company's accounting system (Figure 18.7).

Example	A company supplies high-quality prints of works of art. The customer is able to search for prints by theme, period, artist and price and images of selected prints can be displayed at various degrees of resolution. Prints are also offered in various sizes. The customer can add prints to a shopping trolley and pay online by credit or debit card. The site automatically confirms orders via e-mail.

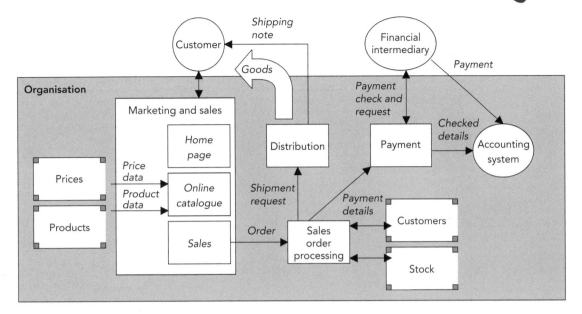

Figure 18.7 Online payment.

For certain intangible goods it is possible to deliver such goods online. Certain intangible goods or products are converging to a digital standard, making the capture, storage and dissemination of media of various types in a digital format.

Examples include (Chapter 8):

- Visual artwork
- Music
- Films
- Broadcast media such as television and radio
- Software

In Figure 18.8 the distribution systems are replaced with an online delivery system. There is also less likely to be a need for a separate stock and products data store. Both product descriptions and the intangible products themselves are likely to be accessed from the products store.

In practice the payment method for such online delivery is likely to be based on a monthly subscription paid through credit or debit details.

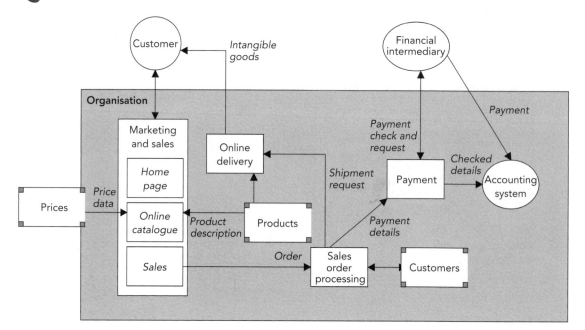

Figure 18.8 Online delivery.

Example   Certain companies pay a subscription charge to sites managing the online delivery of software. Subscription entitles the company to download upgrades of key software products.

18.10 CUSTOMER PROFILING AND PREFERENCING

Customer relationship management has become a popular philosophy in the recent management science literature (see below). Winning new customers and keeping existing customers happy is seen to be critical to organisational success. To enable this an organisation's information systems need to track all customer interactions with a company from initial enquiries through making orders to the whole range of after-sales services that might be offered to and consumed by the customer. This will also probably involve integration of the customer-facing systems with a customer profiling and preferencing system. This information system will dynamically build a profile of a customer and on the basis of this continuously adjust the profile to offer the customer individualised goods and/or services (Figure 18.9).

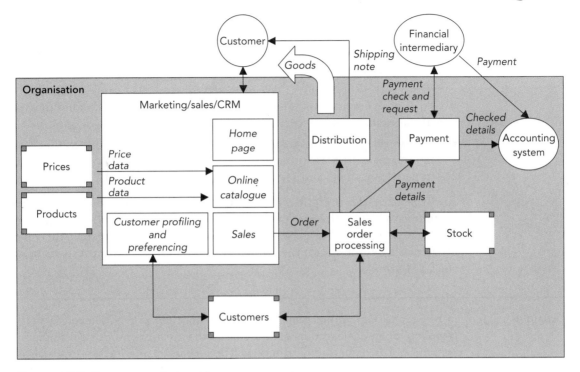

Figure 18.9 Customer relationship management.

Examples

Many Internet booksellers now use customer-profiling systems. E-mail details combined with a previous purchase history enables the site to e-mail customers with details of new books in their area of interest, perhaps offering special discount schemes for established customers.

W H Smith, a major UK retailer, uses a piece of customer tracking software on its Web site. This software tracks whether customers are accessing competitor's sites and strategically places messages on these sites promoting the company's superior pricing and product schemes.

18.11 CUSTOMER RELATIONSHIP MANAGEMENT

In the modern business world, with increasing degrees of competition and the associated globalisation of business, the customer is a key focus. Customer relationship management (CRM) concerns that set of activities that support the customer chain. Hence it is sometimes known as customer chain management. CRM is an attempt to establish long-term relationships with customers.

It is useful to consider CRM as a system composed of three interrelated processes:

- *Customer acquisition*. This comprises the set of activities and techniques used to gain new customers. Customer acquisition activities overlap with e-marketing (Chapter 21) in terms of e-business.
- *Customer retention*. This refers to the set of activities and techniques used to maintain relationships with existing customers.
- *Customer extension*. This consists of the set of activities and techniques used to encourage existing customers to increase their level of involvement with a company's products and services.

All these activities are critically dependent on good data – knowing who your customers are, what they are purchasing, how satisfied they are with the company and what they want in terms of future services and products. Hence, there has been an increasing emphasis on the implementation of information systems to support the CRM process.

Examples

In terms of a high street bank, customer acquisition primarily involves persuading people to open bank accounts or purchase other financial products with the financial institution. Customer retention may involve the bank in offering services such as multi-channel access to bank accounts. Customer extension may involve the bank in offering aggregated products such as combined bank accounts and mortgages.

In 1997 MeritaNordbanken was formed from the merger of Merita Bank of Finland and Nordbank of Sweden. At the time of this merger the company was arguably the most developed electronic bank in the world (Peppard, 2000). It offers customers a large number of different e-banking access devices including telephone, PC, WAP mobile and interactive digital television banking. Financial products are geared around a customer's life events such as studies, going abroad and retirement. MeritNordBanken is now part of the Nordea group.

18.11.1   CUSTOMER ACQUISITION

Customer acquisition for e-business clearly involves the process of attracting customers to Web sites. Hence e-marketing is a critical aspect of CRM. However, customer acquisition also involves attempting to persuade the customer to engage in a dialogue with the company. Through such dialogue the company's systems can build up a profile of the customer in terms of the products/services she is interested in, her demographic profile and her general purchasing behaviour.

18.11.2 CUSTOMER RETENTION

In terms of e-commerce, customer retention has the related goals of retaining customers (repeat customers) and persuading customers to keep using the online channel of communication (repeat visits). Two factors are critical to retention: customer satisfaction and customer loyalty.

One technique used in customer retention is the personalisation of e-mail content. Customers are able to receive personalised alerts of particular products or services in which their profile has indicated an interest. Such alerts may also offer discounts or other added-value services in a bid to persuade customers to return to a B2C site.

18.11.3 CUSTOMER EXTENSION

It might be argued that B2C e-commerce in general and CRM in particular are a natural consequence of the increasing customer focus of organisations. Porter (1985) has argued that the value delivered to the customer is the key feature of contemporary business. Hence it is not surprising to find companies attempting to reorient their processes and systems around an overt customer focus as opposed to a traditional focus around events such as orders and sales. Having an integrated approach to both front-end and back-end customer information systems means that companies can identify repeat customers, identify their behaviour and on the basis of this information offer personalised packages of products and/or services to such customers in the hope that they will continue to conduct business with the company.

Example | Consider an insurance company that sells a number of financial products such as life insurance, car insurance and home insurance to its customers. Traditionally the insurance company structured its information systems around policy types, such as life, car and home. Hence it proved difficult for such a company to determine which customers were purchasing more than one type of insurance with the company. It also meant that the insurance company sent a renewal notice for each type of policy to which a customer subscribed. The systems have recently been restructured around the customer. This means that the company can now tell which are its most valued customers and has initiated various schemes such as discount packages in order to attempt to retain this business.

Question | *How important is customer relationship management as an element of business strategy and how important is it for companies to invest in CRM systems? Does the importance of CRM vary by industry sector?*

18.12 ⊙ BENEFITS OF B2C E-COMMERCE

Implementing B2C e-commerce is likely to be a customer chain strategy for the business (Chapter 22). Benefits will be factored into a strategic evaluation of such implementation (Chapter 25). Benefits of B2C e-commerce can be considered either from the viewpoint of the consumer or from that of the business.
From the consumer side, benefits include:

- Access to goods and services from the home or other remote locations.
- The possibility of lower cost goods and services.
- Access to a greater variety of goods and services on offer.

From the business side, benefits include:

- Lower transaction costs associated with sales.
- Access to global markets and hence to more potential customers.
- Opportunities for disintermediation leading to lower costs for customers.

Example

An online banking transaction costs a fraction of the cost of a transaction that goes through a teller at a high street bank. Not surprisingly, a number of the major high street banks now offer online services to their customers. For the customer of the bank advantages include being able to check online balances, transfer money between accounts immediately and being able to pay bills online.

Question

Which is the most significant benefit of B2C e-commerce for business and why?

18.13 ⊙ PROBLEMS OF B2C E-COMMERCE

Problems or costs are also likely to be factored into an evaluation of a customer chain strategy. Some key problems of B2C e-commerce include:

- Having a sufficient customer base online.
- The costs of re-engineering back-end systems around a customer focus.
- The costs of integrating back-end systems and processes with B2C sites.
- The costs of ensuring the security of online transactions and access to personal data.

Examples

Access to the Internet is variable across the social classes, In the UK, as much as 70% of higher-income groups have access to the Internet. As little as 7% of the lower income groups have such access.

A lot of so-called 'dotcom' companies which sprang on to the scene in the late 1990s had a strong marketing presence but failed to deliver satisfactory levels of performance to their customers in terms of straightforward business activities such as distributing goods quickly and efficiently to customers. Much of this appears to have been due to a lack of integration between back-end and front-end systems in such companies.

Question	*Which is the most significant problem for modern business in the area of B2C e-commerce?*

18.14 ⊚ B2C BUSINESS MODELS

In our discussion of the typical B2C systems of a company we have focused on one particular business model for B2C e-commerce which Timmers (1999) calls an e-shop. An e-shop is a single firm selling their products or services online. In an e-shop, increased revenue is sought through access to a larger market, offering a larger range of products or offering longer opening hours (24 × 7). Lower costs may result from the use of low-cost warehouses, volume discounts on purchases and improved inventory management.

However, Timmers argues that there are a number of other business models for B2C operations. These include:

- *E-malls*. An e-mall is a business model in which a range of businesses share a Web site for the provision of e-services. Effectively it amounts to a form of inter-organisational information system. Increases in revenue are sought in much the same way as for an e-shop. Cost-savings are expected through sharing the implementation and maintenance costs of front-end systems.

- *Third-party marketplace*. In this business model a third party firm provides Internet marketing and transaction services for other firms. This is frequently used by an established company that wants an entry-level exposure in e-commerce without major costs of implementation and maintenance. Revenue generation is typically through membership fees, fees per transaction or a percentage of transaction value.

- *E-procurement*. Electronic tendering of goods and services. This is a popular process strategy that we shall consider in Chapter 19.

- *Value chain integrators*. These companies offer a range of services across the value chain. The services are integrated and companies may outsource major parts of their customer chain or supply chain activities to such companies.

- *Value chain service providers*. These companies specialise in a particular function within the value chain, such as electronic payments, inventory management and logistics. Companies employing such companies save on having to provide such services themselves. Providers of these services normally accrue a fee or a percentage of the services provided from the company.

- *Information brokerage.* Companies specialising in the provision of information to consumers and to businesses to help such individuals and organisations to make buying decisions or for business operations. Revenue models include membership fees, advertising fees and cross selling.
- *Trust and other services.* These companies authenticate the services and products of other companies provided on the Web. Revenue models typically involve some form of membership fee.

Examples   Some examples of particular B2C business models include: http://www.amazon.com/ (e-shop); http://www.indigosquare.com/ (e-mall); http://www.ups.com/ (value chain service providers); http://www.which.com/ (consumer services); and http://www.truste.com/ (trust services).

In November 2002 Tesco.com – the online arm of the food retailer Tesco – saw its sales rise to £10 million. In the UK, 100,000 households now order their goods regularly through the Web site.

There are clearly degrees of overlap between these business model types, such that certain business models form natural clusters. Timmers classifies the business models in terms of the number of functions provided and the level of integration of such functions and the degree of innovation required to implement a given business model.

Example   E-shops have low functional integration and low innovation. Value chain integrators offer high functional integration and demand sophisticated levels of e-business innovation.

Question   *Which of the above business models for B2C e-commerce do you think will be the most sustainable and why?*

18.15 CASE STUDY: AMAZON

Amazon.com is probably the most cited example of a company that has excelled at B2C e-commerce. Amazon.com was launched on the Web in June 1995 by Jeff

Bezos. Bezos obtained the backing of venture capitalists in Silicon Valley to start the operation. He chose to name his site after the world's longest river because Amazon according to Bezos was set to become the world's largest bookstore. At the time of Amazon's entry into the market it had no significant rivals. Within one year the company was recognised as the Web's largest and best bookstore. From the start Amazon offered a range of value-added services to its customers. For instance:

- Personal notification service for customers requesting particular titles.
- A recommendations section where customers can recommend titles in various categories to other customers.
- An awards section which lists books that have won prizes.
- An associate program where other sites could link to Amazon to sell their own selections.

At the start Bezos warned investors that they were unlikely to make a profit in the first five years of operation. However, Amazon has engaged in an aggressive expansion strategy. For instance:

- It has acquired a number of additional retail outlets such as toys and CDs.
- It has provided a facility for online auctions of small goods.
- It introduced zShops in 1999. Such a facility allows any individual or business to sell through Amazon.com – a form of C2C trading.
- It has invested in a number of dotcom companies such as Pets.com and Drug-store.com.
- It created Amazon Anywhere – a mobile e-commerce initiative using WAP technology.
- It has opened a number of distribution centres and operations around the world.

Currently the company is claimed to be the Internet's number one retailer. However, Bezos has indicated that he considers Amazon to be a technology company first and a retailer second. Hence the key differentiating factor for Amazon over the conventional retailer is the Internet and Web. Not surprisingly, the company has to innovate ceaselessly in terms of technology. Having said this, Amazon must ensure that the back-end systems managing its supply, sales and distribution processes work effectively.

The company provides a number of levels of functionality through its Web site:

- *Search features*. The company provides searchable catalogues of books, CDs, DVDs, computer games etc. Customers can search for titles using keyword, title, subject, author, artist, musical instrument, label, actor, director, publication date or ISBN.
- *Additional content*. The company offers a vast range of additional content over and above its products; for example, cover art, synopses, annotations, reviews by editorial staff and other customers and interviews by authors and artists.
- *Recommendations and personalisations*. The Web site attempts to personalise the customer experience by greeting customers by name and offering instant and

personalised recommendations, bestseller listings, personal notification services, and purchase pattern filtering.

- *1-Click™ technology.* This is the company's term for a streamlined ordering process reliant on previous billing and shipment details captured from the customer.
- *Secure credit card payment.* Amazon utilises secure server software that encrypts payment information.
- *Fulfillment.* Most of the company's products are available for shipping within 24 hours.

18.16 SUMMARY

- Business to consumer or B2C e-commerce refers to the attempt to support the organisation's customer chain with ICT.
- B2C focuses on the ICT-enablement of the key processes in the customer chain: pre-sale, sale-execution, sale-settlement and after-sale.
- We may think of an organisation's experience of B2C e-commerce as moving through a number of distinct stages of increasing complexity which support the various phases of commerce:
- A company will first use the Internet for information-seeking and communication.
- More sophisticated companies will establish a marketing presence on the Internet.
- Companies may eventually put an online catalogue of their products and/or services on a Web site.
- Online ordering and online payment are two distinct additional levels of functionality that can be provided on a company B2C site.
- Customer relationship management systems may enable a company to better track all interactions between a company and their business.

18.17 ACTIVITIES

- **(i)** Find one other example of B2C e-commerce.
- **(ii)** Access a B2C site and attempt to assign the features you find to the phases of the customer chain.
- **(iii)** Consider a company known to you. Determine at what stage it is in as far as B2C e-commerce is concerned.
- **(iv)** In terms of some company determine what information is searched for using the Internet.
- **(v)** Find a Web site for an SME in your local area. Determine how successfully it markets itself through the Internet.

(vi) Find a Web site with an online catalogue. Describe the features of the online catalogue.

(vii) Make a list of the sort of goods you can order over the Internet and what you may not. Reflect on the types of products characteristic of markets and hierarchies.

(viii) Certain persons refuse to release their credit or debit card details online. Examine how serious a threat this is to B2C e-commerce.

(ix) Visit the Amazon site and attempt to determine what forms of customer profiling they employ.

(x) Investigate the range of CRM systems offered by vendors.

(xi) Determine what the level of discounting on the price of goods is available by ordering via an Internet site.

(xii) In your personal network investigate the levels of access to the Internet.

(xiii) Using Timmer's types of business model for B2C e-commerce, identify a specific company operating in each area.

(xiv) Try to categorise Timmer's types of business model in terms of some other dimensions besides functional integration and degree of innovation.

18.18 REFERENCES

ABS (2000). *Business Use of Information Technology*. Australian Bureau of Statistics.

De Kare-Silver, M. (2000). *E-Shock 2000: the Electronic Shopping Revolution; Strategies for Retailers and Manufacturers*. Basingstoke, Macmillan.

Hawking, P. and Fisher, J. (2002). The state of play of the websites of large Australian companies. *European Conference on Information Systems*, Gdansk, Poland.

Peppard, J. (2000). Customer relationship management in financial services. *European Management Journal*, **18**(3), 312–327.

Porter, M. E. (1985). *Competitive Advantage: Creating and Sustaining Superior Performance*. New York, Free Press.

Timmers, P. (1999). *Electronic Commerce: Strategies and Models for Business to Business Trading*. Chichester, John Wiley.

CHAPTER 19

BUSINESS TO BUSINESS (B2B) ELECTRONIC COMMERCE

I always keep a supply of stimulant handy in case I see a snake – which I also keep handy.

W. C. Fields (1890–1946)

Advice is the only commodity on the market where the supply always exceeds the demand.

Anonymous

LEARNING OUTCOMES

After reading this chapter, you will be able to:

- Define B2B e-commerce
- Indicate how it services supply chain processes
- Describe the influence of B2B on pre-sale activity
- Describe some of the activities supported by Extranets
- Outline some of the benefits of B2B e-commerce
- Outline some of the problems of B2B e-commerce

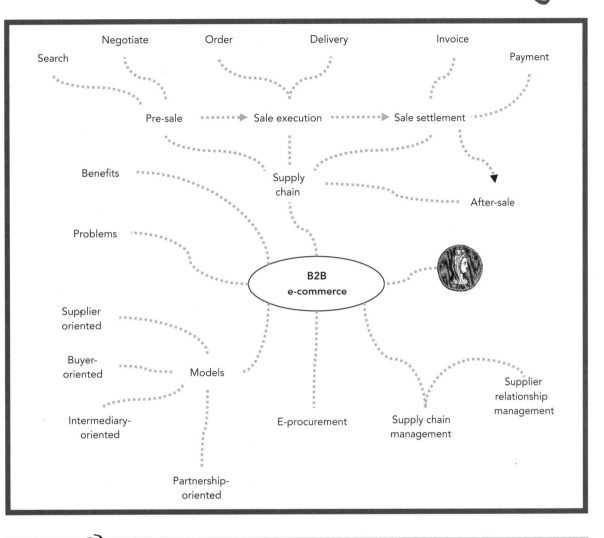

19.1 ◎ INTRODUCTION

B2B e-commerce concerns ICT enablement of the supply chain. B2B e-commerce has been undertaken for a number of decades in that businesses have used electronic records to transfer documentation using standards in the area of electronic data interchange (Chapter 8). More recently the Internet and its associated technologies have been used to transfer data between companies.

It has been argued that B2B e-commerce is even more critical to economies than B2C e-commerce (Cunningham, 2002). It is estimated that the value of B2B e-commerce transactions is typically ten times the value of B2C e-commerce transactions (Wise and Morrison, 2000). Hence ICT innovation has potentially enormous value for organisations engaging in activities in this area.

In this chapter we consider some of the major ways in which the supply chain may be enabled through ICT. We conclude with an examination of some of the key benefits and problems associated with B2B e-commerce. In Chapter 22 we consider the specific process of procurement and the e-business issues associated with this key process.

Example   The Australian Bureau of Statistics found that in 2000 the estimated total value of sales/orders in Australia was $5.1 billion with the majority of transactions being business to business (ABS, 2000).

19.2 THE SUPPLY CHAIN

Business-to-business (B2B) commerce is primarily a buy-side issue. B2B e-commerce represents the attempt to use ICT to improve the supply chain processes of organisations. Traditional aspects of the supply chain, such as the execution and settlement of sales have been conducted electronically for a number of decades using technologies such as EDI. Much of the current interest in this area has been in the use of Internet technologies to enable the pre-sale activity within the supply chain. Enabling technologies in this area include the concept of an Extranet and the recent interest in extensible markup language (XML) (Chapter 8).

Example   The computer hardware manufacturer Dell engages in supply chain innovation including customisation of hardware and direct retailing to customers. Customers may order a personal computer through a Web site that provides an online catalogue of products. Customers can also enter details of specific configurations of hardware they require through this Web site. Such build-to-order retail requires assembly plants around the world (Austin, Texas; Limerick, Eire; Penang, Malaysia) close to suppliers such as Intel (chips), Maxtor (hard drives) and Selectron (motherboards). Order forms follow each PC across the factory floor. Online customer support is provided. The Dell site provides order and courier tracking and pages of technical support related to the tagging of machines.

Much discussion of B2B e-commerce is directed at supporting the repeat commerce model (Chapter 17). Here a company sets up an arrangement with a trusted supplier to deliver goods of a certain specification at regular intervals (Figure 19.1). Each of the phases of the repeat commerce model may be impacted upon by B2B e-commerce:

- *Search*. Buyers within organisations detailing features of the product or service required will complete online forms. This may then be submitted via the corporate Intranet for requisition approval. After requisition approval the purchasing

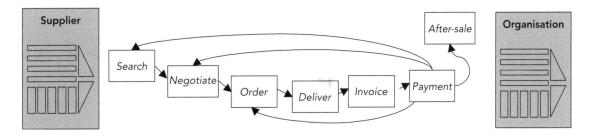

Figure 19.1 The supply chain.

department will issue a request for quote to potential suppliers. Nowadays this may be conducted on an online bulletin board that connects buyers and sellers.

- *Negotiate.* After all bids have been received a vendor is selected probably using some software that ranks bids on the basis of chosen key features of the bid.
- *Order.* The supplier is notified of a successful bid and a purchase order is electronically transmitted to the chosen supplier.
- *Delivery.* After delivery of goods the stock control system is automatically updated.
- *Invoice and payment.* After receiving the invoice from the supplier the company arranges an electronic funds transfer with the supplying company.
- *After-sale.* Supplier relationship management systems monitor all interactions with suppliers and can be used to check on the performance of particular suppliers.

This approach to B2B e-commerce is primarily modelled on the economic model of an electronic hierarchy (Figure 19.1) and can be considered to be an extension to the supplier-facing information systems described in Chapter 6. More recently, forms of market-based trading are infiltrating the B2B sector leading to an overlapping of B2B and B2C business models and technical infrastructure.

Question	*Is the supply chain as significant for service-oriented organisations? Is B2B e-commerce important for such organisations?*

19.3 B2B E-COMMERCE INFRASTRUCTURE

B2B e-commerce is a natural extension of the informatics infrastructure of commercial organisations. In Chapter 6 we referred to such information systems as supplier-facing information systems.

Purchase order processing and payment processing systems normally handle the settlement and execution stages of the commerce cycle. Such information systems are an established part of the information systems architecture of most medium to large organisations. Such systems have also used standards for the electronic transfer of documentation with suppliers. Electronic data interchange (EDI) is a technology that has been used for B2B e-commerce for a couple of decades. More recently, extensible markup language (XML) has been proposed as a replacement technology for EDI (Chapter 8).

Example

In the UK the E-GIF (Electronic Government Interoperability Framework) is being proposed as an XML-based standard set of technical specifications to enable electronic communication between public sector bodies and their suppliers.

The pre-sale and after-sale stages of the commerce cycle have been the most open to innovation in B2B e-commerce. Requisitioning, request for quote and vendor selection are part of what we previously called a supplier relationship management information system (Chapter 6). It is in this area that most of the discussion of B2B e-commerce occurs.

Figure 19.2 illustrates the relationships between the supplier-facing systems of supplier relationship management, procurement and purchase order processing, and other infrastructure systems such as accounting and stock control. This emphasises that successful B2B e-commerce relies on integration with back-end information systems.

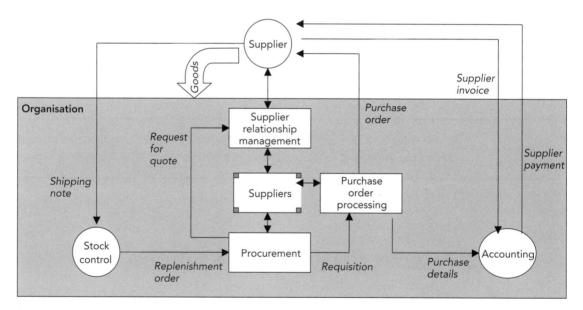

Figure 19.2 Integration of B2B systems with the IS infrastructure.

| Question | Why are pre-sale and after-sale the most potent areas for B2B e-commerce currently? |

19.4 ⊚ SUPPLIER RELATIONSHIP MANAGEMENT

Supplier relationship management (SRM) is sometimes referred to as supply chain management (Meier, 1995) and involves the coordination of all the supply chain activities of the company including relationships with suppliers.

Supply chain management is a generalisation of inbound logistics (Chapter 3), the management of material resources supplied to the organisation. It is also sometimes used to encompass outbound logistics, the management of resources supplied by the organisation to its customers. Just as customer relationship management can be seen to include e-marketing, supplier relationship management can also be seen to include e-procurement (Chapter 22).

Traditionally, management of the supply chain has been organised in terms of hierarchies. Hierarchies coordinate flow by controlling and directing it at a higher level in management hierarchies. Hence companies set up networks of established suppliers and manage such networks as a part of the organisation's management regime. With the rise of the Internet and the Web there has been an increasing trend for supply chain management to move more closely towards market-oriented models (see below).

| Examples | The UK supermarket chain Sainsbury's engaged in a radical rethinking of its supply chain issues during the late 1990s. One result of this is the development of Sainsbury's Information Direct, a portal site for 360 of its major suppliers. Suppliers can use the site to plan product promotions or to track how current promotions are performing. The portal is updated with sales data every day. The site also enables suppliers to deploy inventory where needed in support of promotions. |
| | Josiah Wedgwood & Sons Limited, founded in 1759 by Josiah Wedgwood, is one of the world's leading manufacturers of quality ceramics. In the mid-1990s the company embarked on an ambitious programme of re-engineering its production and supply chain processes around information systems. Wedgwood traditionally used a push model for its production. Production levels were set on the basis of a monthly forecast of expected sales. The company changed the process to a pull model in which products were only manufactured when stock levels triggered an order to replenish. This model was cascaded down to major suppliers in which low stock levels of materials such as lithographic transfers initiated orders to suppliers. |

| Question | What sort of organisations are likely to benefit from B2B e-commerce the most? |

B2B commerce traditionally relies on trusted relationships between a company and either one or more established suppliers. In recent times there have been moves to introduce market models into the supply chain. In terms of pre-sale activity the Internet has enabled four distinct models for B2B e-commerce to occur:

- *Supplier-oriented B2B.* This is sometimes referred to as sell-side B2B e-commerce and effectively this is mirror-image of B2C or buy-side e-commerce. Typically, supplier-oriented B2B e-commerce involves one supplier and many potential purchasers and will take place for small item and volume purchases. One of the most popular forms of supplier-oriented B2B is the e-shop – the promotion of the supplier's products or services through the Internet (Chapter 18).

- *Buyer-oriented B2B.* In this approach a consumer opens an electronic market on its own server. It then invites suppliers to bid on the supply information displayed on the site. Hence one buyer tenders for products among many potential suppliers. As such it is sometimes referred to as buy-side B2B e-commerce. This scenario can be expanded into e-procurement (Chapter 22) in which the later stages in the supply chain are handled electronically.

- *Intermediary-oriented B2B.* In this model an intermediary runs effectively a subset of an electronic market where buyers and sellers can meet and exchange products and services. As such this form of B2B e-commerce involves many-to-many exchanges and is also referred to as B2B e-marketplaces or B2B hubs.

- *Partnership-oriented B2B.* The three previous models are all effectively market-oriented in the sense that they are designed for many-to-many exchange. The traditional model of B2B e-commerce is modelled on an electronic hierarchy. Here an established relationship exists between a company and its supplier. The relationship is likely to be supported by some form of integration of information systems. The Extranet is a modern version of such integration.

Example

Many small companies use the Internet to purchase goods and services in much the same way that the average consumer would. This is an example of supplier-oriented B2B.

An example of intermediary-oriented B2B is Unitec (Ordanini and Pol, 2001). Unitec was founded 13 years ago as a traditional supplier to the automobile industry. It has now established itself as an outsourcing supplier specialising in supply chain management and logistics. It became an intermediary-oriented B2B site in 1997 and has two offices in Europe – one in Augsburg, Germany and the other in Saubadia, Italy. Unitec aggregates the catalogues from multiple suppliers and therefore acts as both a one-stop shop for buyers and a low-cost distribution channel for suppliers. The system allows buyers to search a database of over 44,000 items from over 3,000 companies and place purchase orders in real-time.

Question	*Which model of B2B e-commerce is likely to be the most sustainable?*

19.6 ◎ INTERMEDIARY-ORIENTED B2B

Intermediary-oriented B2B is a key form of reintermediation (Chapter 14) in the supply chain and can be conducted in a number of ways including:

- *Vertical portals.* Vertical portals aggregate buyers and sellers around a particular market segment. They produce revenue through subscription, advertising, commission and transaction fees.
- *Internet auctions.* B2B auction sites enable buyers and sellers to negotiate the price and terms of sales. The seller holds inventory, but the auction site handles fulfilment of goods and the exchange of payment.
- *E-malls/e-stores.* These are general portals run by third parties offering a range of products/services from suppliers for customers. An e-mall is effectively a collection of e-shops.

Example	WIZnet is an example of a B2B portal. It maintains full content catalogues for some 20,000 suppliers.

Question	*Would you predict that forms of reintermediation such as the above will increase in the future?*

19.7 ◎ EXTRANETS

An Extranet is an extended Intranet. Extranets can be considered as a series of connected Intranets between the organisation and important stakeholders such as suppliers, distributors, business partners and remote employees. An Extranet provides secure access to the data of an organisation to its external stakeholders.

Examples	FedEx maintains an Intranet that tracks the packages of customers. A limited part of this Intranet is made available to the customer, thus avoiding the company from engaging in time-consuming handling of enquiries.

General Motors has placed information kiosks in some of its major dealerships allowing customers to check on new automobile products.

Extranets are particularly useful for ensuring effective information flow to partner organisations and individuals. For instance:

- *Suppliers*. Trusted suppliers may be given access to a company's inventory through an Extranet. The supplier may then be alerted of falling stock levels and will be better able to plan its own production on the basis of predicted demand.
- *Distributors*. These stakeholders may be able to query warehouse databases directly via an Extranet. This will enable the distributor to better plan the fulfilment of orders to customers.
- *Remote employees*. Salesmen of a company may be able to query the company's stock while on the road through an Extranet. They are then able to determine precise delivery times for customers. This may be achieved through traditional connections between laptop computers and telephone lines or through the new generation of Internet-enabled mobile phones. Predictions are that this area of mobile-commerce or m-commerce will be a growth area over the next decade.

Question

What is the relationship between Extranets and the idea of the virtual or network organisation?

19.8 ⊚ THE BENEFITS OF B2B E-COMMERCE

Implementing B2B e-commerce is a supply chain strategy for organisations (Chapter 22). B2B e-commerce has been driven by potential benefits that include:

- *Lower purchasing costs*. Traditionally purchasing is a complex, multi-layered process. E-commerce promises lower costs by lowering the costs of transactions and through economies such as the consolidation of purchases.
- *Reduced inventory*. Through just-in-time initiatives, e-commerce allows companies to lower their levels of inventory, thus reducing the costs of warehousing.
- *Lower cycle times*. Cycle time is the time it takes to build a product. Electronic links between companies enable partners to have shorter lead times, speedier product design and development, and faster ordering of components.

Example

Many automobile manufacturers now have electronic links between design teams sited around the world. Blueprints for a particular component can be despatched from one site, say in the UK, to a research and development unit in Japan which is able to prototype and test the component quickly, leading to faster cycle times.

Question   *Which of the above benefits is likely to be the most significant for companies and why?*

19.9 ⊚ THE PROBLEMS OF B2B E-COMMERCE

B2B E-commerce still suffers from some key technical problems that include:

- *Development and maintenance of documentation standards.* EDI has proven effective for the transfer of electronic documentation between medium to large companies. However, it is considered to be generally expensive to implement and therefore out of the reach of the small business. XML is an important vehicle for defining standards for electronic documentation. Advances in defining standards have been made in certain industrial areas, but many areas still lack standardisation.

- *Ensuring secure transfer of data.* Much commercial data associated with commerce is confidential in nature. Hence technologies such as VPNs (Chapter 7) are typically employed to ensure the secure transfer of data. Again, such technologies can prove prohibitive for the small to medium-sized enterprise. Recently attempts have been made to promote technologies such as encryption and digital certificates for use over the Internet. However, a number of concerns still exist over the viability and effectiveness of such technology for commercial transfer of data.

- *Ensuring secure access to Extranets.* For companies employing Extranets suitable measures, both technical and social, must be put in place to prevent the loss of valuable company data.

Question   *Which of the above problems is likely to be the most significant for companies and why?*

19.10 ⊚ CASE STUDY: CISCO

Cisco was founded in 1984 at Stanford University by husband and wife team Leonard Bosack (who developed early router technology) and Sandra Lerner and three colleagues. Cisco is generally regarded as the leader in the market for internetworking equipment (routers) – a key technology supporting the Internet

The technology supplied by the company enables customers to build large-scale, integrated computer networks. Growth of the company has been driven by the surge in data traffic on the Internet. The company initially targeted universities, aerospace companies and government facilities, relying on word-of-mouth and contacts. The market for routers opened up in the late 1980s and Cisco became the first company to offer reasonably priced high-performance routers. It went public in 1990 and initiated an acquisitions strategy to broaden the range of products offered (e.g. ATM switching).

Cisco has implemented an e-business strategy to enable fast integration of its supply-chain with key business processes. The supply chain is critical to the business, as Cisco's manufacturing operation globally consists of 34 plants, only two of which are owned by the company. Suppliers make up to 90% of the subassembly of Cisco products and 55% of the final assembly. This means that suppliers regularly ship finished goods directly to Cisco customers.

A key component of Cisco's B2B e-commerce strategy is integration of its ERP systems with key suppliers. Suppliers use their ERP systems to run their Cisco production lines, allowing them to respond to demand from Cisco in real time. This is enhanced by the introduction of Cisco Manufacturing Online, an Extranet portal that allows partners to access real-time manufacturing information, including data on demand forecasts, inventory and purchase orders.

Such a technical infrastructure means that changes in parts of the supply chain are communicated almost instantaneously to the company. For instance, if one supplier is low on a component then Cisco can analyse its supply chain for excess supplies elsewhere. Changes in forecast demand are also communicated in real time, enabling suppliers to respond immediately to requests for products or materials.

Payments to suppliers are triggered by a shop floor transaction in the ERP system indicating that production is complete. The transaction initiates an analysis of inventory to determine the value of components sold by suppliers and triggers an electronic payment to suppliers. Annual benefits from the use of this ERP system integration are estimated to be in the realm of millions of dollars of savings per year.

Cisco has also engaged in B2C e-commerce innovation. It has introduced a Web portal known as Cisco Connection Online which consists of a dynamic online catalogue, a facility for ordering and configuring products online, a status agent which allows customers and retailers to track orders, a customer service section, a technical assistance section and a software library. The company currently estimates that it earns 75% of its $20 billion sales through its portal. The portal is also indicated as contributing to a 20% reduction in overall operating costs.

19.11　SUMMARY

- B2B e-commerce represents the attempt to use ICT to improve elements of the supply chain of organisations.
- A typical supply chain process includes activities such as search, negotiate, order, delivery, invoice and payment, and after-sale.

- B2B e-commerce systems must be built on a sound back-end information systems infrastructure.
- Supply chain management has arisen as a distinct philosophy within organisations.
- Three distinct models of pre-sale activity in B2B e-commerce include supplier-oriented B2B, buyer-oriented B2B and intermediary-oriented B2B.
- Intermediary-oriented B2B can be conducted in a number of ways including: vertical portals, Internet auctions and e-stores.
- Extranets are extended Intranets and are normally built to improve information flow and communication with external stakeholders.
- B2B e-commerce has been driven by potential benefits that include lower purchasing costs, reduced inventory and lower cycle times.

19.12 ACTIVITIES

(i) Access the Dell site and check out the facilities available.

(ii) Find an example of supplier-oriented or buyer-oriented B2B.

(iii) Find one example of a vertical portal, Internet auction or e-store.

(iv) Find one other example of an Extranet.

(v) Try to determine the effective uses for an Extranet in an organisation known to you.

(vi) In terms of an organisation known to you investigate whether it uses any forms of B2B e-commerce – even if it is as simple as e-mailing suppliers with orders. Try to identify the key benefits of such electronic activity for the company. If the company does not undertake any B2B commerce currently try to identify the potential.

(vii) Find a company using B2B e-commerce. Identify any problems they may be experiencing.

19.13 REFERENCES

ABS (2000). *Business Use of Information Technology*. Australian Bureau of Statistics.

Cunningham, M. J. (2002). B2B: How to Build a Profitable E-commerce Strategy. Cambridge, MA, Perseus.

Meier, J. (1995). The importance of relationship management in establishing successful inter-organisational systems. *Journal of Strategic Information Systems*, **4**(2), 135–148.

Ordanini, A. and Pol, A. (2001). Infomediation and competitive advantage in B2B digital marketplaces. *European Management Journal*, **19**(3), 276-285.

Wise, R. and Morrison, D. (2000). Beyond the exchange: the future of B2B. *Harvard Business Review*, Nov/Dec, 86–96.

CHAPTER 20

CONSUMER TO CONSUMER (C2C) ELECTRONIC COMMERCE

It is only an auctioneer who can equally and impartially admire all schools of art.

Oscar Wilde, *The Critic as Artist*

The community stagnates without the impulse of the individual. The impulse dies away without the sympathy of the community.

William James

LEARNING OUTCOMES

After reading this chapter, you will be able to:

- Describe key elements of the community chain and its basis in social networks and social capital
- Distinguish between an e-community and a virtual community
- Describe some of the features of an e-community
- Relate some of the features of a virtual community
- Outline forms of C2C e-commerce

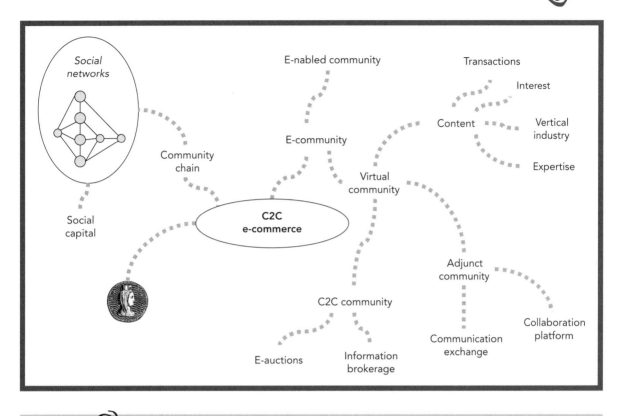

20.1 INTRODUCTION

The Internet is a domain not only for business-to-business or business-to-consumer e-commerce, but also for consumer-to-consumer (C2C) e-commerce. We may define C2C e-commerce as ICT enablement of aspects of the community chain. In a way it is the most radical form of e-commerce, since it overlaps with non-commercial activity in the area of community. Hence there is the need in this chapter to consider definitions of community and the basis of this concept in social networks and social capital.

Commercial and non-commercial organisations are attempting to incorporate aspects of their community chain into their operations or are attempting to formulate new business models embedded in various social networks external to the organisation.

Many forms of C2C e-commerce revert to earlier models of markets and trade in which products and services are exchanged between individuals, where the fixed price model of products and services breaks down and where in some instances trade reverts to earlier forms of economic exchange such as barter. C2C commerce is a many-to-many commerce model. It typically involves the exchange of low-cost items and monetary transactions. With C2C e-commerce this form of trade, which typically survives in local marketplaces, is opened up to global access.

In this chapter we consider a definition for community and use this definition to distinguish between an e-nabled community, virtual community and an adjunct community. It is to adjunct communities that many businesses are now turning to increase levels of value associated with their products and services. We examine C2C e-commerce in terms of this context and consider various auction models on which this activity is based.

20.2 ⊚ THE COMMUNITY CHAIN

People have argued over the term *community* and its key features for centuries (Tonnies, 1935). We will maintain that one of the fundamental features of community is that it is founded on social networks. A social network is a network in which the nodes are people and the links or relations are various forms of social interaction and/or social bonds. Consider Figure 20.1. In this figure we have represented individuals as circles and links as lines. Suppose each line is taken to represent a friendship relation. Hence in net 1 the line between individual a and individual b indicates that a is a friend of b and vice versa.

In examining the three nets in Figure 20.1 the individuals considered remain the same but a transformation occurs through nets 1 to 3. More people are connected in a friendship network in net 3 than in net 1. Suppose we also overlay relationships of trust, collaboration and cooperation. In a community we would expect the connectivity – a measure of the interconnectedness of the nodes in a network – in all four types of social network to be high. Hence net 3 is closer to most definitions of a community than net 1 in Figure 20.1.

In recent literature authors have argued that communities generate value just like organisations and hence it becomes possible to consider a chain of value that a community generates. However, the value of a community lies not in its physical or financial capital but in its social capital. Putnam (2000) defines social capital as being:

> features of social organisation such as networks, norms and trust that facilitate coordination and cooperation for mutual benefit

Capital is traditionally defined as the financial assets available to a company. It is hence a key resource for production. Social capital is the productive value of people

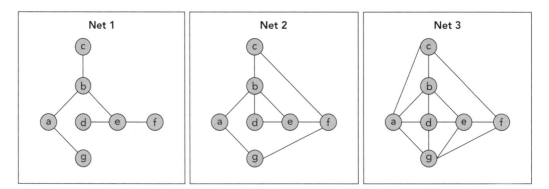

Figure 20.1 Social networks.

engaged in a dense network of social relations. Social capital consists of those features of social organisation – networks of secondary associations, high levels of interpersonal trust, reciprocity - that act as resources for individuals and facilitate collective action. Therefore, it is argued, a community rich in social capital is more likely to possess effective civic institutions and more likely to be effective at maintaining law and order.

A common theme in the literature on social capital and community is that changes towards the mass globalisation and urbanisation of society have led to a decline in community and hence a consequent decline in social capital.

Question	*What is the relationship between the connectivity of a social network and the variety of a system?*

Examples	For instance, Putnam documents the decline in the civic life – membership of clubs, sports, voluntary and political associations – of the USA over the past three decades which he has taken to be symptomatic of a decline in social capital.
	The terrorist attacks on the World Trade Center on 11 September 2001 shocked the world. Many individuals used electronic mechanisms and media to contact loved ones and to exchange information. Some 30 million North Americans (one third of all US Internet users) turned to e-mail, chat rooms and online fora to write eye-witness descriptions, offer words of comfort and engage in debate (Preece, 2002).

These two concepts of a social network and social capital help us to understand some of the different definitions of the concept of an electronic community (e-community). On the one hand, ICT is seen either as an enabler or disabler of traditional forms of community – an e-nabled community. On the other hand, ICT is seen as offering the potential for newer forms of community based on communication networks – the virtual community.

- *E-nabled community*. Community is normally established on the basis of frequent and prolonged interaction between individuals resident in a clearly delineated geographical area. This form of community chain addresses the rise of communication networks and considers whether they are vehicles for re-creating community and social capital in local areas. Some argue that communication networks are a threat to existing forms of social capital and community; others that they provide a new basis for social capital and community.
- *Virtual community*. The Internet and the Web were initially established for free information exchange between dispersed actors around the globe. Some have begun to consider such dispersed networks or individuals and organisations as examples of electronic communities. In such virtual communities social networks are constructed through electronic rather than face-to-face communi-

cation. Such social networks may be dispersed geographically and have a much more specific area of focus than traditional communities.

Examples

Penrhyndeudraeth (http://www.penrhyndeudraeth.co.uk/) is a small town in North Wales with a population of just over 1800 people. Residents and businesses in Penrhyndeudraeth have been given financial support to buy PCs and get access to the Internet. Grants were given to a total of 50 households and businesses in the Penrhyndeudraeth area to help purchase a PC, printer, modem and software. They were also given assistance to help pay their telephone bill. The aim of the project is to accelerate the take-up of ICT by proactively encouraging the community to get online.

Ennis, County Clare, is a town in the mid-West of Eire which has become known as Ireland's 'Information Age Town' (IDEA, 2002). Since 1997 Ennis has benefited from a £15 million investment by Eircom. The aim has been to develop an ICT infrastructure across a range of areas including residents, local business, community, education, the public sector and the private sector. For instance, all households in the town have been offered subsidised personal computers and Internet access, all schools in the locality have had personal computers supplied and a broadband ring has been established in the town.

Ferlander and Timms (2001) report on an ongoing project based in a marginalized community in Stockholm, Sweden. A local community network has been established with the aim of improving the social capital in the community, especially with regard to disadvantaged groups.

As a generalisation, public sector organisations have particularly been interested in making connections between their e-business activities and initiatives in the area of e-nabled community. Such forms of e-community are seen as offering the potential for the stimulation of local economies particularly in disadvantaged areas.

Example

Local authorities in the UK are required to produce community strategies. Many are producing e-community strategies as part of this process. Such e-community strategies typically incorporate plans to use Web sites to encourage the electronic procurement of services and products from local suppliers.

In contrast, private sector organisations have particularly been interested in connecting to the second form of e-community – that of a virtual community. The idea is that various forms of value produced by the community chain may support and encourage commerce. It is only comparatively recently that the Internet and

Web have been used as vehicles for commerce and trade/business purposes. C2C e-commerce mediates between pure forms of trade and pure forms of information exchange.

Question	*What business potential is there in an e-nabled community?*

<h2>20.3 ⊚ VIRTUAL COMMUNITIES</h2>

Rheingold (1995) defines virtual communities as 'social aggregations that emerge from the Net when enough people carry on those public discussions long enough, with sufficient human feeling, to form webs of personal relationships in cyberspace'.

It could be argued that one of the first virtual communities was the community of academics that started to use the Internet (Chapter 9) in the early 1970s to share data, exchange messages and collaborate together on various research programmes.

We shall argue that virtual communities are founded in social networks and produce social capital just like traditional communities. However, there is still some question as to whether the bonds in the social network of a virtual community are as strong and the social capital produced as great as those produced in traditional communities. This is because there are a number of differences between virtual communities and traditional communities:

- *Space*. Traditional communities are normally established on the basis of long residence by individuals in a prescribed geographical region. Virtual communities break geographical boundaries. Individuals are effectively nodes in a communication network.

- *Form of communication*. In traditional communities the dominant form of communication between community members will be face-to-face conversation. In virtual communities various forms of communication may be employed – e-mail, chat, telephone conversation, video-conferencing etc.

- *Focus*. The focus of a traditional community will be diverse but all located around a particular geographical area. The focus of virtual communities is likely to be much more specific in nature but spans the globe.

It is possible to produce various typologies of virtual communities. For instance, virtual communities can be formed in terms of different types of the focus of content provided on Web sites such as:

- *Transactions*. Many sites are established to facilitate the buying and selling of products and services and to deliver information that is related to the completion of transactions.

- *Interest*. Many Web sites focus on areas such as theatre, sports, science fiction or fantasy.
- *Vertical industry*. Web sites locate around key industrial areas such as accounting or manufacturing.
- *Expertise*. Occupational groups may focus around key areas of expertise such as waste management.

Example	An example of a virtual community focused around areas of common interest is Globe.com (http://www.theglobe.com/). This is an international online community with a number of specific interest groups such as a game site for children and an educational site directed at parents and grandparents.

Virtual communities are now being used to enhance conventional e-commerce activity – what we shall call adjunct communities. Virtual communities are also being used to form new forms of C2C e-commerce – what we shall call C2C communities.

Example	Examples of virtual communities of both forms can be found at http://www.compugraph.com/vircom.html.

Question	*Are virtual communities viable?*

20.4 ADJUNCT COMMUNITIES

Certain electronic businesses are attempting to foster and support virtual communities. Adjunct communities are forms of virtual community that focus around the relationships between customers and the business (Armstrong and Hagel, 1996). The key benefits to business are that by creating and supporting such virtual communities businesses will be better able to build membership audiences for their products and services. Certain features of social capital, such as increased support amongst members of a virtual community, can be particularly beneficial to companies. Enhanced levels of trust in a virtual community may support increased levels of trade. These forms of social value may increase customer loyalty and trust with a company.

Timmers (1999) argues that there are two business models appropriate for adjunct communities:

- *Communication exchange.* Timmers confusingly calls this a virtual community. This business model attempts to add value to products and services through communications between a community of members. The company provides an environment in which members can partake in unedited communication and information exchange. Revenue is generated through membership fees, advertising revenue and cross-selling of products and services.

- *Collaboration platforms.* These enable collaboration between individuals and organisations and typically provide a set of tools and an information environment for collaboration.

Examples Examples of communication exchanges can be found at http://www.vertical.net/. Typical uses for collaboration platforms are in collaborative projects for design and engineering or to support virtual teams. An example can be found at http://www.egroups.com/.

Question *What value is created in an informal exchange of communication between members of a virtual community?*

20.5 C2C COMMERCE

Other business models focus more precisely on C2C trading. C2C communities focus around customer-to-customer relationships of exchange. C2C commerce involves trade of typically low-cost items between complex networks of individual actors. Revenues from C2C communities may be generated through advertising, transaction fees and membership fees.

Timmers argues that there are two main business models appropriate for C2C e-commerce. These include:

- *E-auctions.* This is the most prominent business model underlying C2C e-commerce and is discussed in more detail below.

- *Information brokerage.* These are companies specialising in the provision of information to consumers and to businesses. They help such individuals and organisations to make buying decisions or with business operations. Revenue models include membership fees, advertising fees and cross-selling.

Examples An example of the use of electronic auctions in the B2C area is http://www.ebay.com/. An example in the B2B area is http://www.qxl.com/.

C2C commerce focuses on aspects of the community chain and involves trade between complex networks of individual actors. Although typically the monetary value of each exchange may be low, added together billions of dollars are traded annually in forms of C2C commerce. Hence C2C commerce is not a new phenomenon. A range of commercial media have been created for this purpose, including:

- *Newspaper classified advertisements*. Users of newspapers typically list items for sale, normally in newspapers distributed on a local basis. Buyers typically inspect items before purchase and may collect and pay for the item in person.
- *Flea markets and garage sales*. Sellers stock and display items for sale typically at their own homes or at organised markets. Buyers are typically browsing for artefacts and will negotiate prices and collect and transport items.
- *Auction houses*. Sellers take items to specialist organisations for sale. Buyers are able to inspect items before an auction. Buyers typically have to pay a registration fee to bid and are required to be at an auction or to nominate a proxy bidder. The highest bidder wins the auction and pays the auction house. The auction house in turn takes a percentage of the sale and pays the balance to the seller.

The value and take-up of C2C e-commerce is likely to be affected by Metcalfe's law. This was originally expressed as a law of computer networks – that the number of cross-connections in a network grows as the square of the number of computers in the network increases. We can equally express this in terms of the community value of a network. The community value of a network grows as the square of the number of users increases. In fact, Metcalfe's law is a statement of the variety of a system described in Chapter 2. It is likely that the variety in a C2C network will strongly influence the take-up and use of such applications. In other words, the more people there are available to communicate with and share goods and information, the more likely it is that people will participate.

20.5.1   AUCTIONS

There are a number of different ways of conducting auctions. These include:

- *Dutch auction*. The seller places one or more identical items for sale at a minimum price for a set period. When the auction ends the highest bidder gains the item at their bid price.
- *Reserve price*. The seller lists a reserve bid price for an item but the buyers do not normally know the reserve price. Buyers are allowed to place bids for any amount above or below the reserve price. The seller has the option to disregard any bids below the reserve price.
- *Reverse auction*. The buyer lists what is required at the price they are prepared to pay. Sellers bid for the business and can remain anonymous. This means that the seller bears the risk of not being successful.
- *Sealed bid auctions*. Bidders are only aware of the reserve price and bid without knowing the amounts of other bids. All bids are automatically opened at a set time, closing the auction, and the highest bidder wins.

Examples	Most of these approaches to organising auctions have been applied in C2C e-commerce. For instance:

- eBay uses a Dutch auction model.

- Priceline.com offers reverse auctions.

- Most e-procurement systems (Chapter 19) use a sealed bid model in tendering.

Question	*Does the auction model of exchange have potential for infiltrating conventional fixed-price models of exchange with the increasing penetration of the Internet?*

20.6 ◉ CASE STUDY: EBAY

eBay is probably the most significant contemporary example of C2C e-commerce. Pierre Omidyar created eBay in September 1995. Using a Web site hosted by Omidyar's Internet service provider, he originally ran the company in his spare time from his apartment. In its early guise eBay was little more than a simple marketplace where buyers and sellers could bid for items. The company took no responsibility for the goods being traded and gave no undertaking to settle disputes between parties.

By February 1996 so many people had visited the site that Omidyar decided to introduce a 10 cent listing fee to recoup ISP costs. By the end of March 1996 eBay showed a profit. Eventually the volume of traffic to the site persuaded his ISP to ask him to move elsewhere. Omidyar decided to transfer the operation to a one-room office with his own Web server and he employed the services of a part-time employee. He also developed software capable of supporting a robust, scalable Web site and a transaction processing system to report on current auctions.

By August 1996 Omidyar had established one of his friends as the first president of eBay. In June 1997 the company approached venture capitalists for funding and secured $5 million. This enabled the company to establish a more extensive management structure for planned expansion. By the end of 1997 more than 3 million items (worth $94 million) had been sold on eBay, amounting to revenues of $5.7 million and an operating profit of $900,000. eBay had an operating staff of only 67 employees at the time.

In its early days eBay undertook only limited marketing and relied on the loyalty of its customer base and word-of-mouth referrals for its increased business growth. Eventually the company began to employ cross-promotional agreements including banner advertising on Web portals such as Netscape and Yahoo! as well as providing an auction service for AOL's classified section. This evolved into a conventional marketing campaign through traditional print and broadcast media in 1998.

In 1999 the company expanded internationally by creating communities in Canada and the UK. This was followed by expansion into Germany, Australia, Japan and France. During this year and into 2000 the company successfully held its position against strong new entrants into the online auctions market such as Amazon.com. The company also moved into the bricks and mortar area with the purchase of a San Francisco based auction house. eBay used this acquisition to move into the higher-price antiques sector of the market. By the end of June 1999 eBay had 5.6 million registered users and had conducted 29.4 million auctions during the previous three-month period. In the third quarter of 2000 $1.4 billion worth of goods were traded on eBay in 68.5 million auctions, which generated $113.4 million in revenues.

At the time of writing approximately 1.5 million people are joining eBay each month from around the world. A survey by eBay in mid-2001 found that 10,000 people in the USA were now full-time eBay traders. It is estimated that now 40,000 people around the globe earn a living in this way.

Essentially the business model is a simple one of providing C2C auctions online. Much of such activity relies on collectors trading small-price items such coins, stamps and militaria. Although the average item sold through these markets constitutes no more than tens of dollars, as a whole billions of dollars are traded every year in the USA in C2C trading.

The concept is to provide a Web site where anyone wishing to buy or sell on eBay must register by providing personal and financial details. Every user of eBay is given a unique identifier. eBay offers a virtual tour of its services, but people can start buying and selling straight away.

Sellers list items for sale by completing an online form. They pay a small listing fee for this privilege. The size of the fee depends on where and how the listing is presented and whether a reserve price is required for the item. Sellers also choose the duration they wish buyers to bid for the item. At the end of an auction, eBay notifies the seller of the winning bid and provides details of the successful bidder to the seller. The buyer and seller then make their own arrangements for payment and delivery of the goods, usually through e-mail. Payment can be made by cash, cheque, and postal order or electronically through a payment service such as PayPal (http://www.paypal.com), now a subsidiary of eBay. eBay charges a percentage of the final value of the transaction. For instance, suppose a seller listed a collection of stamps for sale at £24.00. The seller might pay approximately 50 pence to eBay to list this collection as a standard item on the Web site. If the collection was sold then the seller would pay 5% of the final sale price to the company.

Since buyers pay sellers before they receive items the business model runs on trust. The eBay feedback system is used to indicate problems with particular users. Users can file feedback about any user on the feedback site. This discourages trade with rogue participants.

The only costs to eBay therefore amount to the costs of computing infrastructure and expenses associated with customer services. eBay keeps no inventory, has no distribution network and does not have to maintain a large amount of staff to make the company viable.

Most of eBay's sellers were serious collectors and small traders who used eBay as their shop-front. eBay enabled them to access a global marketplace for trading of collectibles. For such a community eBay set up the eBay Café. This comprised a chat room where users of the site could communicate and exchange information. Such a facility proved useful to the company in being able to monitor customer reaction to various company initiatives. For instance, changes in pricing were frequently adversely commented on in such fora. eBay also used its customers to post answers to frequently answered questions (FAQs) on its bulletin boards and even employed some active and knowledgeable users of its site to provide e-mail help to its new customers.

In an attempt to develop trust and loyalty amongst its customer community eBay established SafeHarbour in February 1998. SafeHarbour offered certain verification and validation of customers, insurance associated with the selling and buying process and certain regulation of sales activity. The company also created My eBay, a tool that customers could use to personalise the site in terms of keeping track of their favourite categories, view items they were selling or bidding on or check their account balance.

Following a number of outages in 1999 the company decided to outsource its back-end infrastructure to an external supplier. It outsourced its Web servers, database servers and routers to these companies with the expectation of having excess capacity for preserving its service. Hence periodic overhaul of the technical infrastructure of the company is critical to its success.

20.7 ◎ SUMMARY

- C2C e-commerce is ICT enablement of the community chain.
- The community chain is founded in social networks and the value it produces is social capital.
- ICT has been used to enable community in local areas.
- ICT is also the infrastructure underlying the rise in virtual communities.
- Public sector initiatives have been interested in enhancing traditional communities with increased ICT use.
- Private sector initiatives have been particularly interested in the community chain as a new revenue source or as a means of adding value to traditional commercial activities.
- Four contemporary models of C2C e-commerce exist: e-auctions, virtual communities, collaboration platforms and information brokerage.

20.8 ACTIVITIES

(i) If you live in what you would class as a community, investigate how much social capital exists in your community. Determine the evidence for such social capital.

(ii) Identify ways of measuring the social capital in a community.

(iii) Try to list a number of the social networks within which you participate.

(iv) Try to find an example of a community Web site and determine what content is provided on this Web site.

(v) Find one or more examples of a virtual community. Analyse it in terms of the features described in the section on virtual communities.

(vi) Identify ways of measuring social capital in a virtual community.

(vii) Find one example of an e-auction. Determine the auction model it employs.

(viii) Find one example of an information brokerage. Determine what information it provides and to whom.

20.9 REFERENCES

Armstrong, A. and Hagel, J. (1996). The real value of online communities. *Harvard Business Review*, May/Jun, 134–141.

Ferlander, S. and Timms, D. (2001). Local nets and social capital. Telematics and Informatics, 18(1), 51–65.

IDEA (2002). *Local E-government Now: a Worldwide View*. Improvement and Development Agency/Society of Information Technology Management.

Preece, J. (2002). Supporting community and building social capital.

Putnam, R. D. (2000). *Bowling Alone: the Collapse and Revival of American Community*. New York, Simon and Schuster.

Rheingold, H. (1995). *The Virtual Community: Finding Connection in a Computerised World*. London, Minerva.

Timmers, P. (1999). *Electronic Commerce: Strategies and Models for Business to Business Trading*. Chichester, John Wiley.

Tonnies, F. (1935). *Gemeinschaft und Gessellschaft*. Leipzig.

E-MARKETING

Half the money I spend on advertising is wasted, and the trouble is I don't know which half.

Lord Leverhulme

LEARNING OUTCOMES

After reading this chapter, you will be able to:

- Define the process of marketing
- Describe the differences between conventional and electronic marketing channels
- Define some of the key phases associated with the planning and implementation of e-marketing
- Describe some of the techniques of Web-based e-marketing
- Discuss the relationship between branding and e-commerce

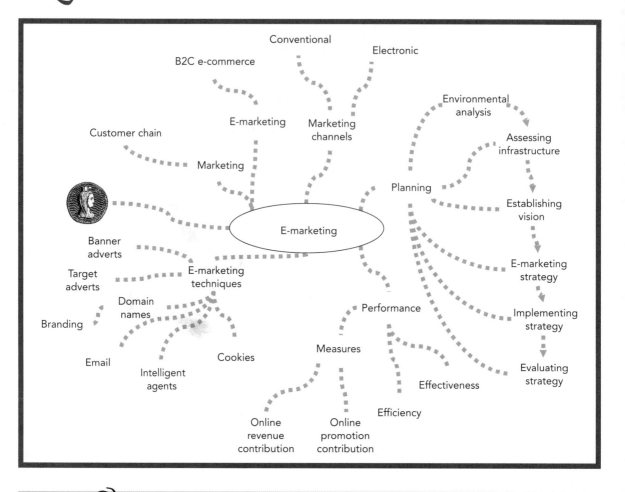

Marketing can be defined as the process of planning and executing the conception, pricing, promotion and distribution of ideas, goods and services to create exchanges that satisfy individual and organisational goals (Brassington and Pettit, 2000). This definition emphasises that marketing is not just an activity that occurs after a product has been produced or after a service has been formulated. In modern business practice, marketing input is important in the design of a product and in the after-sales process.

The Internet and ICT systems offer innovative ways of engaging in pre-sale activity with the customer. One of the most significant of such activities is the electronic marketing (e-marketing) of goods and services. In terms of customer relationship management (Chapter 18), e-marketing is particularly directed at customer acquisition, but is also relevant to customer retention and extension.

Marketing strategy is typically an important part of organisational strategy. Hence, e-marketing strategy is likely to be a critical component of any e-business strategy (Chapter 24).

Traditionally marketing has been focused on the transmission of messages to potential customers through channels such as television, radio, newspapers, and magazines and more recently through direct-selling approaches using the telephone. Such approaches to marketing are characterised by being:

- *Push.* A company disseminates the material to a perceived market of potential customers.
- *Passive.* Traditional modes of advertising require potential customers to find an advert either through browsing or through some more directed search.
- *Linear.* The marketing material is scripted and is expected to be delivered in some linear sequence as a package.
- *Event-driven.* The material tends to be delivered at a specific point in time.
- *One-to-many.* The material is typically 'broadcast' from one source to many potential customers.
- *Information-weak.* This refers to the fact that it is typically difficult to gather direct data on the effect of a traditional marketing product on a given population.
- *Location-dependent.* Typically marketing is dependent on the location of the business and the marketing agency.

Example

Take an advertisement placed in relevant newspapers and magazines to promote a new type of car produced by an automobile company. The company pays to have the advertisement produced by a graphics company (scripting) and is likely to make key decisions on the types of newspapers and magazines to place the advertisement in on the basis of the intended customer base for the car (push). As a multinational automobile manufacturer it will probably decide to run separate marketing campaigns in each of the countries it sends to (location-dependent). These decisions will be predicated on the assumption that potential customers will come across the advertisement while reading their newspaper or magazine (passive). The company will pay the print companies to place the advertisement for a particular day – perhaps timed to coincide with some launch event for the car (event-driven). Since it appears in all copies of the particular newspapers and magazines it is effectively a broadcast of the advertisement. Advertising agencies have to engage in a number of *post hoc* techniques to attempt to capture evidence of the impact of particular advertisements, such as interviewing a sample of customers (information-weak).

In contrast, electronic marketing uses electronic delivery and thus tends to be characterised by being (Bickerton *et al.*, 2000):

- *Pull.* Potential customers themselves access the material.
- *Aggressive.* Such advertising involves actively seeking out customers and initiating some form of contact with them.

- *Interactive*. The potential customer can communicate with the company about its products and services. There is also potential for customising the material for particular customers.

- *Time-independent*. The marketing material can be accessed 24 hours a day 365 days a year.

- *One-to-one/one-to-many/many-to-many*. The material can be accessed in different contexts in a one-to-one or one-to-many relationship between the potential customer and the business or in a many-to-many way between the customer audiences themselves.

- *Information-strong*. Because of the transaction-based nature of e-commerce sites a vast amount of data can be captured which relates customer searching with eventual purchase.

- *Location-independent*. Marketing via the Internet can be achieved on an international scale from one location.

However, a Web site will not prove effective as a marketing tool without sufficient numbers of people accessing it. Hence e-marketing cannot be divorced from traditional promotional activities. Such promotional activities have to be undertaken over and above the creation of a Web site to achieve sufficient levels of traffic to the site. Once a sufficient level of traffic has been produced then a number of e-marketing techniques may be applied.

Example | Union Bank of Norway (UBS) uses a customer-centred strategy based on ICT to personalise marketing to customers in its branches. As soon as a customer walks into a branch of UBS they have to swipe their bank card through a terminal and are issued with a personalised ticket for queuing. This ticket links directly to the bank's data systems. Such systems identify the customer and tailor advertisements on video screens above the bank teller at that particular customer. For example, if the customer has recently applied for a mortgage the screen might display details of life insurance products.

Question | *Will the traffic to Web sites ever reach a position where it will become possible to replace conventional channels of marketing solely with e-channels?*

21.3 PLANNING AND IMPLEMENTING E-MARKETING

Good marketing is reliant on good planning. Planning for e-marketing will be an important part of general e-business planning (Chapter 23). The product of e-marketing planning will be a strategy for e-marketing. Such planning will include (Chaffey *et al.*, 2000):

- *An analysis of the environment for e-marketing*
  This will involve determining the demand for e-commerce in particular market segments. It will also involve close attention to the behaviour of competitors and partners such as intermediaries in this area.

  Market or customer segmentation is the process of identifying the characteristics of different segments of the population to which a company sells or wishes to sell its products or services. On the basis of this analysis it then attempts to determine particular marketing requirements for each customer segment. Seybold (1999) argues that there are five key questions companies should ask themselves in relation to segmentation:
  - Who are our customers?
  - How are their needs changing?
  - Which do we target?
  - How can we add value?
  - How do we become first choice for the customer?

- *An assessment of current internal infrastructure available to the company for e-marketing*
  This will involve evaluating the performance of the current infrastructure and determining the feasible options available to a company in terms of extending its e-marketing infrastructure.

- *Establishing a vision for e-marketing*
  This will involve setting clear objectives for the use of e-marketing in terms of online contribution to company performance and the marketing mix of product, price, place and promotion (McCarthy, 1960):
  - *Product.* For intangible and tangible products and services (Chapter 8) companies will be looking to offer added-value associated with using electronic channels.
  - *Price.* Pricing strategies for products and services should reflect the capabilities of electronic channels. Savings in transaction costs will typically be passed on to the consumer in terms of discounts.
  - *Place.* Due consideration should be given to the most appropriate place to promote goods and services through electronic channels.
  - *Promotion.* This will involve consideration of the integration of electronic promotional channels with conventional promotional channels. It will also concern decisions about the appropriate mix of online with conventional promotion.

Examples

Value could be added to products within electronic delivery channels by improving searching facilities to online catalogues or providing more personalised products.

In terms of pricing, companies may offer discounts for using online ordering or differentiate pricing more dynamically in terms of time of purchase or customer segment. EasyJet.com operates a dynamic pricing policy for its ticketing based on advance booking to its flights and on customer demand.

Placing decisions will involve consideration of whether to disintermediate or reintermediate in particular markets; it will also involve decisions as to the integration of a companies promotional strategies with that of its partners.

Promotional decisions will critically concern the amount of investment to be made in e-marketing as opposed to traditional marketing. EasyJet has used newspapers to offer discounts for advance booking. Potential customers collect tokens from the newspaper and then contact the company via telephone or the Web.

- *Specifying an e-marketing strategy*
  This will involve detailing the part that e-marketing (Chaston, 2001) plays in general e-business strategy (Chapter 24).
- *Implementing an e-marketing strategy*
  This will involve building a technical infrastructure for e-marketing and putting the associated human activity systems in place.
- *Evaluating e-marketing contribution*
  This will involve monitoring the performance of e-marketing in terms of defined objectives such as online contribution (see below).

Question
In what ways is the marketing mix likely to be different for intangible as opposed to tangible products and services?

21.4 THE BENEFITS OF E-MARKETING

The objectives set for e-marketing must clearly be established in terms of a clear path for performance improvement. Any e-business change in an organisation must be evaluated. In Chapter 27 we shall argue that all such change should be evaluated strategically. In other words, the introduction of an e-marketing system should be analysed in terms of its expected costs and benefits.

Typical expected benefits from e-marketing can be divided into those impacting on efficiency and those impacting on efficacy. Such benefits include:

- *Efficiency improvement*
  - Savings in the costs of producing advertising material.
  - Savings in the costs associated with the delivery of promotional material.
  - Ability to include much more information content in promotional material and make it interactive.
  - Ability to promote products and services globally, 24 hours a day, 365 days a year.

- *Efficacy improvement*
  - The ability to reach more potential customers with e-marketing material.
  - The ability to capture more detailed information about customer purchasing behaviour and the impact of promotions.
  - The ability to integrate promotional activity more directly with sales activity.
  - The ability to target particular customer segments in terms of promotional material.

In terms of the effectiveness of e-marketing, there are a number of ways of estimating in financial terms the benefits from e-marketing. One approach is to measure the online revenue contribution of e-marketing. This is an attempt to estimate the impact of remote electronic access channels on sales of goods or services. It is normally expressed as a percentage of the overall revenue derived from online sales over a given time period.

Example

Companies who make a considerable investment in electronic service delivery might typically expect a contribution of 25–75% from online sales. Cisco systems claims to sell 75–90% of its billion dollar sales online.

A variant of online revenue contribution is the idea of online promotion contribution. This might be expressed as an estimate of the proportion of new or retained customers who use remote access channels to organisation systems and complete an order for a good or service with a company. This is frequently expressed as the reach of particular electronic services among an organisation's customer base.

Question

What type of business is likely to have a high online revenue contribution?

21.5 THE TECHNIQUES OF WEB-BASED E-MARKETING

Web sites are now the primary approach for e-marketing. The main techniques of Web-based e-marketing include (Hardaker and Graham, 2001):

- *Banner advertising on Web sites*. Banner adverts are so-called because they are usually displayed across the top of some Web-page. These are one-to-many passive advertisements that are encountered by the user merely by accessing a Web page.

- *Target advertisements on Web sites*. These are one-to-many active advertisements in the sense that the user must click on something in order to be taken to the particular advertisement page. Certain banner advertisements may also be click-through.

- *Use of the company's brand name as a domain name.*
- *Registering the Web site* with a number of search engines so that the company's online material is easy to locate.
- *Use of e-mail to directly contact existing customers* with offers or promotions. Use of direct e-mail is a one-to-one aggressive promotion strategy.
- *Use of e-mail to contact potential customers* from purchased mail lists.
- *Use of intelligent agents* to track how customers use a Web site, build profiles of customers and take actions on the basis of profiling, such as suggesting particular information resources.
- *Use of cookies* (Chapter 15) to collect data about customer behaviour.

Example   The major Web portals such as AOL and Yahoo use both banner and target advertisements.

Banner advertisement campaigns may involve placing such adverts on many different forms of Web site, such as portals, generalised news services and special interest sites. Certain large online companies may utilise a large-scale network of affiliates. Affiliates will place small target advertisements on their Web sites, encouraging users to redirect to the home page of the major company for certain products and services.

Example   Amazon claims that it generates as much as a quarter of its income through its affiliate network.

Question   *There is a big push in many countries to reduce the amount of unsolicited e-mails. What consequence does this have for e-marketing?*

21.6 E-MARKETING REVENUE

Companies are likely to make charges for advertisements on their Web sites. This may form an important revenue stream for a Web-based intermediary such as a Web portal or affiliate. Generally there are three main ways of charging for online advertising:

- *Flat fee*. This is a traditional model for advertising revenue. Here a set fee is charged for placing the advertisement for a set time period.
- *CPM*. Cost per thousand Presentation Model is a method of billing based on the number of advertisements viewed.
- *Click through*. This is relevant to target advertisements and involves billing on the basis of the number of consumers who click through to the particular advertisement.

21.7   BRANDING

Brands are classic examples of signs (Chapter 4). The logo or brand name of a company is an example of a symbol. Generally speaking such symbols signify certain referents such as particular products or the whole of company activity. However, particular logos or brand names are also associated with a range of other connotations or concepts, such as perceived company values and behaviour. In the online world it is particularly important to ensure that a brand is used to maximum effect. This may involve:

- Copyrighting the brand.
- Registering an existing and well-recognised brand name as a domain name.
- Registering the domain name with the most-used search engines.
- Ensuring that the domain name returns high in the lists of returned results to users of search engines.
- Monitoring access from search engines and adjusting strategies to maintain a presence.

Example   EasyJet attempts to place its name on all the possible locations it can to promote its activities. For instance, the company's URL is painted on the side of its Boeing 737 fleet of aeroplanes.

Question   *How does cyber-squatting (Chapter 16) damage the potential for e-marketing?*

21.8   CASE STUDY: EASYJET

In 1994 Stelios Haji-Ioannou launched easyJet as a low-cost air carrier. In 1998 Stelios created easyGroup as a holding company for a number of additional high-demand/low-margin businesses. It is reported that the company has a typical profit margin of only £1.50 per customer. Initially, in order to keep running costs low, the company used the single sales channel of the telephone. The group now uses the Internet as a low-cost sales channel, but it is also significant to the branding of the company as being focused on e-commerce.

easyJet offers high-frequency services on short- and medium-haul routes within Europe. It sees itself as a no-frills airline and has designed its business processes to avoid complexity. For example, it maintains single fares on flights, only offers fares one way, offers no in-flight refreshments, operates out of less used and consequently less congested airports and does not issue tickets but relies on booking numbers. To achieve this the company relies heavily on close integration between its front-end sales systems and its back-end revenue management systems.

Haji-Ioannou originally pronounced that the Internet was for nerds. However, in April 1998 the company introduced its Web site easyJet.com. By August 1999 the site accounted for 38% of ticket sales. This meant that the company had exceeded its target of 30% of sales online by 2000. The transition to running the Web site proved relatively smooth. This was because easyJet was a 100% direct phone sales company and as such it was reasonably straightforward to integrate the Web site with its booking system. The savings the company makes through online booking have enabled the company to offer typical discounts of £1.00 to customers who book online.

The parent holding company of easyJet (easyGroup) launched easyInternetcafé, a chain of 400-seat capacity Internet cafes. Although the cafes are run as a separate business the original intention was to enable people with no Internet access the capability to buy online from easyJet. easyInternetcafé customers visit the easyJet Web site for free but pay a nominal charge for other Internet usage. This strategy of attempting to get their customers online has meant that within two years of introducing its transactional Web site the company was selling two thirds of its seats online.

easyJet varies the mix of its promotional campaigns. It frequently runs Internet-only campaigns in newspapers designed to improve online sales. It ran the first of this type of promotional campaign in February 1999 with impressive results. Readers of the *Times* were offered 50,000 seats at discounted prices. Within the first day 20,000 of the seats had been sold; 40,000 were sold within three days.

The Web site is also used as a public relations facility. For example, journalists wishing to learn about changes to company policy or strategy are referred to the Web site. This saves the company employing a specialist PR company.

21.9 SUMMARY

- Marketing can be defined as the process of planning and executing the conception, pricing, promotion and distribution of ideas, goods and services to create exchanges that satisfy individual and organisational goals.

- E-marketing is the use of electronic channels for the delivery of promotional material.

- Traditional marketing channels are characterized by being push, passive, linear, event-driven, one-to-many, information-weak and location-dependent.
- E-marketing channels are characterized by being pull, aggressive, interactive, time-independent, one-to-many and many-to-many, information-strong and location-independent.
- Planning for e-marketing includes environmental analysis, assessment of current infrastructure, establishing a vision for e-marketing, specifying an e-marketing strategy, implementing strategy and evaluating e-marketing contribution.
- E-marketing can generate efficiency (reduced cost of marketing) and effectiveness (greater customization of promotional material) gains for organizations.
- Techniques for Web-based e-marketing include the use of banner advertisements on Web sites and the use of e-mail to contact potential customers.
- E-marketing revenue can be achieved through flat fee, CPM or click-through models.
- Branding of domain names is a significant component of successful e-marketing.

21.10 ACTIVITIES

(i) Produce a brief statement of the characteristics of a traditional promotional channel such as a television advert.

(ii) Produce a brief statement of the characteristics of an e-marketing promotional channel such as a banner advertisement.

(iii) Generate a list of the efficiency improvements relevant to a particular organisation's use of e-marketing.

(iv) Generate a list of the effectiveness improvements relevant to a particular organisation's use of e-marketing.

(v) Access a particular Web portal and determine what e-marketing techniques are used.

(vi) In terms of a particular e-marketing technique, try to determine the revenue model used.

21.11 REFERENCES

Bickerton, P., Bickerton, M. and Simpson-Holey, K. (2000). *Cybermarketing: How to Use the Internet to Market Your Goods and Services*. Oxford, Butterworth-Heinnemann.

Brassington, F. and Pettit, S. (2000). *Principles of Marketing*. Harlow, Pearson.

Chaffey, D., Mayer, R., Johnston, K. and Ellis-Chadwick, F. (2000). *Internet Marketing*. Harlow, Pearson.

Chaston, I. (2001). *E-marketing Strategies*. Maidenhead, McGraw-Hill.

Hardaker, G. and Graham, G. (2001). *Wired Marketing: Energizing Business for E-commerce*. Chichester, John Wiley.

McCarthy, J. (1960). *Basic Marketing: a Managerial Approach*. Homewood, IL, Irwin.
Seybold, P. (1999). *Customers.com*. London, Random House.

E-PROCUREMENT

I glory

More in the cunning purchase of my wealth

Than in the glad possession.

Ben Jonson, *Volpone*

After reading this chapter, you will be able to:

- Describe the typical activities in the conventional procurement process
- Describe some of the key features of electronic procurement
- Relate a number of key benefits of electronic procurement

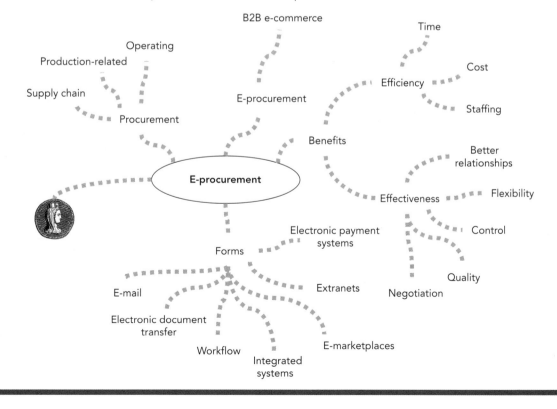

22.1 INTRODUCTION

The pre-sale activity of search, negotiate and order in the supply chain (Chapter 3) is frequently referred to under the umbrella term of *procurement*. Sometimes the term is used to refer to all the activities involved in the supply chain. Hence procurement is an important business process in the value chain and involves the purchasing of goods and services from suppliers at an acceptable quality and price and with reliable delivery.

Electronic procurement (e-procurement) refers to the use of ICT to enable the whole of the procurement process (Rajkumar, 2001). E-procurement is a specific and important feature of B2B e-commerce (Matin *et al.*, 2001) (Chapter 19).

In this chapter we consider some of the key differences between conventional procurement and e-procurement. In terms of this distinction we examine some of the key areas of performance improvement possible with this form of e-commerce. This leads us to examine various forms of e-procurement and suitable technologies for supporting this e-business strategy.

22.2 THE CONVENTIONAL PROCUREMENT PROCESS

It is possible to distinguish between two types of procurement performed by companies (Chaffey, 2002):

- *Production-related*. Production-related procurement is designed to support manufacturing operations. As such, procurement must be geared to fulfilment of long-term needs, generally involves the procurement of customised items and is frequently undertaken through building regular relationships with suppliers. As such, procurement for production-related activities tends to be organised in hierarchies (Chapter 14).
- *Operating*. Non-production or operating procurement is conducted to support all the operations of the business. Such procurement is designed to fulfil immediate needs typically for commoditised items. As such, relationships with suppliers tend to be irregular and temporary. Hence operating procurement is frequently organised in terms of markets (Chapter 14).

Historically, procurement has been a human-intensive process involving activities such as:

- Requesting quotations
- Submitting purchase orders
- Approving and confirming orders
- Shipping
- Invoicing
- Payment

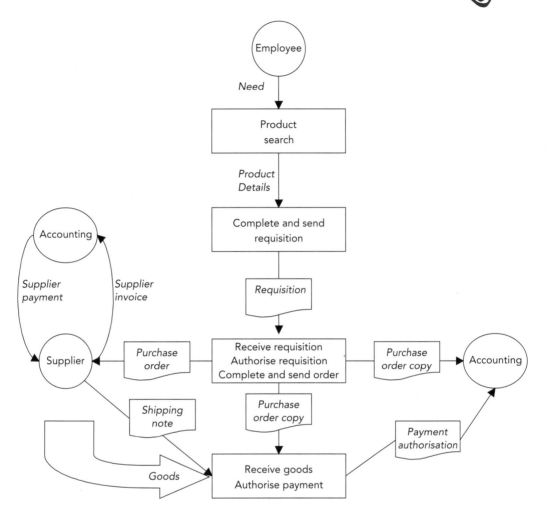

Figure 22.1 The traditional procurement process.

Traditionally, procurement has been performed by a specialist purchasing department typically employing many people using paper documentation, the telephone and fax to communicate with suppliers. A model of a traditional procurement process is illustrated in Figure 22.1.

Employees first search for a product matching a particular need. Details of the product are then entered on a requisition form, which is sent for authorisation to the purchasing department. This department produces a purchase order which is sent to an established supplier. The supplier despatches goods to the company with an attached shipping note. When the goods have been checked a payment authorisation is issued to the accounting department, which pays the supplier.

It is possible to analyse the performance of this process in a number of ways. One approach is to analyse the average time taken to conduct each of the activities in this process.

Assume we have analysed the process illustrated in Figure 22.1 and arrived at the following timings for key activities:

Activity	Average time
Search for product and product identified	1 hour
Complete requisition	10 minutes
Send requisition	24 hours
Receive requisition	12 hours
Authorise and complete order	24 hours
Send order	24 hours
Delivery from supplier	24 hours
Receive goods	24 hours
Check goods	24 hours
Authorise Payment	10 mins
Total	**6 days 80 minutes**

It is important to recognise that this estimate of the average duration of the procurement process is large because of the inherent delays embedded within the current process. Key delays are evident in the receipt of paperwork and goods. For instance, items of documentation such as requisitions may sit in a person's in-tray for up to 12 hours before receiving attention.

Figure 22.2 illustrates a process that has been redesigned with the use of ICT. We are assuming here that employees are able to order directly from supplier Web sites. It therefore represents a model of a typical e-procurement process.

The same sort of analysis may be conducted for this electronic procurement process. The analysis is presented in the table below.

Activity	Average time
Search for product and product identified	20 minutes
Complete order	10 minutes
Delivery from supplier	24 hours
Receive goods and check goods	10 minutes
Issue payment	10 mins
Total	1 day 50 minutes

It is evident that the speed at which procurement may be accomplished is significantly increased.

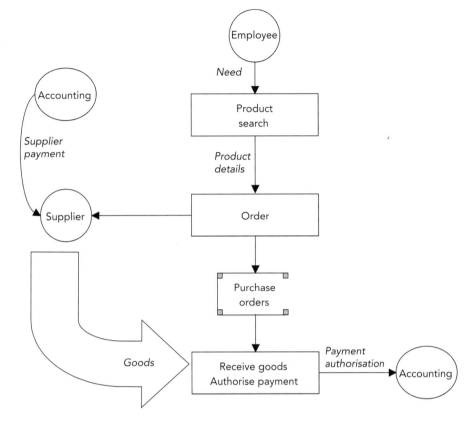

Figure 22.2 A model of an e-procurement process.

Example   Hammer and Champy (1993) describe an accounts payable process (part of a traditional procurement process) at the Ford motor company that was re-engineered. The accounts payable department originally employed 500 employees. A competitor's accounts payable department had five people. Hence, Ford set out to reduce the workforce by hundreds to match its competitors. To do this it re-engineered the invoicing process using ICT.

In the old process the purchasing department wrote an order and sent a copy to accounts payable. Later, when the materials control department received goods, it sent a copy of the receiving document to accounts payable. Meanwhile the vendor sent an invoice to accounts payable.

The accounts payable department was hence involved in matching 14 data items between the receipt order, the purchase order and the invoice before it could issue payment to the vendor. In fact, this department spent most of its time trying to sort out mismatches between these three documents.

The new process was built using the principle of invoice-less processing. In the new process, the purchasing department now entered order information into a database. No copy of this data was sent to anyone internally. When goods arrived at the receiving dock, a receiving clerk checked the material against the outstanding purchase record in the database. If they matched, he accepted the goods and payment was automatically sent to the vendor. If they did not match, the order was returned. Hence matching of only three data items was required – part number, unit of measure and supplier code – between a purchase order and a receipt order. Consequently, Ford achieved a 75% cut in head count.

Question

Besides the time it takes to complete tasks in the process, what other measures of the efficiency of the procurement process might be employed?

22.3 BENEFITS OF E-PROCUREMENT

Typical benefits from electronic procurement may be divided into efficiency improvements and efficacy improvements.

- *Efficiency improvement*
  Typical efficiency improvements include:
  - *Savings in the time taken to undertake procurement.* This is frequently referred to as the cycle time between order and supply. A user of an e-procurement system can complete a requisition quickly, since much of the needed data (such as product codes, descriptions and prices) will be available from integrated systems.
  - *Reductions in error rates.* Reduced rekeying of data between systems eliminates costly and time-consuming work.
  - *Resource savings*, such as in the cost of paper and postage required in traditional procurement.
  - *Staffing savings*, such as in the number of staff needed to be employed in the purchasing department.
  - *Reduction in knock-on costs.* Electronic procurement may introduce savings in related processes and systems such as a reduction in the costs associated with warehousing and inventory.
  - *Reduction in pricing.* Electronic procurement facilitates a reduction in the cost of goods procured due to organisations being able to find the best suppliers at the best prices for particular goods and services.
- *Efficacy improvement*
  Typical efficacy improvements include:

- *Greater flexibility*. Organisations may be able to change their choice of suppliers more frequently in the face of changing market circumstances.
- *Greater control*. Automatic processes of authorisation can be built into e-procurement systems and clear audit trails established.
- *Better quality products and services*. Removal of many burdensome administrative activities can free up purchasing staff to pursue value-added activities such as monitoring and improving product/service quality with major suppliers.
- *Better relationships*. E-procurement offers the potential of improving information flow between buyers and sellers. Certain procurement strategies will involve a long-term relationship with established suppliers. This enables integration of systems between buyer and seller with consequential improvements in efficiency and effectiveness.
- *More effective negotiation*. E-procurement systems enable companies to capture purchasing data more effectively. Such data can be combined with other data collected about suppliers, such as delivery times. This enables the organisation to better negotiate quantities, suppliers and prices.
- *Better information*. Because data can be captured on all the stages of procurement, organisations can conduct sophisticated analyses of spending and better plan strategy in this area.

Examples

Public sector organisations such as the UK Inland Revenue procure large amounts of goods and services from suppliers. In Wales, the public sector is the largest procurer of goods and services. It has been estimated that organisations in the public sector may save as much as 40% on the average procurement transaction by conducting some or all of the activities in the procurement process electronically.

Electronic procurement also offers performance improvement in the area of effectiveness. As a key business process, improvements in this area are likely to provide knock-on effects to other related business processes such as inventory control and production. Hence in such terms the use of e-procurement may have a significant effect on the overall profitability and competitiveness for a company.

Because of its key potential for performance improvement, an e-procurement strategy is likely to be a key component of an organisation's e-business strategy (Chapter 24).

Example

The UK central civil government (OGC, 2002) has developed the vision that all central civil government purchasing transactions should be able to be transmitted securely over the Internet between government and suppliers. Such communication should also be based on using interoperable systems based on common standards. The key aim is to achieve value for money from procurement. To achieve such a vision the Office of Government Commerce has developed a strategy that comprises three core elements:

- *E-hub*. This constitutes a technical infrastructure for e-procurement including a single access point for suppliers to central government customers, a server that provides a translation service between government and supplier systems and a data warehouse to enable analysis of government purchasing patterns.

- *Framework agreements*. A number of framework agreements for e-commerce solutions meant to provide interoperable systems operating to government standards and interfacing with key financial systems.

- *Support*. The Office of Government Commerce provides support to government departments in developing e-procurement.

Question	*Is it possible to identify the most important efficiency or efficacy improvement produced through e-procurement?*

22.4 FORMS OF E-PROCUREMENT

It is possible to distinguish between three broad categories of e-procurement, roughly corresponding to the activities of the procurement process:

- *Electronic sourcing*. These forms of electronic procurement include electronic tendering systems that enable organisational agents to create requests for quotation (RFQ). Electronic RFQs can then be issued to suppliers. Forms of electronic auction may then be utilised to source best-priced contracts with suppliers.

- *Electronic purchasing*. Once a contract with a given supplier is awarded, a number of tools may be used to search catalogues, select desired goods or services, place them in an electronic shopping basket and automatically raise a requisition or purchase order.

- *Electronic payment*. Invoices may be issued in XML format from a supplier once goods have been despatched. Once the buyer has received the goods the invoice can be automatically matched to the purchase order for price and to the goods received for quantity. Various electronic payment systems may then be used to transfer payment to the supplier.

To facilitate standardisation of data and hence effective analysis for management information, many forms of e-procurement will use standard commodity classification coding. Such standard coding schemes may also enable faster searching for a particular item among a range of possible suppliers. Commodity coding is the assignment of standard codes to item records (at the part number level) and to purchase orders (at the purchase order line item level).

Example	There are various coding schemes available:

- *CPV.* Common procurement vocabulary used in the EU in public procurement to group together the products of similar producers

- *EAN.* European article number, widely used in association with a standard for bar-coding

- *UN-SPC.* United Nations Standard Product and Services Code which provides a hierarchically organised product classification system.

For example, a UN-SPC code for a mobile phone would be 43.17.15.12, which decodes as:

43 – Communications and computing equipment

17 – Hardware and accessories

15 – Telephony equipment

12 – Mobile telephone

Question   *What forms of market models are most appropriate for electronic sourcing?*

22.5 TECHNOLOGIES FOR E-PROCUREMENT

Electronic procurement can be achieved in a number of different ways and companies may phase in use of key technologies throughout the supply chain:

- *E-mail.* The simplest level of e-procurement is the replacement of paper-based and telephone communication with communication via e-mail between the supplier and the purchasing company.

- *Workflow.* Workflow systems can be used to improve the flow of documentation such as requisitions and authorisation in purchasing activities.

- *Electronic document transfer.* Companies may use electronic document standards such as EDI or XML (Chapter 8) for purchasing transactions.

- *Integrated back-end systems.* Integrated purchase ordering and accounting systems (Chapter 5) can significantly improve these critical parts of the procurement process. ERP systems (Chapter 11) are frequently used to coordinate key support for procurement activities.

- *Electronic payment systems.* Companies may use credit-based payment systems for monetary exchanges accompanying purchases (Chapter 8).

- *Extranets.* The traditional model of procurement with established suppliers through some form of electronic hierarchy is also a significant source for organisational improvement. The use of Extranets can substantially improve the flow of information between supplier and purchaser and enable more effective coordination of key business processes.

- *Electronic marketplaces*. More sophisticated forms of electronic procurement involve the use of electronic marketplaces (Kaplan and Sawhney, 2000). These are exchanges in which organisations can search for suppliers and negotiate prices for goods and services. Electronic marketplaces may be organised vertically in terms of a particular industry or horizontally in terms of a particular class of users or a particular class of goods and services. Electronic marketplaces may also be public, in which case any organisation may participate, or private, in the sense that commerce is restricted to particular members of the marketplace (Chapter 19).

22.6 CASE STUDY: SCHLUMBERGER

Schlumberger is the world's largest oil service company. In 2000 it had revenues of $8.5 billion and 60,000 employees spread across 100 countries. In the late 1990s it introduced a Web-based procurement system into its largest division – oilfield services.

The system consists of two parts. The first part enables company employees to search online catalogues of common products such as office supplies using the company Intranet. Such catalogues are cut-down versions of the full catalogue from the supplier and only display items that have had special prices negotiated. Once the employee has chosen an item the system automatically creates a requisition, routes the order to the appropriate person for approval and transforms the requisition into a purchase order. The second part of the system provides access for employees to a marketplace of hundreds of suppliers. Each buyer is able to customise this marketplace of products and prices to their needs.

The e-procurement system is based on Commerce One Buysite and Marketsite software. Buysite is used for product selection and approval. Marketsite is used to handle transactions between buyer and seller.

Key performance improvements were experienced with the introduction of this e-procurement system. For example:

- Lower costs associated with the placing of orders because employees act as their own purchaser.
- Lower cost of goods purchased through negotiation of lower prices.
- Greater flexibility in that the company is able to access a larger range of suppliers.

22.7 SUMMARY

- The pre-sale activity of search, negotiate and order in the supply chain is frequently referred to under the umbrella term of *procurement*. Sometimes the term is used to refer to all the activities involved in the supply chain.
- Electronic procurement (e-procurement) refers to the use of ICT to enable the whole of the procurement process.
- Significant efficiency, effectiveness and efficacy improvement is possible through e-procurement.
- Forms of e-procurement include e-sourcing, e-purchasing and e-payment.
- Forms of e-procurement technology include use of e-mail, workflow, integrated systems, Extranets and electronic marketplaces.

22.8 ACTIVITIES

(i) Examine and analyse the whole of or part of some procurement process known to you in terms of the time taken to complete activities.

(ii) Identify key ways in which the procurement process may be re-engineered through ICT.

(iii) Determine what forms of e-procurement are suitable for operational as opposed to production-related procurement.

(iv) Detail the forms of e-procurement used by an organisation known to you.

22.9 REFERENCES

Chaffey, D. (2002). *E-business and E-commerce Management*. Harlow, Pearson Education.

Hammer, M. and Champy, J. (1993). *Reengineering the Corporation: a Manifesto for Business Revolution*. London, Nicholas Brearley.

Kaplan, S. and Sawhney, M. (2000). E-hubs: the new B2B marketplaces. *Harvard Business Review*, **78**(3), 97–108.

Matin, A., Gerard, P. and Lariver, C. (2001). Turning the supply chain into a revenue chain. *Harvard Business Review*, **79**(3), 20–22.

OGC (2002). *A Guide to E-procurement for the Public Sector*. London, Office of Government Commerce.

Rajkumar, T. M. (2001). E-procurement: business and technical issues. *Information Systems Management*, Fall, 52–60.

PART **5**

THE SOCIAL INFRASTRUCTURE FOR E-BUSINESS

When society requires to be rebuilt, there is no use in attempting to rebuild it on the old plan.

John Stuart Mill, *Coleridge*

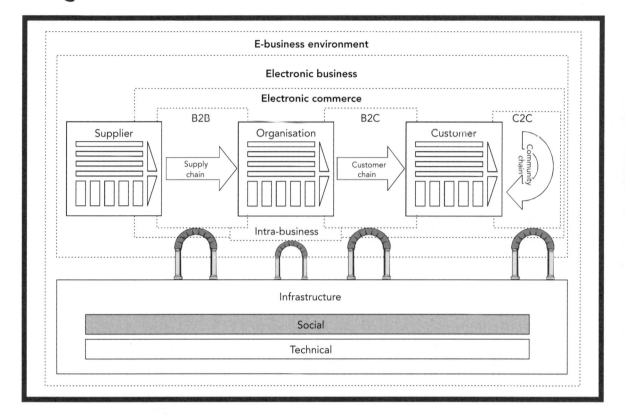

As is evident from the e-business domain model presented above, the social infrastructure for e-business consists of those human activity systems central to supporting the conduct of e-business. As well as the conventional competencies in areas of human activity, such as finance, sales and production, the e-business must develop informatics competencies if it is to survive in the market-place. This is a reflection of the socio-technical nature of e-business. These include competencies in e-business planning, management, development and evaluation.

Figure P5.1 illustrates the relationships between these critical processes. In systems terms, these processes can be can be envisaged in terms of a hierarchy of control (Chapter 3) – e-business planning is a control system for e-business management, which in turn is a control system for project management, which in turn is a control system for e-business development.

E-business planning (Chapter 23) is the process of deciding upon the optimal e-business infrastructure for some organisation and of engaging with the transformation of one e-business infrastructure into another. E-business infrastructure includes both human activity systems infrastructure and informatics infrastructure. The key output from e-business planning is e-business strategy. The planning process should also include performance monitoring – information fed back from the management process – which is critical to the ongoing evaluation of strategy.

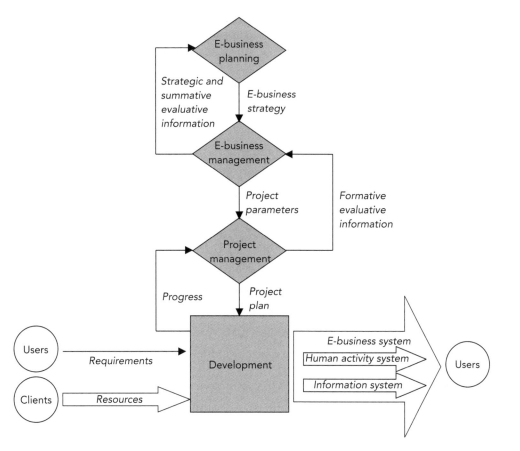

Figure P5.1 The relationship between e-business planning, management and development.

Two forms of management are delineated on Figure P5.1 – general e-business management and project management. E-business management (Chapter 25) is the process of putting plans into action and monitoring performance against plans. E-business management will define, resource and implement a portfolio of projects. Individual projects need to be managed as autonomous fields of activity and progress reported to general management processes. We particularly focus upon a critical layer of organisational informatics known as information management in this chapter and argue that the modern interest in so-called knowledge and content management is really a contemporary reawakening of the importance of managing information effectively and the relevance of various ICTs to this task.

E-business development (Chapter 26) is the process of implementing the plans documented in strategy and resourced from management. E-business systems are socio-technical systems consisting of information systems and the human activity systems they support. Such systems will be constructed by a development organisation. Detailed requirements are likely to be supplied by potential users of such systems and key resources will be supplied by clients of the development organisation – usually managerial groups.

E-business strategy (Chapter 24), project parameters and project plans are all control inputs in this hierarchy of control. Development progress, project reports (formative evaluation) and strategy evaluations (summative and strategic) are all forms of control signal in feedback processes. Figure P5.1 is meant to emphasise that planning, general management, project management and development are continuous processes. As in any human activity system it is important that the feedback loops work effectively for the social infrastructure of e-business to be a viable system. Information systems are equally critical to such processes as to conventional business processes such as sales and manufacturing.

One critical sub-process within management is that of evaluation. Evaluation is the process of assessing the worth of something. At the highest level, evaluation is critical to the continuous assessment of strategy. At the lowest level, evaluation is critical to the assessment of ICT systems within their context of use and application, namely human activity systems. It is for this reason that various forms of evaluation relevant to e-business are discussed in Chapter 27.

The major point to be made in this part of the work is that effective e-business planning, management, development and evaluation is critical for the effective alignment of human activity systems, information systems and ICT in business.

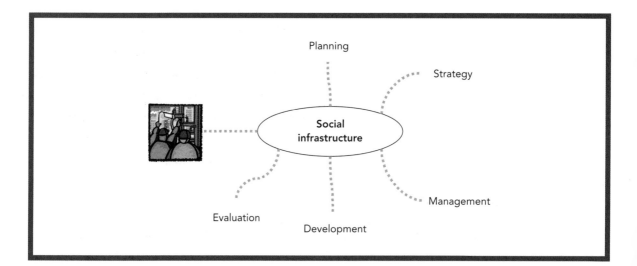

E-BUSINESS PLANNING

In preparing for battle I have always found that plans are useless, but planning is indispensable.

Dwight D. Eisenhower

You can never plan the future by the past.

Edmund Burke, *Letter to a Member of the National Assembly*

LEARNING OUTCOMES

After reading this chapter, you will be able to:

- Define the process of e-business planning
- Describe a number of alternative approaches to conducting e-business planning
- Relate the generic activities of planning
- Describe a number of approaches to generating a vision for e-business

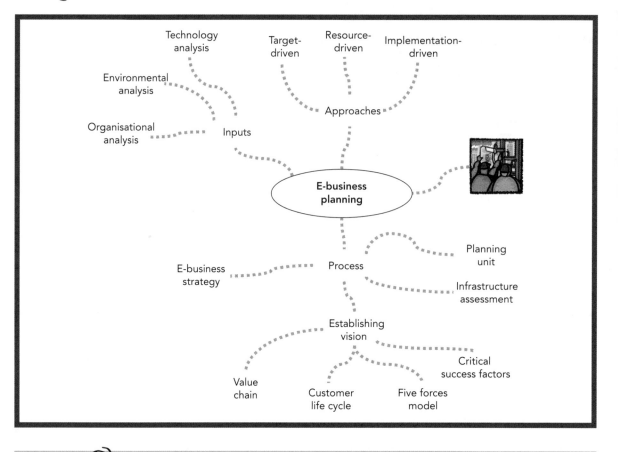

E-business planning is the process of deciding upon the optimal e-business infra-structure and of engaging with the transformation of one e-business infrastructure into another. E-business infrastructure includes both human activity systems infrastructure and informatics infrastructure. The key output from e-business plan-ning is e-business strategy. The key inputs are forms of organisational, technolog-ical and environmental analysis. The planning process should also include performance monitoring – information fed back from the management process. This is critical to the ongoing evaluation of strategy.

In this chapter we consider a conventional target-driven approach to e-business planning. We focus particular attention on techniques for establishing a strategic vision for e-business.

Three major forms of strategic analysis input into the planning process: organisa-tional analysis, environmental analysis and technological analysis (Figure 23.1):

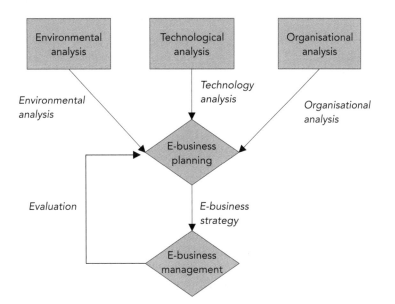

Figure 23.1 Inputs into the e-business planning process.

- *Organisational analysis* feeds information concerning the shape of current organisational activities and plans for changes to such activities. Part of this activity will be an assessment of e-business infrastructure (see below).
- *Environmental analysis* inputs information concerning current and future trends in the immediate environment of the organisation – economic, social and political trends affecting the organisation (Part 3).
- *Technology analysis* will provide information concerning the trends in information and communications technology that are likely to impact upon the organisation in the short- to medium-term future and stimulate needed change in its technical infrastructure (Part 2).

Example

In the financial services sector an environmental analysis may highlight opportunities and threats posed by deregulation of key areas. A technology analysis may highlight the potential of critical technologies such as CRM systems for customer retention. An organisational analysis may identify key problems with business processes such as response time to customer enquiries.

The objective of e-business planning is to develop an e-business strategy. The practical output of e-business planning is a document or a document set that describes strategy in this area. E-business planning will also receive input from management in the form of various types of evaluation conducted on the performance of the organisation.

Questions   *In what way would you propose organising the analysis of environment, technology and organisation? Are specialist roles required for these sort of analyses?*

There are three major approaches to the planning of e-business strategy (Ward and Peppard, 2002) (Figure 23.2):

- *Target-driven.* This is a top-down approach to the planning of strategy. Here strategy is directed through goals or targets set. Consideration is then given to ways of achieving targets and resources needed to conduct activities.

- *Resource-driven.* This is a bottom-up approach to strategy. Here strategy begins with available resources. Activities are specified in terms of these resources and goals achieved in relation to activities.

- *Implementation-driven.* This is a middle-out approach to strategy. Here means and ends are continually assessed and adjusted over time in the shaping of activities.

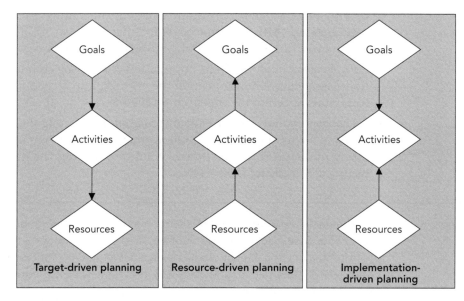

Figure 23.2 Three approaches to planning of strategy.

Example   In target-driven planning the organisation establishes a mission for itself consisting of a series of measurable objectives, such as to improve profitability by 5% in three years. A series of activities are then planned to achieve these goals, such as to decrease inventory levels through the introduction of an integrated inventory and production information system. Resources then have to be provided to support the planned activities in terms of development and project management resources such as programmers, hardware and software.

Question   *What advantages do you think lie with each approach to planning?*

23.4 THE PROCESS OF E-BUSINESS PLANNING

The top-down or target-driven approach to e-business planning is certainly the best documented and hence it is the approach to which we devote the most attention in this chapter. Some generic activities for the e-business planning process are listed below. These phases can be adapted to resource-driven and implementation-driven approaches.

- Setting up a planning unit and approach.
- Assessment of the current e-business infrastructure.
- Establishing a vision for e-business.
- Specifying the e-business strategy.

The form of an e-business strategy is discussed in Chapter 20. Therefore we devote most attention here to the remaining phases of planning.

23.5 SETTING UP A PLANNING UNIT AND APPROACH

To develop an e-business strategy an organisation first usually evaluates a number of existing planning methods, and then generally selects a method for planning or customises its own. The organisation then usually sets up an e-business planning unit consisting of various organisational stakeholders. It relies on the training provided by the method to guide the planning study. Next the unit carries out the multiple phases of the study, generally lasting several months. It uses existing documentation and interviews with organisational stakeholders to define its current business processes. It also studies how the current information systems support these processes. Using its documented understanding, the unit then identifies and prioritises its key information systems for the future technical infrastructure together with an implementation schedule. It prepares a report that includes a plan with recommendations for hardware, software, data, communications and personnel support.

Any planning process must begin with an assessment of the current situation. Current performance is compared with a set of objectives. Business and informatics objectives would be expected to result from an e-business planning exercise.

E-business planning is a socio-technical exercise in the sense that all four layers of organisational infrastructure need to be examined: human activity systems, information, information systems and ICT. The current performance of these layers needs to be established and definitions for future performance and the shape of associated performance management systems needs to be established.

In Chapter 3 we referred to the fact that systems of whatever form generally exhibit some form of control that enables the system to adapt to changes in its environment. Control can be viewed in terms of a monitoring subsystem that regulates the behaviour of other subsystems. This monitoring or control subsystem ensures defined levels of performance for the system through imposing a number of control inputs upon the system. Control is normally exercised in terms of some defined measures of performance. A monitoring subsystem may only work effectively if there are defined levels of performance for the system. Such performance levels will be defined by higher-level systems.

This issue of control is normally expressed in the business literature as the process of performance management. Performance management is the process of measuring past action (Neely, 1998). The assumption is that past action determines current performance. Performance can be measured in terms of three main types of measure – of efficacy, efficiency and effectiveness (Checkland, 1999). The level of performance that an organisation attains is a function of the efficacy, efficiency and effectiveness of the actions it has undertaken. To measure performance effectively an organisation needs to construct performance management systems. Such systems rely on a supporting infrastructure of data acquisition, collation, sorting, analysis, interpretation and dissemination. They normally rely on the definition of key performance indicators (KPIs) for the system in question.

Neely argues that there are four main reasons for the measurement of performance:

- *Checking position*. This includes comparing position with other comparable organisations.
- *Communicating position*. This may be an important part of regulatory regimes in key public and private sectors.
- *Confirming priorities*. Identifying how far an organisation is from achieving its goals.
- *Compelling progress*. Measuring progress, releasing reward tied to progress, communicating priorities and initiating change.

Question	*Why are good definitions of performance critical for compelling change in organisations?*

The term *benchmarking* is particularly associated with the first of Neely's reasons for performance measurement. It is frequently referred to as competitive benchmarking or best practices benchmarking. Such benchmarking is likely to be an important part of any e-business planning.

Eccles (1991) published an influential paper in the *Harvard Business Review* entitled 'The performance management manifesto'. In this paper he heralded a performance measurement revolution and predicted that 'within the next five years, every company will have to redesign how it measures its business performance'. According to Eccles, 'benchmarking involves identifying competitors and/or companies in other industries that exemplify best practice in some activity, function, or process and then comparing one's own performance to theirs'.

He also identified five critical areas of activity for the performance management revolution:

- Developing an information infrastructure
- Putting the technology in place to support this architecture
- Aligning the incentives with the new system
- Drawing on outside resources
- Designing a process to ensure that the other four activities occur

Example	Probably the widest used performance measurement system for local e-government is the Best Value Performance Indicator (BVPI) set of key performance indicators for electronic service delivery – BVPI 157. This performance management system defines ten major types of interaction (transactions) between the customer and local government:

- *Providing information* (such as opening times of libraries and contact details of council members)

- *Receiving payments* (such as council tax payments, business rates and parking fines)

- *Making payments* (such as paying benefits, payments to creditors and providing student loans)

- *Receiving feedback* (such as complaints and consultation)

- *Regulation* (such as the issuing of licences and permits)

- *Making an application* (such as for planning approval or housing benefit)

- *Making a booking* (such as booking a squash court or making an appointment to see a social worker)

- *Paying for goods* (such as for stationery or equipment)

- *Access to community, professional or business networks* (such as providing links to the National Health Service, tourism networks or local businesses)

- *Procurement* (such as arranging and maintaining contracts, tenders, auctions and orders with external agencies)

A large grid is available to the authority that plots as many as 70 different forms of service type against these interaction types. The ten types of interaction are not applicable to every type of service. Service types include:

- Adoption and fostering

- Business rates

- Council tax

- Disabilities

- Electoral registration

- Footways and pavements

- Housing repairs

- Industrial services

- Jobs

- Leisure services

- Members information

- Planning

- Refuse and waste collection and disposal

- Social services

- Tourist information

- Youth service

Authorities are asked to evaluate on a regular basis the percentage of interactions with the public that are being delivered through electronic service delivery against transaction type and service type. The percentages are then averaged against transaction type to provide an overall profile of electronic service delivery in each authority. For example, an authority may produce the following profile:

Providing information	80%
Receiving payments	30%
Making payments	20%
Receiving feedback	70%
Regulation	10%
Making an application	55%

Making a booking	28%
Paying for goods	20%
Access to community	10%
Procurement	15%

Authorities are expected to benchmark their performance in these terms over a number of years in order to be able to demonstrate progress in electronic local government.

To summarise, performance assessment or measurement can be conducted in terms of three forms of performance improvement: efficacy, efficiency and effectiveness. The difference between these performance measures is illustrated in Figure 23.3.

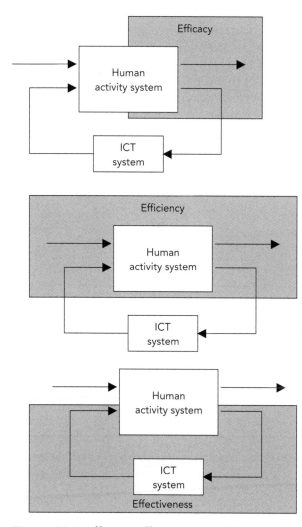

Figure 23.3 Efficacy, efficiency and effectiveness.

23.6.1 EFFICACY

Efficacy is a measure of the extent to which a system achieves its intended transformation. Porter would argue that for any company such a transformation involves delivering greater value to the customer of that organisation. Hence efficacy is primarily focused on the outputs from an organisation. Efficacy gains are typically measured in terms of improvements in the quality of the service or product of a particular company.

23.6.2 EFFICIENCY

Efficiency tends to equate, at least in terms of commercial organisations, with an economic model of the firm. Efficiency is a measure of the extent to which the system achieves its intended transformation with the minimum use of resources. Efficiency gains can be achieved in a human activity system through doing more with the same resources or the same with less resource. Hence efficiency gains can be measured in terms of comparing inputs against outputs using a systems model of the organisation. If inputs and outputs can be expressed in numeric terms then efficiency can be expressed as the ratio of inputs to outputs (Efficiency = Inputs/Outputs).

In the traditional open systems model of organisations capital and labour are the two inputs that the organisation takes from its environment. A micro-economic model of the firm permits capital to be freely substituted for labour to produce similar levels of output or production. Such models predict that ICT can be freely substituted for labour, thereby introducing cost savings.

| Example | Replacement of labour with ICT is a traditional intra-business model of efficiency. The idea of determining the online revenue contribution of e-marketing (Chapter 21) is one key performance indicator for e-commerce that focuses on both efficiency and effectiveness gain. |

Another type of economic model of the firm is based around the idea of transaction costs. Transaction costs are those costs incurred by the organisation when it buys in the marketplace. Firms seek to reduce transaction costs particularly by reducing the costs associated with using markets such as locating and communicating with suppliers, maintaining contracts and obtaining information on products. ICT can help firms reduce the costs associated with such activity.

| Example | Reduction of transaction costs associated with commercial activity through the use of ICT is the typical argument made in support of e-commerce, either buy-side or sell-side. |

23.6.3   PROFITABILITY

As far as commercial organisations are concerned, both efficiency and efficacy are strategies to make more money, i.e. to increase profitability. Efficiency and efficacy gains will lead to more customers and will improve the competitive position of the company.

Efficiency, efficacy and consequently profitability all have to be measured and monitored. Successful companies are those that institute both single- and double-loop learning (Chapter 3) instituted in single- and double-loop feedback mechanisms. Such feedback mechanisms rely on information collected, stored and disseminated through information systems. Hence, information systems and their associated ICT systems are critical to modern organisational performance. The key question is how we measure the effectiveness of information and ICT systems in organisations?

23.6.4   EFFECTIVENESS

Effectiveness is a measure of the extent to which the system contributes to the purposes of a higher-level system of which it may be a subsystem. In terms of the effectiveness of a particular company, if the company is a member of a larger business group then this concerns measuring the contribution it makes to group profitability. If it is an autonomous entity, effectiveness might be assessed in terms of the competitive position of the company in its key markets through competitive benchmarking (Chapter 14). In terms of the relationship between information system and the human activity system it supports, effectiveness concerns measuring the impact of such a system on the purpose of human activity in the area of the organisation it is seen to be contributing to. Much of the discussion of the effectiveness of information systems is directed at attempting to determine the strategic advantage that such systems offer to the business.

Example   Consider some of the benefits of e-commerce considered in Chapter 17. Cost and time savings are primarily efficiency gains. Connection and quality improvements are primarily efficacy gains. Strategic improvements such as improvements in company competitiveness are primarily gains in effectiveness.

Traditionally performance measurement systems have focused on measuring tangible efficiency gain in terms of financial measures (Chapter 27). More recently companies have attempted to build more holistic performance measurement systems that encompass efficacy, efficiency and effectiveness concerns. One of the most famous is that known as the balanced scorecard (Kaplan and Norton, 1992).

The balanced scorecard was invented by Robert Kaplan and David Norton and has taken the business and consulting world by storm. It maintains that if an organisation has a good, well-balanced measurement system, information should be available which allows business personnel to answer four main questions:

- *The financial perspective.* How do we look to our shareholders?
- *The customer perspective.* How do our customers see us?
- *The internal perspective.* What must we exceed at?
- *The innovation and learning perspective.* How do we continue to innovate and create value?

It is argued that these questions should be approached sequentially and in terms of each perspective a few key performance indicators should be utilised. The balanced scorecard has been proposed as a useful instrument for the assessment of e-business concerns.

Question

Which of the three types of performance measure do you think is the most difficult to define in practice?

Examples

An example of some key performance indicators that have relevance to the performance assessment of CRM systems are customer acquisition rate, customer retention rate and customer satisfaction measures.

The European Union's Information Society strategy – eEurope 2005 – (EC, 2002b) is based on four prongs of policy implementation. One of these prongs is benchmarking of progress based on the formulation of a number of key indicators for the Information Society. The objective of developing and using such indicators is as an aid to policy development. The eEurope 2005 plan specifies 14 policy indicators and 22 supplementary indicators (EC, 2002c). The indicators are organised into categories corresponding to the eEurope policy areas. Examples include:

- A1 – % of households or individuals having access to the Internet at home
- B3 – % of businesses having a Web site/homepage
- D1 – number of basic public services fully available online
- G1 – % of enterprises total turnover from e-commerce
- I1 – % of individuals with Internet access who having encountered security problems
- J1 – % of enterprises with broadband access

23.7 ESTABLISHING A VISION FOR E-BUSINESS

Establishing a vision for e-business normally involves assessing the competitive advantage that information systems may deliver. A number of frameworks have been proposed for assessing competitive advantage afforded by information systems such as:

- Critical success factors
- Five forces model
- Customer life cycle
- Value chain (discussed in Chapter 14)

23.7.1 CRITICAL SUCCESS FACTORS

Any organisation needs to identify areas in which it has relative superiority, and to use that superiority both to create barriers to entry as well as to launch strategic offensives. One popular method of doing this is the critical success factor concept or CSF. A CSF is a factor that is deemed crucial to the success of a business. Consequently, CSFs are those areas that must be given special attention by management. They also represent critical points of leverage for achieving competitive advantage. There are normally only a few CSFs – perhaps between three and eight – for each organisation. CSFs follow the 80/20 rule – that only a few issues really count in terms of organisational effectiveness.

CSFs are usually contrasted with CFFs or critical failure factors. A CFF is an aspect of the organisation, the poor management of which is likely to precipitate organisational failure.

Example

A CSF for a chain of high street jewellers is likely to be location of its outlets. A CSF for a health authority is likely to be the quality or standard of service it gives to its customers – patients.

A CFF for the high street jeweller chain is likely to be a high amount of shrinkage in consumer demand. A CFF for a health authority might be poor coordination of its staff, particularly subcontracted staff.

CSFs and CFFs are useful ways of identifying areas for the maximal application of information systems and ICT.

Example

A high street jeweller chain, for instance, would benefit from an information system that enabled managers to select optimal locations for their stores based on factors such as population density and the state of local economy. In contrast, a health authority would benefit from an information system that ensured the efficient work scheduling of nursing staff.

Question	*What would be likely critical success factors for a university?*

23.7.2 FIVE FORCES MODEL

Another framework for assessing competitive advantage is based on the work of Porter and Millar (1985). They argue that a successful firm shapes the structure of competition by influencing five primary forces. These five forces are presented below with a brief analysis of the effects of e-business upon them (Porter, 2001):

- *Industrial rivalry; the competitive position of rival organisations.* Bricks and mortar companies in certain sectors such as banking, travel and insurance have already experienced increasing competition with the rise of clicks-only organisations such as online banks. In many sectors there has also been increased disintermediation; in others, significant amounts of reintermediation through electronic delivery channels.
- *Customer bargaining power.* Electronic trading increased the bargaining power of customers in the sense that they are able to search for and examine a wider array of goods and services. This appears to have a collective effect of driving down prices in markets.
- *Supplier bargaining power.* Supplier bargaining power may decrease with the increasing adoption of B2B e-commerce. Companies may insist that their established suppliers use electronic communication to improve supply chain efficiency. Also, the switching cost to alternative suppliers may be reduced with the rise of B2B hubs.
- *Barriers to entry; threat of new entrants.* It is argued that the start-up costs of entering digital markets are less significant than conventional markets, and consequently the barriers to entry are reduced and the threat of new entrants is increased. However, as the dotcom crash demonstrated, maintaining a sustainable online presence appears to be just as difficult, if not harder, than a maintaining a conventional market presence.
- *Threat of substitutes.* In the e-business arena the rise of digital products (such as digital music) and the increasing degree of digital convergence pose major threats to companies' products. In terms of services, new business models for electronic service delivery threaten existing delivery channels.

Many combinations of these factors, such as low industrial rivalry, high barriers to entry and low buyer bargaining power, can lead to sustainable, above-average, long-term profits. Electronic business can be used to achieve such goals by:

- Changing the basis of competition
- Strengthening customer relationships
- Overcoming supplier problems

- Building barriers against new entrants
- Generating new products or services

Examples

Customer information systems for marketing and sales can have a strategic impact by:

- Winning customers from the competition by using a large customer database.

- Use of market research databases to target customer 'need'.

- Use of telemarketing and direct mailing to improve sales.

- The cost of setting up and maintaining an accurate customer database can be a considerable barrier to entry.

- Introducing electronic shopping as a new service.

The rise of the Internet and the Web has lowered barriers to entry in key industries such as financial services. For instance, while many German banks offer home banking via the Internet, the first totally Internet Bank – Net.B@nk – was created in 1998 by seven Sparda banks (http://www.netbank.de/). Initially capitalised with just $11.03 million, it offers basic banking plus non-financial third-party products. The core product is the 'negic' account – a current account with an overdraft facility, a savings account, fixed-term deposit and a transaction account for securities held on deposit.

23.7.3   THE CUSTOMER RESOURCE LIFE CYCLE

Ives and Learmonth (1984) define an information system as being strategic if it changes a company's product or the way a firm competes in its industry. They use the idea of a customer resource life cycle to identify potential strategic information systems. This model considers a firm's relationship with its customers (the customer chain) and how this relationship can be changed or enhanced by the strategic application of ICT.

The customer resource life cycle is discussed as a sequence of 13 stages:

1. *Establish requirements*. To determine how much of a resource is required.
2. *Specify*. To detail the attributes of the required resource.
3. *Select a source*. Locate an appropriate supplier for the resource.
4. *Order*. To order a quantity of the resource from the supplier.
5. *Authorise and pay*. Before a resource can be acquired, authority for the expenditure must be obtained and payment made.
6. *Acquire*. To take possession of the resource.
7. *Test and accept*. The customer must verify the acceptability of the resource before putting it to use.
8. *Integrate*. The resource must be added to an existing inventory.

9. *Monitor*. Ensure that the resource remains acceptable while in inventory.

10. *Upgrade*. If requirements change, it may be necessary to upgrade resources.

11. *Maintain*. To repair a resource, if necessary.

12. *Transfer or dispose*. Customers will eventually dispose of a resource.

13. *Account for*. Customers must monitor where and how money is spent on resources.

23.8 ⊚ CASE STUDY: THE UK NATIONAL HEALTH SERVICE

The idea of a customer resource life cycle is relevant to both private and public sector organisations, such as the UK National Health Service (NHS). In this setting, the patient is the primary health service customer. The patient consumes a health service resource. A possible customer resource life cycle might then be:

- *Requirements specification*. ICT can be used as a means to aid the general practitioner (GP) and the patient in establishing what health resource is required and what quantity of the resource is required.
- *Selection*. A series of options can be presented to the patient regarding, for instance, a number of hospitals able to offer a given treatment.
- *Order*. The GP would be able to query a hospital's elective admission system to find out when a stay is feasible at the hospital. If it suits the patient a provisional booking could be made on the system.
- *Authorise and payment*. Appropriate routines would update the treatment accounts of the hospital and the budget of the general practice.
- *Acquire*. When the patient arrives for his stay in hospital his details would be transferred from the GP's system to the patient administration system of the hospital.
- *Test*. The patient would be given a listing of the proposed treatment and requested to sign it off.
- *Integrate*. The consumption of the health care resource would be added to the patient history held at the centralised register of the region.
- *Monitor and upgrade*. Preliminary investigation may change the initial prognosis leading to modification of the original health care plan. Any changes or additions to the plan would be recorded by hospital systems.
- *Maintain*. Regular checkups will be made of patients to ensure effective functioning. Such checkups will be notified to patients by the GP system, and the results recorded by the system.
- *Accountability*. The patient receives a report of every treatment concluded with the cost it has associated with the health service budget.

23.9 SUMMARY

- E-business planning is the process of deciding upon the optimal e-business infra-structure for an organisation.
- Three major forms of strategic analysis input into the planning process: organisational analysis, environmental analysis and technological analysis.
- There are three major approaches to the planning of e-business strategy: target-driven, resource-driven and implementation-driven.
- E-business planning is a process comprising setting up a planning unit and approach, assessing the current e-business infrastructure, establishing a vision for e-business and specifying the e-business strategy.
- Assessment will involve determining and using three main types of performance measure: efficiency, effectiveness and efficacy.
- Establishing a vision for e-business normally involves assessing the competitive advantage that information systems may deliver. A number of frameworks have been proposed for assessing competitive advantage afforded by information systems, such as critical success factors, five forces model, customer life cycle, and value chain analysis.

23.10 ACTIVITIES

(i) Write a brief description of what you feel should be included in any organisational analysis.

(ii) Write a brief description of what you feel should be included in any environmental analysis.

(iii) Write a brief description of what you feel should be included in any technology analysis.

(iv) Determine how planning is best described in an organisation known to you – target-, resource- or implementation-driven.

(v) Determine whether there is a specific unit devoted to planning in an organisation known to you. Determine the way it is organised.

(vi) In terms of an organisation such as a university, attempt to develop a series of efficiency, effectiveness and efficacy measures.

(vii) Attempt to apply one of the approaches to establishing an e-business vision to a public sector organisation such as a university.

23.11 REFERENCES

Checkland, P. (1999). *Soft Systems Methodology: a Thirty Year Retrospective*. Chichester, John Wiley.

EC (2002b). *eEurope 2005: an Information Society For All*. Brussels, European Commission.

EC (2002c). *eEurope 2005 Benchmarking Indicators*. Brussels, European Commission.

Eccles, R. G. (1991). The performance measurement manifesto. *Harvard Business Review*, Jan/Feb, 131–137.

Ives, B. and Learmonth, G. P. (1984). The information system as a competitive weapon. *Communications of the ACM*, **27**(12), 1193–1201.

Kaplan, R. S. and Norton, D. P. (1992). The balanced scorecard: measures that drive performance. *Harvard Business Review*, Jan/Feb, 71–79.

Neely, A. (1998). *Measuring Business Performance*. London, Economist Books.

Porter, M. E. (2001). Strategy and the Internet. *Harvard Business Review*, **79**(3), 63–78.

Porter, M. E. and Millar, V. E. (1985). How information gives you competitive advantage. *Harvard Business Review*, **63**(4), 149–160.

Ward, J. and Peppard, J. (2002). *Strategic Planning for Information Systems*. Chichester, John Wiley.

24

E-BUSINESS STRATEGY

To conquer the enemy without resorting to war is the most desirable. The highest form of generalship is to conquer the enemy by strategy.

Sun Tzu, *The Art of War*

After reading this chapter, you will be able to:

- Distinguish between strategic and tactical decision-making
- Distinguish between an organisation, an informatics strategy and an e-business strategy
- Distinguish between strategic analysis, choice and implementation
- Relate a number of organisational strategies
- Describe a number of the elements of an informatics strategy

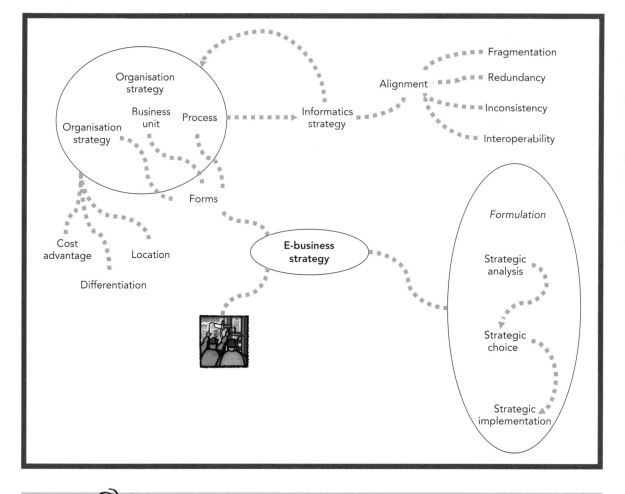

24.1 ⓔ INTRODUCTION

E-business concerns itself with the juncture of ICT and the organisation. Therefore e-business must concern itself with the development of both the strategy for the organisation and the strategy for informatics. E-business strategy is an amalgam of both organisational and informatics strategy.

In this chapter we first consider the difference between strategy and tactics. Then we distinguish between organisation strategy, e-business strategy and informatics strategy. We consider some of the key phases of strategic thinking and discuss a number of organisational strategies relevant for e-business. We conclude with a consideration of some of the features of good informatics strategy.

24.2 ⓔ STRATEGY AND TACTICS

The term *strategy* has historical roots in military operations. According to the *Oxford English Dictionary*, strategy is the art of a commander-in-chief; the art of projecting and directing the larger military movements and operations in a campaign. Strategy is seen to differ materially from tactics. Tactics belongs only to the mechanical movement of bodies set in motion by strategy. The term strategy is now very much used in the same sense in which it is used in the military but directed towards organisational and particularly business activities.

Ansoff (1965) defines strategic decisions as being primarily concerned with external rather than internal problems of the firm and specifically with selection of the product mix which the firm will produce and the market to which it will sell. Strategic decisions are concerned with establishing an 'impedance match' between the firm and its environment, or, in more usual terms, it is the problem of deciding what business the firm is in and what kinds of business it will seek to enter. In systems terms strategy concerns issues surrounding the viability of organisations.

Over the last twenty to thirty years managers within organisations have become very much concerned with developing explicit organisation strategy and with initiating effective ways of planning and implementing strategy (Porter, 1996). Much recent e-business literature has followed this trend and concerns itself with how strategies for information, information systems and ICT can be developed which align themselves with organisation strategy.

Examples

Some examples of strategic e-business decisions include:

- How much are we going to invest in information systems and ICT over the next three years?

- How much development, maintenance and support for our ICT infrastructure is to be sourced internally or outside?

- To what extent are we going to develop a separate e-business organisation?

Question

What is the relationship between a business model and a business strategy?

24.3 ORGANISATION STRATEGY, E-BUSINESS STRATEGY AND INFORMATICS STRATEGY

The UK Institute of Directors believes that there are a number of key differences between organisation strategy and e-business strategy (Institute of Directors, 2000):

- *Planning horizon*. Organisational strategy tends to work with a 3–6 year horizon for planning. Because of technological progress, e-business strategy may only be able to work with a 3–6 month planning horizon.

- *Planning process*. Organisational strategy tends to be produced in a one-off or periodic manner. E-business strategy has to be cyclical in nature reflecting continuous interaction between technical and social infrastructure.
- *Business focus*. Organisational strategy has traditionally focused on production of goods. E-business strategy focuses on information and customer focus.

Question   *What consequences do these distinctions have for the conduct of e-business planning in organisations?*

We would argue that there are at least three different viewpoints as to what e-business strategy constitutes (Lord, 2000). There is no one correct view of what e-business strategy represents. The appropriate viewpoint is defined by organisational context. In other words, e-business strategy will depend on the context of an appropriate business model (Chapter 3) for the e-business.

- *E-business strategy is organisation/corporate strategy*. In this viewpoint there is little or no distinction between organisation strategy and e-business strategy. This definition is appropriate if the e-business is effectively the entire corporation. In practice it may only be applicable if a traditional 'bricks and mortar' company attempts to establish a complete re-engineering of its processes around ICT or a new greenfield e-business is established – a clicks-only strategy.
- *E-business strategy is business unit strategy*. In many companies the e-business strategy may only be applicable to a particular business unit. For example, some companies run their e-businesses as separate but parallel operations.
- *E-business strategy is a process strategy*. A key organisational process or human activity system, or perhaps an integrated set of such processes, may be chosen for radical redesign with ICT innovation. For example, a company may decide that it wishes to concentrate on redesigning its supply chain or customer chain processes with ICT innovation. We would argue that this is the most ubiquitous form of e-business strategy currently.

Examples   The e-business strategy of a company like Amazon.com, because of its role as a dotcom, is almost certainly going to be the same as its organisation strategy. In other companies, supply chain management (Chapter 19) or customer relationship management (Chapter 20) may be developed as an e-business strategy. Or a specific area of e-commerce such as B2C or B2B e-commerce might be chosen. These may be business unit or process strategies depending on the makeup of the organisation.

It should be apparent from the above discussion that e-business strategy is subtly different from but dependent upon informatics strategy.

An informatics strategy defines the structure within which information, information systems and information technology are to be applied within an organisation over some future time frame. An informatics strategy can be divided into three major layers:

- *Information strategy*. This details the information needs of the organisation and processes necessary to collect, produce, store and disseminate information.
- *Information systems strategy*. This consists of a specification of the information systems needed to support organisational activity in the areas of collection, storage, dissemination and use of information.
- *ICT strategy*. This consists of a specification of the hardware, software, data, communication facilities and ICT knowledge and skills needed by the organisation to support its information systems.

In classic models of informatics strategy formulation the ideal of alignment between organisation strategy and informatics strategy is attempted. Ideally, four layers of strategy mutually support the other. A strategy for human activity systems in the organisation (organisation strategy) will be supported by the three layers of informatics strategy. The information needed by the organisation will determine the information systems it requires. In turn, the information systems needed will determine the ICT infrastructure required.

Question   *What potential problems exist in adopting a top-down approach to strategy-making?*

The notion of alignment normally suggests that business strategy formulation should ideally come before informatics strategy formulation, as illustrated in Figure 24.1. Organisation planning is the process of formulating an organisation

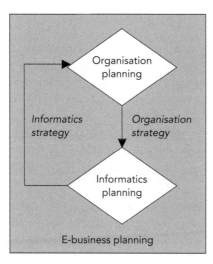

Figure 24.1 The relationship between organisation and informatics planning.

strategy. Informatics planning is the process of formulating an informatics strategy. An organisation strategy will critically affect the direction of an informatics strategy. However, in the modern business world organisational and informatics strategy are typically in a mutual cycle of reinforcement. The formulation of an informatics strategy is likely to critically affect the formulation of future business strategy. E-business planning is therefore a socio-technical activity. We are assuming of course that such planning will include review of not only internal but also external processes. Hence e-commerce strategy will be subsumed by e-business strategy.

Example

Part of an organisation's informatics strategy might be to develop an electronic commerce infrastructure for the electronic delivery of the company's products or services in the future. The relative success of this strategy in terms of increasing sales or opening up new customers will influence future business decisions about organisation strategy.

The success of the Italian motorcycle manufacturer Ducatti's e-commerce strategy led it to review the role of its physical dealerships. In Japan it decided to remove the sales function of its dealership operation entirely, leaving it only with the marketing and after-sales service.

24.4 ⊚ STRATEGIC ANALYSIS, CHOICE AND IMPLEMENTATION

According to Johnson and Scholes (2000) the formulation of business strategy involves three interdependent activities. Figure 24.2 represents these activities in a linear sequence:

- *Strategic analysis*. This involves analysis of the environment, expectations, objectives, power and culture in the organisation and organisational resources. Strategic analysis involves determining the organisation's mission and goals. Strategic analysis involves answering the questions 'What should we be doing?' and 'Where are we going?'.
- *Strategic choice*. This involves generating strategic options, evaluation of such options and the selection of a suitable strategy to achieve the selected option. Strategic choice involves answering the question 'What routes have we selected?'.
- *Strategic implementation*. This involves organising resources, restructuring elements of the organisation, and providing suitable people and systems. Strategic implementation comprises determining policies, making decisions and taking action. It involves answering the questions 'How do we guide our collective decisions to get there?', 'What choices do we have?' and 'How shall we do it?'.

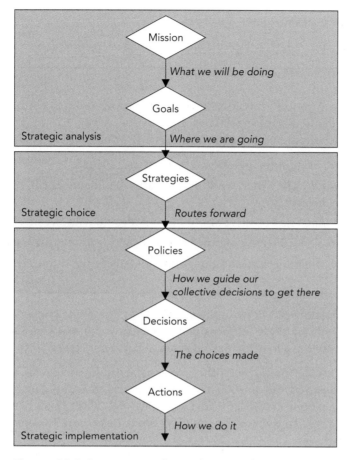

Figure 24.2 Strategic analysis, choice and implementation.

Strategic thinking as exemplified in the activities described above is normally documented in terms of an organisation's mission statement. This will have a limited number of statements of future intention. In terms of each statement of intention a number of goals may be formulated. For each such goal a number of strategies or routes forward may be planned. Each strategy has to be made operational in a series of policies or plans. Plans, in turn, are collections of decisions that involve a series of actions. Hence strategic planning involves constructing a hierarchy of goals, strategies, policies, decisions and actions.

Example   **Mission**: to be the industry cost leader

Goal: achieve staff productivity gain of 5% within three years

Strategy: reduce time lost due to ill health

Policy: maintain a healthy workplace

Decision: ban smoking

Action: inform staff, put up the signs and police the decision

---

An organisation's mission statement at various levels of the hierarchy consists of a limited number of objectives stipulated as a guide to future intention. Such objectives should be SMART objectives:

- *Specific*. Each objective should be clear and focused.
- *Measurable*. The objective should clearly include means by which achievement will be measured.
- *Achievable*. The objective should be achievable with organisational resources.
- *Realistic*. The objective should be realistic in terms of organisational constraints.
- *Timely*. The objective should contain details of the duration of achievement.

Example

An example of a SMART e-business objective might be to implement a new packaged CRM system by the e-business unit (specific) within one year (achievable, realistic, timely) with the aim of increasing average customer retention by 10% (measurable).

The UK retailer group Kingfisher owns established companies such as Woolworth, B&Q and SuperDrug. In 2000 it set itself the objective of growing its sales through e-commerce from £40 million to £1.5 billion by 2004. This constitutes 10% of the group's sales. To achieve this the retail group has created a separate division known as e-Kingfisher.

Question

What consequences might arise from not specifying a mission statement in terms of SMART objectives?

24.5 ORGANISATIONAL STRATEGIES

In commercial environments an organisation takes up a particular position in relation to its competitors. This we might define as the competitive position of the organisation. The development of organisational strategy in terms of the business normally has its prime objective as being the improvement of this competitive position and probably the sustainability of the business in the long term. This is normally expressed as the attempt to gain competitive advantage.

According to Porter (1985) competitive advantage can be gained by engaging in one or more of three generic organisational strategies:

- *Cost advantage strategy*. This essentially aims to establish the organisation as a low-cost leader in the market. The organisation aims to sell its products or services cheaper than its competitors. This may be achieved in a number of ways, such as concentrating on areas involved in improving overall efficiency via better planning.

- *Differentiation strategy*. The organisation undertaking this strategy aims to differentiate its product or service from its competitors. The aim is probably to establish among customers in the marketplace the perception that the organisation's product or service is better in some way than its competitors. This may be through improving quality and reliability relative to price, better market understanding, image promotion etc.

- *Location strategy*. A location strategy involves the organisation attempting to find a niche market to service. A niche market is one where no other organisation currently has an established presence. This may be achieved in a number of ways: by producing innovations in products or services or by placing distribution, marketing and information outlets in areas not utilised currently.

Examples

E-business strategies can be closely aligned with one or more of such generic organisational strategies. For example:

- A number of UK banks have set up online banking facilities as a form of cost advantage strategy. There are a number of reasons why online banking offers performance improvements for high street banks. One of the most significant is the low cost of banking transactions online compared with traditional banking services. Hence online banking can be seen as a form of strategic information system for such businesses.

- American Airlines (AA) used computer and communications technology to build an entirely new business. Hence this constituted a differentiation for AA. It developed a reservation system that listed the flight schedules of every major airline in the world. Of the 24,000 automated travel agents in the USA, 48% used the system. The reservation system displayed AA flights on any particular sector on the screen before any other airline's flights. This took advantage of the reservation clerk's natural tendency to choose the first flight offered. This information system proved so successful that an anti-trust case was brought against AA by other airlines.

- Tesco has established itself as the UK market leader in the electronic retail of foodstuffs – a successful location strategy. Customers may order foodstuffs over the Internet and have them delivered to their door the same day. This service has now become a key part of the company's future business strategy and has formed a critical part of its alliance with a major US food retailer.

These three generic strategies have to be implemented in terms of organisational changes. Hence lower-level organisational strategies have to be put in place to achieve cost advantage, differentiation or location improvements. Modern organisations may be subject to a number of such lower-level organisational strategies:

- *Low-cost production.* This is an efficiency strategy generally directed at cost advantage.
- *Focus on quality and service.* This is an effectiveness strategy directed at differentiation.
- *Globalisation*: developing a global focus for your products and/or services. In different ways organisations may utilise globalisation strategies for cost advantage in terms of their supply chains and for differentiation or location advantage in terms of their customer chains.
- *Right-sizing.* Finding appropriate organisational structures for particular changes in environments. This is primarily a cost advantage strategy, but is also possibly a differentiation or location strategy.
- *Customer intimacy.* Building better relationships with customers. A clear differentiation strategy.
- *Supplier intimacy.* Building better relationships with suppliers. A possible cost advantage strategy.
- *Just-in-time manufacturing.* Keeping inventory levels at a minimum through efficient supply chains. This is primarily a cost advantage strategy.

Examples

Flexible manufacturing may constitute a low-cost production strategy for business. Providing a multi-channel access centre to the goods and services of a company may constitute a quality service strategy. Globalisation is clearly fundamental to the rationale for much e-commerce. Virtual organisations may constitute an example of right-sizing. CRM and SCM constitute customer intimacy and supplier intimacy strategies respectively. Electronic procurement may be critical to just-in-time manufacturing.

Questions

What is the relationship between customer intimacy and customer relationship management? What is the relationship between supplier intimacy and supplier relationship management?

24.6 INFORMATICS STRATEGY

Many informatics projects are closely linked to organisational strategy; many are not. In ideal terms business or organisational strategy should be a key driver of informatics strategy.

An informatics strategy can be subdivided into three critical elements: an information strategy, an information systems strategy and an ICT strategy.

Example

Mission: to be the industry cost leader

Goal: achieve staff productivity gain of 5% within three years

Strategy: reduce the time to process a customer transaction

Policy: improve systems integration

Decision: introduce a corporate-wide ERP system

Action: Set up and resource an implementation project

The objective of informatics planning is to develop strategy in each of these three areas. The practical output of informatics planning is a document set that describes strategy in these three areas. An informatics strategy can be described as being the structure within which information, information systems and ICT are intended to be applied within the organisation. Such a strategy should establish an organisation's long-term infrastructure that will allow information systems to be designed and implemented efficiently and effectively. An informatics strategy is particularly directed at avoiding fragmentation, redundancy and inconsistency among information systems in the organisation, while increasing the interoperability of such systems. The strategy should hence be directed at ensuring an effective 'fit' between an organisation and its information systems.

One of the proposed benefits of having an explicit informatics strategy is to encourage a closer fit between an organisation's activities and its information systems. The question remains how do we measure this fit? Four aspects of an organisation's informatics infrastructure that may be measured and which can be used to determine elements of fit are the levels of fragmentation, redundancy, inconsistency and interoperability in the informatics infrastructure:

- *Fragmentation*. Poor fit is evident in the situation in which data is fragmented across information systems, usually because IS emulates structural divisions within the organisation and because organisational units put up barriers of ownership around data sets. Fragmentation may also be evident in processing where separate ICT systems communicate through manual interfaces.

- *Redundancy*. Poor fit is evident when large amounts of data are unnecessarily replicated across information systems, usually because interfaces do not exist between systems causing the same data to be entered many times. Redundancy may also be present when separate systems perform the same effective processing on data.

- *Inconsistency*. Poor fit is evident when the same data is held differently in different systems or processed differently by different systems, leading to inconsistencies in the ways in which information is produced, stored and disseminated.

- *Interoperability*. The property of interoperability is related to the other three. Generally speaking those systems that are fragmented, redundant and inconsistent are likely to suffer from poor levels of interoperability. This refers to the level to which systems communicate and cooperate within the infrastructure.

Situations subject to fragmentation, redundancy and inconsistency create a series of information 'islands' within the organisation. The existence of such islands makes it difficult to model the organisation in terms of its information. Hence operational managers find it difficult to plan effectively on a day-to-day basis and strategic managers (Chapter 3) find it difficult to plan for the medium- and long-term future.

Question | *Is it possible to develop measures of the fit between an organisation and its information systems?*

24.7 ◉ E-BUSINESS STRATEGIES

Models of the growth of informatics infrastructure in organisations have been used for a number of years to aid strategic thinking relating to the application of ICT (Nolan, 1990). Similarly, growth models for e-business have been and can be used as templates for e-business strategy (Wilcocks and Sauer, 2000). They typically provide a number of key stages from early experimentation with e-business issues to full engagement with e-business. Some of these growth models focus on ICT issues and some focus more on business issues. Such growth models can be useful in a number of ways:

- They provide an aid to enable organisations to understand e-business change.
- They can be used by organisations to engage in competitive benchmarking in relation to e-business.
- They provide an aid to strategy making in the e-business area.

Example | In Chapter 17 we provided a model of B2C e-commerce with the following stages: information-seeking, marketing presence, online catalogue, online ordering, online payment, online delivery and customer relationship management. This offers a simple template that small and medium-sized organisations in particular may seek to emulate in developing their e-business strategy. Effectively it offers a process strategy for the customer chain activities.

The UK Prime Minister announced in 1997 that by 2002, 25% of dealings with government should be able to be carried out by the public electronically. These targets were later revised in the Modernising Government White Paper (Cabinet Office, 1999), which initially set a target of 100% electronic service delivery by 2008. In March 2000 the Prime Minister Tony Blair announced that this target was to be brought forward. The UK government has now set a target that by 2005 all (100%) of government services that can be delivered electronically will be delivered electronically.

Critical to initiating this e-government agenda was the creation of the Office of the e-Envoy in September 1999 and the appointment of the e-Envoy himself, Andrew Pinder, in January 2001. The Office has responsibilities across the whole e-agenda, particularly e-commerce and e-government.

In April 2000 the e-government strategic framework (Cabinet Office, 2000) was published, requiring all central government departments to produce e-business strategies. These are intended to show how each department plans to implement e-government and to achieve electronic service delivery targets. The first draft was required in October 2000. From July 2001 departments are required to report progress against e-business strategies to the Office of the e-Envoy every six months.

The Inland Revenue is the UK government department responsible for collecting and administering taxation. This government department has attempted to be at the forefront of e-government in the UK by transforming its performance using ICT. This is evident in much of the strategic thinking emanating from the leadership within the organisation. For instance, the current chairman of the board presents four indicators that the organisation will use to determine how well it has transformed itself over the next few years:

- The receipt of clean data from customers will allow the Inland Revenue to remove work that adds little value to the organisation and consequently release people to work at the front line of customer care.

- Increasing the organisation's capability to deliver services electronically and increasing the take-up of such services by customers.

- Increasing use of knowledge management so that its staff have better guidance, which in turn enhances its customer service capabilities.

- Information and data management to enable it to progress towards the 'joined up government' vision. That is, to develop seamless, quality services and make best use of the data it receives.

The department set out its first e-business strategy in 2000 (National Audit Office, 2002). The key features of this strategy were:

- The development of a number of electronic channels for different customer groups with clear incentives to encourage the use of such channels. As part of this strategy the organisation intends to offer improved e-services to the UK taxpayer, thus reducing the burden of compliance on individuals and organisations.

- The use of intermediaries such as the National Association of Citizens Advice Bureaux, the Post Office and software suppliers to provide bespoke services to the customers of the organisation.
- Greater integration of its services with those of other departments and the provision of its services through commercial and government portals.
- Transformation of staff roles to focus on support for the customer through electronic tools.

In 2001 the Inland Revenue revised its strategy, keeping the fundamental principles above but making the following additions:

- Transformation of the organisation around a focus on the customer and a philosophy based in customer relationship management.
- Creating a technical framework that will deliver e-services in a modular but integrated fashion.

The Inland Revenue has established three targets for its e-business strategy:

- 50% of services were to be available electronically by 31 December 2002. By this time the organisation aimed to offer basic secure e-services and to have developed plans for organisational change based on such services.
- 50% take-up of its services by 2005. By 2004 the organisation aims to have significantly increased take-up of its core services and have delivered significant benefits from such services.
- All its services will be available electronically by 31 December 2005. By this date the Inland Revenue aims to have achieved a significant business transformation, with most customer transactions being conducted electronically.

24.9 ⊚ SUMMARY

- Strategic decision-making is focused on the future and the environment of the organisation.
- Organisation strategy is a detailed plan for future action.
- Planning is the process of formulating strategy; management is the process of implementing strategy.
- Business strategy should drive informatics strategy.
- Informatics strategy is a detailed plan for future informatics activities.
- Organisation strategy should determine what information is relevant.
- Information strategy should determine what information systems are important.
- Information systems strategy should determine which information technology is relevant.

24.10 ACTIVITIES

(i) Find two examples of strategic decisions made by an organisation.

(ii) Find two examples of tactical decisions made by an organisation.

(iii) In terms of the goal expressed in the example in this chapter, determine some other strategies, policies, decisions and actions that might be formulated in terms of this goal.

(iv) Determine whether there may be any information strategies that might contribute to this goal.

(v) In terms of an organisational goal such as improving worker productivity, determine what other strategies, policies, decisions and actions that we might have in terms of this goal.

(vi) Determine whether there are any information strategies that might contribute to this goal.

(vii) List two SMART informatics objectives.

24.11 REFERENCES

Ansoff, H. I. (1965). *Corporate Strategy*. New York, McGraw-Hill.

Cabinet Office (1999). *Modernising Government*. London, The Stationery Office.

Cabinet Office (2000). E-government – a Strategic Framework for the Public Services in the Information Age. London, Cabinet Office.

Institute of Directors (2000). *E-business: Helping Directors to Understand and Embrace the Digital Age*. London, Director Publications.

Johnson, G. and Scholes, K. (2000). *Exploring Corporate Strategy: Text and Cases*. Englewood Cliffs, NJ, Prentice Hall.

Lord, C. (2000). The practicalities of developing a successful e-business strategy. *Journal of Business Strategy*, **21**(2), 40–47.

National Audit Office (2002). *Better Public Services Through E-government*. National Audit Office.

Nolan, R. L. (1990). Managing the crisis in data processing. *The Information Infrastructure*. Cambridge, MA, Harvard Business Review.

Porter, M. E. (1985). *Competitive Advantage: Creating and Sustaining Superior Performance*. New York, Free Press.

Porter, M. E. (1996). What is strategy? *Harvard Business Review*, Nov/Dec, 59–78.

Wilcocks, L. and Sauer, C. (2000). *Moving to E-business*. London, Random House.

E-BUSINESS MANAGEMENT

Management is nothing more than motivating other people.

Lee Iacocca

Management by objectives works if you first think through your objectives. Ninety percent of the time you haven't.

Peter F. Drucker

LEARNING OUTCOMES

After reading this chapter, you will be able to:

- Distinguish between the management of human activity systems and the management of the informatics infrastructure
- Describe various forms of information management
- Outline the key features of data administration
- Outline the key features of knowledge management
- Outline the key features of content management

410

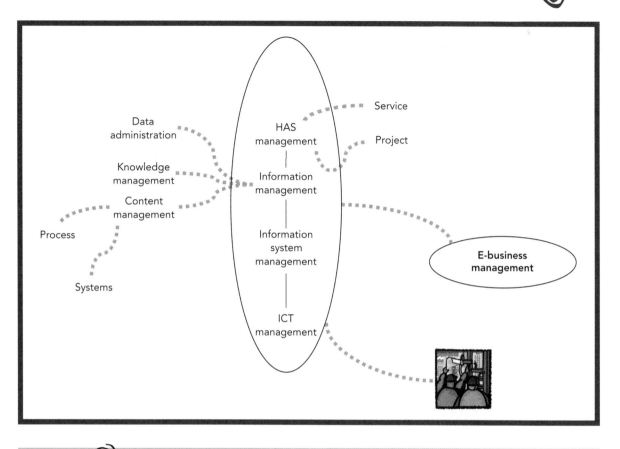

Data administration

Knowledge management

Content management

Process

Systems

HAS management

Information management

Information system management

ICT management

Service

Project

E-business management

Planning is the process of determining what to do over a given time period. Managing is the process of executing, evaluating and adapting plans in the face of contingencies. In systems terms, planning provides the key parameters for control, while management constitutes the exercise of control.

In this chapter we distinguish between e-business management and informatics management. We particularly focus upon a critical layer of informatics management known as information management. We shall argue that the modern interest in so-called knowledge and content management is really a contemporary reawakening of the importance of managing information effectively and the relevance of various ICTs to this task.

We may distinguish between the general management of the human activity systems of some organisation and the specific management of the informatics infrastructure of some organisation. Hence e-business management concerns both general business management and informatics management (Figure 25.1).

25.2.1   BUSINESS MANAGEMENT

In terms of general business management the focus on organisational change through ICT is critical. A key emphasis has been on the redesign of so-called business processes with ICT (Hammer, 1996). In this conception, an organisation is a human activity system or a series of human activity systems. Such human activity systems or business process are amenable to redesign through the use of ICT as a change agent. Such process redesign is likely to involve the following activities:

- *Process mapping*. This involves constructing a high-level map of organisational processes and indicating on such a map key process boundaries. Some form of systems modelling notation is normally used for this activity.

- *Process selection*. From the process map particular processes or sub-processes need to be prioritised in terms of the importance of redesign to them. Three sets of criteria may be used to rank processes for redesign: the health of the process, its importance to organisational performance and the feasibility for redesign.

- *Process design*. This will involve the re-engineering team identifying the problems with the existing process, challenging assumptions about ways of doing things and brainstorming new approaches to organisational activity. Design workshops will be held in which various stakeholders will participate.

- *Process specification*. This generally involves the modelling of both existing processes and the design of new processes using some agreed representation formalism such as a systems modelling notation.

- *Process implementation*. This is probably the most difficult phase of process redesign and involves introducing new work practices and associated technologies into the organisation.

The first three stages constitute unfreezing activities in the sense that they involve studying current inadequacies in organisation activities and generating plans for new ways of doing things (Lewin, 1947). The last two stages constitute freezing activities in the sense that they involve specifying a new process in some detail and implementing the new process within the organisation.

Question   *What sort of knowledge skills does an e-business manager require compared to a general business manager?*

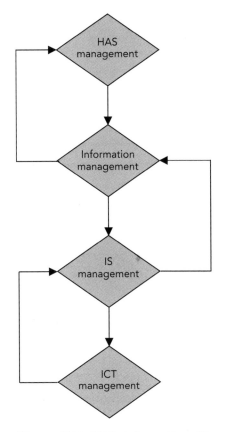

Figure 25.1 HAS, information, IS and ICT management.

25.2.2   INFORMATICS MANAGEMENT

In terms of informatics management Michael Earl (1989) has distinguished between three forms of management – information management, information systems management, and ICT management (Figure 25.1):

- *Information management* is concerned with the overall strategic direction of the organisation and the planning, regulation and coordination of information in support of this direction.
- *Information systems management* is concerned with providing information handling to support organisational activities.
- *ICT management* is concerned with providing the necessary technical infrastructure for implementing desired information handling.

For many organisations information, information systems and ICT services will be organised in one function. This function, service or department will be particularly involved in setting up and managing development projects. It will also be critically involved in evaluating ICT systems for the organisation in various ways.

| Example | A key aspect of information management is determining that suitable standards exist for the representation of data about an organisation's activities. For example, one part of a company may store customer data in terms of surname. Another part of the company may store customer data in terms of some assigned identifier. Key value, particularly in terms of the integration of systems, would be derived if both functions stored and accessed customer data in the same way. |

| Question | *Are three types of role required in organisations to manage information, information systems and ICT?* |

25.3 INFORMATION MANAGEMENT, KNOWLEDGE MANAGEMENT AND CONTENT MANAGEMENT

In recent years many organisations have recognised the importance of information and effective management of this critical resource. The rise of information management is a recognition that:

- Information is critical to the effective operation of human activity systems.
- Information is critical to measuring the performance of human activity systems (Chapter 23).
- Information is a critical organisational resource in itself and should be managed in a similar manner to other organisational resources, such as human resources and material resources (plant and machinery).

A number of terms have been used to describe various approaches to what we call information management. We consider three within this chapter:

- *Data administration*. The administration of the data resource.
- *Knowledge management*. The management of organisational memory.
- *Content management*. The management of Web-based material.

We shall argue that all three are fundamentally forms of information management. They all concern themselves with the administration of various aspects of the information resource of organisations. Such resource may be embodied in a range of ICT, including databases, data warehouses and Intranets.

| Question | *Is it appropriate to use the term information management to encapsulate the management of data, knowledge and Web content? In what way do they all constitute or relate to information?* |

25.4 ⊚ DATA ADMINISTRATION

Data administration is that function concerned with the management, planning and documentation of the data resource of an organisation (Gillenson, 1991). Data administration is concerned with the management of an organisation's meta-data, that is, data about data. It is a function that deals with the conceptual or business view of an organisation's data resource.

The key concept in the move towards data administration has been that data, like capital, personnel etc., should be treated as a manageable resource. In other words, data is a critical commodity in an organisation's attempt to compete in the open marketplace. In this sense, the data administration function is seen as a key part of the data and information management strategy of organisations (Beynon-Davies, 2003).

Example

Why is data such a critical resource for organisations? Consider the case of a university. Without data, such as what students it has, what students are taking which modules and what grades students have achieved, a university is unable to operate effectively. However, consider the case in which:

- Different university departments or schools maintain their own distinctive collections of data with their own distinctive definitions for data items.

- Data is frequently missing or incomplete.

- Data is frequently out of date.

- There is incomplete knowledge among staff as to what data is collected and where it is kept.

In such situations staff may spend a substantial amount of their time resolving data problems. Such situations demonstrate the key need for an organisational function tasked with managing the data resource.

Data administration is not only important for internal processes within organisations. It is also critical to effective data sharing between organisations. Hence, it is particularly critical for effective B2C and B2B e-commerce. Key innovations such as e-procurement could not occur without organisational standards for data storage and transfer.

Example

Data sharing between the institutions of the public sector is critical to effective e-government. For instance, in the UK data held by the Immigration Service needs to be shared effectively with local authorities, the Benefits Agency, the Inland Revenue, and Customs and Excise to enable effective handling of fraud, illegal working and smuggling. Likewise, data sharing between the Driver and Vehicle Licensing Agency and the Department for Work and Pensions is critical to enable disabled motorists to claim Vehicle Excise Duty exemptions more easily (Cabinet Office, 2002).

| Question | *What is the relationship between data sharing and data standardisation?* |

25.5 🌀 KNOWLEDGE MANAGEMENT

Acknowledging the vast amount of literature considering the question of what is knowledge, we provide a working definition of knowledge here for the purposes of explanation and relate it to a definition of information and data. Tsitchizris and Lochovsky (1982) define information as being 'an increment of knowledge which can be inferred from data'. Information therefore increases a person or group's knowledge of something. Note that this definition interrelates the concepts of data, information, knowledge and people:

- *Data are facts.* A datum, a unit of data, is one or more symbols that are used to represent something.
- *Information is interpreted data.* Information is data placed within a meaningful context.
- *Knowledge is networked information.* It is derived from information by integrating information with existing knowledge.

Recently it has been argued that knowledge is a significant resource for organisations (Alavi and Leidner, 2001) because:

- Increased knowledge leads to increased capability to perform effectively. Knowledge is one of the major assets of an organisation.
- Knowledge is complex and usually difficult to imitate. Therefore it has the potential to generate long-term and sustainable competitive advantage for organisations.
- Loss of personnel with significant amounts of knowledge through retirement, downsizing etc. is a significant loss to the organisation. Hence there has been much emphasis on capturing, storing and sharing knowledge throughout the organisation to militate against staff turnaround.
- Knowledge must be created by organisations. Hence organisations need to invest in organisational learning – the processes by which organisations acquire new knowledge.

Individuals clearly acquire knowledge that improves their performance in specific fields. The question is to what degree is it appropriate to speak of human groups and in particular organisations as having knowledge. One useful concept is that of organisational memory. This is what an organisation knows about its processes and its environment. The knowledge in an organisation's memory is a critical resource for organisations in that it enables effective action within economic markets.

Question | *What is the relationship between organisational memory and processes of control in organisations?*

We may distinguish between three forms of organisational knowledge in terms of the accessibility of the knowledge (Liebowitz, 1999):

- *Explicit knowledge*. This is readily accessible, documented and organised knowledge.
- *Implicit knowledge*. Accessible through querying and discussion but needing communication.
- *Tacit knowledge*. Accessible only with difficulty through elicitation techniques.

We may also distinguish between declarative knowledge (knowing what) and procedural knowledge (knowing how).

If knowledge is networked information then information is clearly a prerequisite to effective knowledge. Knowledge management can be considered as being the topmost layer of management processes in organisations reliant on effective information management.

Knowledge management effectively consists of the following key processes (Davenport and Prusak, 2000):

- *Knowledge creation*. The acquisition of knowledge from organisational members and the creation of new organisational knowledge.
- *Knowledge codification/storage*. The representation of knowledge for ease of retrieval.
- *Knowledge transfer*. The communication and sharing of knowledge amongst organisational members.

Clearly the aim of such processes is to make as much tacit and implicit knowledge as possible explicit. It is also directed at formulating clear strategies for organisational learning.

Given the pyramid established for informatics management, knowledge management will clearly rely on an effective ICT infrastructure within a particular organisation. Information and communication technologies such as Intranets, groupware, data warehousing and data mining are all much discussed as relevant technologies for knowledge management.

Example | BG – formerly British Gas – created an enterprise portal to aid the process of forming information around project teams. Each user also has a personal portal that provides links to all the virtual teams to which the individual belongs. The company has also used mobile devices such as palmtops to distribute information to dispersed managers.

Question	*In what way is effective knowledge management critical to the virtual or networked organisation?*

25.5.1   ORGANISATIONAL LEARNING

The concept of organisational learning or the learning organisation, like many management science concepts, is one that seems open to many different interpretations. In recent times it has become particularly associated with the work of Peter Senge at the MIT Center for Organisational Learning (Senge, 1990). In this section we particularly wish to utilise some of the concepts developed in the earlier work of Argyris and Schön (1978) on organisational learning which has a direct correspondence with some distinctions made in Chapter 3.

Argyris and Schön define organisational learning as occurring when: '...members of the organisation act as learning agents responding to changes in the internal and external environments of the organisation by detecting and correcting errors in organisational theory-in-use, and embedding the results of their inquiry in private images and shared maps of the organisation'.

Argyris and Schön distinguish between organisational single-loop learning and double-loop learning. In single-loop learning, individuals respond to error by modifying strategies and assumptions within constant organisational norms. Such learning is directed at increasing organisational effectiveness. In double-loop learning, response to detected error takes the form of a joint inquiry into the organisational norms themselves. The purpose is to resolve the inconsistency between existing norms and make a new set of norms realisable. In both cases, organisational learning consists of restructuring organisational action.

We would argue that single-loop learning is a form of single-loop feedback in organisations. In contrast, double-loop learning is a form of double-loop feedback.

This perspective on organisations treats them not as static entities but as collections of individuals that engage in the active process of organising. Individuals are continually engaged in the attempt to know the organisation and to know themselves in the context of the organisation. The emphasis is on the process of organising, not the entity of organisation.

25.6 ◎ CONTENT MANAGEMENT

The face of the modern organisation is presented through its Web sites. Hence it is critically important for the content of such sites to be well managed. Content management is the organisational process that manages the maintenance of Web-based material. Two dimensions are critical to establishing the case for content management: the volatility of content and the visibility of content.

- B2C (sell-side) e-commerce sites tend to be highly volatile. The content on such sites is updated on a continuous and regular basis. Content is likely to include products, prices and promotions. B2C sites are also likely to be highly visible. The prime purpose of such sites is to attract and keep customers.

- B2B (buy-side) e-commerce sites tend to be less volatile. This is because the content will be less subject to change. The content on such sites tends to remain constant for a reasonable period of time in the sense that the content is updated on a less frequent basis than for B2C sites. B2B sites are also likely to be less visible by their very nature than B2C sites. They are normally designed to be used by a limited range of stakeholders, such as authorised suppliers.

The more volatile and visible the Web site the more important it is for an organisation to establish a content management process. Such a process will ensure that updated content is accurate, relevant and timely.

Question | How would you expect C2C sites to relate to these dimensions of volatility of content and visibility of content?

25.6.1 CONTENT MANAGEMENT PROCESS

Any content management process is likely to include the following stages:

- The creation of content, including its presentation. This will be conducted by a team of content producers including technical staff and representatives of business units.

- The review of content by stakeholders such as the Web manager, marketing manager and legal department. Such stakeholders will ensure that the content adheres to Web-based and marketing standards for the company as well as ensuring that the content does not infringe any laws (Chapter 16).

- The testing of content on a test site. Ideally content should not be released until it has been thoroughly tested. This will normally be done on a test machine.

- The release of content to a live site. The release of content should only occur after full review and testing. The organisation may also wish to ensure that the release is being planned to coincide with other organisational activities.

The organisation may wish to establish time-scales on this process. The time-scales may vary depending on the package of content to be released.

Example   A factual error may demand updating in a matter of a few days. Planned releases of news items may occur once every month. Updates to product information may be released every two months.

Question   *Why is content management so critical to the e-business?*

25.6.2   CONTENT MANAGEMENT SYSTEMS

A range of ICT tools are now available to support the content management process. In a particular organisation such tools may be integrated to form a complete content management system. For example:

- *Content production.* Tools such as Microsoft FrontPage and Macromedia Dreamweaver enable content and its presentation to be produced and updated rapidly.
- *Workflow.* Workflow tools such as Lotus Notes may enable the flow of producing, distributing and checking content to be somewhat automated. A clear audit trail can be established of the authorisation of content.
- *Databases.* Many volatile and visible Web sites are now integrated with back-end database systems. Updates to the Web site, such as product descriptions and pricing, can be achieved by updating data in the database, which is then reflected on the Web site.

25.7   CASE STUDY: DEUTSCHE BANK'S HRBASE

Deutsche Bank has its headquarters in Frankfurt, Germany, and is among the world's leading financial services companies (Heier and Borgman, 2002). However, approximately half of the staff of the company is employed outside Germany and hence coordination and collaboration of staff across the globe is a key issue for the organisation.

The Human Resources (HR) division of the company is responsible for corporate development, staffing, personnel development, compensation and benefits, and supporting infrastructure such as human resource information systems. In the late 1990s the HR division felt the need for greater transparency of its structure and functions and improved communications. They established a department – HR Kinetik – as a means of achieving these goals, and as part of this department's strategy an Intranet-based knowledge management system was planned known as HRBase.

The fundamental idea of HRBase was to capture certain HR employee information such as career phases, skills, interests, languages, and details of current roles and projects. The intention was to use the corporate Intranet to enable easy information exchange and interaction among staff on human resource issues. For this purpose staff were encouraged to create their own Web pages, including project sub-pages.

It was felt that this knowledge management system would help achieve a number of aims:

- Make the division's structure more transparent.
- Foster better communication within the HR division.
- Contribute to a corporate culture of trust, innovation and teamwork.
- Improve knowledge sharing with a consequential lowering of project costs.
- Provide a common information repository and facilitate information sharing.

The development of HRBase began formally in February 2000 and was contracted to Deutsche Software. The system began piloting among a selected group of HR regions in the company in June 2000. The system was rolled out worldwide in the division in September of that year. At the end of January 2001 some 1500 users had registered with the system and set up their individual home pages – more than 80% of employees worldwide. However, in evaluating early use of the system most users reported that the knowledge management system did not add much value to their HR work. One of the prime reasons cited was the lack of integration between HRBase and other corporate systems. These concerns were taken on board by the division and HRBase is being changed accordingly.

25.8   SUMMARY

- E-business management concerns both general business management and informatics management.
- Three levels of informatics management are important: information management, information systems management and information technology management.
- A number of terms have been used to describe various approaches to what we call information management: data administration, knowledge management and content management.
- Data administration is that function concerned with the management, planning and documentation of the data resource of some organisation.
- Knowledge management concerns the effective management of organisational memory.
- Content management is the organisational process that manages the maintenance of Web-based material.

25.9 ACTIVITIES

(i) In terms of some organisation known to you attempt to delineate some of the differences between human activity systems management, information management, information systems management and ICT management.

(ii) Investigate whether some organisation engages in data administration, knowledge management and content management.

(iii) Investigate whether an organisation known to you impose any standards for the collection and representation of key organisational data.

(iv) Attempt to portray necessary components of the organisational memory of an organisation such as a university.

(v) Consider the content management processes either existing or potential of an organization such as a university.

25.10 REFERENCES

Alavi, M. and Leidner, D. (2001). Knowledge management and knowledge management systems. *Management Information Systems Quarterly*, **25**(1), 107–136.

Argyris, C. and Schön, D. A. (1978). *Organizational Learning: a Theory of Action Perspective*. Reading, Addison-Wesley.

Beynon-Davies, P. (2003). *Database Systems*, Basingstoke, Palgrave.

Cabinet Office (2002). *Privacy and Data Sharing: the Way Forward for Public Services*. London, Cabinet Office.

Davenport, T. H. and Prusak, L. (2000). *Working Knowledge: How Organisations Manage What they Know*. Boston, MA, Harvard Business School Press.

Earl, M. J. (1989). *Management Strategies for Information Technology*. Hemel Hempstead, Prentice Hall.

Gillenson, M. L. (1991). Database administration at the crossroads: the era of end-user-oriented, decentralised data processing. *Journal of Database Administration*, **2**(4), 1–11.

Hammer, M. (1996). *Beyond Re-Engineering: How the Process-Centred Organisation is Changing Our Lives*. London, HarperCollins.

Heier, H. and Borgman, H. P. (2002). Knowledge management systems spanning cultures: the case of Deutsche Bank's HRBase. *European Conference on Information Systems*, Gdansk, Poland.

Lewin, K. (1947). Group decision and social change. *Readings in Social Psychology* (eds. T. M. Newcomb and E. L. W. Hartley). New York, Holt, Rinehart & Winston, pp. 340–344.

Liebowitz, J. (ed.) (1999). *Knowledge Management Handbook*. Boca Raton, FL, CRC Press.

Senge, P. M. (1990). The Fifth Discipline: the Art and Practice of the Learning Organisation. New York, Doubleday.

Tsitchizris, D. C. and Lochovsky, F. H. (1982). *Data Models*. Englewood Cliffs, NJ, Prentice Hall.

E-BUSINESS DEVELOPMENT

What we learn to do we learn by doing.

Aristotle

LEARNING OUTCOMES

After reading this chapter, you will be able to:

- Describe the key phases of the e-business development process
- Outline the key functionality of a development information system
- Understand the importance of the development organisation to effective project management
- Describe the key elements of the development toolkit
- Relate the complexity of Web-based development

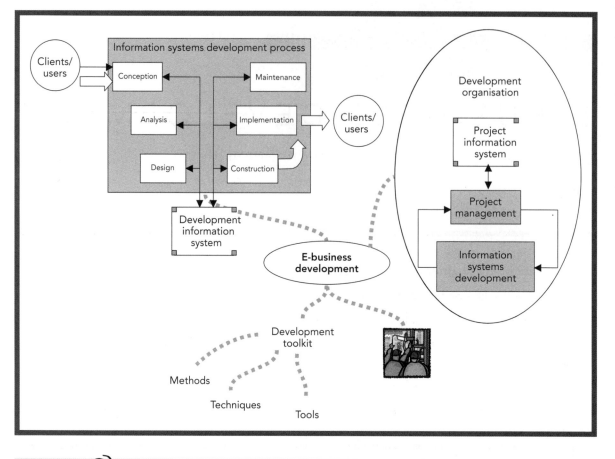

E-business development is that human activity concerned with the design, construction and implementation of key aspects of the e-business infrastructure of an organisation. The key inputs into the system are ICT resources and developer resources. The key output is an information system. A number of key activities are involved in the development process, including conception, analysis, design, construction, implementation and maintenance. A specialist organisation is normally required to undertake information systems development and a toolkit of methods, techniques and tools is required by the developer to engage in these activities.

This chapter is intended to provide an overview of a large and complex field. The reader is referred to (Beynon-Davies, 2002) for more discussion of development issues.

E-business development is that socio-technical system concerned with the design, construction and implementation of key aspects of e-business infrastructure for an

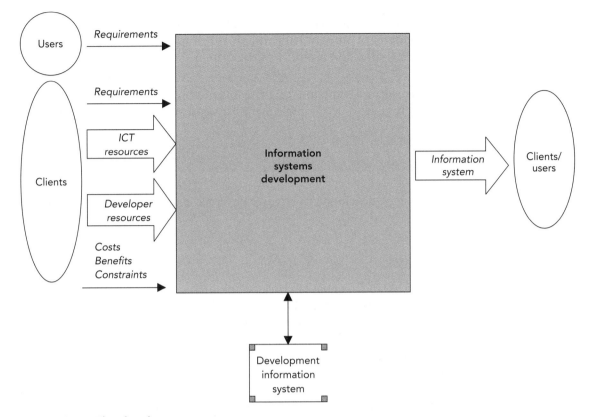

Figure 26.1 The development process.

organisation. This critical human activity system for modern business is represented in Figure 26.1. The key inputs into the system are ICT resources and developer resources. ICT resources may comprise systems construction tools or software packages. Developer resources include not only people but also a toolkit that includes methods, techniques and tools available to the developer.

The key outputs are an ICT system and its associated human activity system. We use the term *information system* to incorporate both these constructs. Information systems in themselves are socio-technical systems since they include both an ICT system and a system of use. Ideally the human activity system and the ICT system should be designed in parallel. The ICT system produced may be a bespoke system or a configured/tailored software package.

Three key types of organisational stakeholder are critical to the development process:

- *Clients*. These are frequently managerial groups involved in setting the major parameters for an IS development project – costs, benefits and constraints. They are critical in providing budgets for projects, used for funding ICT and developer resources.

- *Users*. The eventual users of an information system are likely to be involved in the development process. They will provide important detailed requirements for the functionality and usability of the system.
- *Developers*. Developers are the persons tasked with analysing, designing, constructing and implementing the information system. They may also have a key part to play in delivering the information system into its context of use.

26.3 ⊙ DEVELOPMENT ACTIVITIES

The process of development involves the activities discussed below (see Figure 26.2).

26.3.1 CONCEPTION

Conception is the first phase in the development process and will follow on from e-business planning (Chapter 23). It is the phase in which the development team produces the key business case for an information system. This is a form of evaluation of the system in strategic terms (Chapter 27). The team also attempts to estimate the degree of risk associated with a project to construct the proposed system. Finally, the team considers the feasibility of the IS project in terms of organisational resources. A project that succeeds in the strategic evaluation, risk analysis and feasibility exercise will pass on to a process of systems analysis.

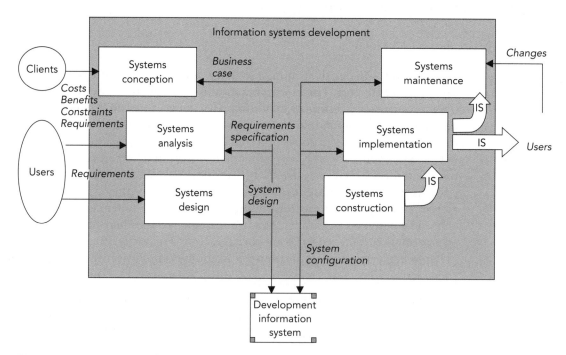

Figure 26.2 Activities of information systems development.

26.3.2 ANALYSIS

Information systems analysis involves two primary and interrelated activities – requirements elicitation and requirements specification. Both sets of activities demand different techniques. Requirements elicitation demands approaches for identifying requirements. Requirements specification demands techniques for representing requirements. Systems analysis benefits from forms of stakeholder participation, especially in the elicitation phase.

26.3.3 DESIGN

Systems analysis provides the major input into systems design. Design is the process of planning a technical artefact to meet requirements established by analysis. Design involves the consideration of requirements and constraints and the selection among design alternatives. Design also benefits from the participation of system stakeholders. Such a design or system specification acts as a blueprint for systems construction.

26.3.4 CONSTRUCTION

This phase involves building the information system to its specification. Traditionally, ICT system construction involves the three related processes of programming, testing and documentation. This may either be conducted by a team internal to the organisation or undertaken by an outside contractor (a form of construction known as outsourcing). Many information systems are now also bought in as a package and tailored to organisational requirements.

26.3.5 IMPLEMENTATION

The process of systems implementation (sometimes called systems delivery) follows on from systems construction. Systems implementation involves delivering an information system into its context of use. Since an information system is a socio-technical system, implementation of such systems involves the parallel implementation of both an ICT system and some form of human activity system. Once a system is delivered into its context of use it will be subject to the process of operation and the process of systems maintenance.

26.3.6 MAINTENANCE

Systems maintenance follows on from systems implementation. Maintenance is the process of making needed changes to the structure of an information system (Burton Swanson, 1992). Maintenance activity may stimulate suggestions for new systems. Hence it may act as a key input into the process of systems conception and thus provides a form of feedback to the process of information systems development

It must be acknowledged that information systems rarely stand still. They may change for a number of reasons:

- In the process of using information systems errors may be found in such systems or changes may be proposed. Fixing errors (bugs) and changing systems is normally classed as maintenance.
- At some point in time a system may be abandoned or need to be re-engineered to fit new organisational circumstances.
- Changes also occur over time in terms of adjustments made to the way both the IS and its context of use works.

Example

Suppose a company wishes to set up an e-commerce Web site. We can map some of the actual activities in the plan for the development of this system against the phases of the development process described above:

- *Conception.* Building the business case for the new e-commerce site; registering the domain name for the site; producing a tender document; issuing the tender; reviewing submissions; awarding the contract.

- *Analysis.* Eliciting key requirements for the site from clients and users; producing key content and presentational requirements for the Web site.

- *Design.* Producing key prototypes of content and presentation; considering changes to work practices; reviewing with users.

- *Construction.* Producing the final HTML pages and graphics; implementing any integration with back-end systems; testing the pages individually and as an integrated set; setting up new organisational structures and processes.

- *Implementation.* Producing a marketing campaign to accompany release of the Web site, updating stationery and registering the site; publishing the site on its appropriate server; putting new organisational processes into action.

- *Maintenance.* Measuring the performance of the site; managing the content over time; reviewing organisational structures and processes.

Question

In what way would you expect these phases to be different for front-end ICT systems development compared with back-end ICT systems development?

26.4 APPROACHES TO INFORMATION SYSTEMS DEVELOPMENT

There are a number of distinct approaches to information systems development. Here we consider alternatives in terms of two major dimensions: type of information systems product and form of sequencing of activities (Figure 26.3).

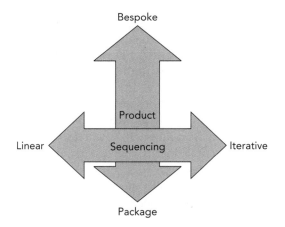

Bespoke

Linear

Product

Sequencing

Iterative

Package

Figure 26.3 Approaches to IS development.

26.4.1   TYPE OF INFORMATION SYSTEMS PRODUCT

In terms of information systems product we may distinguish two main types of development activity: bespoke development and package development.

In bespoke development an organisation builds an information system to directly match the requirements of the organisation. This may involve programming the entire system or the organisation may build a system out of pre-established components. Bespoke development normally offers the organisation the opportunity to closely match some information system to organisational processes. The main disadvantage is that the organisation must make a considerable investment in developing the information system in terms of particularly maintaining a suitably skilled internal informatics service.

In package development an organisation purchases a piece of software from a vendor organisation and tailors the package to a greater or lesser extent to the demands of a particular organisation. A software package is a software application designed to encapsulate the functionality necessary to support activity in a generic business area and may be customisable to a specific organisation's needs. Hence package development introduces a reversal of the place of organisational process. Generally speaking organisational processes have to be adapted to the requirements of some package.

Example

For small companies development of systems from scratch is not normally a feasible option because of lack of sufficient resources. Hence such companies will either buy in a package or employ the services of an external contractor to produce a system. However, even for these alternative approaches to development, the key phases above have to be followed. For instance, it is critical that companies make a business case for the purchase of a package just as they would if they were proposing to construct the system themselves.

26.4.2   FORM OF SEQUENCING

By sequencing we mean the way in which the various phases of the development process are organised. We may distinguish between two broad forms of sequencing: linear and iterative.

The linear model of the development process is indicated in Figure 26.4. Here the phases discussed above are strung out in a linear sequence with outputs from each phase triggering the start of the next phase. In the first three phases the key outputs are forms of system documentation. In the last three phases the outputs are elements of an information system.

The linear model has been particularly popular as a framework for large-scale development projects. This is mainly because a clear linear sequence makes for easier project planning and control (see below). The major disadvantages of the approach lie in the difficulties associated with changing early analysis and design decisions late in a project.

The iterative model of the development process is illustrated in Figure 26.5. In this model systems conception triggers an iterative cycle in which various versions of a system (prototypes) are analysed, designed, constructed and possibly implemented.

The iterative model has been particularly popular among small to medium-scale projects. Iteration, the construction of prototypes (prototyping) and significant amounts of user involvement, seem to reduce the risk associated with ICT innovations and generate stronger commitment from system stakeholders. However, because it is frequently uncertain in an iterative approach how much resource will

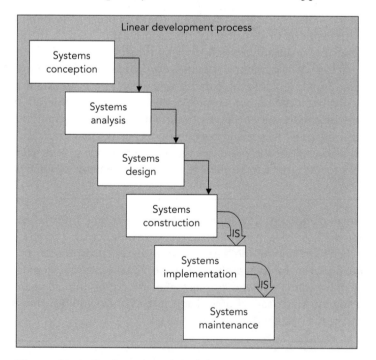

Figure 26.4 The linear model of development.

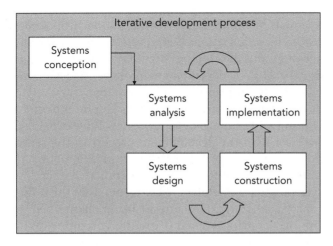

Figure 26.5 The iterative model of development.

need to be devoted to the project, iterative approaches generally appear to suffer from more difficult project planning and management.

The distinction made above between the forms of development makes clear that no single approach to development is applicable to all types of circumstance. Hence e-business projects are likely to use a range of approaches, depending upon development resources, the scale of the project and whether the systems work impinges on the front-end or back-end ICT infrastructure.

Examples

Generally speaking, large-scale back-end projects, perhaps implementing a large corporate database system, are likely to use a linear, bespoke model of development. In contrast, major modules within an ERP system are likely to be developed using a linear package approach.

Front-end ICT systems, particularly those that are Web-based, are likely to adopt iterative approaches because of the time pressures associated with such projects as well as the high levels of interactivity required from such systems.

Question

Large companies are also attracted by package development. What sort of advantages do you think are seen to lie in package development for such companies?

26.5 DEVELOPMENT ORGANISATION

Development is normally organised in terms of projects. A project is any concerted effort to achieve a set of objectives. All projects comprise teams of people engaging in the achievement of explicit objectives, usually within some set duration. Most informatics work in organisations is structured in terms of projects, and thus planning, management and development will normally be conducted as projects. In this chapter we focus on development projects. A development project is any concerted effort to develop an information system.

The initiation of development projects will be done as part of an organisation's e-business planning and management processes. Project management (O'Connell, 1996) will interact with the development process in the sense that it acts as the major control process for development (see Figure 26.6).

Project control is a type of formative evaluation (Chapter 27). The aim of project control is to ensure that schedules are being met, that the project is staying within budget and that appropriate standards are being maintained. The most important objective of project control is to focus attention on problems in sufficient time for something to be done about them. This means that continual monitoring of progress must take place. This is normally achieved through the provision of regular progress reports from the development process.

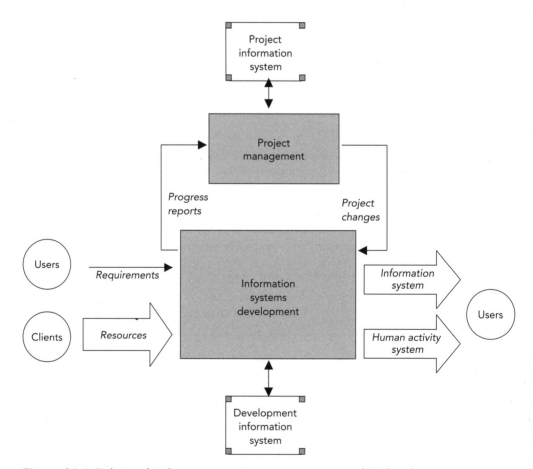

Figure 26.6 Relationship between project management and IS development.

Figure 26.6 illustrates the need for two major forms of information in support of development. The actual process of development itself needs documentary support to enable collaboration between the development team. The process of managing a project also needs its associated information system. This will store not only project plans but also data concerning progress against plans.

Prior to the initiation of the development process a development team is assembled. A number of development roles will be critical to particular phases of the development process:

- *Business analyst.* This role undertakes organisational analysis and systems conception activities such as cost–benefit analyses and risk analysis.
- *Systems analyst.* This role undertakes feasibility study, analysis and design activities.
- *Project manager.* This role is concerned with managing the development process as a unit.
- *Programmer.* This role undertakes construction and maintenance activities.
- *Change manager.* This role undertakes implementation activities.

Various representatives of other stakeholder groups, particularly clients and end users, are also likely to form part of the development team, either throughout the development process or at key points in the life of the information system.

The development or project organisation may utilise native employees of the organisation or outsource the development to an external organisation in various ways. In general terms we may distinguish between a number of distinct types of informatics outsourcing (Lacity and Hirschheim, 1993):

- *Body shop.* This is the type of outsourcing in which contract programmers are brought in to supplement informatics personnel in the organisation.
- *Project.* Here outside vendors are used to develop a new system.
- *Support.* This is the type of outsourcing in which vendors are contracted to maintain and support a particular application system.
- *Hardware.* Organisations may choose to outsource hardware operations, disaster recovery and network management.
- *Total.* This is 'keys to the kingdom' outsourcing, implying outsourcing of the entire informatics service – the development, operation, management and control of informatics processes for a company.

The central focus of outsourcing is the contract negotiated with an external supplier. This contract is normally executed as a service-level agreement.

Example | Many companies have outsourced the development and maintenance of their Web site to external companies. This is primarily a form of project outsourcing.

Some companies will also outsource the 'hosting' of their Web site with an external supplier. Hence hardware, software, communications and data are being outsourced in this case.

Question | What sort of problems do you think might emerge in outsourcing informatics in organisations?

26.6 DEVELOPMENT INFORMATION SYSTEM

A development information system is essential to ensure the effective operation of the human activity system that is the development process. Any reasonable-sized development project will need a consequent information system to support communication between teams of developers, to feed up into a project management and an e-business management process and to communicate with other stakeholder groups such as users and business managers. Such an information system consists of both system documentation and project documentation. System documentation acts as a model of the developing system; project documentation acts as a model of the development process. The key point here is that all information systems in a sense model elements of other systems. Such elements may be artefacts or organisational activities.

26.7 DEVELOPMENT TOOLKIT

Humans evolved from *Homo habilis* – man the toolmaker. We make tools in order to aid in the construction of artefacts and to extend our physical and mental grasp. Therefore, to undertake any development effort the information systems developer needs a toolkit. Such a toolkit will consist of methods, techniques and tools for supporting the activities of the development process – conception, analysis, design, implementation and maintenance.

Methods, techniques and tools are what we might call supporting 'technology' for information systems development (Beynon-Davies, 1998). The term *technology* is used here in its broadest sense to refer to any form of device that aids the work of some person or group of persons.

- *Methods*. These constitute frameworks which prescribe, sometimes in great detail, the tasks to be undertaken in a given development process. Methods are used to guide the whole or a major part of the development process.
- *Techniques*. These form the component parts of methods in that they constitute particular ways of undertaking given parts of a process. Techniques are normally used to guide activity within one phase of the development process.

- *Tools*. By tools we primarily mean here available hardware, software, data and communication technology for engaging in some part of the information systems development process or its set of associated external activities. Tools are frequently used to support the application of particular techniques.

Examples

Structured Systems Analysis and Design Method (SSADM) constitutes a method for the analysis and design of information systems while PRojects IN Controlled Environment (PRINCE) comprises a method for project management.

Entity–relationship diagramming is an established analysis technique, while PERT is an established project management technique. For Web site development storyboarding is a much-used analysis and design technique.

Microsoft Access is an established tool for systems construction, while Microsoft Project is an established tool to aid project managers. In terms of Web-based development many support tools exist, such as Microsoft FrontPage.

26.8 WEB-BASED DEVELOPMENT TOOLS

A variety of tools are available to support the work of Web-based systems development. Generally speaking, such tools support the phases of construction, implementation and maintenance of Web sites. Such tools include:

- *Text and graphics editors*. These are general-purpose packages for the editing of text and graphics files. They may be used to edit HTML documents and associated graphics files in various formats.
- *Specialised HTML editors*. Modern word processing packages generally have ways of producing HTML tags from document formatting. Usually, however, such facilities are not as flexible as those found in specialised tools for the production and maintenance of HTML documents.
- *Advanced graphics tools*. Such tools are particularly used by graphics designers to produce high-quality graphics and animations.
- *Site maintenance tools*. Such tools provide advanced HTML editing facilities such as style templates combined with functionality that make for easier tracking of changes and testing.
- *Front-end/back-end integration tools*. Such tools provide means of connecting Web pages to back-end systems, particularly DBMS (Chapter 11).
- *E-commerce site tools*. These constitute packages for the development of site functionality, such as electronic shopping baskets.

Examples	• *Text and graphics editors* – Microsoft Notepad and Microsoft PhotoDraw 2000
	• *Specialised HTML editors* – Microsoft FrontPage Express
	• *Advanced graphics tools* – Adobe Photoshop, Macromedia Flash and Director/Shockwave
	• *Site management tools* – ColdFusion and Dreamweaver
	• *Front-end/back-end integration tools* – Dreamweaver UltraDev and Lotus Notes
	• *E-commerce site tools* – Lotus Domino Merchant Server and Microsoft Site Server Commerce

26.9 THE COMPLEXITY OF WEB-BASED DEVELOPMENT

The development of Web sites for B2C, B2B, C2C or intra-business purposes is one of the major forms of e-business development undertaken by contemporary organisations. Therefore it maps onto the model of the development process described above, must be conducted by some form of development organisation, must be project-managed suitably and produces both an information system and an associated human activity system as its output.

A Web site is fundamentally a front-end ICT system for an organisation. It is also likely that there will be significant degrees of integration between this front-end ICT system and the back-end ICT infrastructure. Hence much Web-based development presupposes the existence of an efficient and effective back-end ICT infrastructure (Chapter 11).

The development of ICT systems is an innovation process based on three sets of actors or agents: producers, the ICT system and its consumers. Each of these actors is arranged in a triangle of dependencies. The ICT system depends on the producers, the producers depend on consumers, and the consumers depend on the ICT system. The ICT system requires the efforts and expertise of the producers to sustain it; the producers are heavily dependent on the provision of support in the form of material resources and help in coping with contingencies from agencies of consumption; consumers require benefits from the ICT system (Figure 26.7).

The three exchange relations between these agents are fundamentally processes of production, consumption and investment. Organisations usually cycle around these relations in various degrees of rapidity, depending on the scale of the system being developed. Sauer (1993) uses this model to understand and explain the ways in which development projects frequently terminate or fail. This occurs when the level of perceived flaws in a developing ICT system triggers a decision to remove levels of investment in a development project.

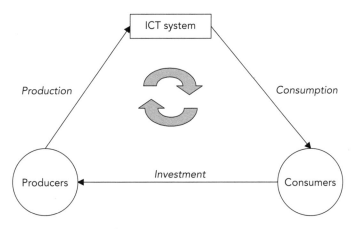

Figure 26.7 Development as an innovation process.

However, the development of Web-based systems is far from straightforward because the network of actors and relations is more complex and uncertain than for 'conventional' ICT systems (Truex *et al.*, 1999).

Firstly, the actors in Web-based development are less easy to define:

- Producers of web-based ICT systems are frequently teams of people with an array of different skills. Such skills may range from film production and graphic design through to programming and database design.

- Consumers of such technology are much less easily 'configured'. In other words, it is much more difficult to decide how to design Web sites that meet the needs of a range of possible user groups including suppliers, customers, employees, partners and regulators.

- Web-based ICT systems consist of integration of complex content and structure. Many organisational Web sites act as effectively front doors to the organisation. As such, the system becomes the visible representation of the organisation and must continually reflect changes in organisational structure and practice.

Secondly, the relations in the network are also more complex:

- The process of producing Web-based ICT systems is subject to rapidity and increasing levels of uncertainty. The typical life cycle for an e-commerce site is of the order of a few months. The requirements of such systems are also likely to change rapidly as organisations attempt to adapt to the rapid changes in the e-business environment.

- The process of consumption is much more diverse. Consumers of Web-based ICT systems may not only be internal stakeholders such as employees. They may include partner organisations such as suppliers.

- The processes by which systems are planned for, financed and managed is much more fluid. Since much Web-based development is outsourced, management processes have to be established with external suppliers and service agreements negotiated for the maintenance of such systems.

Question	What business consequences are there from this portrayal of the increasing complexity of development as an innovation process?

26.10 ⊙ CASE STUDY: DEVELOPMENT OF A PUBLIC RELATIONS SYSTEM AT BT

In this section we provide a short description of a Web-based development and discuss details of the development activity undertaken.

BT is the largest telecommunications provider in the UK. This development project was conducted for the public relations department (PRD) within this company by members of the information systems division. PRD is the department within BT that deals with all press and public relations throughout the organisation. It is distributed across a number of regions of the UK.

BT has a large internal development organisation that again is distributed throughout the company. The system being developed was the second iteration of a system for intra-organisational communication. The system consisted of a diary, a project management module, and a project management 'manual'. The term project here refers to a PRD project, not to an IS project. The system was aimed at the control of public relations campaigns (called variously projects and programmes) against corporate objectives. The basic objective was to provide an online resource for all members of PRD. The avowed aim was to ensure that 'nobody could do their jobs without having their computer switched on'; meaning that all outside communications from PRD should be done with reference to the information system.

In very broad technological terms this IS project can be characterised as the development of an Intranet or knowledge management system. System development tools included HTML editors and the Perl Unix scripting language. Both developers and users performed development work of a sort. The two developers did all their work using workstations and Perl, while customers used PCs for running HTML editors and office applications.

The development team consisted of two developers and five users. Interestingly, the project manager was a business user. Both users and developers were closeted together for three weeks and expected to deliver a working system at the end of that time. All the work on the project was conducted in an office geographically remote from both the developers' and customers' normal places of work. All the team members stayed in the same hotel during the working week and some travelled back home at weekends.

Since users and developers shared the same workspace, much use was made of informal design devices such as low-technology prototypes for the design of system functionality. Developers would also make some changes to prototypes dynamically at their workstations while in conference with users.

Project management particularly involved techniques such as wash-up sessions. Typically occurring towards the end of a working day, a wash-up session broadly involved the following activities:

- Review of day's progress with regard to objectives set.
- Review of what had not been completed and hence remained to be done.
- Generating and documenting what was to be done the next day and who was to do it – a so-called to-do list.
- Documenting the ways in which requirements were being met in a log maintained by the project manager.

At the start of each working day team members would first inspect the to-do list and then go off to their individual workspaces to conduct work. Periodically, and on an *ad hoc* basis, groups would be formed to address design issues.

The development process was overtly iterative in nature. The only documentation produced consisted of informal/group documentation devices such as to-do lists. Prototyping was used throughout the project, including *in situ* modification of prototypes. The involvement of both the user and developers on the project team was focused purely on the development effort for the project duration. Formal review sessions were used on a daily basis. Formative evaluation of prototypes occurred informally throughout each working day.

26.11 SUMMARY

- The process of e-business development can be seen as being made up of a number of generic phases: conception, analysis, design, construction, implementation and maintenance.
- A development information system is essential to ensure the effective and efficient operation of the human activity system that is the development process.
- Development is normally organised in terms of projects. A development project is any concerted effort to develop an information system.
- To undertake any development effort the information systems developer needs a toolkit. Such a toolkit will consist of methods, techniques and tools for supporting the activities of the development process.
- Sustained and invasive Web-based development is likely to be more complex than conventional development because of the variety of actors and the diversity and rapidity of relations between actors.

26.12 ACTIVITIES

(i) Try to identify a piece of development work and identify the key inputs and outputs for this process.

(ii) Find a past information systems development project. Determine how closely the project undertook activities similar to the phases described in the life cycle.

(iii) In terms of a development project known to you, determine whether it used a linear or an iterative approach.

(iv) In terms of a development project known to you determine whether it used a bespoke or a packaged approach.

(v) Determine whether there are any specific methods for Web-based development.

(vi) Determine the range of Web development tools available.

26.13 REFERENCES

Beynon-Davies, P. (1998). Information Systems Development: an Introduction to Information Systems Engineering. London, Macmillan.

Beynon-Davies, P. (2002). *Information Systems: an Introduction to Informatics in Organisations.* Basingstoke, Palgrave.

Burton Swanson, E. (1992). *Maintaining Information Systems in Organisations.* Chichester, John Wiley.

Lacity, M. and Hirschheim, R. (1993). *Information Systems Outsourcing: Myths, Metaphors and Realities.* Chichester, John Wiley.

O'Connell, F. (1996). *How to Run Successful Projects II: the Silver Bullet.* Hemel Hempstead, Prentice Hall.

Sauer, C. (1993). *Why Information Systems Fail: a Case Study Approach.* Henley-on-Thames, Alfred Waller.

Truex, D., Baskerville, R. and Klein, H. (1999). Growing systems in emergent organizations. *Communications of the ACM,* **42**(8), 117–123.

E-BUSINESS EVALUATION

The life which is unexamined is not worth living.

Plato, *Dialogues, Apology*

After reading this chapter, you will be able to:

- Define e-business evaluation
- Distinguish between evaluating the functionality, usability and utility of information systems
- Distinguish between strategic, formative and summative evaluation and place these forms of evaluation within the development process
- Discuss some of the key ways of assessing the utility of Web-based ICT systems

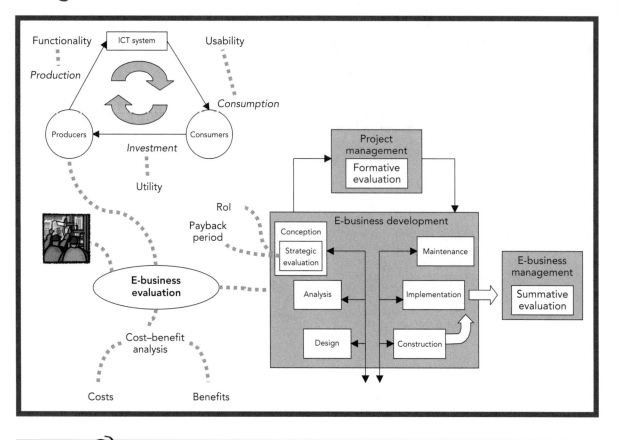

27.1 ⊙ INTRODUCTION

This chapter considers the critical question of how we determine that our infra-structure for e-business is successful. To answer this question we must evaluate our systems at various levels. In this chapter we distinguish between a number of distinct forms of e-business evaluation. First, we consider evaluating some of the distinct features of an information system. Then we consider three processes of evaluation closely aligned with the model of the development process discussed in Chapter 26. At the end of the chapter we focus on the critical problem of evaluating the worth of Web sites and consider the relevance of some of the approaches discussed.

27.2 ⊙ EVALUATION

Evaluation is the process of assessing the merit, value or worth of something (Pawson and Tilley, 1997). As a process it is commonly employed in the context of a coordinated programme of interventions in some domain. As such it is likely to make judgements about a programme's efficacy, efficiency and effectiveness (Chapter 2). Evaluation should normally be based on systematic data collection and analysis and is likely to be designed for use in future planning and management. Therefore evaluation is critically part of the control processes within organisations and is important for adjusting internal activities and technologies to changes in the environment.

The introduction of e-business is typically a programme of intervention using ICT to engender business change (Agrawal *et al.*, 2001). Hence, e-business evaluation is difficult because it comprises a form of socio-technical evaluation. It involves evaluating technical artefacts (ICT systems) in their context of use and application (human activity systems). We focus on the mediating system in this chapter – that of an information system – to enable us to encompass these two views of e-business evaluation.

An information system may be evaluated in terms of its functionality, usability and utility. We may also consider evaluation in terms of three evaluation processes that lie at different points in the development life cycle: strategic, formative and summative evaluation.

Questions   *Many commentators would argue that organisations are not very good at evaluation. Why do you think this might be the case? What barriers must be overcome for successful evaluation?*

27.3   FUNCTIONALITY, USABILITY AND UTILITY

Conventional approaches to evaluation focus on the evaluation of information systems or components. We can distinguish between three dimensions on which an information system should ideally be assessed.

- *Functionality*. Does the information system do what is required? Assessing the degree to which a system is functionally complete and consistent is a classic concern of systems development (Chapter 26). In general system terms functionality is normally an efficacy concern.

- *Usability*. Is the information system usable by its intended population? Assessing the usability of systems has become important with the continuing progress and use of graphical user interfaces and multimedia interfaces popular within Web-based systems. In general system terms usability is normally an efficiency concern.

- *Utility*. Does the information system deliver business benefit for the organisation? Assessing the utility of an information system is something which most organisations conduct at the pre-implementation stage of a project but seldom thereafter. However, this form of evaluation is becoming increasingly important because of the greater pressure being placed on the management of e-business to account for its activities. In general system terms utility is normally an effectiveness concern.

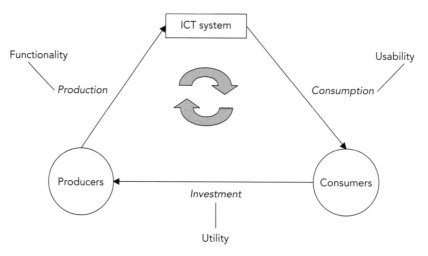

Figure 27.1 Functionality, usability and utility.

In terms of the development cycle for ICT systems discussed in Chapter 26, functionality, usability and utility can be seen to relate to the key processes of production, consumption and investment (Figure 27.1).

Functionality is a feature or guiding principle for the process of producing ICT systems. Usability is primarily an assessment made by the consumers of some ICT system. The assessment of the utility of some ICT system investment must be made both prior to construction and after delivery of a system.

Question	*Many information systems have failed to return satisfactory levels of benefits to costs. Why should this be the case?*

It is possible to distinguish critical forms of evaluation aligned with the model of the development process. Figure 27.2 makes a distinction between three types of evaluation activity in this way:

- *Strategic evaluation.* Sometimes referred to as pre-implementation evaluation, this type of evaluation involves assessing or appraising an information system investment in terms of its potential for delivering benefit against estimated costs. This is fundamentally part of the systems conception process and is primarily concerned with assessing utility.

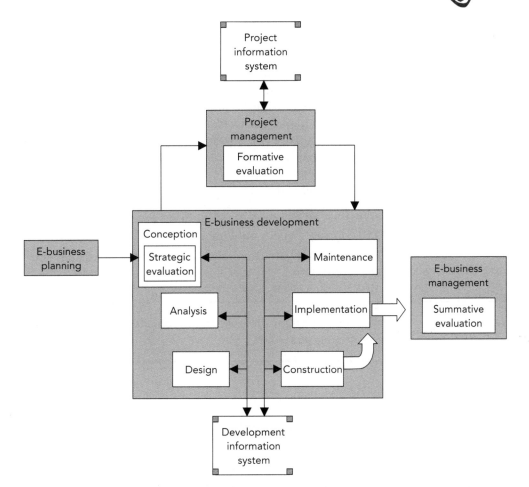

Figure 27.2 Strategic, formative and summative evaluation.

- *Formative evaluation.* Formative evaluation involves assessing the shape of an information system while in the development process itself. Traditionally, formative evaluation will be part of the project management process. Within iterative approaches to development, formative evaluation may be used to make crucial changes to the design of an information system. Formative evaluation is primarily concerned with assessing the functionality and usability of an information system.

- *Summative evaluation.* This type of evaluation occurs after an IS has been implemented. For this reason it is sometimes referred to as post-implementation evaluation (Kumar, 1990). Ideally, summative evaluation involves returning to the costs and benefits established in strategic evaluation after a period of use of the IS. It is a critical activity within effective e-business management.

27.5 ⊚ THE UTILITY OF WEB SITES

A Web site is a key example of a front-end ICT system. Once a Web site is up and running it is important to assess the utility of this system. This would normally be conducted in some form of summative evaluation and periodically reviewed as part of content management strategy (Chapter 25).

Measuring utility in this area is a complex issue because it involves assessing the contribution that the ICT system makes to its encompassing information systems and human activity system. Normal approaches to measuring the worth of a Web site include (Alexander, 2000):

- Collecting data about site visitor activity.
- Collecting data about outcomes.
- Collecting data on the stakeholder experience using extrinsic instruments (Keeney, 1999).

Question

Is it possible to assess the utility of a Web site without some clear idea of its place within business strategy?

27.5.1 COLLECTING DATA ABOUT SITE VISITOR ACTIVITY

Site visitor activity is normally defined in terms of the number of visitors to the site and the paths such visitors take through the content. One approach is to analyse the contents of a server log file. This file records every hit (a download of an item of data) made on a site. A log file analyser can then be used to build a profile of hits over time.

However, hits are a crude measure of usage because if a page is made up of five items of graphics and one item of text, the server log records six hits against the site by one stakeholder. More refined measures are page impressions and site visits. A page impression records a hit as one person viewing one page. A site visit records one hit on one Web site by one person. Such statistics can be produced by log analysers such as Easyminer.

Yet another approach is to use a browser-based approach. Here a short piece of code is inserted into a Web page. When accessed by a user the program runs within the browser and records access to each Web page by the user.

27.5.2 COLLECTING DATA ABOUT OUTCOMES

Outcomes are the key transactions that affect the business such as online enquiries, orders and payments.

Even if a site is used merely for marketing purposes the company is likely to want to know what contribution a site is making to outcomes. Outcome measures clearly call for close integration between front-end and back-end ICT systems. An integrated ICT infrastructure should be able to begin to provide answers to questions such as:

- How many initial online enquiries turn into eventual sales?
- What effect does the Web site have on online sales?
- How many customers purchase online that also purchase within our stores?

27.5.3   COLLECTING DATA ON THE STAKEHOLDER EXPERIENCE USING EXTRINSIC INSTRUMENTS

Extrinsic instruments are the conventional tools of marketing research and include questionnaire surveys and focus groups. The fundamental purpose of such research is to build profiles of customers and establish their attitudes to the e-business experience provided by a company. This might also include some attempt to measure the 'quality' of some Web site in terms of an established instrument (Barnes and Vidgen, 2000). An external company specialising in 'auditing' Web sites may frequently conduct such an approach.

27.6   STRATEGIC AND SUMMATIVE EVALUATION OF E-BUSINESS

Assessing the utility of a Web site is one part of the process of evaluating the efficacy of e-business. Evaluation of e-business is normally expressed in terms of projects and is normally undertaken in terms of an analysis of the costs and benefits associated with such projects. The costs of an information system concern the investment needed in the information system. The benefits of an information system concern the value that the organisation gains from having an information system. Simplistically, if benefits outweigh costs then the project and system are regarded as successes. If costs outweigh benefits then the system and project are classed as failures (Chircu and Kauffman, 2000).

It is useful to make the distinction between two types of costs and benefits associated with information system projects: tangible or visible costs/benefits and intangible or invisible costs/benefits. Tangible costs or benefits are frequently referred to as visible costs/benefits because they are reasonably straightforward to measure. Intangible costs or benefits are frequently referred to as invisible costs/benefits because most organisations experience difficulty in assigning actual measurable quantities to such costs and benefits.

Example | In terms of the development of a Web site, tangible costs may be the salary costs associated with the development team. Intangible costs may be the user and management involvement in development. A tangible benefit may be increased numbers of sales for particular product lines. An intangible benefit might be an increase in customer satisfaction.

The important point to make is that the costs of an information system must be taken into account over its entire life, not solely in terms of its development cost. Frequently organisations forget that the initiation of an information system means a permanent commitment to costs in terms of continuing resources being committed to the operation and maintenance of the information system.

Example
Producing and publishing a Web site is not the end of the matter for an organisation. A company must make a continuous commitment to manage the content on the site and upgrade it periodically with the latest technologies.

Some form of cost–benefit analysis is therefore critical to assessing whether or not the process of developing an information system is a worthwhile investment.

Most of the established techniques for evaluating information system investments focus on tangible costs and benefits and thus are directed primarily at assessments of efficiency gain. Two of the most popular are return on investment and payback period.

27.6.1 RETURN ON INVESTMENT

The return on investment (RoI) associated with an IS project is calculated using the following equation:

RoI = Average (Annual net income/Annual investment amount)

Hence to calculate an RoI one must be able to estimate the income accruing from the introduction of an IS and the cost associated with an IS for a period into the future. The average of this ratio of annual costs to benefits is then taken to indicate the value of the IS to the organisation.

27.6.2 PAYBACK PERIOD

Payback period still assumes that one is able to estimate the benefit of the introduction of an IS to the organisation for a number of years ahead. Benefit is measured in terms of the amount of cash inflow resulting from the IS. Payback is then calculated on the basis of:

Payback = Investment – Cumulative benefit (Cash inflow)

The payback period is equal to the number of months or years for this payback figure to reach zero. Clearly the assumption here is that those systems that accrue financial benefits the quickest are the most successful.

Example

Typical tangible costs associated with the development of a B2C e-commerce Web site and that might be used in an ROI or calculation of payback period include:

- Hardware costs

- Software costs

- Costs of development team

- Costs of project management

- Training costs

- Promotional costs

- Maintenance costs

Typical tangible benefits associated with the development of a B2C e-commerce Web site and that might be used in an RoI or calculation of payback period include:

- Reduction in costs associated with marketing such as catalogues

- Reduction in costs associated with support materials such as leaflets, forms etc.

- Lower number of inaccurate orders

- Staff savings

- Reduction in number of complaints

Question

Many commentators have argued that the benefits of ICT are frequently intangible in nature. What consequences does this have for effective evaluation of ICT?

27.7 CASE STUDY: STRATEGIC EVALUATION OF ELECTRONIC VOTING

The performance of electronic voting (Chapter 7) will depend on the technologies involved and the changes made to the human activity system. Let us assume that the UK government decides to implement a version of remote electronic voting providing the following access mechanisms to a remote voting server:

- Personal computers from the home with Internet access
- WAP-enabled mobile devices
- Voting kiosks provided in public places such as libraries and supermarkets

Clearly the implementation of such a technical infrastructure will have a major impact on the human activity system of electoral voting. We may strategically assess some of the costs and benefits of such a change. Typical benefits might include:

- Cost savings in terms of reduction in personnel needed to run polling stations.
- Cost savings in terms of reduction in personnel needed to run and count ballots.
- Reduction in number of spoilt ballots.
- Reduction in time to produce results.
- Increased convenience in the sense that votes may be cast from any location in the UK or the world, thus making it easier for groups such as the disabled, the elderly and overseas voters.
- Increased convenience in the sense that the period of voting might be extended to 24 hours or perhaps even a week.

Typical costs might include:

- The cost of producing suitable levels of authentication through such measures as PINs, passwords and smartcards.
- The cost of creating a secure back-end infrastructure for the collection and storage of votes on a national scale.
- The cost of ensuring a robust back-end infrastructure in the sense of ensuring availability of systems throughout the period of the election. Such costs will include employing a suitable level of technical personnel support to operate and administer the technical infrastructure.
- The cost of creating a secure front-end ICT system/Web site for the casting of votes.

In the short to medium term the costs of creating a suitable technical infrastructure for remote e-voting may outweigh the tangible benefits. This is particularly the case if the investment in specialised devices such as voting kiosks is made purely for general and local elections. Clearly if double-loop thinking is employed, enabling a redesign of certain aspects of the democratic process, then e-voting becomes a much more practicable option. For instance, if regular referenda/consultations are required for major policy-making then the importance of an effective technical infrastructure for voting becomes critical to the democratic process.

27.8 SUMMARY

- Evaluation involves assessing the worth of something.
- An information system may be assessed in terms of its functionality, usability and utility.
- There are three main processes associated with information systems evaluation: strategic evaluation, formative evaluation and summative evaluation.
- Strategic evaluation involves assessing or appraising an IS/IT investment in terms of its potential for delivering benefit against estimated costs.
- Formative evaluation involves assessing the shape of an IS while in the development process itself.

• Summative evaluation involves returning to the costs and benefits established in strategic evaluation after a period of use of the IS.

27.9 ACTIVITIES

(i) Choose an information system known to you. Identify one feature of functionality, usability and utility for the system.

(ii) Choose an information system known to you. Attempt to estimate the benefits associated with the system and the costs associated with its development.

(iii) Attempt to calculate RoI and payback period for a Web development project known to you.

(iv) Find and describe one example of strategic evaluation.

(v) Find and describe one example of formative evaluation.

(vi) Find and describe one example of summative evaluation.

27.10 REFERENCES

Agrawal, V., Arjona, L. D. and Lemmens, R. (2001). E-performance: the path to rational exuberance. *The McKinsey Quarterly*, **2001**(1), 31–43.

Alexander, S. (2000). E-metrics. *Computerworld*, **34**, 64.

Barnes, S. J. and Vidgen, R. T. (2000). WebQual: An exploration of Web site quality. *Eighth European Conference on Information Systems*, Vienna.

Chircu, A. M. and Kauffman, R. J. (2000). Limits to value in electronic commerce-related IT investments. *Journal of Management Information Systems*, **17**(2), 59–80.

Keeney, R. L. (1999). The value of Internet commerce to the customer. *Management Science*, **45**(1), 533–542.

Kumar, K. (1990). Post implementation evaluation of computer-based information systems: current practices. *Communications of the ACM*, **33**(2), 236–252.

Pawson, R. and Tilley, N. (1997). *Realistic Evaluation*. London, Sage.

BIBLIOGRAPHY

ABS (2000). *Business Use of Information Technology*. Australian Bureau of Statistics.

Agrawal, V., Arjona, L. D. and Lemmens, R. (2001). E-performance: the path to rational exuberance. *The McKinsey Quarterly*, **2001**(1), 31–43.

Alavi, M. and Leidner, D. (2001). Knowledge management and knowledge management systems. *Management Information Systems Quarterly*, **25**(1), 107–136.

Alexander, S. (2000). E-metrics. *Computerworld*, **34**, 64.

Anahory, S. and Murray, D. (1997). *Data Warehousing in the Real World: a Practical Guide for Building Decision-Support Systems*. Harlow, Addison-Wesley.

Ansoff, H. I. (1965). *Corporate Strategy*. New York, McGraw-Hill.

Anthony, R. A. (1988). *The Management Control Function*. Boston, MA, Harvard Business School Press.

Argyris, C. and Schön, D. A. (1978). *Organizational Learning: a Theory of Action Perspective*. Reading, Addison-Wesley.

Armstrong, A. and Hagel, J. (1996). The real value of online communities. *Harvard Business Review*, May/Jun, 134–141.

Ashby, W. R. (1956). *An Introduction to Cybernetics*. London, Chapman & Hall.

Bakos, J. Y. (1997). Reducing buyer search costs – implications for electronic marketplaces. *Management Science*, **43**(12), 1676–1692.

Bakos, J. Y. (1998). The emerging role of electronic marketplaces on the Internet. *Communications of the ACM*, **41**(8), 35–42.

Bandyo-Padhay, N. (2002). *E-commerce: Context, Concepts and Consequences*. Maidenhead, McGraw-Hill.

Barnes, S. J. and Vidgen, R. T. (2000). WebQual: An exploration of Web site quality. *Eighth European Conference on Information Systems*, Vienna.

Barrette, S. and Konsynski, B. R. (1982). Inter-organisational information sharing systems. *MIS Quarterly* (Fall).

Beer, S. (1966). *Decision and Control: the Meaning of Operational Research and Management Cybernetics*. Chichester, John Wiley.

Beer, S. (1972). *Brain of the Firm: the Managerial Cybernetics of Organisation*. London, Allen Lane.

Beer, S. (1985). *Diagnosing the System for Organisations*. Oxford, Oxford University Press.

Bell, D. (1972). *The Coming of the Post-industrial Society*. Reading, MA, Addison-Wesley.

Berners-Lee, T. (1999). *Weaving the Web: the Past, Present and Future of the World Wide Web by its Inventor*. London, Orion Business Publishing.

Berson, A. and Smith, S. J. (1997). *Data Warehousing, Data Mining and OLAP*. New York, McGraw-Hill.

Beynon-Davies, P. (1998). Information Systems Development: an Introduction to Information Systems Engineering. London, Macmillan.

Beynon-Davies, P. (2002). *Information Systems: an Introduction to Informatics in Organisations.* Basingstoke, Palgrave.

Beynon-Davies, P. (2003). *Database Systems,* Basingstoke, Palgrave.

Bickerton, P., Bickerton, M. and Simpson-Holey, K. (2000). *Cybermarketing: How to Use the Internet to Market Your Goods and Services.* Oxford, Butterworth-Heinnemann.

Bradley, S. P. and Nolan, R. L. (eds.) (1998). *Sense and Respond: Capturing Value in the Network Era.* Boston, MA, Harvard Business School Press.

Brassington, F. and Pettit, S. (2000). *Principles of Marketing.* Harlow, Pearson.

Brunn, P., Jensen, M. and Skovgaard, J. (2002). e-Marketplaces: crafting a winning strategy. *European Management Journal,* **20**(3), 286–298.

Bryant, A. and Colledge, B. (2002). Trust in electronic commerce business relationships. *Journal of Electronic Commerce Research,* **3**(2), 32–39.

Burnham, D. (1983). *The Rise of the Computer State.* New York, Random House.

Burton Swanson, E. (1992). *Maintaining Information Systems in Organisations.* Chichester, John Wiley.

Bush, V. (1945). As we may think. *Atlantic Monthly,* **176**, 101–103.

Buzan, A. (1982). *Use Your Head.* BBC Books, London.

Cabinet Office (1999). *Modernising Government.* London, The Stationery Office.

Cabinet Office (2000). E-government – a Strategic Framework for the Public Services in the Information Age. London, Cabinet Office.

Cabinet Office (2002). *Privacy and Data Sharing: the Way Forward for Public Services.* London, Cabinet Office.

Cassidy, J. (2002). *Dot.con: the Real Story of Why the Internet Bubble Burst.* London, Allen Lane/Penguin Press.

Castells, M. (1996). *The Rise of the Network Society.* Massachusetts, Blackwell.

Chaffey, D. (2002). *E-business and E-commerce Management.* Harlow, Pearson Education.

Chaffey, D., Mayer, R., Johnston, K. and Ellis-Chadwick, F. (2000). *Internet Marketing.* Harlow, Pearson.

Chaston, I. (2001). *E-marketing Strategies.* Maidenhead, McGraw-Hill.

Checkland, P. (1999). *Soft Systems Methodology: a Thirty Year Retrospective.* Chichester, John Wiley.

Checkland, P. (1987). *Systems Thinking, Systems Practice.* Chichester, John Wiley.

Chen, S. (2001). *Strategic Management of E-business.* Chichester, John Wiley.

Chircu, A. M. and Kauffman, R. J. (2000). Limits to value in electronic commerce-related IT investments. *Journal of Management Information Systems,* **17**(2), 59–80.

Ciborra, C. U., Braa, C., Cordella, A., Dahlbom, B., Falla, A., Hanseth, O., Hepso, V., Ljunberg, J., Monteiro, E. and Simon, K. A. (2000). *From Control to Drift: the Dynamics of Corporate Information Infrastructures.* Oxford, Oxford University Press.

Clemons, E. K., Croson, D. C. and Weber, B. W. (1996). Reengineering money: the Mondex stored value card and beyond. *International Journal of Electronic Commerce,* **1**(2), 5–31.

Conklin, E. J. (1987). Hypertext: an introduction and survey. *IEEE Computer,* **2**(9), 17–41.

Coyle, D. and Quah, D. (2002). *Getting the Measure of the New Economy.* London, The Work Foundation.

Crabtree, J., Nathan, M. and Reeves, R. (2002). *Reality IT: Technology and Everyday Life.* London, The Work Foundation.

Cram, C. M. (2001). *E-commerce Concepts.* Boston, Thomson Learning.

Cunningham, M. J. (2002). B2B: How to Build a Profitable E-commerce Strategy. Cambridge, MA, Perseus.

Currie, W. (2000). *The Global Information Society.* Chichester, John Wiley.

Daft, R. L. (2001). *Organization Theory and Design.* Cincinnati, OH, South-Western College Publishing.

Daum, B. and Scheller, M. (2000). Success with Electronic Business: Design, Architecture and Technology of Electronic Business Systems. Reading, MA, Addison-Wesley.

Davenport, T. H. (1998). Putting the enterprise into the enterprise system. Harvard Business Review, July/Aug, 121–131.

Davenport, T. H. (2000). Mission Critical: Realising the Promise of Enterprise Systems. Boston, MA, Harvard Business School Press.

Davenport, T. H. and Prusak, L. (2000). Working Knowledge: How Organisations Manage What they Know. Boston, MA, Harvard Business School Press.

DAVIC (2002). http://www.davic.org/.

David, W. (2000). E-commerce – Strategy, Technologies and Applications. Maidenhead, McGraw-Hill.

De Kare-Silver, M. (2000). E-Shock 2000: the Electronic Shopping Revolution; Strategies for Retailers and Manufacturers. Basingstoke, Macmillan.

De man, A.-P., Strenstra, M. and Vallenda, H. W. (2002). e-Partnering: moving bricks and mortar online. European Management Journal, 20(4), 329–399.

Department of the Environment Transport and the Regions (2001). Delivering Local Government Online. London, HMSO.

Dreyfus, H. L. (2001). On the Internet. London, Routledge.

DTI (2000). Statistical News Release, Small and Medium Enterprise (SME) Statistics for the UK, 1999, Department of Trade and Industry.

Dutta, S. and Bison, B. (2001). Business transformation on the Internet: results from the 2000 study. European Management Journal, 19(5), 449–462.

Earl, M. J. (1989). Management Strategies for Information Technology. Hemel Hempstead, Prentice Hall.

EC (1996). Commission recommendation of 3 April 1996 concerning the definition of small and medium-sized enterprises, European Commission: 4–9.

EC (2002a). eEurope Benchmarking Report. Brussels, European Commission.

EC (2002b). eEurope 2005: an Information Society For All. Brussels, European Commission.

EC (2002c). eEurope 2005 Benchmarking Indicators. Brussels, European Commission.

Eccles, R. G. (1991). The performance measurement manifesto. Harvard Business Review, Jan/Feb, 131–137.

Ellsworth, J. H. and Ellsworth, M. V. (1997). Marketing on the Internet. New York, John Wiley.

Emery, F. E. (ed.) (1969). Systems Thinking. Harmondsworth, Penguin.

Emery, F. E. and Trist, E. L. (1960). Socio-Technical Systems. Management Science, Models and Techniques (ed. C. W. Churchman and M. Verhulst). New York, Pergamon.

Ferlander, S. and Timms, D. (2001). Local nets and social capital. Telematics and Informatics, 18(1), 51–65.

Fisher, J. G. (2001). E-business for the Small Business. London, Kogan Page.

Foley, P., Ximena, A. and Shazad, G. (2002). The digital divide in a world city: a literature review and recommendations for research and strategy development to address the digital divide in London. London, Greater London Authority.

Gates, B. (1999). Business @ the Speed of Thought. London, Penguin Books.

Gillenson, M. L. (1991). Database administration at the crossroads: the era of end-user-oriented, decentralised data processing. Journal of Database Administration, 2(4), 1–11.

Gloor, P. (2000). Making the E-business Transformation. London, Springer-Verlag.

Greenstein, M. and Vasarhelyi, M. (2002). Electronic Commerce: Security, Management and Control. New York, McGraw-Hill.

Gulati, R. and Garino, J. (2000). Getting the right mix of bricks and clicks for your company. Harvard Business Review, May/Jun, 107–114.

Hagel, J. and Rayport, J. (1997). The new infomediaries. The McKinsey Quarterly, 4, 54–70.

Hale, R. and Whitham, P. (1997). Towards the Virtual Organisation. London, McGraw-Hill.

Hammer, M. (1996). *Beyond Re-Engineering: How the Process-Centred Organisation is Changing Our Lives*. London, HarperCollins.

Hammer, M. and Champy, J. (1993). *Reengineering the Corporation: a Manifesto for Business Revolution*. London, Nicholas Brearley.

Hanson, W. (2000). *Principles of Internet Marketing*. Cincinnati, OH, South-Western College Publishing.

Hardaker, G. and Graham, G. (2001). *Wired Marketing: Energizing Business for E-commerce*. Chichester, John Wiley.

Hawking, P. and Fisher, J. (2002). The state of play of the websites of large Australian companies. *European Conference on Information Systems*, Gdansk, Poland.

Heeks, R. (ed.) (1999). *Reinventing Government in the Information Age: International Practice in IT-Enabled Public Sector Reform*. London, Routledge.

Heier, H. and Borgman, H. P. (2002). Knowledge management systems spanning cultures: the case of Deutsche Bank's HRBase. *European Conference on Information Systems*, Gdansk, Poland.

Hiu, K. L. and Chau, P. Y. K. (2002). Classifying digital products. *Communications of the ACM*, **45**(6), 73–79.

Hoffman, D. L. and Novak, T. P. (2000). How to acquire customers on the Web. *Harvard Business Review*, **78**(3), 179–190.

Hoque, F. (2000). *E-enterprise: Business Models, Architecture And Components*. Cambridge, Cambridge University Press.

IDEA (2002). *Local E-government Now: a Worldwide View*. Improvement and Development Agency/Society of Information Technology Management.

Institute of Directors (2000). *E-business: Helping Directors to Understand and Embrace the Digital Age*. London, Director Publications.

Ives, B. and Learmonth, G. P. (1984). The information system as a competitive weapon. *Communications of the ACM*, **27**(12), 1193–1201.

Johnson, G. and Scholes, K. (2000). *Exploring Corporate Strategy: Text and Cases*. Englewood Cliffs, NJ, Prentice Hall.

Jones, B., Gray, A., Kavanagh, D., Moran, M., Norton, P. and Seldon, A. (2000). *Politics UK*. Cambridge, Cambridge University Press.

Kalakota, R. and Robinson, M. (1999). *E-business: Roadmap for Success*. Reading, MA, Addison-Wesley.

Kalakota, R. and Whinston, A. B. (1997). *Electronic Commerce: a Manager's Guide*. Harlow, Addison-Wesley.

Kaplan, R. S. and Norton, D. P. (1992). The balanced scorecard: measures that drive performance. *Harvard Business Review*, Jan/Feb, 71–79.

Kaplan, S. and Sawhney, M. (2000). E-hubs: the new B2B marketplaces. *Harvard Business Review*, **78**(3), 97–108.

Keeney, R. L. (1999). The value of Internet commerce to the customer. *Management Science*, **45**(1), 533–542.

Kent, W. (1978). *Data and Reality*. Amsterdam, North-Holland.

Klein, S. (1997). Introduction to electronic auctions. *International Journal of Electronic Markets*, **4**(7), 3–6.

Kling, R. and Allen, J. P. (1996). Can computer science solve organisational problems? the case for organisational informatics. In *Computerisation and Controversy: Value Conflicts and Social Choices* (ed. R. Kling). San Diego, CA, Academic Press.

KPMG (2002). *Is Britain on Course for 2005?* London, KPMG Consulting.

Kumar, K. (1990). Post implementation evaluation of computer-based information systems: current practices. *Communications of the ACM*, **33**(2), 236–252.

Lacity, M. and Hirschheim, R. (1993). *Information Systems Outsourcing: Myths, Metaphors and Realities*. Chichester, John Wiley.

Laudon, K. C. and Traver, C. G. (2002). *E-commerce: Business, Technology, Society*. Boston, Addison-Wesley.

Lewin, K. (1947). Group decision and social change. *Readings in Social Psychology* (eds. T. M. Newcomb and E. L. W. Hartley). New York, Holt, Rinehart & Winston, pp. 340–344.

Liebowitz, J. (ed.) (1999). *Knowledge Management Handbook*. Boca Raton, FL, CRC Press.

Lord, C. (2000). The practicalities of developing a successful e-business strategy. *Journal of Business Strategy*, **21**(2), 40–47.

Lucey, T. (1997). *Management Information Systems*. London, Letts.

Malone, T. W., Yates, J. and Benjamin, R. I. C. (1987). Electronic markets and electronic hierarchies. *Communications of the ACM*, **30**(6), 484–497.

Malone, T. W., Benjamin, R. I. and Yates, J. (1989). The logic of electronic marketplaces. *Harvard Business Review*, **67**(3), 166.

Margetts, H. and Dunleavy, P. (2002). *Cultural Barriers to E-government: Academic Article in Support of Better Public Services Through E-government*. London, National Audit Office.

Markus, M. (2000). Paradigm shifts: e-business and business/systems integration. *Communications of the AIS*, **4**(10).

Martin, J. (1996). *Cybercorp*. New York, American Management Association.

Matin, A., Gerard, P. and Lariver, C. (2001). Turning the supply chain into a revenue chain. *Harvard Business Review*, **79**(3), 20–22.

May, P. (2000). *The Business of E-commerce: from Corporate Strategy to Technology*. Cambridge, Cambridge University Press.

McAfee, A. (2000). The Napsterization of B2B. *Harvard Business Review*, Nov/Dec, 18–19.

McCarthy, J. (1960). *Basic Marketing: a Managerial Approach*. Homewood, IL, Irwin.

Means, G. and Schneider, D. (2000). *MetaCapitalism: the E-business Revolution and the Design of 21st-Century Companies and Markets*. New York, John Wiley.

Meier, J. (1995). The importance of relationship management in establishing successful inter-organisational systems. *Journal of Strategic Information Systems*, **4**(2), 135–148.

Moore, K. and Ruddle, K. (2000). *New Business Models – the Challenges of Transition. Moving to E-business: the Ultimate Practical Guide to E-business* (eds. L. Wilcocks and C. Sauer). London, Random House.

Morath, P. (2000). *Success @ E-business*. London, McGraw-Hill.

Mukhodadhyay, T. (1993). Assessing the economic impacts of electronic data interchange technology. *Strategic and Economic Impacts of Information Technology Investment* (eds. R. Banker, R. J. Kauffman and M. A. Mahmood). Middletown, PA, Idea Publishing, pp. 241–264.

National Audit Office (2002). *Better Public Services Through E-government*. National Audit Office.

NAW (2001). *National economic development strategy. In search of economic growth, social justice and sustainable and balanced development*. A Consultation Paper, The National Assembly for Wales.

Neely, A. (1998). *Measuring Business Performance*. London, Economist Books.

Nolan, R. L. (1990). Managing the crisis in data processing. *The Information Infrastructure*. Cambridge, MA, Harvard Business Review.

Norris, M. and N. West (2001). *eBusiness Essentials*. Chichester, BT/John Wiley.

O'Connell, F. (1996). *How to Run Successful Projects II: the Silver Bullet*. Hemel Hempstead, Prentice Hall.

OECD (2000). The Bologna Charter on SME policies: enhancing the competitiveness of SMEs, In *The Global Economy: Strategies and Policies*. Bologna, OECD.

OGC (2002). *A Guide to E-procurement for the Public Sector*. London, Office of Government Commerce.

Ordanini, A. and Pol, A. (2001). Infomediation and competitive advantage in B2B digital marketplaces. *European Management Journal*, **19**(3), 276-285.

Pawson, R. and Tilley, N. (1997). *Realistic Evaluation*. London, Sage.

Peppard, J. (2000). Customer relationship management in financial services. *European Management Journal*, **18**(3), 312–327.

Peszynski, K. J. and Thanasankit, T. (2002). Exploring trust in B2C e-commerce: an exploratory study of Maori culture in New Zealand. *European Conference on Information Systems*, Gdansk, Poland.

Pinker, S. (2001). *The Language Gene*. Harmondsworth, Penguin.

Porter, M. E. (1985). *Competitive Advantage: Creating and Sustaining Superior Performance*. New York, Free Press.

Porter, M. E. (1996). What is strategy? *Harvard Business Review*, Nov/Dec, 59–78.

Porter, M. E. (2001). Strategy and the Internet. *Harvard Business Review*, **79**(3), 63–78.

Porter, M. E. and Millar, V. E. (1985). How information gives you competitive advantage. *Harvard Business Review*, **63**(4), 149–160.

Preece, J. (2002). Supporting community and building social capital. *Communications of the ACM*, **45**(4), 37–39.

Putnam, R. D. (2000). *Bowling Alone: the Collapse and Revival of American Community*. New York, Simon and Schuster.

Rajkumar, T. M. (2001). E-procurement: business and technical issues. *Information Systems Management*, Fall, 52–60.

Reichheld, F. F. and Schefter, P. (2000). E-loyalty: your secret weapon on the Web. *Harvard Business Review*, **78**(4), 105.

Rheingold, H. (1995). *The Virtual Community: Finding Connection in a Computerised World*. London, Minerva.

Rowley, J. (2002). *E-business: Principles and Practice*. Basingstoke, Palgrave.

Sardar, Z. and Ravetz, J. R. (eds.) (1996) *Cyberfutures: Culture and Politics on the Information Superhighway*. New York University Press.

Sauer, C. (1993). *Why Information Systems Fail: a Case Study Approach*. Henley-on-Thames, Alfred Waller.

Sawhney, M. and Parikh, D. (2001). Where value lies in a networked world. *Harvard Business Review*, **79**(1), 79–86.

Schneier, B. (2000). *Secrets and Lies: Digital Security in a Networked World*. Chichester, John Wiley.

Scott-Morton, M. S. (ed.) (1991). *The Corporation of the 1990s: Information Technology and Organisational Transformation*. New York, Oxford University Press.

Senge, P. M. (1990). The Fifth Discipline: the Art and Practice of the Learning Organisation. New York, Doubleday.

Seybold, P. (1999). *Customers.com*. London, Random House.

Shields, M. G. (2001). *E-business and ERP: Rapid Implementation and Project Planning*. New York, Wiley.

Simon, H. A. (1976). *Administrative Behavior: a Study of Decision-making Processes in Administration*. New York, Free Press.

Singh, S. (2000). *The Science of Secrecy*. London, Fourth Estate.

Singleton, S. (2001). *Ecommerce: a Practical Guide to the Law*. Burlington, VT, Gower.

Sowa, J. F. (1984). *Conceptual Structures: Information Processing in Mind and Machine*. Reading, MA, Addison-Wesley.

Stamper, R. K. (1973). *Information in Business and Administrative Systems*. London, Batsford.

Stamper, R. K. (1985). Information: mystical fluid or a subject for scientific enquiry? *The Computer Journal*, 28(3).

Tapscott, D. (1996). *The Digital Economy: Promise and Peril in the Age of Networked Intelligence*. New York, McGraw-Hill.

Tapscott, D. (1998). *Growing up Digital: the Rise of the Net Generation*. London, McGraw-Hill.

Timmers, P. (1998). Business models for electronic marketplaces. *Electronic Markets*, **8**(1), 3–8.

Timmers, P. (1999). *Electronic Commerce: Strategies and Models for Business to Business Trading*. Chichester, John Wiley.

Tonnies, F. (1935). *Gemeinschaft und Gessellschaft*. Leipzig.

Truex, D., Baskerville, R. and Klein, H. (1999). Growing systems in emergent organizations. *Communications of the ACM*, **42**(8), 117–123.

Tsitchizris, D. C. and Lochovsky, F. H. (1982). *Data Models*. Englewood Cliffs, NJ, Prentice Hall.

Turban, E. and King, D. (2003). *Introduction to E-commerce*. Upper Saddle River, NJ, Prentice Hall.

Turban, E., Lee, J., King, D. and Chung, H. M. (2000). *Electronic Commerce: a Managerial Perspective*. Upper Saddle River, NJ, Prentice Hall.

Turner, C. (2000). *The Information E-Conomy*. London, Kogan Page.

UK Online (2002). *In the Service of Democracy: a Consultation Paper on a Policy for Electronic Democracy*. HM Government.

Venkatraman, N. (2000). Five steps to a dot.com strategy: how to find your footing on the Web. *Harvard Business Review*, **41**(3), 15–25.

W3C (1999). *HTML 4.01*. World-Wide Web Consortium.

W3C (2000). *XML 1.0 2nd Edition*, World-Wide-Web Consortium.

Waddington, C. H. (1977). *Tools for Thought*. St Albans, Jonathan Cape.

Ward, J. and Peppard, J. (2002). *Strategic Planning for Information Systems*. Chichester, John Wiley.

Whiteley, D. (2000). *E-commerce: Strategy, Technologies and Applications*. Maidenhead, McGraw-Hill.

Whyte, W. S. (2001). *Enabling E-business: Integrating Technologies, Architectures and Applications*. Chichester, John Wiley.

Wiener, N. (1948). *Cybernetics*. New York, Wiley.

Wilcocks, L. and Sauer, C. (2000). *Moving to E-business*. London, Random House.

Williams, R. L. and Cothrel, J. (2000). Four smart ways to run online communities. *Sloan Management Review*, **41**(4), 81–101.

Wise, R. and Morrison, D. (2000). Beyond the exchange: the future of B2B. *Harvard Business Review*, Nov/Dec, 86–96.

Witten, I. H. and Frank, E. (2000). *Data Mining*. San Francisco, CA, Morgan Kaufmann.

Zuboff, S. (1988). *In the Age of the Smart Machine: the Future of Work and Power*. London, Heinemann.

GLOSSARY AND INDEX

Term	Definition	Pages
Authorisation	The facilities available for enforcing database security.	216
Awareness	A precondition of electronic delivery. Stakeholders must be aware of the potential benefits of electronic delivery.	15, 251–2

B

Term	Definition	Pages
B2B	Business to business. *See* Supply chain.	
B2B e-commerce	The use of e-commerce in the supply chain.	18–19, 293–4, 324–33
B2C	Business to customer/consumer. *See* Customer chain.	
B2C e-commerce	The use of e-commerce in the customer chain.	17–18, 293, 303–20
Back-end ICT system	A core ICT system involved in manipulating the key data for the organisation.	13, 190
Back-end information system	A core transaction processing information system concerned with supporting the internal processes of an organisation.	89
Back-end information sytems infrastructure	The core set of transaction processing information systems in organisations.	86–96
Balanced scorecard	A popular form of organisational evaluation which benchmarks against an holistic measurement system.	387–8
Bandwidth	A measure of the amount of data that can be transmitted along a communication channel in a unit of time. Normally measured in bits per second.	130
Benchmarking	Sometimes called competitive practices benchmarking. The process of comparing performance against other comparable organisations or processes.	382–4
Bespoke development	The development style in which an organisation produces a new information system to directly march the organisation's requirements.	429
Branding	The process of using some form of sign to identify a product or service provided by an organisation.	357
Bricks and mortar business	Businesses in the sense that they have a physical presence usually in terms of buildings where they can be located.	60
Broadband	A term generally used to describe a high-bandwidth communication channel.	130, 135
Browser	A program that allows users to access and read Web-documents.	175–6
Bulletin board	Web facilities that permot users to post items to a central access area.	182
Bus network	A form of network topology in which devices are connected to a main communication line known as a bus.	134

Term	Definition	Pages
Business model	A business model specifies the structure and dynamics of a particular enterprise, particularly the relationship between different stakeholders, benefits and costs to each and key revenue flows.	59–60, 319–20
Business process	*See* Human activity system	
Business strategy	*See* organisation strategy	
Buyer-oriented B2B	Consumer opens electronic market on its own server and requests bids.	330

C

Term	Definition	Pages
C2C e-commerce	Consumer to consumer e-commerce. ICT enablement of aspects of the community chain.	19, 294–5, 336–45
Capacity	*See* Bandwidth	
Cash commerce	Cash commerce occurs when irregular transactions of a one-off nature are conducted between economic actors. In cash commerce the processes of execution and settlement are typically combined.	17, 290–1
Chat	Technology enabling near synchronous many-to-many communication over the Internet.	169, 207
Cisco	A leading in the market for inter-networking equipment.	333–4
Clicks and mortar businesses	Businesses that still maintain a physical presence but also offer services and products accessible by clicking online.	60
Clicks-only businesses	Businesses that have emerged entirely in the online environment.	60, 129
Client	A key type of organisational stakeholder. Clients sponsor and provide resources for the construction and continuing use of some information system.	76, 425
Client–server	An applications architecture in which the processing is distributed between machines acting as clients and machines acting as servers.	126, 202–4
Closed system	A system that does not interact with its environment.	35
Commerce	A process consisting of pre-sale, sale execution, sale settlement and after-sale activities.	289
Communication channel	The medium along which messages travel.	123–4, 130–2
Communication subsystem	Layer of an IT system concerned with communications. That part of an ICT system enabling distribution of the processing around a network.	74
Communication technology	Technology used for communication. This forms the interconnective tissue of information technology. Communication networks between computing devices are essential elements of the modern ICT infrastructure of organisations.	8, 72

Term	Definition	Pages
Community chain	The community chain is based on informal social networks of individuals and is a major force underlying C2C e-commerce.	6, 54, 338–41
Comparator	A mechanism that compares signals from sensors with control inputs.	39
Competitive position	An organisation takes up a particular position in a market defined by its activities and relationships with its competitors, suppliers, customers and regulators.	237
Competitor	A key type of organisational stakeholder. Key organisations in the same industrial sector or market that compete with an organisation.	77, 234
Concept	The idea of significance. The collection of properties that in some way characterise the phenomena.	69
Conception	A phase of the development process. Determining the costs and benefits associated with a proposed information system.	426
Construction	A phase of the development process. Traditionally ICT system construction involves the three related processes of programming, testing and documentation.	427
Consumer	An actor (individual, group, organisation) which consumes a good or service. *See* Customer.	297
Consumer behaviour	The behaviour of consumers, particularly decision-making, in the commercial process.	297–9
Content management	Content management is the organisational process that manages the maintenance of Web-based material.	419–20
Contract	An agreement between actors which is enforceable in law.	266–7
Control	The mechanism that implements regulation and/or adaptation in systems.	7, 35–6
Control inputs	Special types of input to a control process that define levels of performance for some system.	37, 40
Control subsystem	That subsystem which regulates the behaviour of a system it is monitoring.	36, 37, 382
Cookie	A data file placed on a user's machine by a Web browser. Used by an organisation's ICT system to monitor interaction.	258
Copyright	Copyright law enables authors of an intellectual property to prevent unauthorised copying of such material. The law applies to physical transactions of written material regardless of its country of origin.	269
Cost advantage	This essentially aims to establish the organisation as a low-cost leader in the market.	403
Cost–benefit analysis	Cost–benefit analysis is critical to assessing whether or not the process of developing an IS is a worthwhile investment.	447–9

Term	Definition	Pages
Credit commerce	Credit commerce is where irregular transactions occur between trading partners and the processes of settlement and execution are separated.	17, 290–1
Credit-based payment systems	Credit-based systems are modelled on conventional payment mechanisms such as the cheque and credit card except that signatures are digital rather than physical.	154
Critical success factor	A factor which is deemed crucial to the success of a business	389
CRM	See Customer relationship management	
Customer	A key type of organisational stakeholder. Consumers of an organisation's products or services.	76, 235
Customer chain	The chain of activities that an organisation performs in the service of its customers. Sometimes referred to as the demand chain.	6, 52, 305–6
Customer profiling and preferencing	A mechanism of customising online products and services for the customer based on detailed information captured about the customer.	314–15
Customer relationship management	The set of activities devoted to managing the customer chain.	105, 314–17
Customer relationship management system	That information system devoted to managing all interactions of a customer with an organisation.	105–6
Customer resource life cycle	A strategic planning framework due to Ives and Learmonth. Also useful in defining elements of the customer chain.	391–2
Customer facing information systems	Front-end information systems used by customers.	104–6
Cybernetics	The discipline devoted to the study of control systems.	36

D

Term	Definition	Pages
Data	Sets of symbols.	7, 8, 68, 72
Data administration	Data administration is that function concerned with the management, planning and documentation of the data resource of some organisation.	415
Data flow	A data flow is a pipeline through which packets of data of known composition flow.	33, 80
Data format	A format for data typically consisting of data structures, data elements and data items.	145–6
Data management	The set of facilities needed to manage data.	190–3
Data management layer	A layer of an ICT system concerned with data management.	74, 190
Data mart	A small data warehouse.	195
Data mining	Data mining is the process of extracting previously unknown data from large databases and using it to make organisational decisions.	195

Term	Definition	Pages
Data model	An architecture for data.	192
Data privacy	Ensuring the privacy of personal data.	13, 214, 257–9
Data protection	The activity of ensuring data privacy.	258–9
Data security	The process of ensuring the security of data.	13, 213–21
Data store	A data store is a repository of data.	80, 91
Data structure	An organisation for the representation of data within some database.	145
Data subsystem	That part of an IT system concerned with managing the data needed by the application. *See* Data management layer.	8, 74
Data type	A categorisation of data defining the format and operations for data.	145
Data warehouse	A data warehouse is a type of contemporary database system designed to fulfil decision-support needs. It utilises large amounts of data from diverse data needs to fulfil multidimensional queries.	195
Data warehousing	The process of building and managing data warehouses.	195
Database	An organised pool of logically related data.	191
Database management system	A suite of computer software providing the interface between users and a database or databases.	191–2
Database system	A term used to encapsulate the constructs of a *data model*, *DBMS* and *database*.	190
Database/Web site integration	The technologies associated with integrating database systems with Web sites.	208–10
Datum	A unit of *data*.	68
DBMS	*See* Database management system	
Decision support database	A database designed to support organisational decision-making.	193
Decision support system	DSS. *See* Executive information system	10, 103
Decision-making	The activity of deciding on appropriate action in particular situations.	55, 298–9
Demand chain	*See* Customer chain	
Design	A phase of the development process. Design is the process of planning a technical artefact to meet requirements established by analysis.	427
Developer	*See* Producer	
Development information system	That information system designed to support the development process.	434

Term	Definition	Pages
E-business management	The process of putting e-business plans into action and monitoring performance against plans.	21, 410–20
E-business planning	The process of deciding upon the optimal e-business infrastructure for an organisation. E-business planning is the process of planning the transformation of one e-business infrastructure into another.	20–1, 352, 377–92
E-business strategy	A plan for the utilisation of e-business within an organisation.	21, 379, 395–406
E-commerce	Electronic commerce. The conduct of commerce using ICT.	4, 17, 281–4, 287–99
E-community	Term used to describe either a traditional community enabled with ICT or a virtual community.	339–40
Economic actor	An agency which engages in economic exchange.	339–40
Economic environment	The markets within which an organisation competes. An economic system is the way in which a group of humans arrange their material provisioning.	14–15, 229–42
Economic relationship	The relationships of exchange between economic actors.	233, 235–7
Economic system	*See* Economic environment	
E-democracy	The use of IS and ICT to improve democratic processes.	17, 272–4
EDI	Electronic Data Interchange: provides a collection of standard message formats and an element dictionary for businesses to exchange data through an electronic messaging service.	91, 146–8, 326, 369
Effectiveness	A measure of the extent to which the system contributes to the purposes of a higher-level system.	7, 38, 387–8
Effector	Components that cause changes to a system's state.	39
Efficacy	A measure of the extent to which a system achieves its intended transformation.	7, 38, 386
Efficiency	A measure of the extent to which a system achieves its intended transformation with the minimum use of resources.	7, 38, 386–7
EFT	Electronic Funds Transfer: a means for transferring money between financial repositories (such as banks or bank accounts.	153, 312
EFTPOS	Electronic Funds Transfer at Point of Sale: a form of EFT where the purchaser is physically at the point of sale.	153
E-government	The use of ICT to enable government processes.	271–3
EIS	*See* Executive information system	
Electronic delivery	A term used to encapsulate the delivery of services and certain products over communication networks.	10–13, 140–55
Electronic government	The use of ICT to enable government administrative processes.	17

Term	Definition	Pages
Electronic hierarchy	A hierarchy in which exchanges on a one-to-many basis are conducted using ICT.	15, 239–40, 330
Electronic payment system	A system for the electronic transfer of monetary data.	151–4, 369
E-mail	Electronic mail. The transmission and receipt of electronic text messages using communication networks.	169, 207, 369
E-mail protocol	A communication protocol for the transfer of electronic mail.	163
E-mall	A collection of e-shops.	331
E-market	An e-market is a market in which economic exchanges are conducted using information technology and computer networks.	15, 152–3, 237–8, 370
E-marketing	The process of planning and executing the conception, pricing, promotion and distribution of ideas, goods and services using electronic channels.	19, 349–57
Employee-facing information systems	Front-end information systems used by employees.	108–9
Encryption	The process of encoding and decoding messages to ensure security of such messages.	218–19
End user	A key type of organisational stakeholder. Persons or groups which use an information system.	76, 426
Enterprise resource planning system	A software package consisting of a set of ICT systems which integrate to form an infrastructure for a company.	196–8
Environment	Anything outside the organisation from which an organisation receives inputs and to which it passes outputs.	3, 13–17, 32, 225–8
E-procurement	A term used to refer to ICT-enablement of key supply chain activities.	19, 361–70
Executive information system	EIS. That type of information system designed to support high-level strategic decision-making in organisations.	10, 103–4
External e-democracy	Used to refer solely to the enablement of democratic processes between members of a political grouping and their governmental representatives.	273
Extranet	Allowing access to aspects of an organisation's Intranet to accredited users.	168, 208, 331–2, 369–70

F

Term	Definition	Pages
Feedback	The way in which a control process adjusts the state of a system being monitored to maintain homeostasis.	40–1
Firewall	A collection of hardware and software placed between an organisation's internal network and an external network such as the Internet.	207, 221

Term	Definition	Pages
Five forces model	A strategic planning framework due to Porter and Millar.	390–1
Formative evaluation	That form of information systems evaluation concerned with monitoring the developing functionality and usability of a product.	445
Fragmentation	A measure of the degree to which data and processing are fragmented among information systems.	405
Front-end ICT infrastructure	The organised collection of ICT systems interacting with key stakeholders.	200–10
Front-end ICT system	An ICT system that supports a front-end information system.	12, 126, 201, 204–5
Front-end information system	An information system which interacts with internal or external stakeholders of the organisation.	101
Front-end information systems infrastructure	That part of the information systems infrastructure concerned with the core front-end information systems of the organisation.	99–112
FTP	File Transfer Protocol. A protocol for transferring files over communication networks.	163, 207
Functionality	What an information system does or should be able to do.	71, 76, 443
G		
Globalisation	The process by which organisations are operating across the globe.	240–2, 248
Goods	Tangible or intangible objects produced by organisations.	54, 142
GPRS	General Packet Radio System. A form of radio communication channel for data transmission with high bandwidth.	136
H		
Hardware	The physical (hard) aspects of ICT consisting of processors, input devices and output devices.	8, 72
Hierarchy	An important systems concept in which a system can be decomposed to form various levels of detail.	15, 232, 233
Homeostasis	The process of ensuring that a system remains regulated within defined limits.	36
Homeostat	A mechanism for ensuring homeostasis.	36
HTML	Hypertext Markup Language. A standard for marking up documents to be published on the WWW.	148–9, 175, 176–7
HTTP	Hypertext Transfer Protocol. An object-oriented stateless protocol that defines how information can be transmitted between client and server.	163, 174
Human activity system	A human activity system is a logical collection of activities performed by a group of people. Systems consisting of people, conventions and artefacts designed to serve human needs.	6, 46–62

Term	Definition	Pages
Human resource management	A secondary process in the internal value chain. This involves the recruiting, hiring, training and development of the employees of a company.	50
Hypermedia	Hypermedia is the approach to building information systems made up of nodes of various media (such as text, audio data and video data) connected together by a collection of associative links.	12, 173–4
Hypertext	A subset of hypermedia concentrating on the construction of loosely connected textual systems.	172, 173–4

I

Term	Definition	Pages
I-commerce	The use of Internet technologies in support of e-commerce.	4
ICT	Information and communication technology. ICT is any technology used to support information gathering, processing, distribution and use. A term used to encapsulate hardware, software, data and communications technology.	7–8, 72–3
ICT infrastructure	The set of interrelated ICT systems used by an organisation.	9, 13, 78, 126, 187–90
ICT strategy	The process of managing the current ICT infrastructure and implementing a new ICT infrastructure.	399
ICT system	An ICT system is a technical system sometimes referred to as a 'hard' system. An ICT system is an organised collection of hardware, software and communications technology designed to support aspects of an information system.	8, 73–5
Impact	A precondition of electronic delivery. Use of remote access mechanisms must reach a critical threshold driving a virtuous cycle.	16, 256
Implementation	A phase of the development process. Delivering an information system into its context of use.	427
Inbound logistics	A primary process in the internal value chain involving the receipt and storage of raw materials and the distribution of such materials to manufacturing units.	50
Inconsistency	A measure of the degree to which data is treated differently in differenct ICT systems.	405
Informatics infrastructure	An informatics infrastructure consists of the sum total of information, information systems and information technology resources available to the organisation at any one time.	9, 187–9
Informatics management	The management of information, information systems and ICT within organisations.	413
Informatics strategy	A definition of the structure within which information, information systems and information technology are to be applied in an organisation.	21, 399–400, 404–6

Term	Definition	Pages
Information	Information is data interpreted in some meaningful context.	7, 68
Information infrastructure	This consists of definitions of information need and activities involved in the collection, storage, dissemination and use of information within the organisation	9, 78, 187
Information management	The management of the information resource of an organisation.	413, 414
Information society	A term very loosely used to refer to the effect of ICT, information systems and information generally on modern society.	15, 248–9
Information system	A system of communication between people. Information systems are systems involved in the gathering, processing, distribution and use of information. A system designed to deliver information for some organisation.	7, 66–81, 425
Information system model	A representation of an information system.	79–81
Information systems infrastructure	The set of interrelated information systems used by an organisation. This consists of the information systems needed to support organisational activity in the areas of collection, storage, dissemination and use.	9, 78, 88, 187
Information systems strategy	That part of an informatics strategy concerned with specifying the future control of an information systems infrastructure and implementation of new elements of this infrastructure.	399
Infrastructure	Systems of social organisation and technology that support human activity.	4, 9, 78–9
Input	The elements that a system takes from its environment.	5, 32, 37
Intangible goods	Goods that fundamentally can be represented as data and and hence can be delivered to the customer electronically.	12, 142, 290
Intangible services	Services that fundamentally represent information services and hence can be delivered to the customer electronically.	12, 142, 142–3
Intellectual property rights	A means of ensuring that creators are able to benefit from their intellectual accomplishments.	268
Interactive digital television	A remote access device. A combination of digital television and an up-channel using conventional telephony.	127
Interest	A precondition of electronic delivery. Stakeholders must be interested in using remote access mechanisms for electronic delivery.	15, 252–3
Interface subsystem	That part of an IT system concerned with managing the user interface.	8, 74
Intermediary	Sometimes known as a channel organisation. An organisation which mediate between other organisations in the value-chain.	51
Intermediary-oriented B2B	An electronic market run by an intermediary for buyers and sellers in a specific area.	330–1
Intermediation	The process of introducing intermediaries into the supply chain.	238

Term	Definition	Pages
Internal e-democracy	The way in which information and communications technology (ICT) can be used to improve internal democratic processes within government.	273
Internal value chain	Those activities internal to the business involved in the production of value.	6
Internet	A set of interconnected computer networks distributed around the globe.	12, 157–69
Internet auction	An auction conducted over the Internet.	331
Internet service provider	ISP. A company supplying connections to the Internet.	166–7
Interoperability	A measure of the degree to which information systems are able to coordinate and collaborate.	405–6
Inter-organisational information system	That form of information system that is developed and maintained by a consortium of companies in some cognate area of business for mutual benefit.	15, 239–40
Intra-business e-business	The use of ICT to enable the internal business processes of the firm.	4
Intranet	The use of Internet technology within a single organisation.	109–11, 168, 206–7
IP address	Internet Protocol address. A unique identifier for the computers on a communications network using TCP/IP.	163–4
ISDN	Integrated Services Digital Network. A broadband communication channel for the local loop.	135
Iterative development	The style of development in which the activities of development cycle around the development of prototypes.	430–1
K		
Knowledge	Knowledge is derived from information by integrating information with existing knowledge. This may be represented as knowledge = object + relation + object.	416
Knowledge codification	The representation of knowledge for ease of retrieval.	417
Knowledge creation	The acquisition of knowledge from organisational members and the creation of new organisational knowledge.	417
Knowledge management	The management of organisational memory. Consists of knowledge creation, knowledge codification and knowledge transfer.	416–18
Knowledge management systems	A group of information technologies used for managing knowledge within organisations.	417
Knowledge transfer	The communication and sharing of knowledge among organisational members.	417
L		
Law of requisite variety	See Requisite variety.	

Term	Definition	Pages
Linear development	In this form of development the phases are strung out in a linear sequence with outputs from each phase triggering the start of the next phase.	430
List server	Technology enabling the easy maintenance of mail lists.	169, 207
Local area network	LAN. A type of communication network in which the nodes of the network are situated relatively close together.	132
Local e-democracy	Local groups use ICT to support democratic activity within the community itself.	274
Local loop	The communication channels between the local telephone exchange and the customer.	135

M

Term	Definition	Pages
Mail list	An organised collection of e-mail addresses.	169, 207
Maintenance	A phase of the development process. Correcting errors in an information system and adapting an information system to changing circumstances.	55–6
Management information system	MIS. A type of information system supporting the tactical decision-making of managers.	10, 103
Management-facing information systems	Front-end information systems used by management.	10, 102–4
Market	A market is a medium for exchanges between buyers and sellers.	14–15, 231–2
Marketing and sales	A primary process in the internal value chain. Marketing is the process of planning and executing the conception, pricing, promotion and distribution of ideas, goods and services to create exchanges that satisfy individual and organisational goals. Sales is the associated activity involved in the management of purchasing activities of the customer.	50
Marketing channel	A channel for the communication of marketing messages.	351–2
Mass deployment database	Databases designed to deliver data to the desktop.	194
MIS	*See* Management information system	
Mobile device	A category of remote access devices including cellular telephones, laptop computers and personal digital assistants.	128
Modulation	A property of a communication channel. A communication signal is either modulated as digital or analogue.	130
MP3	MP3 stands for Motion Picture Experts Group-1 Level 3. This format employs an algorithm to compress a music file, achieving a significant reduction of data while retaining near CD-quality sound.	155

Term	Definition	Pages
Multi-channel access centres	An organisational hub for various access mechanisms.	129
Multimedia kiosk	A remote access device. Specialist access points to services provided on the Internet.	128
N		
Napster	A software application that enabled users to locate and share digital music in MP3 format.	155, 242–3
Negative feedback	The monitoring subsystem monitors the outputs from the system and detects variations from defined levels of performance. If the outputs vary from established levels then the monitoring subsystem initiates some actions that reduce the variation.	41
Newsgroup	Technology for enabling threaded discussions between many-to-many users.	169, 207
Non-credit-based payment systems	Non-credit-based payment systems are designed to encourage the exchange of micro-payments electronically.	153–4
Non-repudiability	A user of an ICT systems should not be able to deny that they have used the system for some commercial transaction.	214
O		
OLAP	Online Analytical Processing. A technology that supports complex analytical processing.	195
Open system	A system that interacts with its environment.	35
Operational database	A database used to collect operational data.	193
Operations	A primary process in the internal value chain involving the transformation of raw materials into finished products.	50
Organisation strategy	The general direction or mission of some organisation.	397–8, 402–3
Organisational informatics	Organisational informatics is that discipline devoted to the study of information, information systems and ICT applied to organisations.	77
Outbound logistics	A primary process in the internal value chain involving the storage of finished products in warehouses and the distribution of finished products to customers.	50
Output	The elements that a system passes back to its environment.	5, 32, 37
Outsourcing	The use of external organisations to produce, maintain or support the whole or a part of the informatics infrastructure.	433
P		
Package development	The style of development in which an organisation purchases a piece of software from a vendor organisation and frequently tailors it to organisational requirements.	429

Term	Definition	Pages
Packet-switched network	A communications network which employs packet switching protocols and technologies. Data is broken into individual packets which are disseminated over a communications network through the application of routers.	161–2
Partner	A key type of organisational stakeholder. Key organisations in the same industrial sector or market that participate in a part-nership arrangement with an organisation.	77, 235
Payroll information system	That back-end information system dealing with the payment of employees of the organisation.	95–6
Performance	The degree to which a system reaches specified levels.	7, 38, 382
Personal computer	A desktop computer used as a remote access device.	127–9
Physical flow	Pipelines for the transmission of physical goods.	32, 80
Political environment	The external environment of the organisation concerned with power and its exercise.	16–17, 263–74
Political system	See Political environment	
Polity	A political system centred on a geographical area.	264
Portal	See Web portal.	
Positive feedback	Positive feedback involves the monitoring subsystem increasing the discrepancy between desired and actual levels of performance.	41
Preconditions for elec-tronic service delivery	A range of social factors, expressed in a sequence, which affect the likely take-up of the electronic delivery of goods and services.	250–6
Privacy	See Data privacy	
Process	Some transformation of input into output. In behavioural model-ling a process is a transformation of incoming data flow(s) into outgoing data flow(s).	5, 32, 37, 80
Process mapping	The activity of analysing and specifying major organisational processes.	412
Process redesign	The process of analysing, redesigning and implementing organi-sational processes.	412
Procurement	A secondary activity in the internal value chain. Procurement is the process of purchasing goods and services from suppliers at an acceptable quality and price and with reliable delivery.	51, 362
Producer	A key type of organisational stakeholder. Teams of developers that have to design, construct and maintain information systems for organisations.	76, 426
Production	That set of activities concerned with the creation of goods and services for human existence.	231

	Definition	Pages
Search engine	A system that allows users to locate Web sites matching keywords.	182
Secure Sockets Layer	SSL. Netscape's attempt to offer a secure channel of communication. It is a framework for transmitting sensitive information such as credit card details over the Internet.	220
Security	*See* Data security	
Semantics	The study of the meaning of signs.	68–70
Sense and respond	A systems view of the organisation which emphasises adaptation to environmental change.	111–12
Sensor	A mechanism that monitors the changes in the environment of a system.	39
Service	Some activity delivered to a stakeholder.	54
SGML	Standard Generalized Markup Language: a generalised markup language for describing the formatting of electronic documents.	148–9
Sign	Anything that is significant. Normally made up of symbol, concept and referent.	68–70
Single-loop feedback	In single-loop feedback the performance plans for a system remain unchanged.	57
Skills	A precondition of electronic delivery. Stakeholders must be suitably skilled in using remote access mechanisms.	254–5
Social capital	Social capital is the productive value of people engaged in a dense network of social relations. Social capital consists of those features of social organisation – networks of secondary associations, high levels of interpersonal trust, reciprocity – which act as resources for individuals and facilitate collective action.	338–9
Social environment	The external environment of the organisation concerned with society.	15–16, 246–61
Social infrastructure	The social infrastructure for e-business consists of those human activity systems central to supporting the conduct of e-business. These include competencies in e-business planning, management, development and evaluation.	4, 19, 373–6
Social network	A network of social relations.	338–9
Social system	*See* Social environment	
Socio-technical system	A technical system embedded in a system of social organisation.	75–6
Soft system	Collections of people undertaking activities to achieve some purpose.	42
Software	This comprises the non-physical (soft) aspects of information technology. Software is essentially programs – sets of instructions for controlling computer hardware.	8, 72

Term	Definition	Pages
Spamming	The process of sending unsolicited e-mails to large numbers of people.	258
SQL	*See* Structured Query Language	
Stages of growth model	A model which defines some key phases in the life of informatics management for some organisation.	406
Stakeholder	The group of people to which an information system is relevant.	76–7
Star network	A network topology in which network devices are connected to a central computer.	133
State	A system's state is defined by all the values assigned to a system's state variables.	33
Stock control information system	An information system for recording details of inventory.	92–3
Strategic evaluation	Sometimes referred to as pre-implementation evaluation, this type of evaluation involves assessing or appraising an information system investment in terms of its potential for delivering benefit against estimated costs.	444
Strategy	Strategy is the art of a commander-in-chief; the art of projecting and directing the larger movements and operations in a campaign.	40, 396–7
Sub-optimisation	Optimising the performance of a component sub-system independently will not generally optimise the performance of the system as a whole.	79
Subsystem	A major part of some system that can be considered in system's terms.	5, 34–5
Summative evaluation	This type of evaluation occurs after an IS has been implemented. For this reason it is sometimes referred to as post-implementation evaluation.	445
Supplier	A key type of organisational stakeholder. Organisations that supply goods and services to an organisation.	77, 234
Supplier relationship management	The management of supply chain activities. Sometimes referred to as supply chain management.	107, 239
Supplier relationship management system	That information system devoted to managing all interactions of a supplier with an organisation.	107
Supplier-facing information systems	Front-end information systems used by suppliers.	106–8, 328
Supplier-oriented B2B	Producers and consumers use the same electronic marketplace. Essentially the same as B2C e-commerce.	330
Supply chain	The chain of activities that an organisation performs in relation to its suppliers.	6, 51, 326–7
Symbol	That which is signifying something.	69

Term	Definition	Pages
Synchronisation	A property of a communication channel. The degree to which the sender and receiver of messages are synchronised.	130
System	A coherent set of interdependent components which exists for some purpose, has some stability, and can be usefully viewed as a whole.	5, 29–44

T

Term	Definition	Pages
Table	*See* Relation	146, 192
Tangible goods	Goods that have a physical form and cannot be delivered to the customer electronically.	142, 290
Tangible services	Services that have a physical form and cannot be delivered to the customer electronically.	143
TCP/IP	Transmission Control Protocol/Internet Protocol is the communications model underlying the Internet.	162–3
Technical infrastructure	The supporting infrastructure of ICTs for e-business.	4, 10–13, 115–19
Technology development	A secondary process in the internal value chain. This involves the activities of designing and improving the product and its associated manufacturing process.	51
Telephony	A category of access device which includes fixed audio and video telephones as well as mobile telephones and fax machines.	126–7
Three-tier architecture	A client–server architecture divided in to three layers: interface, business and data.	203, 204–5
Transaction	A logical unit of work. A transaction transforms a database from one consistent state to another consistent state. Transactions are major ways of recording service delivery.	11, 54, 144–5, 233
Transaction processing system	TPS. A type of information system supporting the operational activities of an organisation.	102
Transaction subsystem	That part of an IT system concerned with communicating between the interface and rules subsystem and the data subsystem.	8, 74
Transactional data	Transactional data is data that records events taking place between individuals, groups and organisations.	233, 249, 257
Trust	Trust is the glue that binds organisations together into a single cohesive unit and keeps them functioning. Trust is also critical to economic transactions between buyers and sellers. Trust is defined in the Oxford English Dictionary as 'a firm belief that a person or thing may be relied upon'.	259–60
Tunnelling technology	Tunnelling technology involves the transmission of data over the Internet using leased lines to the local ISP. With the use of encryption, authentication and other security technologies such an approach can be used to produce a Virtual Private Network (VPN) over a wide area network.	168, 208, 221

Term	Definition	Pages
U		
Uniform Resouce Locator	URL. A unique identifier for a document placed on the Web.	164
Usability	An information system's usability is how easy a system is to use for the purpose for which it has been constructed..	71, 76, 443
Use	A precondition of electronic delivery. Stakeholders must regularly use remote access mechanisms in core areas of life.	16, 255
User interface	*See* Interface subsystem	
Utility	The worth of an information system in terms of the contribution it makes to its human activity system and to the organisation as a whole.	71, 76, 443, 446–7
V		
Value	A general term used to describe the outputs from an organisation.	6
Value-added network	VAN. A type of communication network in which a third party creates and maintains a network for other organisations.	132
Value chain	An organisation's value chain is a series of interdependent activities that delivers a product or service to a customer.	6, 49–51, 96
Variety	A measure of the complexity of a system. The number of possible states a system may take.	33, 227
Vertical portal	These normally provide the same functionality as horizontal portals but for a specific market sector.	181, 227
Viable system	A term used by Stafford Beer to describe a system capable of surviving in a volatile environment.	58–9
Virtual community	A community consisting of a network of actors on some communication network.	339–42
Virtual organisation	An organisation built on an ICT infrastructure that enables collaborative e-working among members. Also referred to as network organisations. Organisations characterised by flat organisational hierarchies, formed around projects and linked together by information technology.	61–2
VPN	Virtual private network. A form of network which employs tunnelling technology to secure data transmission over the Internet.	168, 208
W		
WAP	Wireless Application Protocol.	128
Web	*See* WWW	
Web page	A term generally used to refer to the presentational aspect of a Web document.	178, 180–1
Web portal	A portal is designed to be an entry point for users into the WWW.	181

Term	Definition	Pages
Web-based development	The process of producing Web sites.	436–8
Web site	A logical collection of HTML documents.	12, 177–80
Wide Area Network	WAN. A type of communication network in which the nodes of the network are geographically remote.	132
WWW	World Wide Web. A set of standards for hypermedia documentation. It now has become almost synonymous with the Internet.	12, 169, 171–82
X		
XML	eXtensible Markup Language. A meta-language for the definition of documents	149–51, 326, 369